GLOBAL ARCHAEOLOGICAL THEORY

Contextual Voices and Contemporary Thoughts

GLOBAL ARCHAEOLOGICAL THEORY
Contextual Voices and Contemporary Thoughts

Pedro Paulo Funari

Campinas State University
Campinas São Paulo, Brazil

Andrés Zarankin

Instituto Multidiciplinar de Historiae y Ciencias Humanas,
Consajo Nacional de Investigacions Cientificas y Technicas
Ciudad Autonoma de Buenos Aires, Argentine

and

Emily Stovel

Ripon College, Ripon, Wisconsin

With the support of

 FAPESP

Fundação de Amparo à Pesquisa do Estado de São Paulo

KLUWER ACADEMIC/PLENUM PUBLISHERS
New York, Boston, Dordrecht, London, Moscow

Library of Congress Cataloging-in-Publication Data

Global archaeological theory : contextual voices and contemporary thoughts / edited by
    Pedro Paulo Funari, Andrés Zarankin, Emily Stovel.
      p. cm.
    Includes bibliographical references and index.
    ISBN 0-306-48650-4—ISBN 0-306-48651-2 (pbk.)—ISBN 0-306-48652-0 (e-book)
    1. Archaeology. 2. Material culture. 3. Ethnology. I. Funari, Pedro Paulo A.
II. Zarankin, Andrés. III. Stovel, Emily.
CC72.G57 2005
930.1′01–dc22   2004049806

ISBN 0-306-48650-4 (hardbound);   0-306-48651-2 (paperback);   0-306-48652-0 (e-book)

© 2005 by Kluwer Academic/Plenum Publishers, New York
233 Spring Street, New York, New York 10013

http://www.kluweronline.com

10 9 8 7 6 5 4 3 2 1

A C.I.P. record for this book is available from the Library of Congress.

Permissions for books published in Europe: permissions@wkap.nl
Permissions for books published in the United States of America: permissions@wkap.com

Printed in the United States of America

Contents

I. Archaeological Theory

II. Archaeological Theory and Methods in Action

III. Space and Power in Material Culture

IV. Images as Material Discourse

V. The Construction of Archaeological Discourse

Global Archaeological Theory

Introduction

Pedro Paulo A. Funari, Andrés Zarankin,
and Emily Stovel

In 1982, Ian Hodder published "Symbols in Action", crystallising a series of ideas that opened the possibility of rethinking archaeology. At a later point, Michael Shanks and Christopher Tilley (1987a and b) published two seminal volumes aimed at reconstructing archaeology as a socially informed and engaged discipline. A similar revitalization of archaeology also took place in the early sixties when Lewis Binford proposed a foundation for scientific archaeology. Processualism diverges from the previous unitary paradigm of New Archaeology in its encouragement of many different approaches, methods and perspectives, and in its explicit political commitment. While 'New Archaeology' considered archaeology a hard science with one explicit and correct way of practicing it, subsequent postprocessualism, including contextual or interpretative archaeology, has led to a plurality of approaches.

The contextual perspective argues that archaeological practice is directly linked to a subjective scholar. The archaeologist connects the past and the present and considers artifacts, archaeological practice and text as discourse. Material culture is considered active in the construction of subjects and subjectivities, in opposition to the processual emphasis on material culture as adaptation to the natural environment and as a passive product of social activity.

1

These two issues—artifact as active text and academic subjectivity—although linked in postprocessualism, do not actually come together unless we argue that all aspects of archaeological investigation are considered historical, contextualized entities; including the researcher, the objects they examine, and the interpretative frameworks they employ.

In fact, postprocessualist scholars seem to consider all aspects of archaeological investigation historical, contextualized entities: including the researcher, the objects they examine and the interpretative frameworks they employ. All are as actively and equally engaged in the construction of culture and social structure as they are in its representation. What is so interesting about this subjective approach is that it incorporates a plurality of readings, thereby implying that different interpretations are always possible (Shanks and Hodder, 1995), and allowing us to modify and change our ideas under the light of new information and/or interpretive frameworks. In this way, interpretations form a continuous flow of transformation and change and thus archaeologists do not uncover a real past but rather construct a historical past (Jenkins, 1995) or a narrative of the past (Funari, 1995).

Twenty years have passed since the publication of "Symbols of Action" and although traditional approaches in archaeology are still widely used, we find that free spaces are created allowing us to get away from the requirement of searching for a 'true past'. New fields and topics which were considered inadequate or even unthinkable at the beginning of the 1980s are now common, such as gender issues, ethnicity, class, landscapes, consumption, and architectural archaeology, among others (Andrade Lima, 1999; Buchli and Lucas, 2001; Delle et al., 2000; Díaz-Andreu and Champion, 1996; Gero and Conkey, 1991; Gilchrist, 1999; Grahame, 1995; Funari, 1993, 1994; Johnson, 1993; Jones, 1997; Leone and Potter, 1999; McGuire and Paynter 1991; Miller, 1987; Miller et al., 1989; Parker Pearson and Richards, 1994; Zarankin, 1999). Of course, some of these have always been studied in archaeology, but now have a new element: a conscious and explicit political interest on the part of the scholar and the subject. Renfrew and Bahn (1993) have even suggested that "nowadays, archaeology is a tolerant church that embraces lot of 'different archaeologies'." The metaphor of a church betrays a Western homogenizing concept that tolerates diversity to a point, but in essence archaeology is increasingly seen as a part of social praxis; diversity, then, becomes an inescapable part of the discipline.

Since the creation of the World Archaeological Congress in 1986, archaeology has acquired both global and ethical dimensions. The attendance of archaeologists from all over the world at the 1st Meeting of Archaeological Theory in South America, sponsored by WAC, and which took place in 1998 in Vitoria (Brazil), reflected a conscious attempt to decentralise the discipline, from an imperialist point of view to an empowering one. This is the basis of the present volume too, having grown though contributions by authors living outside the so-called Western imperialist core. From our standpoint, archaeological theory is a global endeavour with a global perspective (Ucko, 1995) and incorporating, above all, a critical political stance. A view from the periphery—be that a geographical (from the most austral country in the world, Argentina) or social periphery (from scholars of the poorer nations)—is fundamental to such a critical stance, since critical experiences and conditions engender critical thought.

Thinking and discussing theory is a much more common practice for the archaeologist than it ever was. South America, in particular, has received and consumed an enormous number of theories developed in Western countries. In recent years, however, there is an increasing realization that theoretical and methodological debates are at the heart of the discipline everywhere such that Latin America is no exception. This book seeks to contribute further to the discussion of archaeological praxis, starting with the gathering of several papers read at the meetings in Vitoria,[1] but including other works as well.[2] Despite the variety of approaches represented here, all of the papers focus on fundamental theoretical issues found in the discipline and thus both engage and represent the very rich plurality of postprocessualism discussed above. We consider archaeology a useful tool for deconstructing homogenous pasts created by master narratives because it explores and empowers all those histories excluded from official normative discourses. The following contributions consider topics such as gender, the meaning of material culture, the archaeology of aesthetics and images, and radical archaeological thought, among others.

Archaeological Theory in Action

The chapters of this book are characterized by a number of themes which are explored in relation to diverse theoretical, methodological, and historical contexts. Five themes are thus explored, followed by a commentary from Matthew Johnson. Issues in archaeological theory are discussed in Section I by four contributors, two of whom are South American. Julian Thomas begins our discussion by exploring the "inherently social character of material culture" and the political focus of archaeological practice, thus setting the groundwork for many of the subsequent papers. He asserts that archaeologists are responsible for cracking open sealed (modern) understandings of the past through understanding past relationships which is itself only accessible by recognizing the active role of objects in the past. And usefully, he asserts that we can and will be rigorous in our model building because although our interpretations are 'subject to our subjectivities', they are also flexible in the face of new phenomena and thus "reality is always symbolically mediated, but this does not make it any less real" (Thomas, this volume).

Exploring another take, Karlsson asks us 'Why is there material culture instead of nothing?'. In answer to this complex question, the author employs Heidegger and distinguishes material culture as a physical representation from the major process in which the material manifestation is only the final result. In essence, he considers both present and past people shared 'Being' such that we come together on the nature and perception of material culture because of that shared existence. Here too we find Guarinello's discussion of the challenges to symbolic archaeology, demonstrating that (almost) new models need revision and reflection, and attempting to provide general characteristics of an 'active symbolic material culture'. Moreover, he critiques the provision of meaning for material culture without written substantiation because, as before, this process allows for the archaeologist to assume their interpretations are in some way similar to prehistoric meanings. To ward against this, we must contextualise our symbolic work with detailed consideration of the (pre)historic conditions that surrounded the symbolic system under study. Finally, Alberione provides an interesting consideration, both in substance and in style, of the recurrent tension between written and material texts/documents in Historic Archaeology and the role of the archaeologist/author in reading and constructing sites. All authors explore the interplay between the two active and in invested participants in an archaeological investigation: scholars and material culture. We conclude, along with Thomas, that this similar activity and political engagement should be explicit and requires a non-Western component.

Section II, 'Archaeological Theory and Methods in Action', offers case studies of and new views on innovative models in contemporary archaeology. Orser, for example, begins from the utility of network theory to the construction of a global historical archaeology to propose that archaeologists must focus on the connections and connectors between people and groups in the past. For a truly complex understanding, we must examine large and small scale connections, including global patterns of social articulation. He provides a good schematic picture of what network analysis can offer archaeology and a brief example of new questions arising from its application in the archaeology of Palmares, Brazil. Funari, on the other hand, compares the urban settlement planning of the Spanish and the Portuguese in the New World. This little explored juxtaposition provides interesting insight into the comparative method and two different symbolic material modes in the colonial past that *still* mark urban environments today. Alberti explores the putative difference between gender and sex with reference to cross-cultural evidence that bodies, sex, and gender are constructed differently by different communities at different times, and that we cannot postulate the existence of a natural body against which social categories are imposed. Here we see that bodies, not just objects, are integral to the construction and representation of world-views. Politis seeks to inject the impact and objects of children to the study of the past by providing key correlates for children's material production and consumption through analogies collected in modern hunter-gatherer communities. Such ethnographic data show that children were significant producers of material culture, especially in residential camps. Finally, Stovel explores the possibility of studying identity construction in the past, and the antagonistic foundations of this new model, through the case of interaction between inhabitants of the Tiwanaku polity and San Pedro de Atacama in northern Chile between 200 and 1000 AD.

The third Section, 'Space and Power in Material Culture', focuses specifically on the relationship between space and power within the active role of material culture in diverse cultures and periods. Lazzari begins by making a critical revision of the use of space in models of exchange in archaeology, proposing the need for a reformulation based in social theory, specifically in the sense that we must consider the possibility of resistance and the construction of status through trade and long-distance interaction. She demonstrates the utility of this reformulation with a case study from the Formative Period (600 BC–AD 1000) in Northwestern Argentina where 'distance' is not seen as an abyss that prehistoric actors needed to 'overcome' in their exchange networks. Rather, different distributions of various material forms suggest that these groups were producing and consuming goods within "a variety of interaction relationships and networks" (Lazzari, this volume) that also served the negotiation of conflict and power.

Acuto and Zarankin consider the manipulation of space in particular as a vehicle for the creation and maintenance of power relations. The former develops the specific spatial mechanisms of domination used by the Inca Empire, including the physical and cultural recalibration of place and hierarchy in the landscape of conquered peoples. He cites the imperial installation of a totally new spatial organization that not only reproduces the power structures of the Inca, but situates them as the ancestral and spiritual foundation of each conquered community. The latter author demonstrates how transformations in the design of public elementary schools in 19th and 20th Century Buenos Aires shared the same principles of restricted access while reflecting an important shift—from a Disciplinary Society to a Control Society—in the understanding of control and socialization which entailed changing perceptions of the role of schools and of the citizens they 'produced'. Senatore, on the other hand, considers the underlying Enlightenment principles evident in the planning and implementation of the Spanish colonization of Patagonia during the 18th Century. There, in the southernmost colony Floridablanca, we see the manifestation of desires to construct and replicate the ideas of a 'modern' society. In all of these cases we are yet again confronted with the simultaneous reflection and construction of 'the social' (lo social) that is found in both the production and consumption of material culture (including texts and otherwise), and of archaeological reports.

Section IV, 'Images as a Material Discourse', deals with the potential of iconographic analysis in archaeological research. Three contributors demonstrate the unique difficulties of this key component of archaeological research. Prous returns to the perennial concern with the validity of modern meanings inferred from prehistoric imagery and how different archaeological schools have produced different interpretations of past imagery. He quite rightly reiterates that meaning is culturally determined, but insists that the time and space that separates us from past peoples should not deter our symbolic analyses. Modern archaeologists can see the symbolic interpretations they produce as heuristic tools useful for approximating past meanings and for understanding *ourselves* better. In other words, he claims (Prous, this volume) that, *"our view of rock art manifestations is more sensitive to their 'artistic' aspect than prehistoric peoples were"*. This is because we express our linkage with a consumerist society in which art is a *"per se* product."* In other words, that our interpretations are culturally determined does not prevent us from understanding the past, nor does it prevent us from understanding the present which is, in the end, the ultimate goal of archaeology. In turn, Chevitarese provides a detailed and fascinating examination of the decline in various motifs characteristic of rural scenes found on Classical Grecian Attic vases during the 5th and 6th Centuries BC. Several formal, design, and thematic changes in the iconography of these vases help us understand long-term, deep-seated tensions between images and conceptualisation of urban *versus* rural environments, and may have been a product of a significant reorientation in Greek society at the time toward more urban interests. In the end, urban values and themes of city life are argued to reflect a growing Athenian imperialism.

As is patently clear, this volume is interested in the relationship between archaeology and politics. Díaz-Andreu (1999) has already commented that political aspects of scholarly knowledge have increasingly entered the core of the discipline. As such, the final section, 'The Construction of the Archaeological Discourse', encompasses a series of papers concerned with this very issue. McGuire and Navarrete consider the differences between the radical archaeologies of North and South America, stating bluntly that Latin American Social Archaeology demonstrates a more critical and 'revolutionary' character than its simply 'rebellious' Anglo-American counterpart, Marxist Archaeology. In fact, Social Archaeology engenders and reflects more political praxis than its more reflective and diffuse northern partner despite a similar dedication to social reform and critical knowledge building because of the intellectual and political history of Latin America, and the current patterns of funding and political activism in each professional sector.

Both Ferreira and Piñón, in turn, see archaeology as a tool of the hegemonic classes during two moments in the formation of the Brazilian nation insofar as it supported oppressive identity regimes that reified race and class differences. In other words, the subjective nature of archaeological investigation, if unquestioned, can reflect and enact modern power imbalances that archaeologists would wish to counteract. Such is the case explored by Noelli, where the excessive dominance of one theoretical and methodological framework in Brazil from the 1960s and 1970s until the present lead to difficulties in articulating archaeological and ethnographic data, certainly in the case of the Jê. Noelli provides a detailed reconsideration of the issue thereby demonstrating the real dangers of relying on one investigative perspective alone. In addition, he opens new avenues for research and confirms the value of proposing multiple interpretive models. It is this intimate historical and political examination of Brazilian archaeology that makes Noelli's contribution so thought-provoking and complementary to a similar analysis provided for Argentina by Podgorny and colleagues. This last paper not only considers the specific adoption of New Archaeological premises in Argentina during the 1960s and 1970s, but it also attempts a rigorous historiography of the discipline, thus avoiding the more common personalized discussions. As a result, the authors provide an intimate picture of the development of two archaeological modes—the cultural historic school and American culturalism—that were actually more integrated that previously thought. Of even more interest is their consideration of the diffusion of academic texts and journals which has rarely been considered in the intellectual histories of Latin America, despite its obvious importance. In fact, they argue that more texts were available to scholars than usually is presumed. Finally, Matthew Johnson provides a commentary on all contributions.

The preceding discussion demonstrates how intertwined much current theoretical work is in archaeology. It also shows that varied and apparently contradictory perspectives share similar underlying interests in political action and scholarly engagement. Theoretical debates are increasingly relevant to archaeologists, and issues of methods, theory, personal and professional goals, data collection and analysis are all integral to this endeavour. The views of contributors coincide and contradict, but this is the nature of a pluralistic science. While total consensus is unlikely, this diversity ensures we are flexible and open to change and that we are conscious of the necessity of this very quality for the promotion of politically engaged research and action.

Most papers in this volume explore 'processes'—of representation, of knowledge construction, of material production and exchange—such that it seems odd to label them 'postprocessual'. In fact, it would appear that postprocessual analyses require even more dedication be applied to archaeological research such that each subjective element, be that object or person, be it in the present or the past, is fully exposed in terms of its social and political ramifications. It is within the detailed process of constructing, producing, representing, and changing that these interests are detected. This volume does not undertake to explore these political underpinnings to excise them and thus attempt a more objective, uncompromised perspective. Instead, it proposes we identify the common political commitment (bad and good) found in the prehistoric and historic production of objects, self and knowledge, such that we can commitment ourselves in the present, and thereby recognize and develop our underlying political engagement.

Here action means not just enacting theory in methods and analysis, but also acting as politically aware and engaged scholars that incorporate diverse critical approaches to improve understanding of the past yet also to improve our contribution through knowledge and deeds to the struggle for the improvement of social conditions in the core and the periphery.

Acknowledgements

We owe thanks to the scholars who contributed chapters to the volume, and to the following colleagues who forwarded papers (sometimes unpublished), exchanged ideas, and helped us in so many different ways: Margarita Díaz-Andreu, Mark Graham, Matthew Johnson, Michael Shanks, Christopher Tilley, Peter Ucko, Amalia Sanguinetti de Bórmida. The ideas expressed here are of course our own, for which we alone are therefore responsible. We must also recognize the important institutional support received from the The World Archaeological Congress, Brazilian National Research Council (CNPq), the São Paulo State Research Foundation (FAPESP, granted to Dr. Funari), the Campinas State University, and the Department of Prehistoric and Archaeological Research of the Argentinian National Science Fundation (DIPA-CONICET).

Notes

[1] Such as those by: Alberti, Karlsson, Lazzari, McGuire and Navarrete, Noelli, Orser, Podgorny et al. Politis, Prous. The same chapters were published in Portuguese and/or Spanish in Funari et al. (1999).

[2] That is, Acuto, Alberione, Chevitarese, Ferreira, Funari, Guarinello, Piñón, Sequeira, Senatore, Stovel, Zarankin.

References

Andrade Lima, T., 1999, El Huevo de la Serpiente: Una arqueología del capitalismo embrionario en el Río de Janeiro del siglo XIX. In *Sed Non Satiata: Teoría social en la arqueología latinoamericana contemporánea*, edited by A. Zarankin and F. Acuto, pp. 189–238. Ediciones del Tridente, Buenos Aires.

Buchli, V., and Lucas, L. G., editors, 2001, *Archaeologies of the Contemporary Past*. Routledge, London.

Delle, J., Mrozowski, A., and Paynter, R., 2000, *Lines that Divide: Historical Archaeologies of Race, Class and Gender*. University of Tennessee Press, Knoxville.

Díaz-Andreu, M., 1999, Nacionalismo y arqueología: del viejo al nuevo mundo. *Revista del Museo de Arqueología y Etnología* Suplemento 3:161–180.

Díaz-Andreu, M., and Champion, T., 1996, *Nationalism and Archaeology in Europe*. UCL Press, London.

Funari, P. P. A., 1993, Memória histórica e cultura material. *Revista Brasileira de História* 13:17–31.

   1994, Rescuing Ordinary People's Culture: Museums, Material Culture and Education in Brazil. In *The Presented Past, Heritage, Museums and Education*, edited by P. G. Stone and B. L. Molineaux, pp. 120–136. Routledge, London.

   1995, A cultura material e a construcao da mitología Bandeirante: Problemas da identidade nacional brasilera. *Ideais* (Campinas) 1:29–48.

Gero, J., and Conkey, M., 1991, *Engendering Archaeology: Women and Prehistory*. Blackwell, Oxford.

Gilchrist, R., 1999, *Gender and Archaeology: Contesting the Past*. Routledge, London.

Grahame, M., 1995, *The House of Pompeii: Space and Social Interaction*. Ph.D. dissertation, Department of Archaeology, Southampton University, England.

Hodder, I., 1982, *Symbols in Action*. Cambridge University Press, London.

Jenkins, K., 1995, *On What is History: From Carr and Elton to Rorty and White*. Routledge, London.

Johnson, M., 1993, *Housing Culture: Traditional Houses in and English Landscape*. Smithsonian, Washington D.C.

Jones, S., 1997, *The Archaeology of Ethnicity: Reconstructing Identities in the Past and the Present*. Routledge, London.

Leone, M., and Potter, M., editors, 1999, *The Historical Archaeology of Capitalism*. Plenum Press, New York.

McGuire, R., and Paynter, R., 1991, *The Archaeology of Inequality*. Blackwell, Cambridge, MA.

Miller, D., 1987, *Material Culture and Mass Consumption*. Blackwell, Oxford.

Miller, D., Rowlands, M., and Tilley, C., 1989, *Domination and Resistance*. Routledge, London.

Renfrew, C., and Bahn, P., 1993, *Arqueología: teorías, métodos y prácticas*. Akal, Barcelona.

Shanks, M., and Hodder, I., 1995. Processual, Postprocessual and Interpretive Archaeologies. In *Interpreting Archaeology. Finding Meaning in the Past*, edited by I. Hodder, M. Shanks, A. Alexandri, V. Buchli, J. Carman, J. Last and G. Lucas, pp. 3–29. Routledge, London.

Shanks, M., and Tilley, C., 1987a, *Reconstructing Archaeology: Theory and Practice*. Routledge, London.

Shanks, M., and Tilley, C., 1987b, *Social Theory and Archaeology*. Polity, Oxford.

Ucko, J., editor, 1995, *Theory in Archaeology: a World Perspective*. Routledge, London.

Zarankin, A., 1999, Casa Tomada: sistema, poder y vivienda familiar. In *Sed non Satiata: Teoría Social en la Arqueología Latinoamericana Contempoánea*, edited by A. Zarankin and F. Acuto, pp. 239–272. Ediciones Del Tridente, Buenos Aires.

Materiality and the Social   1

Julian Thomas

In this contribution I intend to consider some problems concerning material things and social relations, which arguably derive from the intellectual structure of our own discipline. Archaeologists, obviously, study the material traces that human beings leave behind them, and on that basis they attempt to understand past societies. Necessarily, this means that we are placed in the position of having to reflect on the relationship between the social and the material, because this directly affects the kinds of statement which we can legitimately make about the past.

It can be argued that our discipline is burdened with a way of thinking which is characteristic of modernity, and which we might characterize as 'Cartesianism'. I will suggest that this actually impedes our understanding of the material culture of the pre-modern past. But at the same time I am aware of the irony that archaeology is itself a product of the modern era. It was the parallel development of commodified, linear work-time and of the nation-state, that fuelled an interest in the origins of particular peoples and nations (e.g., Trigger, 1989). However, I do not wish to argue that there was a particular point at which the western world 'became modern'. Rather, I suggest that modernity represents a particular relationship between people and their world which gained coherence over a long period of time (Foucault, 1984).

As Bruno Latour (1993) argues, one of the characteristic elements in modern thinking has been a separation or segmentation of the rich and complex elements which make up the world into distinct and bounded categories. And the understanding is that the things which surround us naturally divide up into classes, which are *discovered* by science, rather than created in discourse. As the range of discursive categories multiplied, so new analytic fields were generated, and archaeology was one of these. With its practice of uncovering the hidden past, and stripping away layers of detritus in order to disclose older and more profound realities, archaeology provides the perfect paradigm for modern thought. Structural linguistics, in its search for the deep generators of language, or Freudian psychoanalysis, identifying the sedimented strata of the personality, have both relied on the metaphor of archaeology in setting up a separation between surface and depth. It seems that as a means of gaining knowledge of the past, archaeology has a model of depth and surface, or of ancient truth needing to be recovered from contemporary ruin, written into its constitution.

I want to argue that the scientific revolution and the Enlightenment did not so much discover the order of nature as *construct* it, and that by implication modern thought has been involved in a general process of alienation. This is not simply an alienation of workers from their products, but of human beings from the world of material things. In this respect, recent ethnographic work has been very instructive in demonstrating the ways in which non-western modes of thought emphasize the *relational* character of existence (e.g., Strathern, 1988). As soon as we are able to divide the world up into bounded categories of things, many of the relationships in which people find themselves are severed, or at least obscured. So people can come to appear as self-sufficient and internally motivated units, and 'their environment' can be reduced to a series of boxes in a flow-chart. Presented as separate entities, things or units can be valorized against each other (Jordanova, 1989). One entity can be held to be more solid than another, or to underlie another, or to give rise to another, or to be more fundamental than another. This is the principle which gives us the logic of economic base and cultural superstructure, unconscious and conscious self, essence and substance, authenticity and superficiality. It is very interesting that in this way of thinking we can equally well argue that biology provides the basis for social life, *or* that deep generative structures provide the basis for human thought. So both materialism and structuralism can be accommodated within these patterns of modern thought: in either case one entity is being set up as primordial in relation to another. One *thing* is presented as a given foundation, and another is assumed to be derived from it. This way of thinking has been described as a metaphysics of substance or presence, since it presents particular objects as being so fundamental that they evade analysis.

From my point of view, the most significant aspects of this way of thinking are the distinctions between culture and nature, and mind and body, which are conventionally associated with René Descartes (Cottingham, 1992). For Descartes, mind and body are different kinds of substance, so that the human being is a 'rational animal', a biological entity onto which some ephemeral extra element has been grafted (Heidegger, 1993). In a similar way, nature is understood as the *given* worldly material which is transformed and enlightened by culture. Culture then represents the cognitive aspects of human progress, which can subdue or dominate nature, the substantial. Our problem is that archaeology is implicated in this process by which we turn the world into objects observed by subjects, but that this process actually renders our subject matter incomprehensible. Archaeologists study *material culture*: something which is, within the Cartesian scheme of things, a contradiction in terms (Thomas, 1996). Consequently, I would argue that archaeology has consistently attempted to reduce material culture to an essence, which then has to be located *either* in the realm of ideas or that of physical presences.

For example, the archaeology of Britain and America in the first half of this century was dominated by forms of culture-history which presented artifacts as the material manifestations of internalized norms and values (e.g., Childe, 1936, 1942). Members of a given culture group shared the same ways of making and decorating pottery because they shared the same mental templates. But because these things were locked away in the sphere of the mind, and because the minds of dead people are now lost to us, the meanings of ancient artifacts are effectively beyond consideration.

I think that we can start to see the extent of these problems if we think for a moment about the way in which Karl Marx discussed materiality. Marx, of course, was one of the great theorists of alienation, but I think that we can argue that his focus on *production* remained deeply modernist in character. Marx recognized that under capitalism objects are severed from their producers through the operation of wage labor, so that they can circulate freely as alienated commodities. However, he maintained the distinction between culture and nature, so that raw materials are seen as having been *taken out of* an essentially passive nature, and transformed into artifacts through the application of human labor. As Marx (1970: 177) puts it, "man ... opposes himself to Nature ... in order to appropriate Nature's production in a form adapted to his own wants."

So Nature constitutes a storehouse of resources, whose utility is realized through the application of human labor. The relationship is an oppositional one, in that the 'work' of nature in producing resources is categorically different from the human action which frees those resources for use.

From an archaeological point of view, the disadvantage of this perspective is that it presents material culture as no more than a product or reflection of society. According to this argument, society logically precedes any material substance which is taken up and transformed into an artifact. As a result, social relations come to be perceived as metaphysical and inter-subjective. If we accept this, archaeological evidence becomes no more than a pale reflection of relationships which are now entirely vanished. And the most that we can hope to do as archaeologists to is find the pattern of those relationships somehow preserved in their material outcomes. However, it is clear that many non-western communities do not acknowledge any distinction between culture and nature, and I think that this should prompt us to think more closely about both social relationships and materiality.

Now, many recent forms of social thought have replaced a concern for social morphology ("the social unit is composed of . . . such-and-such") or social structure ("the social unit is underlain by . . . such-and-such") with a framework based on social practice. In these perspectives, the social becomes something which people *do*. One way of expressing this is to say that social life involves the *working* of relationships. This, hopefully, conveys a sense of people's *engagement* in social conduct. The notions of social morphology and social structure both tend to promote the perception of society as something which is *thing-like*— a bounded entity, if you like (Laclau and Mouffe, 1987). A shift toward social practice therefore has significant implications. Firstly, the social ceases to have any grounding essence, and it is seen instead as reproducing itself through continual performance. Secondly, it is evident that diverse social practices such as agriculture, exchange, ritual and craft production will rarely involve exactly the same groups of people, and need not all be bounded within the same social group. Different activities may have distinct yet overlapping constituencies. These may cut across lines of gender, ethnic affiliation, age and class. Indeed, each of these group identities may be seen as, to some extent, the outcome of social practice, rather than purely a pre-existing framework within which social life is conducted. Shirley Strum and Bruno Latour (1987) put this very nicely, by suggesting that we are never 'in' a society so much as struggling to define one. So the effect of this insight is to remove 'society' from its pre-eminent position as an *object* of analysis, replacing it with 'the social', which is an unbounded field or space. As a result, this concern with practice brings about a shift from a focus on entities to one on relationships.

Now, one of the better-known examples of an approach to social life which stresses relationships over entities is Michel Foucault's work on power (Foucault, 1977, 1978, 1980). Foucault argues against what he calls the 'juridical' conception of power, which sees it as something which can be held and dispensed by a ruler, principally as a means of restricting the actions of others. Power, he says, is not a thing or a commodity, and it cannot be held, stored or monopolized. It is a relational network in which people find themselves immersed. It also is not separate from other kinds of relationships—power is immanent in all forms of relationality. Moreover, power is not a contract that people enter into from outside. People do not create power relationships: power relationships produce people. By that I mean that we come to recognize ourselves as human subjects because the language that we use to talk about ourselves, the ways of acting and communicating, and the cultural stereotypes that make us intelligible to others are all imposed on us: they are all effects of power. In this sense, power restricts us, but it also facilitates our actions. All of the things which our culture imposes on us—from means of statement to forms of identity— become the resources through which we realize our own goals and objectives.

If we accept that the social is a field of relationships rather than a bounded entity, I think it becomes easier to recognize the inherently social character of material culture. The social is a hybrid, which mixes up human and non-human elements (Latour, 1993). Human activities are rarely conceived and executed by a single person, or brought to fruition within a single mind. More often, we use ideas and materials which have been affected by the actions of others, negotiate with others to define the form that the project will take, and channel our intentions through material things in bringing about our design. So, for instance, writing an academic paper involves engaging with books and papers written by others (which exist in a material form), discussing ideas with colleagues, and writing on a computer—with much of the content emerging in the act of writing itself. The process involves the negotiation of a series of alliances and associations, both with people and with objects. So you could say that you have a productive alliance with the computer, which is maintained until the printer ribbon breaks, or whatever. I would suggest that all of these connections are social in character, and that "socialness' extends to all of the relational involvements in which human beings are implicated.

Material culture is therefore not simply a product of society, it is *integral to* society. It follows that materials which remain from the past are more than evidence for a vanished entity: they are a part of that entity which is still here with us in the present. As such, of course, they are re-contextualized. Back in the 1960's and 70's, when many archaeologists were trying to claim a scientific status for the discipline, it was maintained that the 'archaeological record' was a kind of laboratory of human behaviour. In other words, archaeological evidence was something inert, which was bracketed off from both the past and the present. I am suggesting quite the opposite: these materials are part of now vanished social formations, and they have a cultural significance in the present. A very clear example of this would be Stonehenge in southern Britain, which both embodies aspects of past social practices, and has a variety of different modern meanings (Bender, 1998). Stonehenge is implicated in various notions of 'Englishness', and it is claimed and presented in various different ways by English Heritage, the National Trust, the Order of Druids, new age travelers, earth mysteries enthusiasts, and so on. To a greater or lesser extent, I would suggest that this is true of all material culture: it is implicated in a set of social relationships, and yet those relationships keep shifting as the historical process unfolds itself. So the task of the archaeologist becomes a twofold one: to attempt to identify through critique the modern understandings within which the evidence is now embedded, and to 're-animate' it through interpretation. Interpretation is an attempt to re-work past relationships, by putting agency back into the material fragments of the past. Necessarily, what one ends up with is a reading of the past which is of and for the present, but I think its also one which is grounded and constrained by the material evidence.

So far, so good. I am arguing in effect that archaeological practice, by engaging with material things, provides a kind of allegory for past social life. However, I should like to complicate matters somewhat by thinking a bit further about the character of materiality.

Philosophically, materiality has often been connected with irreducibility: that which exists materially simply *is* (Butler, 1993). This, after all, is the foundation of empiricism. However, it may be a mistake to imagine that simply because we can see and touch a thing we can grasp it in its entirety. That much would imply an unmediated transfer of objective information into the brain. This might be a description of the way in which a very sophisticated machine might function, but I do not think that it is how human beings operate in their world. When we apprehend the world, we do so through language, symbols, and concepts. If we were to want to argue that 'the real world exists independently of language', for instance, we still have to do so through the medium of language. However, this does not condemn us to insisting *either* that there is a real material world which can be transparently apprehended by consciousness, *or* that there is only language and signification. It is important to tread a fine line between these two extreme positions. Language does not bring the world into being, or create a fantasy existence which hides reality from us. Instead, language is the means by which the material world is revealed to us. We can recognize things because we have the concepts at our disposal to apprehend them. Where our concepts are inadequate to grasp what we encounter, we create new ones. So reality is always symbolically mediated, but this does not make it any less real.

What this means in practice is that when we have an experience of some phenomenon, we experience it 'as' something or other. We hear birdcall, we taste honey, we feel a walking-stick, we smeel the pine trees, and so on. The experience and its interpretation are coextensive. It is only when something is incomprehensible, through its unfamiliarity, that we focus on it analytically and try to define what it might be. Even then, it tends to be our available stock of language which gives us the resources through which we rationalize our new experience. Robert Mugerauer gives a very good example of this process when he describes the earliest European travelers and colonists entering the American west. Unable to describe the alien land-forms which they encountered in the vocabulary of Old World landscapes, they resorted to an architectural lexicon of 'vaults', 'spires' and 'crenellations' (Mugerauer 1985).

This suggests that materialization is not just given; it is a *process*, in which the physical world is gradually disclosed to us (Hull, 1997). Of course, we are never aware of all of the objects that surround us at once: our concern is directed toward things with which we are involving ourselves at a given time. This is principally a matter of the tasks and projects in which we are involved. So cleaning the floor directs my interest to the broom that I use, even though my absorption in the task might mean that this involvement is implicit and unconsidered (Heidegger, 1962). Thus two senses of 'mattering' are interconnected: we are aware of things matter-ing (being material) because they 'matter to us', they are significant. So signification does not merely describe or reflect materiality, it provides the conditions under which materiality can be recognized and make sense. This begins to break down any idealist notion that language and symbols operate in a rarefied cognitive realm, separate from material reality. Signification, or discourse, is something which happens in the real world, and which articulates relationships between real things.

Of course, it follows from what I have been arguing already that signifying practices are implicated in relations of power and knowledge. Our differential positioning as people, and our differential access to knowledge provide us with distinct ways of giving voice, and varied chances of being recognized as an authoritative speaker. Similarly, inscriptions and material symbols are more or less likely of being recognized depending upon the conditions under which they are encountered. So it follows that materialization is an effect of power. Judith Butler (1993) has documented the way in which human bodies have to perform in approved ways, citationally repeating a regulatory norm, in order to secure cultural intelligibility as a 'man' or 'woman'. The alternative is to lie outside what can be readily comprehended, in abjection. But even artifacts will be understood in different ways by people who come to them with different understandings which emerge from different social experiences. Occupying different positions in the network of power, people will interpret their material surroundings in different ways. In understanding my give rise to hegemonic struggles over the definition of reality. However, it would be a mistake to argue in these circumstances that one group has a true appreciation of the situation, while another is laboring under false consciousness.

So, to try to come to some sort of conclusion, I have suggested that modern thought, which separates the mental and the material, or society and nature, into distinct spheres makes the enterprise of interpreting material things appear both too easy and too difficult. The empiricists believed that the status of objects was self evident. I am suggesting a much more complex situation, which makes the study of artifacts at once more challenging and potentially more rewarding. Human social life is inherently relational:everything we do, and everything we are is realized through relationship. The material world is not extrinsic to those relationships, and artifacts are implicated in the ways that we create meaning and carry out our everyday lives. For an archaeologist, this means that the task of attempting to understand the past becomes more like anthropology. We attempt to engage with the material evidence, just as the ethnographer enters into a conversation with his or her informants. But at the same time, I am suggesting that the apprehension of the material world is a social phenomenon. How things are materialized depends upon the language, the concepts, the experiences, and the power relations which converge on a particular experience. So just as we cannot look back at the ancient past and imagine that those people understood their own bodies in the same way as we do in the present, we equally cannot imagine that the significance of material culture is fixed and changeless. This underlines the point that the conversation between past and present that is involved in interpretation is one which can never be fully completed. The more we know about a past material world, the more we are likely to find that we fall short of a total understanding.

References

Bender, B., 1998, *Stonehenge: Making Space*. Berg, London.

Butler, J., 1993, *Bodies That Matter: On the Discursive Limits of "Sex"*. Routledge, London.

Childe, V. G., 1936, *Man Makes Himself*. Watts, London.

1942, *What Happened in History*. Penguin, Harmondsworth.

Cottingham, J., 1992, Cartesian Dualism: Theory, Metaphysics and Science. In *The Cambridge Companion to Descartes*, edited by J. Cottingham, pp. 236–256. Cambridge University Press, Cambridge.

Foucault, M., 1977, *Discipline and Punish: The Birth of the Prison*. Vintage, New York.

1978, *The History of Sexuality. Volume 1: An Introduction*. Peregrine Press, London.

1980, Truth and Power. In *Power/Knowledge*, M. Foucault, pp. 109–133. Harvester, Brighton.

1984, What is Enlightenment? In *The Foucault Reader*, edited by P. Rabinow, pp. 32–50. Peregrine, Harmondsworth.

Heidegger, M.,1962, *Being and Time*. Translated by J. Macquarrie and E. Robinson. Blackwell, Oxford.

1993, Letter on Humanism. In *Martin Heidegger: Basic Writings* (2nd edition), edited by D.F. Krell, pp. 213–265. Routledge, London.

Hull, C. L., 1997, The Need in Thinking: Materiality in Theodor W. Adorno and Judith Butler. *Radical Philosophy* 84: 22–35.

Jordanova, L., 1989, *Sexual Visions: Images of Gender in Science and Medicine between the Eighteenth and Twentieth Centuries*. Harvester Wheatsheaf, London.

Laclau, E. and Mouffe, C., 1987, Post-Marxism without Apologies. *New Left Review* 166: 79–106.

Latour, B., 1993, *We Have Never Been Modern*. Harvester Wheatsheaf, London.

Marx, K., 1970, *Capital, Volume 1*. Lawrence and Wishart, London.

Mugerauer, R., 1985, Language and the Emergence of the Environment. In *Dwelling, Place and Environment*, edited by D. Seamon and R. Mugerauer, pp. 51–70, Columbia University Press, New York.

Strathern, M., 1988, *The Gender of the Gift*. University of California Press, Berkeley.

Strum, S., and Latour, B., 1987, Redefining the Social Link: from Baboons to Humans. *Social Science Information* 26: 783–802.

Thomas, J. S., 1996, *Time, Culture and Identity: An Interpretive Archaeology*. Routledge, London.

Trigger, B. G., 1989, *A History of Archaeological Thought*. Cambridge University Press, Cambridge.

2

Archaeology and the Meanings of Material Culture

Norberto Luiz Guarinello

Whether considered as a more anthropological or more historical discipline, archaeology is a science of objects, which one nowadays more commonly calls 'material culture'. No matter how we define culture, though, it involves communication and meaning and the archaeologist's task may be defined as that of extracting, or rather of proposing meanings to objects produced by human cultures. That task is surrounded by great difficulties, quite different from those presented by written texts or oral tradition. It is now almost common sense that objects communicate, or are rather means for communication, either between contemporaries (their producers and users) or through time, as monuments from the past that we try to transform into documents. Since the 60's Semiotics and Anthropology have been trying to decipher the world of things by imagining it is structured like a language, with its own grammar, syntax, and vocabulary. In archaeology, the most daring experiment in this sense was perhaps that of David Clarke (1968, 1972), but it had no followers and the parallel between language and material things seems in fact to lead to a dead end. More recently, the emphasis in archaeological theory has shifted from language, understood as a signic system, to symbolic systems, with all the complexities associated with the interpretation of symbolic meanings. Considering material culture as a symbolic system opens an extraordinarily fertile field of investigation, but poses new

19

problems and difficulties. It the last of these I wish to explore further here.

The growing interest in symbols is a recent phenomenon. The so called New Archaeology, still largely predominant in the USA and the Americas, is a case in point. In the 60's and 70's, new archaeologists were more interested in establishing what they thought were the scientific foundations of the discipline. They employed a once fashionable method—the so-called hypothetico—deductive method—and developed a view of the evolution of human societies which centered on ecological or adaptive factors. Even if they did not totally disregard ideology or symbolism, they tended to treat them as a sub-system of society, dependant on technology or adaptive forces. Their interpretation of past societies was based on models of a universal character: on any given level in the evolutionary scale, societies in the same adaptive situation would display the same correlations or regularities between technology, social organization and social symbols or ideology. Symbols were not forgotten, but surely they were not the main concern (cf. Binford, 1983).

Since the late 80's, however, things have changed rather swiftly. Archaeology has entered postmodernity and the focus of innovative theory has moved to England, particularly to Cambridge, where Ian Hodder assembled a group of young, thought-provoking archaeologists whose work has been most influential. The 'postprocessual school' has some interesting characteristics (see Shanks and Hodder, 1995) that warrant further consideration:

1. Their theoretical basis is sought from outside archaeology, mainly from continental philosophers like Foucault, Derrida, Bourdieu and even Nietsche (Bapty and Yates, 1990; Tilley, 1990).
2. Discourse is their main theoretical category. Everything is considered discourse or text, be it material culture or the works of contemporary archaeologists.
3. Science is regarded with suspicion, as an instrument of power which imposes a western attitude on the rest of the world, or the scientists' own views onto the general public.
4. They tend to disregard technological or adaptive factors as being less important than symbolic ones, that is to say, than the meanings of material culture.

So the meaningful character of material culture has come to the forefront of archaeology. Objects are no longer considered simple and passive reflections of technology or social organization. Material culture is considered to be an active, structuring dimension of human societies and its meanings, as a fundamental dimension of human life. At times, it seems to appear as the determining one. However, in order to interpret the meanings of material culture, they totally reject the comparative, cross-cultural and evolutionary presuppositions of the old New Archaeology.

To postprocessual archaeology, every human culture has its own symbolic structure that can only be understood in its own terms, that is to say, in the very specific context that produced it. The only way of interpreting the meaning of material culture would be to recreate the specific contexts in which the objects were meaningful, thus to make a contextual analysis of them. Material culture is considered to be structured much like a text, or rather to be a text, with all the difficulties a text poses to the reader, with all the infinite readings a text offers to the readers (Hodder, 1990).

This conception of material culture has some interesting points. On one hand, it seems very pessimistic in its emphasis on the opacity of material culture, on the difficulties it encounters in comparing different contexts, on the multiple possible readings it admits and proposes. On the other hand, it is also too optimistic in its boldness in exploring the symbolic dimension of material culture and the robustness of the readings they propose. Their assumption is that the local context would certainly supply, to the attentive archaeologist, all the keys to the interpretation of the objects they find.

Nonetheless, their actual interpretations of the meanings of ancient objects do not always seem convincing. Moreover, they do not ever keep to the reading methods they propose. In fact, from their theoretical papers one would expect very thick descriptions of archaeological contexts which would be the key to the revealing of the symbolic meanings of the objects found therein. In practice, we find little of this. Ian Hodder, for instance, has recently turned his attention to the early Neolithic of Southeastern Europe and the Middle East (Hodder, 1992). This period represents to him the domestication of man in Europe. His central idea is that in order to domesticate plants and animals, these societies had first to domesticate themselves and that they achieved this by material and symbolic means. So, the female statuettes abundantly found in early Neolithic sites are regarded as instrumental to and a statement of this process of domestication. He appropriately rejects the old interpretation of them as symbols of the Mother Goddess. But his own interpretation is not without its methodological faults. How does he extract meaning from the female statuettes? Well, it is a complex operation. His point of departure is the assumption that these societies were organized by the opposition between house and wilderness (in his words *domus* x *agrios*). To settle in houses, societies had to be afraid of the wilderness. So, terrible symbols of the wild were put inside their houses. The statuettes of women are also found within the houses, as opposed to the terrible images of the wilderness: "the metaphor of the women was a central part of the idea of *domus*" (Hodder, 1992: 246) so they are proof that women were associated with the house, with home, cooking and agriculture. Hodder oscillates between seeing this association as a sign of women's power in that society or rather, of their submission (Hodder, 1992: 257). He really proposes both in successive papers, only to reject them both and to conclude that his own interpretations were based on a sexist, male's outlook (Hodder, 1992: 258). More importantly, when he does propose an interpretation he employs universal categories and not contexts! Sheer archaeological context seemed to be unable to reveal the meaning of the statuettes. And in fact, his interpretation is based on a binary opposition (home-wild) very like those of Levi-Strauss (culture-nature) or even those employed by Leroi-Gourhan in his interpretation of Paleolithic rock art (Leroi-Gourhan, 1985). It is true that he argues that this categories are particular to this area and period, but they are not in any way contextual or particular, but very abstract ones (as Hodder himself admits, 1992: 251).

By these critical remarks I do not intend to deny the relevance and importance of postmodern archaeology and the significance of the questions they put to all archaeologists and social scientists. But before trying to interpret the symbolic meaning of material culture or even proposing it as the main task for archaeology, we should pay more attention to what symbols are and, above all, to what limits the archaeological documents themselves impose on their study. After all, what do we mean by affirming that material culture is symbolic? That is a difficult question. The very definition of symbol is debatable. One can find many definitions of it in the literature of the Social Sciences, among anthropologists, psychoanalysts, philosophers, semioticians and even archaeologists. Some people equate sign and symbol with the linguistic sign, so that symbols seem to have an arbitrary but very precise and circumscribed meaning; that is, they refer to precise, identifiable things. The majority however, use symbols in relation to specific kinds of sign, which are not completely arbitrary, but are produced by metaphors, analogies, metonymies, etc. Symbols in this view express things that may not be precise or rather, they allude to things which cannot be expressed by words. They communicate in specific ways, quite unlike the linguistic sign. Such are religious symbols, or those of psychoanalysis, either Freudian or Jungian. (Augé, 1982; Dévereux, 1979; Maquet, 1982).

This second meaning of symbols seems more useful for interpreting material culture; symbol as an allusion, a reference to things not expressed and not necessarily expressible by words, as signs with a surplus of meaning. These symbols may be very private and particular, but they are always a statement of social meanings, of shared beliefs, common identities or even social conflicts. We are surrounded by these social symbols, they give us unity and a sense of a common life. In terms of material culture, symbols are objects especially invested with emotion, objects that serve to communicate. But is all communication symbolic? Do all cultural objects function as symbols? I do not believe so. As I see it, there are many levels of meaning in the objects. Any object is part of a human transaction, be it in its production, distribution or consumption, and so all objects are means of communication. But some of their meanings are unintentional, others are consciously employed to communicate, others yet are explicitly produced to communicate. If we forget for a moment that objects may be differently invested in their meanings (from unnoticeable to highly effective), we can reduce the meanings of objects to different spheres.

The most concrete one is functional. Objects indicate their use by their material, form, and decoration. The meaning of a cooking pot is to cook. Form seems determined by function as an almost signic relationship. That is the way Moles (1972) analyses table services and the arbitrary meaning of each piece within a set. One may suppose a code behind the objects which is structured like a language by the sheer play of opposition in their forms. Of course this is mostly true of service sets; that is, groups of objects associated with a specific activity and with specific functions within it. That is not true of all material culture. Archaeological interpretation at this level of meaning poses specific problems given the high degree of arbitrariness in the form/function relationship found in all human societies. In effect, different cultures employ different objects to execute similar functions, like forks and chopsticks, or similar objects to do quite different things. So frequently we cannot predict the functional meaning of an object from a foreign culture just through its form.

On a more general level, objects are a fundamental part of social communication, joining people together or pulling them apart. They are everywhere; they constitute the world we live in. They are the products of humans yet are themselves socially productive. Objects approximate and differentiate groups of people in the process of their production, either by the sheer division of labor between sexes or age groups or through different forms of class exploitation; they create and reinforce relationships through their distribution and exchange within and between societies and they materialize and express social positions through their consumption. Objects even unintentionally express and are the materialization of social identities and differences. We can propose to identify a group, a tribe, a series of tribes by their pottery, haircut, dressings, funeral practices, houses and so on. At the individual level, we can sometimes identify a potter by his style, even if this particularization was unintentional.

Modes of consumption also intentionally express identities and differences and the spans of identities and differences admitted in a given society or between societies. Objects classify human beings, include or exclude, substantiate and express identity and differences in gender, age, occupation, religious beliefs, football teams, birthplace, wealth or lifestyles. Objects offer a range, more or less open to individual choice, of possibilities to communicate social identities and differences, to large sectors of society as well as to the individual consumer of modern societies. The distribution of objects reflects and materializes in this way the structure of a society. The important point is that their meaning depends on a code which is not in themselves, but is produced elsewhere, in the social relationships which constitute a society. Objects are thus not structured like a text, as the postprocessualist would say (i.e., Hodder, 1990). They have no internal code, no unifying meaning or authorship, no frozen meaning to be differently read. Different societies will have different structures of objects, some more egalitarian, some highly differentiated in forms, functions, qualities and quantities. The interpretation of the meaning of material culture depends on the interpretation of the society producing and using it.

At a more abstract and profound level, objects can loose precise reference values and signify or communicate a structured code outside their meaning. Arrangements of objects may produce very complex sets of meanings by way of allusion, metaphor, analogy, in a very imprecise, impressionistic manner. This is an everyday experience. When we enter someone's house, the objects inside it and the house itself enable us to classify their owner in a general way, as rich or poor, middle-class, blue or white collar, and to have a feeling of the tastes of the occupants. But this perception is not a precise one, it is always open to different interpretations. The objects themselves and their arrangement produce an ambiguous discourse, an almost polyphonic one. As many authors have already pointed out, from different perspectives, we organize our world and express ourselves through the use and arrangement of certain objects, but the structures we find in the objects are more symbolic than signic (Baudrillard, 1968; Douglas and Isherwood, 1979).

At last, there are specific objects which are produced precisely for their shared symbolic content, like artistic (aesthetic) and religious objects, or recently created national symbols. These are the most difficult for the archaeologist to decipher. Their meanings are not strictly structured nor fixed but metaphorical, paradigmatically structured, meaningful only to specific partners in often ritualized use. These intentional symbols have always had a surplus of meaning; they synthesize beliefs and emotions; they are highly affective and can represent quite different things to different people even in the course of a single event or within the same ritual in which they are employed. Their meanings can be socialized in very different degrees, from very particular symbols, impressed in specific objects to which individuals attribute unshared meanings, understandable only to themselves, to those which can encompass the collective emotions of a whole group of people.

Material culture is thus a complex matter. In a sense, it means much more than its meanings. It is a fundamental part of human existence and of social relations: it is a means to action over the world and over people, it enables and forbids people to take part in social practices, it signals and symbolizes, it expresses, it indicates, it classifies. It, or parts of it, may have different meanings, from very private to social ones, more exclusive or more widely shared; meanings that may be contrastive or even contradictory within a given society; meanings, it must be said, are never given, they are interpreted, imposed or negotiated. Objects are thus a matter of power relations, as has been repeatedly stressed by archaeologists over the last few years. The control over objects, be it in their production, distribution, or consumption, is a way of controlling the social practices of everyday life and defining the production of meaning within a given society. It is part of the permanent self-structuring process of any society.

The process of interpreting material culture may seem easier to those who believe in the universal character of symbols, who treat symbols as the statement of the human mind and psyche in general, like psychoanalysts and structuralists. Some very interesting interpretations have been made using these assumptions, concerning for instance myths or religious symbols. I find them, however, highly speculative and they do not appeal to my taste.

Be that as it may, the interpretation of material signs and symbols does remains a major concern for archaeologists. I think we should be more cautious about our interpretations. Today it seems old-fashioned to remember the famous ladder of inference proposed by Hawkes in 1954, but it remains valuable. For Hawkes, archaeology would find it increasingly difficult to understand the meanings of objects as it progressed from technological questions through economic, social and finally ideological ones. I think he was essentially right.

As has been seen, my examples have been drawn from prehistory. That is because prehistorians are confronted with greater difficulties than classical archaeologists in interpreting their materials. After all, classical archaeologists do have written texts. I do not entirely agree with Moses Finley (1989), to whom prehistory was an almost impossibility, and medieval and contemporary Archaeologies perfectly useless. But I do agree with him that Classical archaeology occupies a special position within the various existing archaeologies. Classical Archaeology has access to a plethora of written sources, together with well known, published, classified, dated archaeological material of excellent quality, together with a long tradition of reflection and analysis behind it that puts it in a very special position within archaeology.

However, while written sources are excellent guides in the study of material culture, they pose their own problems to archaeological interpretation. In fact, objects and texts, even if produced by the same society in the same period, are different dimensions of reality and their relationship is never immediate (Andren, 1998). Material culture is neither a reflection of literature/written culture, nor its illustration. As we saw, it has its own levels of meaning. This is true of objects in general and particularly of iconography, which I take here as an example.

Iconography, or the imaging of objects, may be decorative or symbolically invested, narrative or paratactic, figurative or abstract. The important point is that it has its own rules. Mythological scenes, for instance, are not mere translations of written myths, they are the statement of myths by way of images. Think of Etruscan iconography and the problems it poses to interpretation: are the images on Etruscan objects from the VII BC merely decorative, or a banalization of Greek myths and art, or a precise reference to Greek myths, or to their own mythical narratives (Camporeale, 1965)? Well, we do not have, after all, the Etruscan texts. But the same uncertainty is present in the interpretation of Athenian iconography from the V and IV centuries BC. Think of the women in Dionysian pottery scenes: are they maenads or nymphs? (Carpenter, 1986, 1997).

In fact, what written sources offer us are just possible interpretations, by contemporary men, of the meanings of some of the objects or images they used to employ and see. They can show us some of the possible or more diffused interpretations, but not the real and only ones. Think only of the apothropaic meaning of the phallus, which Latin literature presents either according to its attractiveness or on its awful ugliness. Sometimes, iconography seems even to contradict written sources, as in the case of the recently recovered paintings at the suburban baths of Pompeii, with scenes of lesbianism.

The truth is that material culture is very resistant to interpretation by archaeologists. Almost by definition, we cannot see the objects in use, we cannot ask the users about the meanings they attributed to them, we cannot attain the deep understanding modern Anthropology would require. So archaeologists have to give them their meaning and suppose that this was the ancient and prevalent one. How to do this? To answer this question we must return to our levels of meaning. Production and technologies may be studied in themselves. Service sets present recognizable structures that we may identify, provided that we establish the right correlation between form and function. On the other hand, to decipher an object as social classifier we need a model of the society which produced, distributed, and consumed it. This may seem a circular argument, but in fact we do need an interpretation of the society prior to the interpretation of the objects through which we intend to understand that society. Finally, to interpret symbols we need written sources, but even they give us but a range of possibilities and not real meanings. The comparative method is important at all these levels, but understandably more in the first. The interpretation of symbols, as defined here, is the most difficult and risky. It depends on a hardy combination of universal and particular contexts. It represents a frontier zone, where explanation becomes understanding, where a dialogue between the past and the present becomes possible, including all the uncertainty of real life. There is no way out; to interpret the meaning of something we must give it its meaning.

References

Andren, A., 1998, *Between Artifacts and Texts: Historical Archaeology in Global Perspective*. Plenum Press, New York.

Augé, M., 1982, *The Anthropological Circle: Symbol, Function, History*. Cambridge University Press, Cambridge.

Bapty, I., and Yates, T., 1990, Introduction: Archaeology and Post-structuralism. In *Archaeology after Structuralism*, edited by I. Bapty and T. Yates, pp. 1–32. Routledge, London.

Baudrillard, J., 1968, *Le système des objects*. Gallimard, Paris.

Binford, L., 1983, *In Pursuit of the Past*. Thames and Hudson: London.

Camporeale, G., 1965, Banalizzazioni etrusche di miti greci—I. In *Studi in Onore di Luisa Banti*, pp. 111–123. L'Erma, Roma.

Carpenter, T. H., 1986, *Dionysian Imagery in Archaic Greek Art: Its Development in Black-Figure Vase Painting*. Clarendon Press, Oxford.

1997, *Dionysian Imagery in Fifth-Century Athens*. Clarendon Press, Oxford.

Clarke, D. L., 1968, *Analytical Archaeology*. Methuen, London.

1972, *Models in Archaeology*. Methuen, London

Dévereux, G., 1979, *Fantasy and Symbol: Studies in Anthropological Interpretation*. Academic Press, London and New York.

Douglas, M., and Isherwood, B., 1979, *The World of Goods*. Basic Books, New York.

Finley, M., 1989, *Arqueologia e História, uso e abuso da História*. Martins Fontes, São Paulo.

Hawkes, C. F., 1954, Archaeological Theory and Method: Some Suggestions from the Old World. *American Anthropologist 56*:155–168.

Hodder, I., 1990, Textos de cultura material y cambio social: una discusión teórica y algunos ejemplos arqueológicos. *Boletin de Antropologia Americana 21:* 25–39.

1992, *Theory and Practice in Archaeology*. Routledge, London.

Leroi-Gourhan, A., 1985, As *religiões da Pré-História*. Edições 70, Lisboa.

Maquet, J., editor, 1982, *On Symbols in Anthropology: Essays in Honor of Harry Hoijer*. Undera, Malibu.

Moles, A., 1972, *Théorie des Objects*. Editions Universitaires, Paris.

Shanks, M., and Hodder, I., 1995, Processual, Postprocessual and Interpretive Archaeologies. In *Interpreting Archaeology: Finding Meaning in the Past*, edited by I. Hodder, M. Shanks, A. Alexandri, V. Buchli, J. Carman, J. Last and G. Lucas, pp. 3–29. Routledge, London.

Tilley, C., editor, 1990, *Reading Material Culture: Structuralism, Hermeneutics and Post-Structuralism*. Basil Blackwell, Oxford.

3

Why Is There Material Culture Rather than Nothing?

Heideggerian Thoughts and Archaeology

Håkan Karlsson

Introduction

The purpose of this paper is to elucidate and discuss a fundamental, ontological question which appears to have been forgotten and simplified in the discourses of contemporary archaeology. This question is, *'Why is there material culture rather than nothing?'* In accordance with its purpose, and the question just put forward, this paper is quite philosophical in nature. It presents a discussion that is probably unfamiliar to most archaeologists. Despite this fact, I would encourage the reader to continue, because the actual discussion leads to further questions that are of crucial relevance both to archaeologists and to archaeology.

Irrespective of which theoretical approach we take, we can easily agree that the past material culture that we deal with as archaeologists exists before our eyes, but what about its Being? By Being, and this is a central point, I do not mean the visibility or appearance of phenomena. In accordance with the later reasoning of the German philosopher Martin Heidegger, I rather refer to Being as the process that makes everything that is manifest, that makes it appear. It is Being that renders possible, and determines, all that is (Heidegger, 1927: 2–15; 1953: 14–15; 1954b: 16–17, 85, 106, 137–149; 1957: 57–67). This argument concerning the ontological difference between Being and beings is probably unfamiliar

29

Figure 3.1. The megalith known as 'The Dwarfs' House', Lindome parish, Västergötland, Sweden.

to most archaeologists, because we usually refer to the Being of material culture as the fact that it is manifest in a physical way. It is there in front of us, it is present before our eyes, and it can be experienced. We do not distinguish between Being and beings.

How then do we conceive of the Being of the megalith shown in Figure 3.1? And how do we conceive of the Being of the illustration itself? In the fact that they are visible and manifest, or in the process that renders them manifest?

Traditional Ontology

Probably most of us would refer to the Being, both of the megalith and of the illustration, in accordance with the first proposal, i.e., as the fact that they are manifest in a physical way. We, then, approach the Being of these beings in the same way as the traditional Aristotelian and Platonic, post-Socratic philosophers. But at the same time we are not aware of Being as the process that renders phenomena manifest. In this traditional approach, Being as process becomes just the visible appearance of phenomena, instead of the crucial process that makes them appear, i.e., there is no awareness of the ontological difference between Being and beings.

This traditional view of Being has been with us since Plato and Aristotle, and it was further developed and strengthened by, for instance, Descartes and Kant. Plato interprets Being as idea, as that which is seen in the visible, the aspects that are offered by the phenomenon in its presence (Plato, 1935: VI, VII). Thus, Plato lets the consequences of Being (the appearance and presence of beings) take the place of Being as process, and Being and being are considered identical. The ultimate outcome of the unawareness of Being as the process of appearance is that the (ontological) difference between Being and beings is forgotten. Being is interpreted by Plato and his successors as the visible appearance of phenomena, while the subjective perception of the present phenomenon becomes central. The idea becomes a paradigm (ideal), and the appearance of a phenomenon is considered to be the emergence of a copy that can be judged in accordance with the ideal. The appearance of something is, from now on, a visible appearance in accordance with an ideal located in human consciousness. This leads to a division of the world into subject and object, into thinking (consciousness) and object (of consciousness), i.e., a division between human thinking and Being as process. Within this framework, the human subject and his or her consciousness are conceived of as a thinking entity that produces representational ideas of the world in which it exists, which means that the world becomes centered on the subject and its production of ideas. We all know the consequences of this anthropocentric ontology, as it comes to us mainly through the reasoning of Descartes and Kant: the objectification and use of human beings and animals, the view of truth as a correspondence between subjective ideasand the subjective perception of objects, the endeavor to find measurable, secure truths that develops through the modern project, and the striving for human control, reason, logic and dominance. In accordance with this, traditional metaphysics or ontology is anthropocentric in its nature, because it considers the human production of ideas to be the center of the world. From this it does not follow that all traditional metaphysics is idealistic in its nature, but rather that the traditions of both idealism and realism argue solely about the ontological status of beings, while they have in common the fact that they do not recognize the unity between Being and human thinking that precedes any distinction between subject and object. In a simplified manner, it can be stated that the main reason for this anthropocentrism is to be found in the unawareness of the ontological difference and the unity between Being (-as-history) and human thinking (Heidegger, 1947: 5–52; 1953: 79–80, 91, 137–140; 1954b: 133–136; 1969: 66–70). Is there an alternative, and what does it look like? Is it possible to conceive of the Being of the megalith in the illustration and the Being of this illustration, not as the fact that they are visible and manifest, but in accordance with the second proposal, as the process that makes them manifest?

Pre-Socratic (Late Heideggerian) Ontology

According to Martin Heidegger's later reasoning, pre-Socratic philosophers such as Parmenides and Heraclitus did not work within the framework of a forgotten-ness of the ontological difference, nor did they neglect Being as the ultimate foundation for everything that is manifest. They did not conceive of the relationship between human beings and Being as contradictory; rather, they viewed the human capacity to think as a response to Being (-as-history). Being was therefore conceived of as the ultimate ground for everything, that is, including our human existence (Heidegger, 1953: 104–111; 1954b: 175; 1957: 14–17).[1] Thus, pre-Socratic reasoning are reversed if compared with the post-Socratic ones. But what does this imply? Are we, as human 'beings', and our thinking determined by Being (-as-history)?

According to Heidegger, Being is responsible for the crucial call that gives us something to think about in the first place. Thus, our thinking is still an activity that takes place in our consciousness, but our consciousness (and our capacity to think) are grounded in Being. Thinking, then, is not a question of the production of representational ideas, but rather of openness towards that which calls upon us to think, an openness in which we let the truth of Being appear against the background of its own initiative. In this context, truth is not conceived of as correspondence, but as disclosed-ness (aletheia). This means—something which is rather unfamiliar to most of us—that it is not we who point to things, but rather things that show themselves to us in the event in which Being, as a process, lets them be seen by us. Accordingly, we can have different opinions concerning a specific phenomenon, but it is Being, as a process, that is the ultimate foundation for the fact that there is a being to have opinions about (Heidegger, 1947: 54–57; 1954b: 33–40, 84–90, 147–149; 1959: 19–20; 1962a: 39–40). For instance, we can interpret the actual megalith as the 'House of the Dwarfs', in accordance with the 17th-century view, or we can interpret it as a grave. And we can interpret the illustration as a reflection of the empirical reality or as some black impressions on a piece of paper. The point is that both the megalith and the illustration are (still) there. This analysis implies that Being, when disclosed by our thinking, is partly identical to, or rather united with, the nature and activity of thinking. The relationship between Being and the thinking of human beings is one of mutual dependence, in which we, as human beings, 'dwell' in Being. This is because Being needs our thinking as an opening from which it can come forth, at the same time as we need the openness of Being (Heidegger, 1947: 111–120; 1953: 75–76; 1954a: 187–204; 1954b: 4–5, 33, 146–149, 158; 1957: 18–19, 23–41; 1959: 49–59).

But how is it possible that a human being can be brought forward in Being, at the same time as a human being resolves for, and receives, the disclosure of its own ground? Heidegger states that our requirement of truth is the foundation for the relationship between us and things, and that this relationship occurs as history (Heidegger, 1957: 64; 1959: 56–60; 1961: 481–485, 489). Here history is to be conceived of as a mode of knowing and not as the happenings and deeds of the world or as the cultural achievements of human beings. The fundamental thing in history is not its sequential nature, but rather historical thinking. We should look for history where the articulation of the nature of things occurs. Such history relates human beings to things, because, through it, things are sustained by the human requirement that they shall become true (unconcealed), at the same time as this requirement of truth means a requirement that the nature of things shall be brought forth. Thus, the articulation of the nature of things is an aspect of the disclosure (truth) of Being as process. But, as already mentioned, human thinking and our possibility of articulating the nature of things is at the same time grounded in Being as process. Thus, Being as process is the source and origin of all articulation and all thought, and therefore also the source and origin of history. In a simplified way, it can be stressed that Being is history (Heidegger, 1947: 81; 1954a: 277; 1969: 1–26, 1989: 494).

Does this mean that Being (-as-history) is the origin of all kinds of thinking about the Being of beings? Is Being the basis for both pre-Socratic and post-Socratic ideas of Being? According to Heidegger, this is exactly how it is. Being has a history (in a more traditional interpretation of the concept) that is grounded in the different historical articulations (ideas) of Being (Heidegger, 1950: 311–317; 1953: 70, 143; 1957: 55–67; 1959: 56–59; 1969: 1–26; 1975). But the point that Heidegger means is that Being as a process (in itself) is dynamic in its nature. Therefore, our historical articulations of Being (grounded in our transcendental structures of experience, i.e. our pre-understanding) is not the foundation for this history; rather, our thoughts are solely the opening from which Being comes forth in different shapes throughout different historical epochs. Therefore both our understanding and our pre-understanding are grounded in Being (-as-history), and not in our (anthropocentric) transcendental structures of experience.

But does this reflection on the dynamics of Being (-as-history) not create a passive human being, who is totally determined by Being and who cannot influence history? The crucial question is, whether we have some kind of freedom within these structures. Heidegger stresses that we cannot influence the turning of Being and that we do not know when this turning will come or whether it will come at all (Heidegger, 1962a: 37–47). But at the same time we still have the opportunity to let beings be what they are. We have the freedom to allow others to become what they are and to accept our mutual dependence. We also have the opportunity to pose fundamental questions about Being (-as-history) and the relationship between ourselves and Being (-as-history). We can prepare ourselves for the turning of Being (Heidegger, 1943: 16–18; 1953: 16–24, 29–30, 120–121, 124–130; 1962a: 37–47). From my point of view, this project, directed towards the fundamental structures of our existence, is the opposite of passivity.

From this, it follows that the actual question ('Why is there material culture rather than nothing?') ought to be answered by saying "Because Being (-as-history) lets it appear through our thoughts".

Contemporary (Post-Socratic) Archaeology

Are these considerations of any relevance to archaeology as a discipline or to us as archaeologists? I believe that they are both relevant and important. This is primarily because the dominant, contemporary, Western, archaeological approaches (cultural-historic, functionalist, Marxist, processual and postprocessual) and the different approaches that can be classified under these simplified headings seem to be more or less anchored in post-Socratic anthropocentrism. For instance, it is obvious that both processualism and postprocessualism conceive of the Being of past remains as the fact that they are visible and manifest, and not as the process that makes them manifest. This is the case whether the meaning that we ascribe to past remains is conceived of as a present, socio-ideological construction or whether it is viewed as a product of scientific methodology. Thus, both processualism and postprocessualism work within the frameworks of post-Socratic metaphysics and anthropocentrism. This implies that, whichever of these approaches we use, we shall be concentrating on beings (things/artifacts) as beings, while remaining unaware of Being (-as-history), i.e., the process or way by which everything that is comes forward in our thoughts. In other words, we are not aware of the (ontological) difference between beings and Being, nor are we aware of the unity between our thinking and Being (-as-history). This implies that both processualism and postprocessualism solely pose consciousness-centered questions to past remains and never answer the questions that emanate from the Being of these beings. This is the case whether we argue from a position where our ideas (independently produced in our consciousness) can be tested and analyzed in a methodological manner against the material reality or whether we claim that our socio-political context forms our ideas and thus the meaning of the material world. This context is still considered as constructed *solely* as a consequence of our human subjectivity, and thus indirectly by our human consciousness. It can therefore be concluded that the primary similarities between processualism and postprocessualism lies in the fact that advocates of these standpoints just argue about the ontological status of beings, while they have in common the fact that they do not recognize the unity between Being and human thinking that precedes any distinction between subject and object.

Needless to say, the dichotomy between subject and object cannot be deconstructed within the framework of these anthropocentric conjectures, nor can the subject become decentered. Processualism focuses upon the reality of the past that we as (independent and isolated) thinking human beings must decode through objective methodologies, and postprocessualism concentrates upon the subjective construction of the past that takes place in our context-dependent consciousness. Thus, the dichotomy between subject and object is unaltered in both approaches, and the anthropocentric concentration upon the human consciousness cannot be deconstructed, because these approaches do not recognize the ontological difference and the unity between Being (-as-history) and human thinking. It may also be stressed that beings, such as past remains, are treated as a form of standing reserve that is always at the disposal of our subjective will. This is the case whether we set them up as independent objects or as subjective constructions.[2] From this, it follows that, within the framework of anthropocentrism, archaeologists seem to use the past and its material culture as just a form of standing reserve that we can handle in accordance with our

will and our desires etc. In other words, the unawareness of the ontological difference and the crucial power of Being (-as-history), inherent
in both processualism and postprocessualism, implies that these approaches are carried out within the same, post-Socratic, metaphysical
framework.

To some of us, the proposed question, and the discussion of this
question presented above, seem to be completely irrelevant: there are
objects of material culture (megaliths as well as illustrations) because we
can see them, touch them or use them in accordance with our ideological or existential projects, etc. The crucial question rather seems to be
how their meaning is considered, as a past or as a present construction?
Of course, I do not deny the epistemological differences between processualism and postprocessualism where these issues are concerned;
the point is that the questions concerning the meaning of material culture are secondary in comparison with the forgotten question that I have
put forward above.[3] The question of whether the actual megalith is a
'House of the Dwarfs' or whether it is a grave is secondary, as is the
question of whether the illustrations in this paper are some black impressions on a paper or a reflection of the empirical reality. This will be
the case as long as we have not tried to answer the primary question
of why these phenomena are there at all.

From this, it follows that contemporary archaeology, or rather contemporary archaeologists, are not aware of, and do not use, the existential potentials inherent in Being, while most of us seem to have come to
halt in the dead end of post-Socratic metaphysics, i.e. in the dichotomies
between subject and object and in anthropocentrism.

A (Late) Heideggerian (Contemplative Archaeological) Approach

Having attempted to shed some light on the complexities in late-
Heideggerian reasoning, I would now like to consider how such a reasoning could influence and enrich our archaeological practice. Needless
to say, the discussion below is just a brief outline, highlighting some relevant themes in this complex issue, and it ought to be stressed that the
structures of these themes are simplified because they are inseparably
interlaced with each other.[4]

Awareness of Our 'Dwelling' in Being (-as-History)

A contemplative archaeology inspired by late-Heideggerian thought
could enrich archaeology primarily because, in a self-reflective manner,
it lets archaeologists understand the ultimate foundations of our human
existence and our human thinking. It lets archaeologists become aware

of the ontological difference, and the unity between Being and beings, i.e., between Being (-as-history) and our human thinking. In other words, this archaeology is under way on the question of thinking, i.e. it thinks about thinking and it is open in relation to Being and lets it appear against the background of its own initiative. At the same time, it follows a middle path, where we need the Being of beings at the same time as the Being of being needs us, or rather our thinking.

Deconstruction of (Post-Socratic) Metaphysics

In a contemplative archaeology, Being is not conceived of as a passive part of beings or as a subjective idea of beings. Being is rather that which calls upon us to think. Through the awareness of our 'dwelling' in Being, this approach presents us with the ability to move beyond the traditional, post-Socratic view of Being, the secondary dichotomies between idealism and realism, constructivism and objectivism, subject and object, and present and past, and to de-center post-Socratic anthropocentrism, (i.e., the division between Being and human thinking) without leaning towards these traditional dichotomies. This approach prepares us to accept that these dichotomies are secondary in relation to the fact that it is Being (-as-history) that is the primary origin of our temporality and our thinking, as well as the ultimate foundation for the coming forth of Being in our thoughts and in our faculty of speech, i.e. the foundation for everything that *is*. In such an approach, one is well aware of the (ontological) difference, and the unity between Being and beings, as well as of the power of Being (-as-history), in other words, of the fact that our 'dwelling' in Being precedes all forms of post-Socratic dichotomy, as well as post-Socratic anthropocentrism. This means that a contemplative archaeology also transcends the traditional, post-Socratic views of the content of concepts such as truth, logic and meaning. Truth and meaning are no longer conceived of as being produced solely as a consequence of the ideas and ideals that dwell and are produced in human consciousness, and the correspondence between these ideals and some objectified beings. Truth and meaning are instead conceived of as the coming forth of Being (*aletheia*) in human thought. Logic is deconstructed as an instrument for the judgment of correct or incorrect thoughts and statements, as a consequence of the fact that thinking is no longer (in the manner of unawareness) divided from Being. In contemplative archaeology, thinking, Being (as *logos*) and truth (*aletheia*) are re-united. Thus, the actual deconstruction is directed at both idealistic and realistic standpoints and at some processual and postprocessual standpoints in contemporary archaeology. The main purpose of this deconstruction is to stress the ontological difference and the crucial relationship and unity between Being and beings, i.e. to stress that Being (-as-history) is the forgotten foundation for all forms of thinking, a foundation that precedes every interpretation of the ontological status of beings.

A contemplative archaeology that lets beings be ought to include a respectful attitude towards other beings (in the form of things or artifacts), when we conceive of them as something other than just a standing reserve that is there simply for our benefit, pleasure or use. The most fantastic thing about past and present artifacts is not *what* they are but rather *that* they are and that they have the same origin as ourselves. It is these beings, or rather their Being, that gives us the framework of our orientation in the world. These beings cannot be conceived of solely as interpreted objects that stand in a dialectic relation to a subjective interpreter, i.e., Being (-as-history) is the foundation of both archaeologists and their thoughts and for the (past and present) material culture. Thus, it is also the foundation of our ability to ascribe meaning to other beings. I do not reject the postprocessual view of the meaning of the past as a present construction. My point is that this construction is grounded in the temporality of ourselves and the beings that we handle and that the ultimate foundation of this temporality is to be found in the Being of beings (Being-as-history) and not *solely* in our subjective (or in the postprocessual case, contextualise) choices. To understand these thoughts, we have to realize that, even though the past and present material culture does not bear any final meaning in itself, it, or rather its Being, is still the source of what archaeologists know and do. We can ascribe different meanings to a specific phenomenon, such as a megalith, but the main point is that it *is* and that it is occupying our thoughts. If it had not been there, its meaning would not have been a problem to us. In accordance with the previous discussions, these remarks must not be understood in a realistic way, because it is Being (-as-history) that is responsible for the fact that there are artifacts, as well as human thinking, rather than nothing. Needless to say, the situation in which Being lets beings emerge through our thoughts is an interlacing between human thoughts and Being.

In other words, Being needs our capacity to think and our 'dwelling' in Being. From this, it may be argued that the interest of a contemplative archaeology lies first and foremost in the coming forth of the Being of beings, through our thinking and our faculty of speech, and not in methodological control, in the search for past meanings or in the present, sociopolitical use of material culture, i.e., the interest is directed towards truth as *aletheia* and our 'dwelling' in Being and truth.

Theoretical Pluralism

I want to suggest that a contemplative archaeology is directed towards the fundamental, ontological grounds for everything that is. Through this sort of contemplation of our relationship to the Being of beings, we can achieve a different understanding of the ontological grounds for everything that is, including the grounds of our own existence and our own thinking. This contemplative archaeology, then, is directed towards the coming forward of Being, not solely in artifacts, but also in theoretical reflections and thought in archaeology. It pays attention to the grounds for different theoretical approaches and interpretations, at the same time as it 'lets these beings be'. Such an archaeology concomitantly fosters theoretical pluralism and leads to the ultimate foundation of this pluralism. Contemplative archaeology thinks about thinking and is aware of and is ready to discuss the anthropocentric standpoints that seem to be the basis of all contemporary, theoretical approaches in archaeology. This is mainly because these anthropological standpoints are at the same time, and on the primary level, grounded in Being (-as-history). Consequently, this discussion is directed not only at the processual and postprocessual standpoints but at all other theoretical standpoints in archaeology. My purpose is not to destroy these approaches and their interpretations, but rather to discuss the fundamental grounds for them.

Preparation for the 'Turning' of Being

In his later analyses, Heidegger emphasizes that we should prepare ourselves and our thinking for the 'turning' of Being and that one part of this preparation is to learn to think in a contemplative manner, i.e. to think about thinking and its foundation in Being (-as-history). Heidegger also stresses that we cannot influence the 'turning' of Being and that we do not know when this 'turning' will come or if it will come at all (Heidegger, 1962a: 37–40; Pöggeler, 1996: 210–212; Stambaugh, 1995: 209–212). These ideas seem to create a passive man, totally controlled by Being (-as-history), but we ought to remember the mutual dependence between a person's thinking and Being. We have also seen above that we can pose fundamental questions about the Being of being and the relationship between thinking and the Being of beings. Thus, we still have the freedom to act within the framework of Being, and we may still allow others to become what they are and to accept our mutual dependence.

Reflection and Critique

A contemplative archaeology is a 'path of preparation' that leads beyond archaeology's contemporary anchorage in traditional, anthropocentric metaphysics. This means that this kind of archaeology is also ready to reflect critically on the consequences of anthropocentrism. For instance, archaeology's calculated connection with contemporary sociopolitics, its use of beings as a standing reserve, and its legitimization of this path towards destruction is a consequence of the unawareness of the ontological difference and the power of Being (-as-history). This means that a contemplative archaeology is also directed at questions concerning the present (ideological) use of beings on the general level, because it ought to show that this use is not primarily grounded in subjectivity but in Being (-as-history). Contemplative archaeology does not avoid the political implications of archaeology; it rather strives to stress their foundations. One of the implications of this is that contemplative archaeology is connected with wide ranges of existential and political discourses, at the same time as it is a preparation for the 'turning' of Being. This archaeology is self-reflective in its nature, because it is anchored in a discussion of the ultimate foundations of our existence and our thinking, as well as of our identities as archaeologists and human beings. Within its framework we are constantly ready to question ourselves and our 'indisputable' doctrines, as well as all other 'indisputable' doctrines, wherever they come from.

Contemplation as 'Method'

A contemplative archaeology does not make any traditional, scientific, methodological claims concerning the way to make people understand the original meaning of the past and its material culture. The thinking about thinking and the awareness of our 'dwelling' in Being (-as-history) that are the central themes of a contemplative archaeology can be conceived of as a sort of 'method', a 'method' that is directed at the existential dimensions of our present life as human beings and as archaeologists and at the grounds of our thinking. If we recognize that our thinking is a response to the call from Being, it is at the same time to be conceived of as a non-anthropocentric 'method' that discloses both beings and the foundations of everything that is, i.e., Being (-as-history). For instance, it can be stressed that, when it comes to a discussion of the contemporary metaphysical views on which we base our existence, the contemplative "method" can help us to reflect critically about the sort of thinking that decides how we view other beings and ourselves. Thus, there is a deconstructive moment of critical questioning immanent in such a contemplative 'method'. This path of contemplation leads us beyond the post-Socratic dichotomy between subject and object, and beyond anthropocentrism and its division between thinking and Being.

Conclusion

Until now, we archaeologists, imprisoned in post-Socratic anthropocentrism, have argued solely about the ontological status of beings, while we have not recognized the ontological difference and the unity between Being (-as-history) and human thinking that precedes this secondary argumentation. Nor have we been aware of the fact that it is

Being (-as-history) that lets phenomena (material culture) come forth through us. In accordance with the reasoning outlined above, our relationship to material culture should not primarily be conceived of as a dialectic relationship. My point is that, even if we orientate ourselves in the world with the help of material culture, the main relationship between us as archaeological interpreters and the interpreted material culture is in our common ground, our 'dwelling' in Being (-as-history), i.e., we orientate ourselves not so much with the help of material culture as with the help of Being. Being (-as-history) enables us both to experience and to construct things. Being lets us deal with beings and create history. We need Being and Being needs us. Thus, the megalith and the illustrations discussed above are not there solely because someone has constructed them in accordance with their (pre)understanding. When it is Being that is the ultimate ground of our (pre)understanding of all phenomena, this includes the (pre)understanding of our own being as persons and as archaeologists.

Some may claim that the discussion and the proposals presented in this text are based upon a theoretical construction or, more precisely, a linguistic fabrication, concerning the ontological difference between Being and beings. What is Being if it is not the fact that beings are manifest but rather the foundation that renders everything that is manifest and that determines all that is? In this context, it would lead the reader astray to try to answer this question, but let us at least begin to approach it through the crucial question: why is there material culture rather than nothing?—I am, you are, the megalith in the illustration is and the illustration is, but why?

Acknowledgements

I would like to thank Anna-Carin Andersson, Per Cornell and Ola W. Jensen for comments on an earlier version of this paper and to Neil Tomkinson and Ymke Mulder for the language revision.

Notes

[1] Heidgger herer refers, above all, to Parmenides, fragments # 5 and 6 (Parmenides, 1951).

[2] For these processual and postprocessual standpoints, see, for instance, the analyses of Binford, Hodder, Shanks and Tilley, etc.

[3] For a more comprehensive discussion of the common metaphysical foundation of processualism and postprocessualism, see Karlsson (1998a, b). For discussions of the epistemological differences between processualism and postproccssualism, see, for instance, Binford, 1982a, b, 1987,1989a, b; Earle and Preucel, 1987; Hodder, 1986, 1991; Shanks,1982; Shanks and Tilley, 1987a, b; Tilley, 1990; Thomas, 1996).

[4] For my discussions of a contemplative archaeology, see Karlsson, 1997a, b and 1998a, b.

References

Binford, L. R.,1982a, Meaning, Inference and the Material Record. In *Ranking, Resource and Exchange*, edited by C. Renfrew and S. Shennan, pp. 160–163. Cambridge University Press, Cambridge.

1982b, Objectivity-Explanation-Archaeology 1981. In *Theory and Explanation in Archaeology*, edited by C. Renfrew, M. J. Rowlands, and B. A. Seagraves, pp. 125–138. Academic Press, New York and London.

1987, Data, Relativism and Archaeological Science. *Man* 22: 391–404.

1989a, Review of Hodder, 'Reading the Past': Current Approaches to Interpretation in Archaeology. In *Debating Archaeology*, edited by L. R. Binford, pp. 69–71. Academic Press, San Diego.

1989b, Science or Séance?, or Processual to 'PostProcessual' Archaeology. In *Debating Archaeology*, edited by L. R. Binford, pp. 27–40. Academic Press, San Diego.

Earle, T. K., and Preucel, R. W., 1987, Processual Archaeology and the Radical Critique. *Current Anthropology* 28: 501–538.

Heidegger, M., 1927, Sein und Zeit (erste Hälfte). In *Jahrbuch für Philosophie und phñomenologische Forschung* VIII, pp. 1–438, Halle.

1943, *Vom Wesen der Wahrheit*. Klostermann, Frankfurt.

1947, *Platons Lehre von der Wahrheit: Mit einem Brief über den 'Humanismus'*. Francke, Bern.

1950, *Holzwege*. Klostermann, Frankfurt.

1953, *Einführung in die Metaphysik*. Niemeyer, Tübingen.

1954a, *Vorträge und Aufsätze*. Neske, Pfullingen.

1954b, *Was heißt Denken?* Niemeyer, Tübingen.

1957, *Identität und Differenz*. Neske, Pfullingen.

1959, *Gelassenheit*. Neske, Pfullingen.

1961, *Nietzsche, Erster Bandk*. Neske, Pfullingen.

1962a, *Die Technik und die Kehre*. Neske, Pfullingen.

1969, *Zur Sache des Denkens*. Niemeyer, Tübingen.

1975, *Die Grundprobleme der Phänomenologie*. Gesamtausgabe Bd. 24. Klostermann, Frankfurt.

1989, *Deiträge zur Philosophie (Vom Ereignis)*. Gesamtausgabe Bd. 65. Klostermann, Frankfurt.

Hodder, I., 1986, *Reading the Past: Current Approaches to Interpretation in Archaeology*. Cambridge University Press, Cambridge.

1991, Interpretative Archaeology and its Role. *American Antiquity* 56: 7–18.

Karlsson, H., 1997a, Anthropocentrism Revisited: a Contemplative Archaeological Critique. *Archaeological Dialogues* 4: 114–119.

1997b, *Being and Postprocessual Archaeological Thinking: Reflections upon Postprocessual Archaeologies and Anthropocentrism*. GOTARC Serie C. Arkeologiska Skrifter 15, Göteborg.

1998a, *Re-Thinking Archaeology*. GOTARC Series B. Gothenburg Archaeological Theses 8, Göteborg.

1998b, Brothers in Arms and Beyond the Secondary Front: A Contemplation upon the Common Metaphysical Foundation of Processual and PostProcessual Archaeologies. In *The Kaleidoscopic Past*, edited by A. C. Andersson, Å. Gillberg, O. Jensen, H. Karlsson, and M. Rolöf, pp. 119–133. Proceedings of the 5th Nordic TAG Conference, Göteborg, 2–5 April 1997, GOTARC Serie C, Arkeologiska Skrifter 16. Institutionen fr Arkeologi, Göteborgs Universitet: Göteborg.

Parmenides, 1951, Fragmente. In *Die Fragmente der Vorsokratiker*, edited by H. Diels, pp. 227–246. Weidmannsche, Berlin.

Plato, 1935, *The Republic*. Heinemann, London.

Pöggeler, O., 1996, Does the Saving Power Also Grow? In *Critical Heidegger*, edited by C. Macann, pp. 206–226. Routledge, London.

Shanks, M., 1992, *Experiencing the Past: On the Character of Archaeology*. Routledge, London.

Shanks, M., and Tilley, C., 1987a, *Re-Constructing Archaeology: Theory and Practice.* Cambridge University Press, Cambridge.

1987b, *Social Theory and Archaeology,* Polity, Cambridge.

Stambaugh, J., 1995, The Turn. In *From Phenomenology to Thought, Errancy and Desire,* edited by B. E. Babich, pp. 209–212. Kluwer Academic Publishers, Dordrecht, Boston and London.

Thomas, J., 1996, *Time, Culture and Identity.* Routledge, London.

Tilley, C., 1990, On Modernity and Archaeological Discourse. In *Archaeology after Structuralism: Post-structuralism and the Practice of Archaeology,* edited by I. Bapty and T. Yates, pp. 127–152. Routledge, London.

4

What Conditions of Existence Sustain a Tension Found in the Use of Written and Material Documents in Archaeology?

José Alberione dos Reis

Reflecting upon the Beginning

A tension will be explored here. 'Tension' implies: a quality or state of that which is tense, stretched with force, extended, stiff. This is the sense which characterizes the state of tension referred to in this paper's title potentially found between written and material documents in the field of archaeology. In fact, it speaks of "tired themes of Archaeology versus History, document versus artifact and whatever it may be" (Johnson, 1999: 23) as unresolved tension leads to tiredness. The situation about this tension is not an end, a completion, nor a termination, but a pause and new beginning in order to continue questioning.

> The same author talks about frequent tensions and fragmentation that permeate archaeological work. These should be seen, however, ". . . as challenging, as productive of new insights into the past, rather than as 'problems' or limitations" (Johnson, 1999: 31).

With this in mind, the present text considers some aspects of this tired but nevertheless persistent tension. It will explore some authors that work on these questions and format a summary of their thoughts. Some observations will be made on what one could think of as a "difference" hanging over this tension, in the documentary sources used in archaeological work. As illustrations of this difference, two case studies will be presented: *Espaço privado e vida material em Porto alegre no século* XI (Private space and material life in Porto Alegre during the 19th century) by Symanski (1998) and *A colonização portuguesa da Ilha de Marajó: espaço e contexto arqueológico-histórico na missão religiosa de Joanes* (The Portuguese colonization of the Island of Marajó: archaeological and historical context and space in Joanes' religious mission) by Lopes (1999). These cases will be studied by focusing on how this tension has been resolved. Unresolved elements of the same tension will provide a conclusion to this interesting debate on fragmentation between material and written documents.

Two exceptions are evident in this reflection upon a beginning. First, the tension explored here is a product of the great divide inserted between Prehistoric and historical Archaeologies.[1] Only Historical Archaeology will be considered here. Second, the style employed in writing this paper may draw one's attention. Without deviating from the academic standards that set the bounds of scientific rigor, such writing conveys the pleasure found from the research.[2]

An Attempt to Open the Words

Independence, support, difference, help, equivalence, subordination, complementarity, and so many other words could be used to attempt to describe the extent of the tension between material and written documents in Historical Archaeology (Funari et al., 1999; Kern, 1991). Below is an attempt to open the paths of these words towards the tired tension, humming along its reach.

The Words without the Things: Theoretical Prolegomena

Written Documents

To begin, one might reflect upon what a written document can be. Since the positivist school of thought,[3] the written document takes precedence as the sovereign source of historical endeavors. At present, however, such a premise has its supremacy shaken by so-called 'source criticism' or, as Veyne (1987: 14) points out, "by no means what the historians call event is seized directly and entirely; it is always completely and laterally, (...) should we say, through the *tekmeria*, the vestiges."

The written document is thus one among many types of "vestiges" of the past. Written documents speaking for themselves represent logical, but subjective choices by the historian, owing to their position in a social structure, their thematic interests, their ideologies. Such an understanding dismantles the imagined impartiality of the documentary source, though not including the existence of gaps, for the possible absence of written documentation of an event is as meaningful as its presence. Thus, one can say that "for the historian, all evidence, be it written, oral, or archaeological, numismatic or epigraphic, is 'document'." (Cipolla, 1995: 43)

There is no document that is impartial, purely objective in its content, innocuous in its narrative. Written documents are material products of historical acts and simultaneously reflect choices by the historian. In this way, Le Goff (1990: 547) points out: "[t]he intervention of the historian who chooses the document, extracting it from the set of data from the past, preferring this to others, giving it a value of testimony that, at least in part, depends on their own position in the society of their time and their mental organization, is inserted in an initial situation that is even less 'neutral' than their intervention."

Thus, the written document is a product from a certain relations of force and power in the past of a given society. This document then passes through the historian's acts, his choices, his silence and occultation, materialized finally as an object embedded in the contextuality of historical production. "The document, therefore, is nothing more to History, this idle matter through which it tries to reconstitute what men have done or said, what past is and what just leaves tracks: it attempts to define in the documentary tissue itself, units, sets, series, relations." (Foucault, 1997: 7)

Material Documents

This is the *leitmotiv* of any archaeological act, even theoretical. In this field, even without the smell of earth and the sound of the trowel, one also works with material documents, even through texts.

Let us wait a little, however. Material documents through an archaeological perspective will be considered more fully later. Here, some mistaken allegations arising from History's point of view about such a source will be presented. They are mistaken for they are based on a pretence of completeness, exemption and the supremacy of the written document as a reflection of human events.

Meneses (nd) presents the following allegations concerning mistakes that occur in the study of the human past (and the present) produced by the nature of material documents: a) material things are incomplete representations of the phenomena of the social universe; b) documents are residual, since an archaeological site contains only vestiges that have undergone an assortment of natural and cultural actions. Such allegations lack a true basis. They just propagate a more fundamental mistake of separating the material from the non-material. It is impossible not to recognize the ubiquity of material/immaterial things that result from all human action, their vestiges and their remains.

On this dichotomy, Moberg (1986: 60) comments that, ". . . the notion of culture is for itself immaterial. Actually, the questions to which the archaeologist looks for the answers concern exactly the immaterial".

An interval. Clarification is now needed. A concept, in the foundation of opening words:

> For social appropriateness, it is convenient to presuppose that men intervene, mold, and give shape to elements from the physical environment, according to cultural norms and purposes. This action, however, is not aleatory, casual, individual, but aligns itself according to patterns, among which objectives and projects are included. Thus, the concept can include artifacts, structures, changes in the landscape, and animated things (a hedge, a domestic animal) and also the body itself as it is subject to this kind of manipulation (deformations, mutilations, signaling, paintings) or, still, its spatial arrangements (a military parade, a liturgical ceremony). (Meneses, nd: 112)

A broad conceptualization, but almost complete. Almost, since the material document/culture relationship leads to what Moberg pointed out above as the "immaterial", the questions to which the archaeologist looks for answers: meanings, symbols, readings. It is important to highlight that not all archaeology looks for answers, let alone formulates questions.

A theoretical school is still strong in archaeology—the historical-cultural school—that contemplates the material document with similar presuppositions as those of the positivist school that sees artifacts speaking for themselves, for example. Here, the material document/culture is to be measured, quantified, dated, arranged in series, narrated and described in a final text of authority based on empirical research. Such text is compared to other texts already known and published and one more link is created in a sequence of geographic distribution of artifacts and their relationship with already identified traditions.[4]

On par with the historical-cultural school yet in disagreement with it, the postprocessual school[5] argues one must 'reading' such culture, searching through its materiality for symbols and meanings. This alleged reading despises this said tired debate, tense in its persistence.

Well, tiredness implies time for a break to catch one's breath and keep on walking. As an aside, Johnson (1999: 26) highlights: "It is almost impossible to present a theoretical basis for an academic argument without some confusion for some people and irritation or unpleasantness for others." It is as though from the sacred altar of artifactual empiricism, representing themselves what archaeological research is, someone exclaimed (and it is usually exclaimed): We want to see how it is possible to read pieces of earthenware!

It is in Hodder (1994) that this emphasis in the real possibility to read material documents/culture is found. It is not isolated artifacts that will facilitate such reading. As it has been said and repeated, archaeology does not dig things, but people. Better still, it digs things from people who are in a broad interrelated context, as it was suggested above in the concept of material document/culture. Hodder (1994: 17) stresses that deduction or inference in archaeology, whatever form it may take, can only come from the material document/culture tension. Therefore, the problem is not only how to read symbolism or meaning, but what kind of archaeology to do to carry out such reading. For that, Hodder says (1994: 140) that "(t)he meanings of material culture are influenced to a great degree by technological, physical and functional consider-ations. The practical and partially non-cultural nature of these factors allows reading the 'text' of material culture much more simply than if it were constituted exclusively by arbitrary linguistic signs. The context of material culture is not only abstract and conceptual, but also pragmatic and non-arbitrary." It is a cumbersome challenge, even leading to irrita-tion or boredom, to make archaeology go beyond formalized empirical description. We must be obstinate and struggle for more abstraction and conceptualization, to understand symbols and meanings in a contextual range of evidence.

Relating material culture to social issues, or what 'types' and ' cul-tures' mean in social terms, is a principal part of the work of Shanks and Tilley (1996). For these authors, so-called 'traditional archaeology', among several postures on these questionings, completely avoids the social meaning of material document/culture. The last 25 years of re-search is characterized by dispute over simple technical classifications on the one side, and seeking meaning of social aspects on the other. Nevertheless, despite the nature of such classifications, the material document/culture divide does not stand merely as a reflection of so-cial practices or cognitive systems, but constitutes an action involving the development and performance of such practices and systems. In answer to these questions, Shanks and Tilley assert (1996: 114) that:

> material culture is structured in relation to a specific social totality and is histor-
> ically and spatially constituted. Individual material culture items are concrete
> and particular. They are, after all, empirical objects. At the same time material
> culture items in the archaeological record are meaningfully constituted and
> linked in structural relationships underlying their physical presence, forming
> a network of cross-references. (. . .) The inter-relatedness of meaning of mate-
> rial culture in the archaeological record refers to the inter-subjectivity of human
> actions.

The previous sections suggest that the debate between the writ-ten document and the material document, in spite of being tired, ac-tually continues to be tense. Perhaps in the current manifestations of Historical Archaeology, such debate seems dull. Or, maybe it hides a confrontation without more theoretical-methodological meaning among the various types of sources (pictorial, cartographic, photographic, oral[6] sources etc.) that support archaeological research. Could this confronta-tion not also be hiding a dispute about knowledge/power between the different fields that produce knowledge within the human sciences? Could this not be a *razzia* between academic discourses, as Foucault (1998: 9) points out, in order to control, select, organize and redistribute procedures that aim to conjure and dominate texts with a normative materiality? These thoughts lurk behind the tiredness, worrying away at this tension. Let us go back to the dispute between written and material documents.

Some Reflections on this 'Documentary' Tension

We will now follow the path of some authors who have explored this tension. While arguing for the impossibility of eradicating the distinction between 'artifact' and 'text' in an attempt to dissolve this tension, Andrén (1998: 113–134) presents five different traditions within Historical Archaeology on this theme:

1. Aesthetic: material culture is seen as the starting point for textual productions;
2. Philological: archaeology is regarded as support for Philology and the resolution of linguistic problems;
3. Historical: where there are insufficient written records, archaeology is employed as a complement to textual production;
4. Historical and Cultural: the presence or absence of texts makes little difference, as archaeology sees the artifact as the main interest and does not seek to fill gaps in written sources;
5. Archaeological: archaeology is used where texts are few of nonexistent, using historical analogies instead.

In his summary of these traditions, the author (Andrén, 1998: 146) comments: "Both artifact and text and the relation between them can be perceived from different points of view, depending on several perspectives and traditions. We can see artifact and text as categories, as objects, as documents, or as discursive contexts and in each one of these perspectives the relations can be defined differently." This author identifies the tension between 'artifact' and 'text' yet defends any problems as a product of different 'perspectives'. In addition to these relations, he considers similarities as analogies: "The specific context of Historical Archaeology is so created in a search for similarities between artifact and text. (...) artifact and text as 'contemporary analogies'" (Andrén, 1998: 156).

In a text-aided book about archaeology, Little (1992) speaks of documentary myths and archaeological research, saying that the latter can demolish historical constructions created and perpetuated by written documents related to human events. Archaeology has the potential to question the purposes of History, as well as particular narratives of the past. To illustrate this point of view, one finds the following in Cipolla (1995: 43): "...a relation between literary testimony and archaeological documentation is not the one between the lord and the slave, as people used to say. archaeological data are a primary source on a par with a text by Tacitus or with an inscription.[7] The historian must acknowledge that these can integrate the literary documentation, contradict it (...), or provide information on the subjects in which the historical records are mute."

The relations between archaeological documents and data can be regarded as interdependent and complementary or as dependent and contradictory (Little, 1992; 1994). As such, Little (1992: 4) says: "(. . .) the adoption of one or another depends on the questions that will be made or the points of view of the interpretation." Here 'relations', 'questions' and 'interpretation' all lie in connection with the tension between written and material documents.

While exploring this "debate about the integration of archaeological and historical evidence", Senatore and Zarankin (1996: 115) present two 'perspectives'—historicist and archaeological—which each deal with this documentary tension in different manners. The historicist perspective does not give importance to the difference between written document/material document; the analysis of the written sources occurs prior to archaeological work. History is complemented by archaeological information, "since this theoretical point of view, archaeology, works as a complement and its contribution to the knowledge of the past is limited to and dependent on the presence of historical evidence." (Senatore and Zarankin, 1996: 118) In the archaeological perspective, it is possible to use written documentation as a source of hypotheses;[8] it focuses distinctively on data obtained from written documents and material documents; it proposes an evaluation of historical sources related to archaeological research. For those who work under this perspective, "the empirical basis is the material evidence. (. . .) the hypotheses must be contrasted with the data generated from the analysis of the archaeological records. (. . .) the elaboration of hypotheses can be effected by taking several sources, among which historical sources can be included." (Senatore and Zarankin, 1996: 119)

As we can see, the tension remains. These two perspectives confront each other when one seeks integration between the two documentary sources.[9] Taking the historicist perspective, we can see archaeology as a technique that emulates History. From the archaeological perspective, the sources are combined and archaeology is relied upon to formulate alternate questions to those of History.

In contrast, Pedrotta and Gomés Romero (1998) point out that both archaeological records and written records are "data" transformed by the researcher in conceptual constructions and therefore are equally important for knowing the past. According to these authors, both the archaeological and written records ". . . are derived from empirical objects and according to certain objectives, goals and procedures of the research." (Pedrotta and Gomés Romero, 1998: 121)

Seeking neither to prefer one over the other nor for their integration, but rather epistemic independence, Kosso (1995) claims that Historical Archaeology is a field that benefits from this situation. Without clarifying what he means by 'epistemic independence',[10] but nonetheless constructing a text on the topic, the author deals with binary couples in tension: archaeology/history, material sources/textual sources, texts/artifacts, text/archaeology.

The benefit enjoyed by Historical Archaeology refers to circumstances in which textual records are not necessarily independent of archaeological records. Both play a supporting role for each other, yet remain epistemically independent (Kosso, 1995: 178). Kosso (1995) further points out that both pieces of evidence require the same need to be seen as conceptual constructions in relation to human events. "Neither one nor another source of information, text or archaeology, is assumed as having more epistemic authority than the other. Each one is useful and persuasive evidence to the other as a result of their mutual independence." (Kosso, 1995: 181) The tension between the two sources is established by the fact that the texts usually speak of short-term events of precise significance, whereas material documents more often deal with long-term events, and/or processes lasting long periods of time.

In conclusion, the author warns against this separation between written and material documents as determination of independence. At the same time, he seems to feel confident about the benefit to Historical Archaeology of this possible epistemic independence: "Using texts and archaeology as complementary evidence does not assure independence, but it is a good place to see it. (. . .) It is possible, although it is not certain, that texts and archaeology can benefit each one of them as independent evidence." (Kosso, 1995: 194)

Ah! A proposal to open words. When one thinks of words as a means of facilitating the opening of overlap, they form endlessly woven, viscous webs, just like the mysteries of black holes. Even so, let us go back to what has been said above about the tension and find what references arise from it. Tiredness of debate, enlargement of concepts, the tension between written document/material document seems insoluble. It passes through epistemic independence, integration, confrontation, equality, submission, relationship, complement, distinction, all words that attempt to cope with, even encompass, such tension. They do not! Artfully among them, however, one is hidden that may, once the web is disentangled, bring some understanding to the tension. It is about 'difference' as a concept of contradiction between written document/material document; about how Historical Archaeology works in a field where the 'difference' between these two documentary sources remains—sometimes more so than others—in terms of their representation of the same events or evidence of human actions (Leone and Crosby, 1987).

Let us go back to the words. To 'differ': to be different, to distinguish, to diverge, to disagree. To 'differentiate': to establish difference or distinction between, to distinguish, to make diverse. Two similar and contradicting verbs, with the noun difference[11] between them: diversity, dissimilarity, divergence.

The tension between the two documentary sources is established by a difference in itself. The same event will be understood on one side by the written document and on the other side by the material document. The difference appears in the production of knowledge about that event. They are independent sources because they are different in this production. All that is different, is different by virtue of something. There is something in the event, transformed and created as textual and material evidence. In this way, Deleuze (1997: 43) points out: "The difference is the state of determination as unilateral distinction. Of difference, it is necessary to say what makes it, or that it is made, as in the statement 'to make the difference'.

The word difference designates two fundamental meanings (Lalande, 1996: 1) a relation between objects of different thoughts—written document/material document; 2) the characteristics that constitute the difference in itself—material text/culture. Therefore, beyond the independence between written and material sources, an epistemic difference is established between them when they aim at sustaining the production of knowledge in the field of archaeology.

Finally, a closing remark with the help of Derrida (1991: 43): "(...) On the other hand, the differences are effects themselves. They have not fallen from the sky entirely ready; they are so little inscribed in a *topos noetos* as they are prescribed in the brain."

So, these prolegomena come to an end about such a theme that is said to be tired, dull and irritating. As we can see, it still has a long path in its inevitable tension towards the haze of differences and contradictions.

The Cases: The Words with the Things

Two cases are presented below that show how this tension between the sources has been dealt with, by passing through their differences. A paper on 'Private Space and Material Life in Porto Alegre in the 19th Century' (Symansky, 1998) was originally presented as a Master's thesis in History a PUCRS in archaeology, under the title "Domestic groups and Consumption Behaviours in Porto Alegre in the 19th century: *Solar Lopo Gonçalves*" (i.e., Lopo Gonçalves Manor). In general, it consists of archaeological research on residential units occupied by family groups. The author analyzed the material elements that had been routinely used and, after having lost their usefulness, were discarded as garbage in the backyard of a house. The author had the possibility of recovering facets of the routine of two domestic groups of a society. The unearthed[12] material items of a 19th century house in Porto Alegre, the *Solar Lopo Gonçalves*, were analyzed from a structure of consumption behavior, aiming at verifying how social and cultural variables, such as the socioeconomic status of a certain group, are manifested in the archaeological record. In addition to the archaeological research, a broad study of the written documentation[13] was conducted, providing information on the lifestyle of the family groups that inhabited Porto Alegre in the 19th century.

For Symanski (1998), the archaeological material represented a source that, in opposition to written records, had not suffered distortions according to the interests and values of the people who produced it.[14] Written documents are regarded as allied with material documents. The written sources were researched privileging information on the material culture. Among them, post-mortem inventories received the most attention because the objective of the research was the study consumption behavior and how variable socioeconomic status is manifested in the archaeological record.

Historical Archaeology, according to Symanski (1998: 16), represents a potentially fertile field that presents a confrontation between "...what was written (documentary sources) and what was done (material sources) (...)." In this way, the author explains a certain discrepancy between the documentary source that is most used in the research—the post-mortem inventories—and the unearthed material items: "There are clear distinctions between the domestic chapters described in inventories and what is commonly found in archaeological records (...). Most of the material found in the archaeological records, in its turn, either is not listed in the inventories or, if it is, its description is so superficial that it hardly allows an identification that is valid for purposes of research for archaeologists" (Symanski, 1998: 122).

The tension between written document/material document, in this case, was approached under alliance and confrontation. Alliance, for the hypotheses where archaeological and the written documentation was regarded as support for its verification. The confrontation came from the discrepancy between the information of the inventories and the information obtained through the unearthed material items. Expectations about the archaeological evidence, that is, that it would reflect the socioeconomic status of the family groups in the researched domestic unit, were not mirrored by the information gathered in the written documents. This was the 'discrepancy': that the inhabitants corresponding to the first domestic group of the researched unit were prosperous merchants and the unearthed material items did not correspond to such an elevated status. This situation required additional exploration of the written documentation. It turns out that the Manor had been considered a rural residence since the beginning of the last headquarters in Porto Alegre, in the 19th century. The author (Symansky, 1998: 247) concludes that: "However, it seems to have been common, in the country area, the maintenance of a way of living more traditionally rustic, even among families with greater purchasing power."

Well, it looks as if there is tension indeed in present Historical Archaeology investigations; either by alliance or by confrontation. It also looks like the difference between written document/material document in the production of knowledge, besides being epistemic, has hidden differences according to the archaeologist's theoretical and methodological expectations and choices; whether in the historicist or archaeological perspective, as Senatore and Zarankin (1996) assert.

'The Portuguese colonization on the Island of Marajó: archaeological and historical context and space in the religious mission of Joanes' was completed as a Master's thesis in History at PUCRS, with a major in archaeology. According to Lopes (1999), this paper studied social relations between the Portuguese conquerors and native American societies located near the mouth of the Amazon River. For this end, the author used the exploratory-inductive and theoretico-inductive methods, focusing on written documentary analyses, material culture from an archaeological site and field survey.

The archaeological research was conducted at a site with prehistoric and historic elements, located on the island of Marajó. It is characterized by two different occupations of the same space: a religious mission—first Jesuit (17th century) and then Franciscan—constructed on an indigenous settlement; and then a military-administrative settlement by the Portuguese Crown (second half of the 18th century). Lopes (1999) carried out archaeological excavation himself for this study. Only one test pit, the result of an archaeological rescue mission carried out in 1986 (*Sítio PA-JO-46: Joanes*), provided archaeological material for this dissertation.

The archaeological data are preceded by consideration of historical sources,[15] geographic charts, radar images, iconography, photographs and the analysis of archaeological material[16] collected from the aforementioned rescue event. As no excavations were conducted, the research involved survey and mapping of the archaeological site exclusively. This circumstance led to a reformulation of the objectives of the research, "aiming at also establishing the hypotheses that arose from the consultation with the written historical sources (primary and secondary) and from the analysis of the archaeological material of Joanes (Lopes, 1999: 12). Well, tension has come up in this research, creating modifications to the initial objectives.

As one of the objectives included understanding the political, economic, social and cultural roles of the missionaries when contacts were made with the indigenous people, "the archaeological posture of analysis" (Lopes, 1999: 15) written documentation was brought in to corroborate and deepening "explanations to the phenomenon studied" (Lopes, 1999: 15). Another approach to resolving the tension between sources involves bringing written document/material document together to subsidize "archaeological posture" and its explanatory constructions. In other words, according to Lopes (1999), the written documentary sources can be seen as providing analytical support to Historical Archaeology. Others would be iconography, photography and maps.

For Lopes (1999), the written document must be considered from an archaeological perspective that not only confirms or contests other documents, exposes gaps, or is used as guidance for the geographical location of an area to be researched. On the contrary, the written document can be compared with the material document/culture, with an archaeological perspective from the beginning, to infer more about the spatial, social and cultural organization of the researched area. In addition to 'subsidize' and ' support', the tension referred to here is also described as 'compare'. This game of amassing words is appetizing, twisting and turning the difference between written document/material document.

Speaking of "verbal meanings" as a statement of symbols and functions, Lopes (1999: 56) has the following conclusion about how he understands the tension of sources form his research in Historical Archaeology: "From a historical-archaeological perspective, our analysis will consider the historical documents and the archaeological vestiges as texts that can be read and interpreted according to their specificity: the historical documents can be approached in a critical way that contemplates the context in which they were produced; the archaeological record, pre-historical and historical text by excellence, must be read coherently from an appropriate theoretical and methodological posture, (. . .)." In addition, Lopes (1999) states that the research concentrated on making an inventory of the written sources as subsidiary sources to archaeological survey and laboratory analyses of material culture from the archaeological salvage endeavor.

In this way, a reading of the tension requires coherence, appropriateness and specificity between written and material documents, interjecting a subtle conceptual veil between differences in the sources, just like the thin and transparent pellicle that separates the layers of an onion. It is always there, making us cry when we peel it, marking the difference in its transparency and limiting the relation to a single event, that is, the onion. Well, we now finish this presentation of words with things. They are mere examples permeated by distinct openings to the words that stress, or better, highlight the continuity of the tension between written document/material document, just like the different tides move towards the same ocean, the same seasons always bring different autumns.

Not to Conclude

Now, at the end of this writing, the author encounters the bitterness of not concluding. Why is this so? It is quite clear that this tension has no conclusion in archaeology. Could it? Considering the peculiar situation of a field where this tension is manifest: Historical Archaeology.

Separating into intrusions: <u>Historical</u> (written document) <u>Archaeology</u> (material document/culture). In the denomination and conformation, the defenselessness that causes the tension of the sources inexorable. It passes by and confirms the difference between them, not of identities nor between identities, but difference between kinds of sources in the production of knowledge about the same happenings with different records for dissimilar events.

In not concluding, perhaps the historical archaeologist can be regarded as a reader-author-producer of texts. A reader of material culture who aims to identify the meanings and symbols held within factors such as genus, class,[17] ethnicity, choices, behaviors, contexts and so on. Consider this: the archaeologist as the reader of the site, an entity created over so many years, through several intentional and non-intentional human actions, through different and active natural processes. Now consider this: the archaeologist as the author-producer of texts about such a site. Such a text is the climax of a long and complicated process beginning with the first visit to the field, the first contact with the written documents, followed by, after several stages, breaking the soils from which the material documents will come, be cleaned, classified, analyzed, synthesized, interpreted, and, finally, published in a text of archaeological authorship.

It is an artful game, that of the site-text, where the representative and different or converging roles of the archaeologist-reader/

archaeologist-author-producer of texts circulate. In this sense, Dyson (1995: 35) suggests the following: "The final result of this entangled combination of human and natural processes has been the creation of a basic archaeological text with its complex combination of distortion and meaning. That is where the archaeologist-reader comes in, whose purpose is to create a new type of text intended for several audiences. (...) the archaeologist becomes not only a reader of the site, but also, since the beginning of the research of the field, as well as from the moment the first report is written, the author of the site."

From the authors presented, as a panorama of the tension, Andrén (1998) states that it is impossible to cease the distinction between written document (text) and material document (artifact). He even suggests that such confrontation is innocuous to the field of Historical Archaeology. Little (1992) mentions the potential archaeology possesses to question presuppositions of History. The tension of the sources takes place through relations that can be interdependent, or complementary and contradictory. Two perspectives—Historicist or Archaeological—are shown by Senatore and Zarankin (1996) when they consider the tension of sources in Historical Archaeology. In opposition to this, Pedrotta and Gomés Romero (1998) sustain an equality of the sources, owing to the fact that they are both conceptual constructions. Finally, Kosso (1995) highlights that an epistemic independence exists between written and material documents. Such a conceptualization was also seen as a difference, possibly epistemic, focusing on the production of specific knowledge of Historical Archaeology.

Through the game of opening words—such as confrontation, relations, support, independence, difference—to explore the tension herein presented, we end up not concluding. Like the field where this knowledge is created even expresses such tension in its peculiar name—Historical Archaeology—where the pressure of the sources is constant throughout, without conclusions. Historical Archaeology accommodates the tension, either through tiredness of the debate or through annoyance.

Acknowledgements

I would like to thank Pedro Paulo de Abreu Funari for his advice and criticism, Fernanda B. Tocchetto, Lúcio Ferreira, and the colleagues who contributed in many ways such that this paper could be written. The author holds sole responsibility for the ideas herein contained.

Notes

[1] A concept: "Historical Archaeology is a text-aided archaeology that uses a combination of archaeological and historical methods, sources, and perspectives to study the recent past." (Fagan, 1996:279)

[2]See, for example, the savory scientific text by Pacheco and Albuquerque (1999: 115–133).

[3]"..., the positivist history considers scientific an inductive method based on absolute empiricism. In the case of history, the historical fact substitutes the experiences. As the facts speak for themselves, their reconstitution is sufficient; (...)" (Burguière, 1993: 614).

[4]Tradition: "A sequence of styles or cultures that develop throughout the time, starting one from another, and forming a choronological continuity." (Souza, 1997: 124)

[5]This school varies from hyper-relativists to moderates. It includes several current theoretical trends arising from Sociology, Semiotics, Structuralism, Philosophy, Marxism, and Feminism, and other disciplines. Emphatically, it has brought to archaeology the dimension of symbolic meanings whose salience and substance vary with different cultural contexts. It upholds the relevance of archeologists as 'builders' of the past according to their own social class, ideology, culture and genre as a good starting point from which they formulate their questions of archeological evidence.

[6]For this source, consult Purser (1992) who interlaces Oral History with Historical Archaeology.

[7]It can be added that 'inscription' refers to all materiality of culture for archaeology.

[8]In this sense, a good suggestion or an example of hypothesis of work from archaeology on 'silences' and 'gaps' in written documents is found in Hall (1999).

[9]Besides the conflicting points that have been presented, a further difficult topic concerns ethnicity in historical Archaeology. On this theme and its inclusion in the tension between written document/ material document, consult Jones (1999).

[10]"It is possible to use 'epistemic' in lieu of 'epistemological'. Epistemic refers to knowledge. We can employ 'epistemic' to characterize a certain type of questions and certain notions that are put forward and used, respectively, when expressions that involve propositional attitudes are studies" (Mora, 1994:1040). On this theme, epistemic/epistemological, consult Audi (1997), Dancy and Sosa (1996), and Japiassu (1976).

[11]Difference is mentioned here in the epistemological sense, in the production of knowledge. For other 'differences', be them ethnic, cultural, religious, economic or social differences; consult Canclini (1999) and Semprini (1999), among others.

[12]The items were as follows: chinaware, glass, bones, metal, ceramics; all acquired through archaeological excavation.

[13]Post-mortem inventories, memories, accounts by travelers, descriptions by chronicles and informants; historical and historiographic sources about Porto Alegre. Architectonic data was used in addition to this documentation.

[14]Seen like this, it would seem as if there were an exemption of conflicts or 'interests' in possible defenselessness of archaeological remains. In this way, it is possible to compare the existence of identifiable relations of power in these same remains which arise from social processes or from the social production of space. In this latter sense, Vargas Arenas and Sanoja (1999) are an important source.

[15]Codices from the Public Archive of Pará were consulted, containing regulations, censuses, several official letters, indexes of royal charters, royal charters and provisions, writs, and orders.

[16]Comprising molded indigenous *caboclo* pottery; bones; metal (coins); earthenware, porcelain and sandstone. The material documentation also contained the ruins of an old religious mission on the site.

[17]Class is still/also a subject for Archaeology. Consult, for example, McGuire and Walker (1999) and Wurst (1999).

References

Andrén, A., 1998, *Between Artifacts and Texts: Historical Archaeology in Global Perspective*. Plenum, New York.

Audi, R., editor, 1997, *The Cambridge Dictionary of Philosophy*. Cambridge University Press, Cambridge.

Burguiére, A., 1993, *Dicionário das Ciências Históricas*. Imago, Rio de Janeiro.

Canclini, N. G., 1999, *Consumidores e Cidadãos: conflitos multiculturais da globalização*. Universidade Federal do Rio de Janeiro, Rio de Janeiro.

Cipolla, C., 1995, *Introdução ao estudo da História Econômic*. Edições 70, Lisbon.

Dancy, J., and Sosa, E., editors, 1996, *A Companion to Epistemology*. Blackwell, Oxford.

Deleuze, G., 1997, *Différence et répétition*. PUF, Paris.

Derrida, J., 1991, *Margens da Filosofia*. Papirus, Campinas/São Paulo.

Dyson, S. L., 1995, Is there a text in this site? In *Methods in the Mediterranean: Historical and Archaeological Views on Texts and Archaeology*, edited by D. E. Small, pp. 25–44. E. J. Brill, Leiden.

Fagan, B. M., 1996, *The Oxford Companion to Archaeology*, New York: Oxford University Press.

Foucault, M., 1998, *A ordem do discurso*. Loyola, São Paulo.

1997, *A Arqueologia do saber*, Forense Universitária, Rio de Janeiro.

Funari, P. P. de A., Jones, S., and Hall, M., 1999, Introduction: Archaeology in History. In *Archaeological History: Back from the Edge*, edited by P. Funari, M. Hall, and S. Jones, pp. 1–20. Routledge, London.

Hall, M., 1999, Subaltern voices? Finding the Spaces between Things and Words. In *Archaeological History: Back from the Edge*, edited by P. Funari, M. Hall, and S. Jones, pp. 103–203. Routledge, London.

Hodder, I., 1994, *Interpretación en arqueología: corrientes actuales*, Crítica, Barcelona.

Japiassu, H., 1979, *Introdução ao pensamento epistemológico*, Francisco Alves: Rio de Janeiro.

Johnson, M. H., 1999, Rethinking Historical Archaeology. In *Archaeological History: Back from the Edge*, edited by P. Funari, M. Hall, and S. Jones, pp. 23–36. Routledge, London.

Jones, S., 1999, Historical Categories and the Praxis of Identity: The Interpretation of Ethnicity in Historical Archaeology. In *Archaeological History: Back from the Edge*, edited by P. Funari, M. Hall, and S. Jones, pp. 219–232. Routledge, London.

Kern, A. A., 1991, *Abordagens teóricas em Arqueologia*, paper presented in roundtable discussion on the Theory of Archaeology, 6th Scientific Meeting of the Brazilian Archaeology Society, Rio de Janeiro.

Kosso, P., 1995, Epistemic Independence between Textual and Material Evidence. In *Methods in the Mediterranean: Historical and Archaeological Views on Texts and Archaeology*, edited by D. E. Small, pp.177–196. E. J. Brill, Leiden.

Lalande, A., 1996, *Vocabulário técnico e crítico da Folosofia*, Martins Fontes, São Paulo.

Le Goff, J., 1999, *História e memória*, Universidade de Campinas: Campinas.

Leone, M. P., and Crosby, C. A., 1987, Middle-Range Theory in Historical Archaeology. In *Consumer Choice in Historical Archaeology*, edited by S. Spencer-Wood, pp. 397–410. Plenum, New York.

Little, B., 1994, People with History. *Journal of Archaeological Method and Theory* 1: 5–40.

1992, *Text-aided Archaeology*, CRC Press, Boca Raton.

Lopes, P. R. do C., 1999, *A colonização portuguesa da Ilha de Marajó: espaço e contexto arqueológico-histórico na missão religiosa de Joanes*, Master's thesis, Pontifícia Universidade Católica do Rio Grande do Sul, Porto Alegre/RS.

McGuire, R. H., and Walker, M., 1999, Class Confrontations in Archaeology. *Historical Archaeology* 33: 159–183.

Meneses, U. T. B. de., nd, *A cultura material no estudo das sociedades antigas*. Universidade de São Paulo, São Paulo.

Moberg, C. A., 1986, *Introdução à Arqueologia*. Edições 70, Lisbon.

Mora, J.F., 1994, *Dicionário de Filosofia*. Ariel, Barcelona.

Pacheco, L.M.S., and Albuquerque P.T. de S., 1999, O Lajedo Soledade: Um Estudo Interpretativo. In *Pré-História da Terra Brasilis*, edited by M.C. Tenório. Universidade Federal do Rio de Janeiro, Rio de Janeiro.

Pedrotta, V., and Gómes Romero, F., 1998, Historical Archaeology: an Outlook from the Argentinean Pampas. *International Journal of Historical Archaeology* 2(2): 113–131.

Purser, M., 1992, Oral History and Historical Archaeology. In *Text-aided Archaeology*, edited by B. Little, pp. 25–35. CRC Press, Boca Raton.

Semprini, A., 1999, *Multiculturalismo*. Bauru/São Paulo: Universidade do Sagrado Coração.

Senatore, M.X., and Zarankin, A., 1996, Perspectivas metodológicas en Arqueología Histórica: reflexiones sobre la utilización de la evidencia documental. *Paginas sobre Hispanoamérica Colonial—Sociedad y Cultura* 3:113–122.

Shanks, M., and Tilley, C., 1996, *Social Theory and Archaeology*. Polity, Cambridge.

Souza, A.M. de., 1997, *Dicionário de Arqueologia*. Associação dos Docentes da Universidade Estácio de Sá (ADESA), Rio de Janeiro.

Symanski, L.C.P., 1998, *Espaço privado e vida material em Porto alegre no século XIX*. Pontifícia Universidade Católica do Rio Grande do Sul (EDPUCRS), Porto Alegre.

Vargas Arenas, I., and Sanoja M., 1999, Archaeology as a Social Science: Its Expression in Latin America. In *Archaeology in Latin America*, edited by G.G. Politis and B. Alberti, pp. 59–75. Routledge, London.

Veyne, P., 1987, *Como se escreve a História*. Edições 70, Lisbon.

Wurst, L., 1999, Internalizing Class in Historical Archaeology. *Historical Archaeology* 33: 7–21.

5

The Reception of New Archaeology in Argentina

A Preliminary Survey

Irina Podgorny, María Dolores Tobías,
and Máximo Farro

The aim of this chapter is to raise a number of questions that may contribute to the future understanding of the impact that the New Archaeology had on archaeological research programs developed in Argentina during the 1970s and 1980s. Far from attempting to define or to criticize of the movement identified as New Archaeology, our intention is to contribute a study that may help to clarify how this movement was understood in Argentina.[1]

Historiographies of Archaeology in Argentina

Most historiographic work of Argentine archaeology has been conducted under the assumption that its research methods and problems are to a large extent the consequence of a demarcation of archaeological sub-areas of study (Podgorny, 1999a). There is convincing evidence suggesting that this has been the case (cf. González, 1985; Politis, 1990), and we have elsewhere discussed the moment at which this criterion emerged (Podgorny, 1999a, b). In fact, during the twentieth century, archaeological research began to be organized on the basis of geographic and regional criteria, following research programs and exhibits in museums. In other words, the division of Argentina into archaeological sub-areas was the result of the local history of archaeological practice and was not derived from its object of study or a methodology defined from the beginning (Podgorny, 1999a).

The research methods and problems may in the first place be related to a specific training in scientific practice and only then to the object of investigation. Methods and techniques are learned before being applied to a specific region. For this reason, the methods do not derive from the region in which they are applied. The object of study, however, could instead be considered as reflecting a relationship between a scientist's training and education and the circumstances of the discipline in which the problem is formulated. Thus, the history of an object of study would be better understood from the perspective of the history of the institutions where disciplines are practiced and taught. Since at least 1919 to 1921, when the Universidad Nacional de Tucumán and del Litoral were founded, three research centers prevailed in Argentina: La Plata, Buenos Aires, and Córdoba. Without going into too many details concerning all events between 1920 to the present, it was only in the 1960s that central and regional universities had their own archaeological research programs. Most archaeological research was conducted from Buenos Aires and/or La Plata, and the area of focus of a particular academic center did not necessarily involve the region of the center's location (i.e., the Valle de Santa Maria Project run by the Universidad del Litoral in the 1960s, cf. Garbulsky et al., 1993).

Several historiographical accounts have assumed that the history of a scientific discipline is a mere consequence of general politics. For the case of Argentina, Guber and Visakovsky (1997, 1997/98) have suggested that one characteristic of the anthropological and archaeological historiographical analysis published in Argentina subsequent to 1983[2] is that explanations of what had occurred in the academic sphere can be found by mere looking at political changes at the national level. In fact, several anthropologists in Argentina, such as Ratier and Ringuelet (1997), claim, with regard to the history of social anthropology, that general social and political conditions determine local academic practice. Along the same lines, it is claimed that these conditions were to be brought to an end and that in 1983, when democracy was restored, a new era opened in the various fields of social research. In the words of Guber and Visakovsky (1996, cited in Visakovsky et al., 1997) "the origins of the degree in anthropology were abridged and subordinated to the memory of the degrees in anthropology during the 'proceso'[3]." In this narrative context, the year 1983 inaugurated not only an era of democracy but also a new era for Argentine Anthropology. This way of writing about the past leads to a moralistic speech about history and does not help in understanding the multiple and complex links which connect science and politics.

Let us remark that there is a tendency among the practitioners of all disciplines to explore the history of the disciplines by drawing from one's own memories or by using the testimony of witnesses from secondary sources or a vague historical frame. This type of work probably bears witness to the groups that by then needed to consolidate after years of exile or that disputed the vacancies now open to them in institutions (Podgorny, 1997/1998), but does not provide a complex nor complete enough picture of the historic process.

As indicated by classic pieces of work in sociology and the history of science, the articulation of political processes and the foundation of academic groups is never direct (cf. Marchand, 1997 for a recent analysis of the development of the classic archaeology in Germany; Vázquez Leon, 1996 for the anthropology of Mexican archaeology; Martínez Navarrete, 1989 and García Santos, 1997 for Spain; Podgorny, 1998). Moreover, foundational speeches are frequent in the history of sciences: some scientists rise in a situation defined by them as finished, and announce a new science. Although these manifestos can be considered landmarks of a change in a material sense, they do not necessarily contain any real change. Whether they fail or become institutionalized, the conditions for this phenomenon should be more closely analyzed. These may include the extant institutional organization, the role played by smaller communities, and in particular the process that leads to the dominance of specific academic groups. Binford's opening speech in the United States of America constitutes a good example of this phenomenon.[4]

In 1994, Orquera (1994: 107) laid out two hypotheses in Argentina to explain the types of investigations in the regions he had studied, and concluded that much of the archaeology of the Pampa, Patagonia and Tierra del Fuego was conducted in response to New Archaeology innovations in the United States (focusing primarily on the work of Binford, Shiffer and, to a lesser extent, Flannery). The nature of this intellectual relationship varied, however, "from militant affiliations to the collective use of certain concepts, and certainly, a skeptical resignation in the face of such dominance". With respect to other schools of archaeological thought, Orquera (1994: 107) asserts that they:

> do not seem to have had an influence on researchers that work in the area, or at least their results cannot be perceived, neither Hodder's contextual post-processualism, nor Shank's and Tilley's hermeneutics of power, the Marxist approach, or an examination of symbolism and ideology. Perhaps the nature of the local materials does not lend itself to such speculations, or the reason may be a strong collective preference on the part of the archaeologists for materialist-positivist trends.

It is worth identifying three aspects of this analysis: first, by the mid-1990's the New Archaeology—in its multiple forms—appeared as a consolidated movement that would have developed as a 'collective option' and that would have determined the reception of other movements in vogue in the international sphere. A second aspect that was not developed by Orquera, who restricted his work to the above mentioned area, is that this "option" appears in relation to other investigations in different regions where the materials are completely different from those of the hunter-gatherer societies of Patagonia. A third aspect arises from this latter point: it would seem as if when studying complex societies that belong to different historical moments both in Patagonia/Pampa and the rest of the country, the practice of archaeology would have to adopt the language of the New Archaeology to be 'contemporary', modern or scientific.[5]

In this chapter, we intend to present a number of issues that will contribute to a better understanding of the processes that led to the above-mentioned hegemony of the New Archaeology in archaeology done in Argentina. We will only consider certain aspects of its institutionalization such as the incorporation of themes of the New Archaeology into courses at Buenos Aires and La Plata universities, and into archaeological investigations. The libraries of anthropology and archaeology at both universities are also considered to determine the arrival of journals and books that discussed New Archaeology.

The analysis of archaeology and sciences of this period in Argentina considers the country to have been isolated from main schools of thought because of the lack of updated material in institutional libraries. It is our interest to test this idea through an examination of the time of arrival of publications in order to detect possible discontinuities and changes in the politics related to the acquisition of books and journals. Some of the ideas and adherence to Argentine and international trends in archaeology will be presented by the authors. The aim of this chapter is to start to build an empirical basis with which we can achieve a more complex understanding of the history of our discipline. Archives, documents, and libraries contain valuable information worthy of use.

Archaeology and Research at the University Level

Although the first university courses in archaeology in Argentina date to the turn of the twentieth century (Fernández, 1979/80: 53), the structuring of the degree of anthropology with archaeology as a specialization at the Universities of Buenos Aires (*Facultad de Filosofia y Letras*) and La Plata (*Facultad de Ciencias Naturales*) was only carried out in 1958 and 1959, respectively. While in the beginning archaeology in Buenos Aires was part of the department of Geography of the *Facultad de Filosofia y Letras* (Buchbinder, 1997: 197), in 1974 it became—together with anthropology—a Historical Sciences degree. During 1974, the latter was composed of three sections: History, Geography, and Anthropological Sciences.[6]

The close union between archaeology and geography in Buenos Aires was consolidated by the work of archaeologist Félix Outes (1879–1939) at the beginning of the 1930s. Outes was then the director of the *Museo Etnográfico of the Facultad de Filosofía y Letras at the Universidad de Buenos Aires* after having been in charge of the Geography section in the same *Facultad* (Podgorny, 1999a, b). Although the inclusion of archaeology as a discipline within anthropology and not within history was influenced by the model of current institutions in the United States, it was also linked to the configuration of these fields in Argentina. Before 1930, archaeology was referred to as 'prehistory' in the meetings of Argentine history, and in the basic educational syllabi and textbooks of national history (Podgorny, 1999b). By the end of that decade, an interest on the part of historians to restrict the object of study, leaving out the past of indigenous societies, had developed. In fact, in 1937 during the Second International Congress of the History of America that was held in Buenos Aires, the 'History of America' was defined in the following way:

> ...from the moment of the discovery which meant the exclusion of the study of the indigenous civilizations considered in their own terms but not in those aspects that closely related them to the historical development that began with the conquest of the continent. (Nosotros, 1937: 3)[7]

On the other hand, although Ferrnando Márquez Miranda (1897–1961)—as well as other archaeologists- resorted in practice to common methods of historical inquiry, he also depicted himself and his discipline as part of the natural sciences. In fact, for Márquez Miranda, the foundational image of Ameghino linked the practice of archaeology to naturalism and to a supposed grudge certain groups in the government held against the sciences (Podgorny, 1997). Let us consider two further aspects: first, during the first years of Peronism, both Márquez Miranda and Francisco de Aparicio were estranged from their academic positions at La Plata and Buenos Aires. Second, in 1947 the *Museo Argentino de Ciencias Naturales de Buenos Aires* released 72,000 objects from archaeological and anthropological collections that had been held in the museum since the nineteenth century (Podgorny, 2000) to the *Museo Etnográfico (Facultad de Filosofía y Letras, Universidad de Buenos Aires)* to be directed by José Imbelloni, who had been previously in charge of the anthropological section of the *Museo Argentino de Ciencias Naturales de Buenos Aires*.[8] Imbelloni's perspective was questioned in journals by the Argentine Communist Party where Ameghino was considered a representative of the scientific view of culture and humanity. On the other hand, during Peronism and outside of university institutions, historians and archaeologists jointly took part in projects such as *Imago Mundi*, a journal of the history of culture interested in debating intellectual problems that were excluded from the education at university. Anthropology, archaeology, ethnology, and ethnography were illustrated in this journal as a separate section of the book reviews.[9] In 1948, Oswald Menghin (1888–1973) arrived in Argentina. Menghin joined the universities of Buenos Aires and La Plata, and when the Peronist government fell, he founded the *Centro Argentino de Estudios Prehistóricos at the Museo Etnográfico* in 1956 (Fernández Distel, 1985: 90). Menghin linked the study of the indigenous past to the European tradition of Prehistory and World History[10] (cf. Kohl and Pérez Gollán, 2002).

Before 1959, archaeological research was mainly promoted by university and national museums. The former included the museums of La Plata (Universidad de La Plata) and the *Etnográfico de Buenos Aires* (Universidad de Buenos Aires), and the latter included the *Museo de Ciencias Naturales Bernardino Rivadavia*. National universities in the Litoral and Northwestern provinces were also involved in archaeological research (cf. Politis, 1992). Furthermore, investigations conducted by private collectors or university post graduate students educated in areas not directly related to archaeology participated, until the 1950s, within this sphere and network created by the museums. With growing professionalization, the disciplinary limits gradually narrowed down (cf. Podgorny, 2000 for a discussion of the situation at the beginning of the twentieth century).

In 1959, CONICET (*Consejo Nacional de Investigaciones Científicas y Técnicas*) was created and sought to form a body of government-employed scientists organized into the different disciplines according to the French model, the CNRS. Due to working conditions, the majority of researchers in Argentina hold in addition to this job, a teaching position at a university that in most cases, especially in the social sciences, provides a space to work as well as libraries. The '*comisiones asesoras*' of the CONICET took charge of the evaluation of research projects and the professional and educational training of young people who wanted to be initiated into scientific practice. Not long after its creation in 1960, the Commission of Social Sciences and Humanities was replaced by three other commissions—among which the vast sphere of the 'Human Sciences' is distributed—with the aim of allowing for a greater consideration of the problems related to them. As a consequence, the committees of Economic Sciences, Legal Sciences and History created in 1959, were eliminated and the three *comisiones asesoras* that still exist today were formed. These are the Commission of Anthropology, Archaeology, and Historical Sciences; that of Social, Economic and Legal Sciences; and the commission of Philosophy, Psychology, Philology, and Education.[11] The presidency of the *comisión asesora* that includes archaeology was held by the Ingeniero José Babini from 1960 to 1966, by the archaeologist Dr. Rex González from 1966 to 1967, by Alberto Espezel Berro from 1967 to 1968, and by the anthropologist Dr. Marcelo Bórmida from 1969 to 1978.[12]

During the decades of interest to the present discussion, the XXXVII Congress of Americanists was held in 1966 in the city of Mar del Plata. The congress had local investigators as its main speakers. It was presided over by Alberto Rex González, with Víctor Núñez Regueiro as its General Secretary[13] and had members from Europe, America, and Asia. This congress represented a shift for its main organizers that consolidated a generation: on the one hand, figures such as Oswald Menghin, José Imbelloni, and Antonio Serrano (presented by the organizers as the heritage of the past, inherited by the younger generations) were given honorary recognition; on the other, the future was identified with the trends followed by young North American researchers such as Betty Meggers and Clifford Evans. In fact, after Imbelloni's eulogy (see endnote 13), these two American investigators—present in Mar del Plata- were also acknowledged as representing "a different generation, still young, with an open and promising future" and that had "already accomplished very respectable scientific work". The speech not only emphasized "the image of a couple united through their love and science" but also the

...renovation and change that some of your ideas have meant to archaeology. Especially in regard to the breakage of the traditional molds, with new interpretations that will allow for a review of old concepts, whatever the end results will be (...). We must as South Americans add something that cannot be overlooked: the affection that Mr. and Mrs. Evans has had for all Latin American things.[14]

The speech also emphasized the support that the Evans were giving to local young people who wanted to be trained with them at the Smithsonian Institution. Alberto Rex González, at 50 years of age, represented not only the bridge between the older and future generations but also the connection between the young and local generations, and what seemed as a promise of renovation in North American archaeology. It is important to emphasize that despite the coup of 1966 which caused the conference to be held in Mar del Plata (as indicated by González in "*Jornadas de 30 años de la Carrera de Antropología*", see Secondary Sources), the discussions of the organizers appealed to the identity of the scientists as a whole that, despite any differences, identified the enemy not in colleagues with different objectives but in the lack of support from institutions and the state. Furthermore, the closing speech of the architect Jorge Enrique Hardoy insisted on the possibility of transforming society by means of knowledge of the Americanist disciplines, and on the problem of the lack of political engagement of Latin American sciences.[15]

González's role as an organizer and a mediator is particularly evident in the *Primer Congreso de Arqueología Argentina*, held in the city of Rosario, province of Santa Fe in May of 1970.[16] Of the twenty seven presentations at this congress, eight were given by González's disciples or corresponded to work done by González alone or together with other members. Only two presentations quote Meggers or Evans' work directly (one by Núñez Regueiro and another by Bernardo Dougherty).[17] At the opening speech, González made reference to the 'naturalist' origins of the local archaeology and the need to abandon the ignorant speculations of fieldwork. He also put emphasis on the moment of redefinition that the discipline was going through, and on the promising future offered by new analytical options such as cybernetics and structural analysis. González presented the emergence of the 'New Archaeology' as a result of these changes and emphasized the need for the specialization and formation of work teams (González, 1970: 26–27).

Oral testimony from different sources and the documents on which these are based from the 1980s and 1990s describe two trends: the cultural historic school, lead by O. Menghin at the *Facultad de Filosofía y Letras de la Universidad de Buenos Aires*, and American culturalism, lead by Alberto Rex González at the museum of the *Universidad de la Plata* and the graduate program in History at the universities of Córdoba and Rosario. However, the different schools had many professors in common and were not characterized by extremely opposing points of view (see Table 5.3 and Appendices 1–3). In fact, some of the course programs at the *Universidad de Buenos Aires* included several references to the work of Meggers and Evans. Moreover, the translation of archaeological literature published in English, French, and German was common in Buenos Aires at the *Facultad de Filosofía y Letras*, a task principally undertaken by two teaching assistants, who later became professors: Osvaldo Chiri and Luis Abel Orquera.[18] Because of the mass production of translations and mimeographed reproductions by companies that survived as a result of the industry of the '*apunte*', students had access to a bibliography in Spanish that was bigger than the one translated by the medium or large editorials of other Spanish speaking countries or than many institutional libraries had.

The translation of material from Europe and English speaking countries into Spanish during the time of our interest has already been indicated by Martínez Navarrete (1989). In Argentina, we must also include the translation of French archaeological and anthropological material by the Eudeba publishing house of the *Universidad de Buenos Aires, Nueva Visión* (with translations of North American material), and the distribution of English and North American archaeological material published by the *Fondo de Cultura Ecónomica*. The lecture notes reproduced at the *Universidad de Buenos Aires* do not seem to have extended beyond the university sphere, with the exception of cases in which the professors worked concurrently at more than one university and would carry their views of translated materials with them. This material was incorporated into institutional libraries in the same way as a journal or a book would be, and could be borrowed or read at the library like any other document from the collections.

Let us discuss the formation of university libraries and investigation in Latin America. Discussions about the scientific and intellectual practice of peripheral countries suggest an isolation of the latter due to the lack of updated material at institutional libraries, as well as an ambiguous relationship generated by an ideal 'Master's library'. The situation in which the investigator subsidizes its own work in order to remedy the lack of updated material by buying or exchanging books gives shape to peripheral work and ultimately leads to that kind of autodidactic pride of not knowing what is produced outside one's own sphere. This may also result in an agreement with other streams or ways of working, or finding one's self trapped in an idealized 'core' library. The lack of acquisition of books on the part of institutions is often used to explain ignorance of or the absence of bibliographic references. This situation, however, does not characterize the real circulation network of material that is primarily based on individual private libraries rather than on university libraries (Podgorny, 1997/8). It would seem that it was mainly in the privately held libraries of professors and investigators where material could be found. The analysis of subscriptions of Argentine institutional libraries to journals reveals a different panorama than those coming from oral testimonies (see Tables 5.1 and 5.2).

The anthropology libraries of Argentine educational institutions developed more with the establishment of a broad exchange network with similar institutions in Europe, the United States, and other countries in the American continent (Lopes, 1997). The reciprocal exchange of publications among academic establishments of South America

Table 5.1. Subscriptions at Museo de La Plata Library (UNLP)

Year	AAnth	AAnt	CA	L'A	Arch	Antiquity
1959	X			X	X	
1960	X			X	X	
1961	X			X	X	
1962	X	X		X	X	
1963	X	X		X	X	
1964		X		X		
1965	X			X		
1966	X			X		
1967	X			X	X	
1968	X			X	X	
1969	X		X	X	X	
1970			X	X	X	
1971	X		X	X	X	
1972	X	X		X	X	
1973	X	X	X	X		
1974	X	X	X	X	X	
1975			X	X	X	
1976	X			X	X	
1977	X	X		X	X	
1978	X	X		X	X	
1979	X	X		X	X	
1980	X	X	X	X	X	
1981	X	X	X	X	X	
1982	X	X	X	X		
1983	X	X	X	X		
1984	X					

AAnth: American Anthropologist
AAnt: American Antiquity
CA: Current Anthropology
L'A. L'Anthropologie (París)
Arch: Archaeology (Archaeological Institute of America, Boston)

allowed the dissemination of written work and the provision of publications for the local libraries regardless of the libraries' budgets. There is still a lack of research focusing on the development of Argentine university libraries that would allow an assessment of the impact of politics within the academy as well as of economic crisis on the acquisition of books, subscriptions and/or the exchange of journals. The data presented in the tables are fragmentary and only intend to give a preliminary view of what happened during those decades, regarding the acquisition of archaeological journals. It can be noted that journals continued to arrive in Argentina with some regularity and that the arrival of new material depended on the mail delivery periods among countries. The prohibition of the use of institutional libraries to professors who had been dismissed during the last military government, especially at the library of the *Museo Etnográfico de la Universidad de Buenos Aires*, is known from oral testimonies.

Nevertheless, library collections do not constitute sufficient evidence to allow for an assessment of what materials were read or who the readers of the different chapters were. However, this would not be

Table 5.2. Subscriptions at Museo Etnográfico (UBA)

Year	AAnth	AAnt	CA	L'A	Arch	Antiquity
1959	X	X		X		X
1960	X	X	X	X		X
1961	X	X	X	X		X
1962	X	X	X	X		X
1963	X	Only 3	X	X		X
1964	X	X	X	X		X
1965	X	X	X	X		X
1966	X	X	X	X		
1967	X	X	X	X		X
1968	X	X	X	X	X	X
1969	X	X	X	X	X	X
1970	X	X	X	X	X	X
1971	X		X		X	X
1972	X		X	X	X	X
1973	X		X	X	X	X
1974	X	X	X	X	X	X
1975	X	X	X	X	X	
1976	X	X	X	X	X	X
1977	X	X	X	X	X	X
1978	X	X	X	X	X	X
1979	X	X	X	X	X	X
1980	X	X	X	X	X	X
1981	X	X	X	X		X
1982	X	X	X	X		X
1983	X	X	X			X
1984	X	X	X			X

an impossible task as in most cases the books contain a stamp with the names of their readers. On the basis of these sources, Binford's 'first readers' were quite a few in number. Binford's work is cited for the first time by Núñez Regueiro and Tarragó in 1972. As it was previously mentioned, Rex González presented the New Archaeology at the *Primer Congreso de Arqueología Argentina* in 1970. Binford's (1962) manifesto was included in Ana María Lorandi's course programs at La Plata (see Table 5.3). Luis Orquera (personal communication) admits to have first introduced Binford's work on the European Mousterian in 1972. As noted by Orquera, information about New Archaeology was not introduced by those who would later most vigorously follow this current as a mark of identity or in their research programs.

Several questions emerge for future investigation. It would be interesting to see if New Archaeology falls within a perspective that attempted to stay away from the European traditions imprinted onto Argentine archaeological practice by Menghin. This possibility could be traced in some of Gonzalez's presentations. It would also be interesting to determine the degree to which the translation of material and the lack of English, French, and/or German knowledge, made the presence of a translator and a mediator between the local reality and the necessary productions from the corc. The degree of communication among the different research centers in Argentina should also be investigated to assess whether or not each university acted as an island. Perhaps

Table 5.3. Chairs of Archaeology/Prehistory at the School Of Natural Sciences (La Plata University) and the First References to "New Archaeology"

Chair Year	Fund. Antr.	Pre VM	Pre I Paleol	Pre II	Pre II Neolit	Pre III	Pre Am I	Pre Am II	Pre Am III	Tecn Inv A	Arq Arg	Pre Gral
1959	Cigliano		Cigliano									
1960	Cigliano		Menghin		Menghin							
1961							Marquez Mir	Marquez Mir	Marquez Mir	Cigliano	Cigliano	
1962									Men. ghin	Cigliano	Cigliano	
1963		Menghin	Menghin	Menghin		Menghin	Rex Gonz			Cigliano		
1964	Chiappe		Menghin	Menghin			Rex Gonz		Rex Gonz	Cigliano	Rex Gon	
1965	Cigliano	Cigliano					Rex Gonz			Cigliano	Rex Gon	
Change of Syllabi							Arq Am 1	Arqueología Americana II				
1966		Cigliano	End of these chairs				Rex Gonz	Rex González				
1967		Cigliano					Rex Gonz	Rex González				
1968		Austral					Rex Gonz	Rex González				
Change of Syllabi												
1969		Austral					Cardich	Lorandi **B**				
1970		Austral					Cardich	Lorandi **B**				
1971		Austral					Cardich	Lorandi **B**				Krapovickas
1972		Austral					Cardich	Lorandi **B**				
1973		Austral					Cardich	Lorandi **B**				
1974		Austral					Cardich	Lorandi **B**				
1975		Austral					Cardich **B**	Lorandi **B**				
1976		Austral					Cardich **B**	Lorandi **B** and **W**				
1977		Austral					Cardich **B**	Lorandi **B**, **W** and **F**				
1978		Austral					Cardich **B**	Carlota Sempé				
1979		Austral					Cardich					
1980		Austral					Cardich					
1981		Austral					Cardich					
1982		Austral **B**					Cardich					
1983		Austral **B**					Cardich					

B: Binford
F: Flannery
W: Watson et al. 1974

isolation would have mainly occurred among disciplines within universities rather than among institutions as is the case of the literature that circulated through sociology and history. Other factors in the society that may have stimulated or inhibited the reception of the New Archaeology cannot be ignored.

To conclude, we would like to emphasize that Argentine archaeological practice is currently perceived as constituted by two opposing sides, such that each one must cancel the other out for the good of science (Boschín, 1991–1992; Boschín and Llamazares, 1986). This view of two opposing groups—in conflict until a final victory is achieved—can be traced even to the origins of the discipline. This language is based, as noted by Guber and Visacovsky for social anthropology, on a reconstruction of the history of the science based on the events that occurred during the military dictatorship. Therefore, it is common to find histories of the disciplines tinted with moral values where modern actors fight the conflicts of the past. To confront this rhetoric would be an excellent first step towards a practice of archaeology in Latin America which acknowledges its true conflicts.

Acknowledgements

Luis Abel Orquera gave us access to his book collection and his memories. We would also like to thank the librarians of the Museo Etnográfico and the Museo de La Plata as well as those who work in the Archives of the Facultad de Filosofía y Letras (UBA) and CONICET for their patience and collaboration. María Isabel Martínez Navarrete and Luis Rossi helped us with part of the bibliography. Some of the material used in this chapter comes from the Acervo Histórico de la Facultad de Ciencias Naturales y Museo, where classificatory and inventory work is being done thanks to an Early Career Grant from Fundación Antorchas (ref. A-13532/1-103).

Appendix 1: References Quoted in Syllabi

Ana María Lorandi

1969: Binford, L., 1962, Archaeology as Anthropology. *American Antiquity* 28(2).
1973: Binford, S., and Binford, L., editors, 1969, *New Perspectives in Archaeology*. Aldine, Chicago. Chapter 1, Part 1.
  Clarke, 1968, *Analytical Archaeology*. Methuen, London
1976: Watson et al., 1974, *El método científico en arqueología*. Alianza, Madrid.
1977: Flannery, K., 1973, Archaeological Systems Theory and early Mesoamerica. In *Contemporary Archaeology: A Guide to Theory and Contributions*, edited by M. Leone. Southern Illinois University Press, Carbondalc.

Cardich, Augusto

1975 to 1978: Binford, L., 1973 Post-Pleistocene Adaptations. In *Contemporary Archaeology: A Guide to Theory and Contributions*, edited by M. Leone, Southern Illinois University Press, Carbondale.

Binford, S., and Binford, L., editors, 1969, *New Perspectives in Archaeology.* Aldine, Chicago.

Appendix 2: Calls for New Faculty Members (Source: Acervo Histórico de la Facultad de Ciencias Naturales y Museo de la Universidad Nacional de La Plata)

1959

"Profesor adjunto en la Cátedra de Prehistoria I (Paleolítico)"
Committee: O. Menghin, A. Rex González and Marcelo Bórmida
Candidate: Eduardo M. Cigliano.

1969

"Profesor Ordinario (adjunto, con dedicación simple para la cátedra de Prehistoria General)" Committee: A. Vivante, A. Serrano and A. Zapata Gollán
Candidates: Delfor Chiappe and Pedro Karpovickas. No results.

"Profesor Ordinario (titular, con dedicación simple para la cátedra Prehistoria del Viejo Mundo)"
Committee: Vivante, J. Schobinger and A. Serrano
Candidates: Antonio Austral.

1971

"Profesor Ordinario (adjunto, con dedicación simple para Prehistoria General)"
Committee: Schobinger, M. Bórmida and Marcelino
Candidates: Antonia Rizzo y P. Krapovickas (selected),

"Auxiliar de Investigación para la cátedra de Antropología general"
Committee: Chiappe, Vivante and Austral
Candidates: María Borrello, R. Raffino, Héctor Pucciarelli, Raquel Saffores de Pabón, Susana Ringuelet, Héctor Calandra y Luis Carbonari. Selected: Raffino, Calandra and Ringuelet.

"Auxiliar de Investigación para la cátedra de Arqueología Americana (Culturas Precerámicas)"
Committee: Cardich, Austral and Ana Lorandi
Candidates: R. Raffino, L. Carbonari and Antonia Rizzo (selected)

"Auxiliar de Investigación para la División de Antropología"
Committee: Vivante, Cardich y Austral
Candidates: Carlota Sempé and H. Calandra (selected).

"Auxiliar de Investigación para la cátedra de Arqueología Americana, culturas Agroalfareras"
Committee: Austral, Cardich, Krapovickas
Candidates: María A. Borrello, Carlota Sempé, Héctor L. D'Antoni and Bernardo Dougherty (selected)

1972

"Jefe de Trabajos Prácticos para la cátedra de Técnicas de la Investigación arqueológica"
Committee: Cardich, Austral and Chiappe
Candidates: R. Raffino.

Appendix 3: Syllabi from Faculty Members of the School of Philosophy and Letters, Buenos Aires University, some examples.

Prehistory, American and Argentine Archaeology, 1975
(*Source:* Biblioteca Museo Etnográfico. FFyL-UBA)

Translator	Year	Author	Source	Language	Country
O.Chiri	1966	Willey	An Introduction to American Anthropology	English	USA
O.Chiri		Rowe		English	USA
O.Chiri	1966	Master	The American Naturalist	English	USA
LAO	1971	Willey	Journal of Quaterny Research	English	USA
O.Chiri	1973	Bryan	An Introduction to American Anthropology	English	USA

Prehistory and American Archaeology

1971: Professor Ciro René Lafón
Note 1554: Biblioteca del Museo Etnográfico de la FFyL UBA

Translator	Year	Author	Source	Language	Editors	Country
O.Chiri	1963	ARG	SMC	English	Meggers-Evans	USA
O.Chiri	1964	Brieger, F.G.	Enc. Intelectuais			USA
O.Chiri	1948	Bennett, W.	Yale U.P in A	English		USA
O.Chiri	1963	Altenfelder Silva F.	SMC	English	Meggers-Evans	USA
O.Chiri	1963	Angulo Valdés, C.	SMC	English	Meggers-Evans	USA
O.Chiri	1967	Lanning, E.	Peru before the Incas	English		USA
	1958	Collier, D.	Revista Colombiana de Arq.	Spanish		Colombia
	1962	Mason, A.	Las antiguas culturas del Perú	Spanish		México
O.Chiri	1963	Estrada, E.	SMC	English	Meggers-Evans	USA
O.Chiri	1963	Meggers	SMC	English	Meggers-Evans	USA
O.Chiri		Kidder, Lumbreras		English		
1972						
LAO	1949	Willey	BAE, Handbook	English	Steward	USA

Sources not Quoted in the Text

Revista de la Sociedad Argentina de Antropología, Buenos Aires.
  1989, Treinta años de la carrera en Buenos Aires (1958–1988). *Jornadas de Antropología*. Universidad de Buenos Aires, Facultad de Filosofía y Letras, Buenos Aires.
Núñez Regueiro, V., 1971, Conceptos teóricos que han obstaculizado el desarrollo de la Arqueología en Sudamérica. *Estudios de Arqueología* (Museo de Arqueología de Cachi, Salta) 1.

Notes

[1] For an analysis of Argentina of the 1960s, see Hora and Trímboli, 1994; Terán, 1991; Halperín Donghi, 1969; Caldelari and Funes, 1997; and Sigal, 1991.

[2] The year 1983 marks the end of thirteen years of military dictatorship, and the beginning of Raúl Alfonsín's presidency.

[3] 'El Proceso' refers to the 'process in which the Nation was reorganized', a term that the military governments used to define themselves.

[4] Binford, L., 1962, Archaeology as Anthropology. *American Antiquity* 28(2).

[5] The criticisms of the New Archaeology should also be taken into consideration. In 1983, the CAEA published Bayard's criticism of this school as a way to compensate for its increasing importance among young Argentine archaeologists.

[6] Syllabus of the career of Anthropological Sciences, file 35.307/74. Archive of the Facultad de Filosofia y Letras.

[7] This omission can be considered unique, particularly when considering that twenty years earlier the *Congreso Americano de Bibliografía e Historia* that took place in Buenos Aires and Tucuman in 1916 included in its two sections 'the pre-Columbian period' (Archive of the Facultad de Ciencias Naturales: carpeta de 1916). In 1937 congresses were divided into those dedicated to pre-Columbian societies and those of the Colonial period: "The Congreso Internacional de Historia de America is an institution designed to promote and relate the activities of academies and historians of the New World. It is primarily a scientific institution that stimulates original research in the areas of American History from the time of the Conquest to the present (Prehistoric and Protohistoric times, and the Discovery are themes that belong to the Congress of Americanists)" (Levene, [1937] 1938:13).

[8] Although the museum had abandoned the model of 'Natural History Museum' since 1930, in favor of one of 'Natural Sciences', the section of anthropology and archaeology was about to open its new exhibition halls when its dissolution was decided. In 1945, the scientific section of the Museum of 'Anthropology, Ethnography and Archaeology' was second—after Zoology—in staff numbers. Head of Archaeology was Eduardo Casanova and honorary head of Ethnography Enrique Palavecino (Universidad de Tucumán). In charge of Numismatics was Aníbal Cardoso, assistants in Archaeology and Anthropology Santiago Gatto, Pablo Haedo, Luis Chillida, and Osvaldo Paulotti. Carlos Vega was the head of the Institute of Native Musicology and his assistants were Isabel Aretz-Thiele and Margarita Silvano de Regoli. There was also a sculptor and modeler (Joaquin Da Fonseca), an assistant in Taxidermy (Secundino Da Fonseca), and two draftsmen (Ismael Astarloa and Eduardo Rios) *(Anales del Museo Argentino de Ciencias Naturales "Bernardino Rivadavia"*, 61. Buenos Aires, Imprenta de la Universidad, 1943–1945). The technical staff was moved to other sections in the museum.

[9]Salvador Canals, Esther Hermitte, and Jorge Graciarena. The cited references were taken from publications of the Wenner Gren Foundation (New York), the American Anthropological Association, Hamburg, Mexico, Paris and were published the year before the reviews appeared in Argentina. Hermitte in "'An Introduction to Anthropology' by Ralph Beals. H. Hoijer (1953)" sustained that the authors "approach the study of culture with a non-historical criterion. On the contrary, their analysis is structural and specialized in the comparison of contemporary cultures, including ours. The value of this publication increases by its discussion of the most important and recent anthropological theories." (*Imago Mundi*, 6, diciembre de 1954:108–109).

[10]"The final objective is the world history of primitive times, that is, of the most ancient period of human development in which the cultural, linguistic, and racial foundations were created, from which humans achieved a historical perception of themselves, and a rational understanding of the cosmos" (Menghin, 1957:1, cited in Fernández Distel, 1985: 91).

[11]Memoria del CONICET, actividades del año 1960. Reseña general de la labor realizada desde febrero de 1958.

[12]Ibid. and "Informaciones del Consejo Nacional. Boletin Mensual de Investigaciones Científicas y Técnicas, enero y febrero 1966".

[13]Dr. Bernardo Houssay, president and founder of the CONICET, was the honorary president and one of the speakers who inaugurated the Congress. Honorary vice-presidents were Padre Guillermo Furlong, S. J.; Maria H. Holmberg, widow of Ambrosetti; and José Imbelloni, who despite his absence due to health reasons was recognized by the organizing commission as 'the most significant Argentine Americanist of his time' (cf. *Actas y Memorias del XXXVII Congreso Internacional de Americanistas*, vol. I:LV, Buenos Aires, 1968). The members of the honorary comission were E. Casanova, H. Greslebin, O. Menghin, and A. Serrano. The vice-president of the organizing comission was Julián Cáceres Freyre.

[14]*Actas y Memorias del XXXVII Congreso Internacional de Americanistas*, vol. I:LV, Buenos Aires, 1968.

[15]Ibid., pp. LX and LXI. For more information on the meaning of the speeches of homage and praises for the History of Sciences, cf. Farro and Podgorny, 1998.

[16]The committee was constituted by González, Antonio Austral, Juan Schobinger, Mario Cigliano, Fernando Gaspary, and Agustín Zapata Gollán (*Actas y trabajos del Primer Congreso Nacional de Arqueología Argentina*, Publisher in Buenos Aires in 1975).

[17]During the mid-1980s Bonnin and Laguens (1984/85) did a bibliometric survey of the type of references used by researchers based on the journal of the Sociedad Argentina de Antropología (Relaciones). Their aim was to prove—from the standpoint of a scientific archaeology—the persistence of 'traditional archaeology' in a context where scholars claimed to have abandoned the past. This study, however, has not been used or cited in later works and it reflects the references used in the 1980s.

[18]Cited in the tables as LAO.

References

Bayard, D., 1983, La nueva arqueología: una historia crítica. *Scripta Ethnologica*, suplementa 2:9–27.

Bonnin, M., and Laguens, A., 1984–1985, Acerca de la arqueología argentina de los últimos 20 años a través de las citas bibliográficas en las Revistas Relaciones y Anales de Arqueología y Etnología. *Relaciones de la Sociedad Argentina de Antropología* 16: 7–25.

Boschín, M. T., 1991–1992, Historia de las investigaciones arqueológicas en Pampa y Patagonia. *Runa* 20: 111–144.

Boschín, M. T., and Llamazares, A., 1986, La escuela Histórico-cultural como factor retardatario del desarrollo científico de la arqueología argentina. *Etnía* 32: 101–156.

Buchbinder, P., 1997, *Historia de la Facultad de Filosofía y Letras Universidad de Buenos Aires*. Eudeba, Buenos Aires.

Caldelari, M., and Funes, P., 1997, La Universidad de Buenos Aires, 1955–1956: lecturas de un recuerdo. In *Cultura y política en los años '60*, edited by E. Oteiza, pp. 17–42. Instituto Gino Germani, Oficina de Publicaciones CBC/ UBA, Buenos Aires.

Farro, M., and Podgorny, I., 1998, Frente a la tumba del sabio: Florentino Ameghino y la santidad del científico en la Plata. *Ciencia Hoy* 8(47): 28–37.

Fernández, J., 1979–1980, *Historia de la Arqueología Argentina*. Anales de Arqueología y Etnología, Universidad Nacional de Cuyo, Mendoza.

Fernández Distel, A., 1985, Prehistoria. in edited by Caea, *Evolución de las ciencias en la República Argentina 1872–1972, X, Antropologí.*, Sociedad Científica Argentina, Buenos Aires.

Garbulsky, E. et al., 1993, Comenzando a recuperar nuestra memoria institucional: Entrevista a Susana Petruzzi. *Revista de la Escuela de Antropología* (Universidad Nacional de Rosario) 1: 93–107.

García Santos, J. C., 1997, La arqueología española de los 80: Una visión de las raíces teóricas. In *La cristalización del pasado: génesis y desarrollo del marco institucional de la arqueología en España*, edited by G. Mora and M. Díaz-Andreu. CSIC- Universidad de Málaga, Málaga.

Gilman Guillén, A., 1988, Enfoques teóricos en la arqueología de los ochenta. *Revista de Occidente* 81: 47–61.

González, A. R., 1985, Cincuenta años de arqueología del Noroeste argentino (1930–1980,: apuntes de un casi testigo y algo de protagonista. *American Antiquity*, 50(3: 505–517).

Guber, R., and Visacovsky, S., 1998, Controversias filiales: la imposibilidad genealógica de la antropología social de Buenos Aires. *Relaciones de la Sociedad Argentina de Antropología* 22–23: 25–53.

Halperín Donghi, T., 1969, *Argentina en el callejón*. Buenos Aires.

Hora, R., and Trímboli, J., 1994, *Pensar la Argentina: Los historiadores hablan de historia y política*. El cielo por asalto, Buenos Aires.

Kohl, P. L., and Pérez Gollán, J. A., 2002, Religion, Politics, and Prehistory: Reassessing the Lingering Legacy of Oswald Menghin. *Current Anthropology* 43:561–586.

Levene, R., 1938, Palabras de los miembros de la mesa organizadora del Congreso reunido en Buenos Aires entre el 5 y el 14 de julio de 1937 en conmemoración del IV Centenario de la fundaciÛn de la Ciudad de Buenos Aires, Academia Nacional de la Historia, Buenos Aires. *II Congreso Internacional de Historia de América* Vol. 1: 13

Lopes, M. M., 1997, *O Brasil descobre a pesquisa científica. Os Museus e as ciências naturais no século XIX*. Hucitec, São Paulo.

Martínez Navarrete, M. I., 1989, *Una revisión crítica de la prehistoria española: la Edad del Bronce como paradigma*. Siglo XXI, Madrid.

Marchand, S., 1996, *Down from Olympus: Archaeology and Philhellenism in Germany, 1750–1970*. Princeton University Press, Princeton.

Nosotros, 1937, *Número extraordinario dedicado al II Congreso Internacional de Historia de América*, suplemento del Número 16. Segunda Época, Buenos Aires.

Orquera, L. A., 1994, *Historia de las investigaciones arqueológicas en Pampa, Patagonia y Tierra del Fuego*. Manuscript.

Podgorny, I., 1997, De la santidad laica del científico: Florentino Ameghino y el espectáculo de la ciencia en la Argentina moderna. *Entrepasados, Revista de Historia* 13: 37–61.

1998, Comments on Heinrich Härke's 'Archaeologists and Migrations: A Problem of Attitude?' *Current Anthropology* 38(5):35–36.

1997/1998, Comentario sobre 'Antropología del mundo contemporáneo: el surgimiento de la antropología de la ciencia' de Cecilia Hidalgo. *Relaciones de la Sociedad Argentina de Antropología* 22–23: 87–90.

1999a, De la antigüedad del hombre en el Plata a la distribución de las antigüedades en el mapa: Los criterios de organización de las colecciones antropológicas del Museo de La Plata entre 1890 y 1930. *História, Ciências, Saúde-Manguinhos* 6 (1): 81–100.

1999b, *Arqueología de la educación: Textos, indicios, monumentos. La presentación de los pueblos indígenas en la educación argentina.* Sociedad Argentina de Antropología, Serie Tesis Doctorales, Buenos Aires.

2000, *El argentino despertar de las faunas y de las gentes prehistóricas. Coleccionistas, estudiosos, museos y universidad en la Argentina (1880–1920).* Eudeba/Libros del Rojas, Buenos Aires.

Politis, G. G., 1988, Paradigmas, modelos y métodos en la arqueología de la pampa bonaerense. In *Arqueología Argentina Contemporánea*, edited by H. Yacobaccio, pp. 59–107. Búsqueda, Buenos Aires.

1992, Política nacional, arqueología y universidad en Argentina. In *Arqueología en América Latina Hoy*, edited by G. Politis, pp. 70–87. Banco Popular, Bogotá.

Ratier, H. E., and Ringuelet, R. R., 1997, La Antropología social en la Argentina: un producto de la democracia. *Horizontes antropológicos* (Histórias da Antropología) 7: 10–23.

Sigal, S., 1991, *Intelectuales y poder en la década del sesenta*, Buenos Aires.

Terán, O., 1991, *Nuestros años sesentas.* Puntosur, Buenos Aires.

Vázques León, L., 1996, *El leviatán arqueológico. Antropología de una tradición científica en México.* Research School CNWS, 44, Leiden.

Visacovsky, S., Guber, R., and Gurevich, E., 1997, Modernidad y tradición en el origen de la carrera de Ciencias Antropológicas de la Universidad de Buenos Aires. *Redes* 4(10): 213–257.

6

Network Theory and the Archaeology of Modern History

Charles E. Orser Jr.

Introduction

In my book *A Historical Archaeology of the Modern World* (1996), I out-lined a general approach intended to help forge a truly global historical archaeology. The gist of my argument was that after about A.D. 1500, conscious agents of colonialism, capitalism, Eurocentrism. and moder-nity created a series of complex, multidimensional links that served to tie together diverse peoples around the globe. My arguments werc, in essence, that it was the interaction of these diverse peoples that cre-ated the many historical manifestations of the modern world, the world which we in fact now inhabit. Central to my argument was the idea that men and women, in the course of their daily lives, create and main-tain the connections that precipitate both cultural change and cultural continuity over time.

I argued then that historical archaeology, to have a truly significant place in today's scholarship, should embrace the issue of global connec-tions, providing empirical studies demonstrating the origin and earliest development of globalization, modernization, and colonialist expansion. I still believe in the essential validity of my general research program (Orser, 1998c), but having outlined the general approach, it is now ap-propriate to devise a concrete framework for conducting archaeological studies of the sort I advocate. Among the many approaches that might be selected or devised, I believe that my research goals can best be accomplished by adopting an approach that is overtly rooted in network analysis adapted both from contemporary anthropology and sociology, and from geography. The purpose of this paper is to present an outline of this approach and to argue for its strength and interpretive potential. I believe that the use of such an approach will permit historical archaeologists to collect, evaluate, and interpret information in new and informative ways. As part of this argument, I also present a brief example from Brazil, focused on the seventeenth-century slave kingdom of Palmares.

A Central Tenet and Its Implications

A central proposition of the kind of analysis I propose rests on the understanding that men and women hold themselves together socially through a series of complex interrelationships that can be modeled as a web. This understanding of human society has a long pedigree in anthropological thought. For instance, early in the twentieth century, French sociologist Emile Durkheim (1915: 426) argued that social units, often identified by analysts as tightly bounded, discrete entities, were in fact broad and far-reaching. As he put it, "There is no people and no state which is not part of another society, more or less unlimited, which embraces all the peoples and all the states with which it first comes in contact, either directly or indirectly". The theme of social interconnectedness was later adopted by British anthropologist A. R. Radcliffe-Brown (1940) and American anthropologist Alexander Lesser (1961). Both scholars took Durkheim's idea further, focusing on the notion of the social network. Radcliffe-Brown (1940: 3) wrote that every individual was part of "a wide network of social relations, involving many other persons", and Lesser (1961: 42) argued that human groups were "inextricably involved with other aggregates, near and far, in weblike, netlike connections." During this period, other social scientists adopted the concept of the social web to develop an explicit "social network analysis." In anthropology, J. A. Barnes (1954) and J. C. Mitchell (1974) were early leaders in developing this approach, and today a full-blown field of social network analysis exists in anthropology and sociology (Wasserman and Faust, 1994). Most recently, anthropologist Michael Carrithers (1992: 11) has used the term 'mutualism' to refer to the idea that social relationships are "the basic stuff of human life".

Following on the heels of Barne's (1954) pioneering study of the social networks created and enacted in a tiny Norwegian fishing village, a number of researchers refined and broadened the idea of the social network by attempting to discover how networks operate, how they are constructed, and how men and women—and social collectives—produce and reproduce the links between them. Further research has shown, for example, that connections can include a wide variety of factors, including kinship, class loyalties and perception, environmental understandings, economic strategies, relations of power, and cognitive understandings (Knoke and Kuklinski, 1982: 15; Schweizer, 1997; Wolf, 1982, 1984).

One of the implications of adopting a network perspective is that it allows investigators to downplay the mysterious effects of culture. In the purely "culturalist" point of view, individuals do things because of their culture. Culture appears to float above them as an ethereal cloud, invisible yet present, inescapably exerting itself on everything people do. The culturalist perspective helps to explain, for example, how colonizers could move from one part of the world to another and create an image of their homeland in a different environment.

Culturalist explanations have been particularly prevalent in archaeology, especially in historical archaeology. Archaeologists studying post-Columbian colonialism have been drawn to the culturalist position because of its apparent ability to explain the transference of culture from one place to another. Accordingly, James Deetz, an accepted leader in the field, has given this perspective a prominent place in the historical archaeologist's interpretive toolkit. Thus, for him, a "cultural landscape" is "that part of the terrain which is modified according to a set of cultural plans" (Deetz, 1990: 2). Within this understanding, human-built landscapes look the way they do 'because of culture'. People shape their physical landscapes in accordance with what makes them comfortable. In colonial situations, then, the transference of culture from one part of the world to another has meant, quite literally, that "At the southern tip of the African continent, one finds a little piece of England" (Deetz, 1990: 1). Given that men and women who traveled the globe took their cultures with them, it only makes sense that they would construct environments that fit their cognitive models of what is proper and right. Thus, the culturalist view neatly explains why structures in one part of the world can look just like those in another. Fort Orange in New York State resembles Forte Orange (Forteleza de Santa Cruz de Ttamaracã) in northeast Brazil because the colonial Dutch built both fortifications. The forts' engineers and builders obviously raised structures that made sense to their cultural understanding of the proper appearance of a fortified place. Another way to say this is that the builders of the forts, *in effect*, lived under their culture's all-pervasive cloud, a fact that the physical things they constructed appears to reflect extremely well.

The culturalist's conception of the cultural landscape seems to make abundant sense, and many historical archaeologists have used this model in their research (see, for example, the papers in Kelso and Most, 1990, and Yamin and Metheny, 1996). Many archaeologists, trained in the anthropological tradition, find comfort in using culture as the final explanation for understanding the way the world works. The built environment, like everything else, reflects culture. This conclusion is perhaps in some measure adequate, but is it enough? Even Deetz (1991: 8) said that historical archaeology will often refute Occam's Razor, meaning, of course, that the simplest explanation may not always be the best. Such is the case with the culturalist explanation.

The culturalist position has indeed found a ready audience among many historical archaeologists, but it contains two significant problems that cannot be ignored. In the first place, the position incorporates a vague notion of culture and gives it explanatory power. Most archaeologists are indeed careful, exacting scholars, but the culturalist position makes it too easy to end an investigation with a simple culturalist 'explanation': "Their culture made them do it".

In other words, the culturalist point of view promotes facile explanations and interpretations to explain otherwise exceedingly complex historical situations. The presentation of simplistic interpretations does no service to the archaeological profession, especially at a time when archaeological budgets are in danger of being reduced or disappearing altogether. The second deficiency with the culturalist perspective is that it tends to downgrade, or even to hide, mutable, historical social relations and to create in their wake seemingly synchronic pictures of the past. Thus, the culturalist may envision a built landscape to represent a cultural imprint that in fact lasts for many years as if frozen in time. Accordingly, when the utopian Harmony Society created their "cultural landscape" at Economy, Pennsylvania, it "symbolized the German homeland from which they were forced to flee" (De Cunzo et al., 1996: 111). While no archaeologist, regardless of interest, is unmindful of diachronic change, the culturalist perspective makes it possible, and indeed easy, to accept some degree of synchronicity. Germans create a timeless little Germany in Pennsylvania, while the English recreate a little England in South Africa. This statement is true to some extent, but overall culture change is difficult to model within a landscape when the entire landscape is viewed as culture's creation.

A network approach openly rejects the culturalist position and proposes instead that landscapes are conscious creations based, not strictly on culture, but on the interactions and associations of male and female agents. An individual's associations and connections are conscious creations that are free to change situationally. In thinking of a physical place, rather than to perceive a cultural landscape—a space created through the vagaries of culture—the network approach understands that physical creations require an intimate knowledge of time and place, built around two interconnected dimensions, the sociohistorical and the socioenvironmental structures. These structures are composed of human-to-human and human-to-environment relations. If we wish, we may refer to the structures as cultural, but only in a nominal manner; the use of 'culture' in this instance has no final explanatory power.

Networks in Archaeology's Past

Interest in the past use of space is not new in archaeology. Beginning with Willey's (1953) pioneering settlement studies in Peru, archaeologists have considered and evaluated where ancient peoples have built their sites and monuments, and many archaeologist have conducted spatial, or locational, analyses in the attempt to explain ancient site distributions (for some examples, see Clarke 1977a; Hodder and Orton 1976; Kent 1984; Zimmerman 1977). It has emerged from these studies, and from those of scholars in other fields, that the notion that where things are not is as important as where things are. Though archaeologists of necessity focus their excavations on the discrete locations where past activities have occurred—where things are—they also understand the significance of where things are not. A classic example can he found in the prehistoric Hopewell Interaction Sphere, a model proposing that prehistoric Native Americans in the midwestern United States (from about 100 B. C. to A. D. 300–350) carried on economic activities within a series of expanding networks. The operating networks included intra-local, inter-local, intra-regional, inter-regional, and even trans-regional manifestations, eventually tying together sites hundreds of kilometers apart (Struever, 1964; Struever and Houart, 1972). This model was created to account for the presence of similar artifacts found great distances from one another, but its creators had an intuitive understanding that the objects moved through space in order to be deposited where they were found. In other words, in order to reach their final resting places, the artifacts had to have occupied a series of different spots along the route.

The need for archaeologists to understand the interconnection between space and place was explicitly noted several years ago by David Clarke (1977b), who described what he termed 'spatial archaeology'. As he defined it, spatial archaeology is:

> ... the retrieval of information from archaeological spatial relationships and the study of the spatial consequences of former hominid activity patterns *within and between* features and structures and their articulation within sites, site systems and their environments: the study of the flow and integration of activities *within and between* structures and resource spaces from the micro to the semi-micro and macro scales of aggregation. (Clarke, 1977: 9; emphasis added)

Clarke's somewhat dated use of the totalizing structures of micro (within structures), semi-micro (within sites), and macro (between sites) levels can be excused, but his basic understanding is generally consistent with the network approach I advocate. Clarke explicitly understood the difference between 'spatial archaeology'—as a pursuit intended to understand the significance of places and spaces—and 'settlement archaeology'—an archaeology directed toward living places. An archaeology directed toward understanding the networks of the past has several similarities with Clarke's spatial archaeology, with the exception being that my approach leans much more heavily on social network theory, a topic not as well formulated twenty years ago as it is today. Though Clarke did not make detailed use of network theory, even as it was then formulated (Haggett and Chorley, 1969), he nonetheless did have an avowed interest in understanding networks in archaeological research (Clarke, 1968: 469–472).

Examples showing the importance of social networks in historical archaeological analysis are not prevalent, but they do exist (Orser, 1998b). Two studies deriving from recent research at Annapolis, Maryland, are illustrative (Shackel et al., 1998). In the first example, Mark Warner (1998) investigates two houses inhabited by African-American families in the late nineteenth and early twentieth centuries. Examining social status and its identification with artifacts is a persistently important topic in historical archaeology. Warner observes that the African-American community did not represent a monolithic culture. On the contrary, the residents of the community appeared to make conscious choices that were socially charged and situationally meaningful. Individuals took certain actions within their community, not because their culture directed them to do so, but because some situational opportunity had presented itself at the time. Warner uses the consumption of tea as an illustration to show that some African Americans consciously selected tea drinking as a strategy to produce direct social benefits. Men and women drank tea, not because tea drinking was some kind of cultural marker, but because its consumption fostered and maintained certain relationships that the consumers deemed helpful to their specific situations. Tea, in essence, helped to create and maintain certain sought-after social connections. In historic Annapolis, then, there existed distinct networks of tea drinkers. One implication of this finding is that the presence of tea cups and saucers at sites associated with African Americans serves to indicate a possible social strategy of real living men and women, rather than the operation of some cultural norm. In another study, Christopher Matthews (1998) shows that the most important architectural designs of Annapolis's elites were those inspired by Andrea Palladio. Matthews argues that because Palladio was an extremely significant creator of the built environment within this prominent Chesapeake city, we must understand the man himself before we can begin to understand his style of architecture. As part of this understanding, we should recognize that Palladio and other prominent architects designed buildings that were idiosyncratic to a certain extent. Though we may suppose that the buildings were idiosyncratic in somewhat culturally constrained ways, it is difficult to argue that the architects produced buildings simply as products of their culture. Palladian architecture is clearly European in form, but is the use of the culturalist's perspective here, as an explanatory tool, truly satisfying? On the contrary, it seems much more interesting and potentially more enlightening to argue that the buildings designed by architectural luminaries were intended to symbolize, create, and maintain social relations between people, and to create boundaries between individuals (see also Leone, 1995; Leone, et al. 1998). As large objects seeking to communicate profound messages, the buildings and the creators behind them were integral elements of social networks. They worked to create social and physical distance between real men and women. In both examples, then, a culturalist interpretation would fall short of providing satisfactory explanations and promoting historical understanding. I believe that much more interesting and powerful interpretations will result from adopting an explicit network perspective.

Clearly, to make network theory useful to archaeological interpretation, archaeologists must devise frameworks that have direct archaeological relevance. Whereas earlier attempts by prehistorians to adopt network approaches in their research have drawn largely from geographic models, the use of written records and oral testimony by historical archaeologists makes it possible to apply some of the approaches from social network theory to studies of post-Columbian history.

The relations put into operation in a sociohistorical setting—encompassing both human-to-human relations and human-to-environment relations—comprise networks. Networks are easy to conceptualize as graphs composed of points connected by lines. In formal network analysis, points are termed 'nodes' or 'vertices', and connecting lines are termed 'links' or 'edges' (Haggett and Chorley, 1969: 5; Wasserman and Faust, 1994: 93). The archaeologist's job is to discover the nature and composition of these relations, to learn how they were expressed in material terms, and to understand these expressions through time. The archaeologist's first task is to develop a conceptual understanding of both kinds of relations, acknowledging the significance of their historical manifestations and accepting that a framework created for one sociohistorical setting will not have universal application.

For archaeological analysis, it is important to remember that human-to-human relations, like human-to-environment relations, are social and spatial at the same time. It is also necessary to understand that many of the relations that archaeologist study will incorporate power in some fashion. This understanding is particularly pertinent for historical archaeologists because the societies they study are usually capitalist in nature or at least have some involvement (willing or unwilling) with the capitalist enterprise.

Capitalist relations necessarily incorporate issues of power. Though it may be easier to conceptualize the enactment of power relations between individuals, we may also observe from our vantage point in the late twentieth century, in view of the destruction of diverse biotic communities during the modern era, that power is also exerted by humans on plant and animal communities (Mander, 1996). Thus, in both human-to-human and human-to-environment relations, we may accept Foucault's statement that "space is fundamental in any exercise of power" (Rabinow, 1984: 252). Where there is space, particularly in a capitalist setting, there is also power. And, the conduct of capitalism is necessarily a spatial pursuit as well as a social and economic endeavor (Scott, 1998; Sheppard and Barnes, 1990).

The introduction of relations of power necessarily raises the issue of ideology. Ideology has been, and most likely will continue to be, a hotly debated topic by scholars, including archaeologists. In this paper, it is not my intention to provide a lengthy discussion of ideology, and for present purposes it is enough to use the classic understanding that ideology serves to misrepresent and to hide social relations between diverse men and women, either individually or collectively. Rather than constituting an immutable force exerted by one class on another, the most sophisticated analysts imagine that ideologies are constantly being redefined both historically and situationally by real historical actors. Most scholars also now accept that ideologies are not created solely by society's elites, preferring instead to argue that every social unit is free to construct and promote its own ideologies. Given this reality, it is pertinent to consider the characteristics and consequences of the clash of ideologies within a society. For historical archaeologists, this clash usually occurs within a capitalist society or in situations where capitalism is being introduced and actively promoted, accepted, and resisted (Orser, 1996: 160–178). Thus, understanding the clash of historically constructed ideologies in capitalist settings necessarily incorporates some knowledge of how power relations are created, enacted, and maintained within complex webs of interaction.

Social relations, power relations, and the construction of ideologies are important archaeological topics because each always occurs at a particular place and at a certain historical time. And, given the nature of archaeological research, the historical manifestations of these relations can be evaluated over time. But before we can make such diachronic studies, we must have a method and a terminology for understanding the synchronic characteristics of the networks themselves. These modeled networks must be firmly rooted in the social and historical realities of the situation under investigation.

As a start, we may say that the locations where social connections are given expression are 'places' While the distance between the places are 'spaces'. In network language, places are nodes or vertices, while spaces are links or edges. Places and spaces can be either actual, physical entities—courtyards, houses, roads—or they can be cognitive structures—kinship ties, associational, memberships, and so forth. In both cases, the humanly constructed places and spaces represent 'spatiality,' a consciously created sociophysical landscape. Spatiality is thus not a naturally occurring phenomenon, simply a place where a culture lives. Rather, it is a "constituted objectivity, a 'lived' reality" (Soja, 1989: 79). Spatiality is ultimately "about the ordering of relations between people" in space and place (Hillier and Hanson, 1984: 2).

Spatiality can be the expression of ideology imprinted on the earth's surface to show that humans "are not so much self-aware as self-and-other aware" (Carrithers, 1992: 60). What this means is that the construction of modern landscapes is a function of the network of relations people maintained both with one another and with the natural environment around them. In constructing their landscapes, men and women are not simply agents of their culture, they are self-and-other aware. Men and women create social and environmental relations within a complex series of interconnected networks, each of which has specific historical meaning. Therefore, added to the idea that ancient roads and transportation routes were "ties that bind" (Hassig, 1991), we may also say that the social connections represented by the roads also bound men and women together. The social ties and the physical links work in tandem.

Scholars from several disciplines have conducted network analysis for many years, but archaeologists in large measure have been reluctant to follow suit. Though many reasons may exist for this lack of application— some of which may be purely personal—at least two reasons immediately spring to mind to explain the archaeologists' general disinterest in network analysis.

In the first place, archaeologists who study prehistory are usually reluctant, often for good reason, to adopt research methods and approaches originally designed to interpret modern settings. Many archaeologists may consider the often great time lengths between the subject of their study and the subject of the model weakens the model's applicability. For example, some archaeologists may be reluctant to use information on the rail systems on nineteenth-century New England in their study of the road system of the ancient American Southwest. Establishing the relevance of the analogy in this case could be extremely difficult. Prehistorians, of course, are well aware of the problem here, and this understanding is probably what lead Clarke (1977b: 28) to argue that "archaeology must develop its own related range of spatial theory" that could articulate with other disciplines examining the use of space.

The second reason why archaeologists may have largely rejected network analysis in their research may stem from the practical considerations of data collection. Simply put, the collection of adequate information is often unrealistic or even impossible when large-scale networks are the intended focus of study (Gorenflo and Bell, 1991: 80). Archaeologists, often facing severe shortages of time and funding, usually do not have the luxury of collecting data from large regions. The collection of information from a large area may take years of research. As an example, Struever's study of the Hopewell Interaction Sphere noted above was only possible after at least two decades of serious archaeological work had preceded him. Archaeologists have always confronted the problems of inadequate data collection, and the problem is acute for network analysis, even when conducted by cultural anthropologists (Sanjek, 1996: 397). The problem only grows more acute when archaeologists begin to think in trans-regional or global terms. Geographer Peter Haggett (1990: 28) nicely summarized the problem when he observed that the "problem posed by any subject which aims to be global is simple and immediate: the earth's surface is so staggeringly large."

The concerns of archaeologists over the collection of adequate information and the application of appropriate models are clearly important to consider. But, though these concerns justifiably trouble prehistorians, they need not be of equal worry to historical archaeologists. The presence of written records and other sources of textual and even oral information makes network analysis considerably more appealing to historical archaeologists. The presence of textual documentation, which may include maps, plats, plans, and written and verbal descriptions, may even decrease the need to conduct large-scale reconnaissance surveys. Every historical archaeologist knows that written records must not be used uncritically, even where physical features are concerned (Milanich, 1998), but most would agree that such materials can be excellent sources of information. In fact, the presence of textual information has often been used as a defining characteristic of historical archaeology. One of the great advantages of using textual and verbal information in historical archaeology is that, where researchers have used them to construct settlement models, they often provide a one-to-one correlation between the model and the archaeological entity under study. Even in cases where direct association does not occur, justifiable confidence in the applicability of the model is often possible because of the similarity in time between the model and the unit of study. Thus, a geographic model of nineteenth-century settlement in Maine, based on written records and field survey, may be applicable to an archaeological study of nineteenth-century settlement in Massachusetts.

Without question, the advantages offered by the presence of textual information give network analysis in historical archaeology great potential. Documents, carefully considered and evaluated, can increase the validity and power of an archaeologist's spatial interpretations. Beyond this simple practical concern, however, network analysis in historical archaeology is even more significant because it can provide empirical grounding to issues that interest many anthropologists and archaeologists today: "layered contexts, multiple voices, and historical processes" (Houseman, 1997: 753). In this sense, the application of network analysis to archaeology, and particularly to historical archaeology, is timely and pertinent.

Network analysis begins with the simple notion, stated above, that men and women create and maintain relationships. Networks of interaction or association exist because individuals have many relationships. These relationships can take the form of 'vertical' and 'horizontal' linkages (Schweizer, 1997: 740). Vertical linkages are those that are hierarchical, and which relate to social units of increasingly larger size. Horizontal linkages, on the other hand, relate to the interconnectedness between various domains within a social unit.

Both horizontal and vertical links are important to consider, but an interest in hierarchical links is especially pertinent to historical archaeology because vertical linkages tie men and women to interregional, extraregional, and even transnational networks of the kind that operated after 1492 (and which still operate). Given the nature of these links, historical archaeologists must adopt a multiscalar approach to study them (Orser, 1996: 184–190). A multiscalar perspective is also needed to examine the horizontal linkages because these connections tie together the political, economic, social, communicative, and other elements of a social body.

A network model and multiscalar analysis go hand in hand. In the course of their daily lives, men and women conduct their actions along a number of different scales and within a diverse number of networks. Out of the infinite number of scales that can exist in any social entity, individuals "comprehend patterns, recognize homogeneity, plan for the future, and operate in the present at specific scales" (Marquardt, 1992: 107; see also Marquardt, 1985). An 'effective scale,' the level at which a pattern or meaning may be discerned, exists for each conscious decision made by the individual (Crumley, 1979: 166).

When conducting an overt multiscalar analysis, a researcher begins at one effective scale and seeks to understand it. Once the analysis is satisfactorily completed, the knowledge is transcended as the analyst moves to another scale. This process is repeated until the investigator is satisfied that all possibilities have been exhausted. As one moves from one scale to another, it often becomes clear that the social entities under investigation maintain their connections across time and space. Historical archaeologists examining the modern world should understand that the agents of colonialism, capitalism, globalization, and Eurocentrism created links that cross-cut several effective scales, both social and physical.

Network analysis gives initial prominence to people and places as nodes and the links that connect them. The resultant network analyses, which clearly must be multiscalar, can be used to model relationships between people and people, people and places, and places and places in both synchronic and diachronic dimensions.

Several key concepts lie at the heart of formal network analysis. In social network analysis, these concepts are, in ascending order: actor, relational tie, dyad, triad, subgroup, group, relation, and social network (Wasserman and Faust, 1994: 17–20). In an archaeological analysis modeled on social network analysis, the analytical concepts might be site, connector, dyad, triad, area, region, relation, and network (Table 6.1).

In social network analysis, the actors are discrete individuals or social units that work collectively. Depending upon the scale of analysis, the individuals can be single men and women in a group or nation-states within a world network. For archaeological analysis, however, it may be most appropriate to consider the actors to be individual men and women since this conception would be consistent with the geographic notion of the site. Though it may be difficult or impossible to conduct research on individual men and women in prehistoric settings, this focus need not cause overwhelming concern for historical archaeology

Table 6.1. Core Concepts of
Network Analysis

Social	Archaeological
actor	site
relational tie	connector
dyad	dyad
triad	triad
subgroup	area
group	region
relation	relation
social network	physical network

because of the presence of supportive, non-archaeological documentation.

Actors are linked together by relational ties. These social connections can be rooted in personal evaluations (such as friendship, respect, a sense of empathy), an association or affiliation (through shared labor, organizational membership), kinship (either real or fictive), or through a power relationship (owner to worker, ruler to ruled). In a geographic sense, the relational ties will be actual physical features that serve to link sites together, such as rivers, roads, causeways, and bridges. The importance of such features in archaeological analysis is "that they can provide tangible evidence of cultural links across geographical space" (Trombold, 1991: 8); they are, in essence, connectors. A dyad, in both social and physical space, refers to the relationship established between two actors or sites. In network analysis, the tie between the two entities is perceived as an integral property of the pair rather than as a feature of either individual (Wasserman and Faust, 1994: 18). Thus, the tie between father and son is a property of both individuals at the same time, just as a road linking two sites originates from both at the same time. In social analysis, it is possible, however, to have "asymmetric dyads" (Wasserman and Faust, 1994: 510–511), where a relationship is only chosen by one of the individuals. As an example, a son who feels abandoned may reject a relationship promoted by his father. Asymmetric dyads may also appear in the landscape, though probably with less frequency. A swiftly running river, connecting two villages, provides an example. In the absence of motor boats, only the villagers living upriver could use the river as a relational tie. The villagers living downstream would have to use another relational tie (a road or path) if they sought interaction with the upriver villagers. The triad, like the dyad, has been the subject of much network analysis. It consists, as the name implies, of three actors, or thinking archaeologically, of three interconnected sites. Following this line of reasoning, a subgroup in social network analysis is comprised of sets of dyads and triads. For archaeological analysis, I have chosen to term the subgroup an 'area,' and the group—composed of several subgroups—a 'region.' This usage is consistent with the notion of the region in geographic network analysis as being an area enclosed by relational links or edges (Haggett and Chorley, 1969: 5).

Elsewhere (Orser, 1996: 131–144), I have explored the problem posed by physical boundaries when using a network approach in archaeology. To paraphrase, I argued that when archaeologists explicitly think about the relational ties between sites and people they may be forced to forget their traditional understanding of what constitutes an archaeological area or region. In line with the proposition that site dyads and triads are distinguished by their connection, I argued that historical archaeologists may be able to consider parts of different continents within the same area or region. Thus, for a certain period of time, it may be argued that colonial Portugal and colonial Brazil, or colonial England and colonial South Africa, were part of the same area or region because of their relational ties. This understanding is quite distinct from the cultural landscape, where what ties areas together is the cognitive, cultural processes of colonizers.

89

NETWORK THEORY

A Brief Example

Given the requirements of a rigorous multiscalar network analysis in archaeology, much more space would be needed to present a complete example here. Nonetheless, it is still important to provide a brief specific example to demonstrate the interpretive power and potential of network analysis in archaeology. Space limitations prohibit a full example, and I understand that my example will be necessarily incomplete and sketchy. But, to demonstrate the value of network analysis I focus on the seventeenth-century kingdom of Palmares in northeast Brazil. As I have pointed out elsewhere (Orser, 1994b, 1996), Palmares provides an excellent case study for an archaeologically informed network analysis.

Palmares was a kingdom built in the present state of Alagoas in northeast Brazil by a number of runaway slaves around 1605. The colonial Portuguese government destroyed the settlement in 1694, but at its height, Palmares is thought to have had as many as 20,000 residents. In 1992 and 1993, I collaborated on an exploratory archaeological study of Palmares with Pedro Funari, and information about this research effort can be found elsewhere (Funari, 1995a, b; 1996a, b; Orser, 1992, 1993, 1994a, b; 1998a; Orser and Funari, 1992).

Palmares was a unified kingdom designed around resistance to enslavement and debasement. At the height of its development, Palmares was composed of ten discrete villages: Amaro, Arotirene, Tabocas (two villages), Zumbi, Aqualtene, Dambrabanga, Subupira, Macaco and Andalaquituche, with Macaco being the seat of the king (Figure 6.1). Research is not advanced enough to indicate precisely how the individual villages were connected. Historical records do clearly show, however, that the Palmarinos maintained continual relations with their environment. One observer who knew the condition of the territory of Palmares in the 1670s described it as "a naturally rugged place, mountainous, and dry, sown with all varieties of trees known and unknown" (Drummond, 1859: 304). The dense forests and the surrounding mountains helped to create Palmares, just as they sheltered and hid the Palmarinos from the invading colonial armies from the coast. At the same time, the environment sustained the people. Historical documents make it abundantly clear that they grew a variety of crops, caught fish, and domesticated fowl. They used the foliage for their homes, their basketry, and their defensive stockades, just as they used local clays to make pottery. Without question, the Palmarinos created and maintained a complex network of relationships with their environment.

At the same time, a series of complex social and power relationships helped to hold the kingdom together. The king of Palmares was a man named Ganga Zumba, and his brother, Gana Zona, ruled the

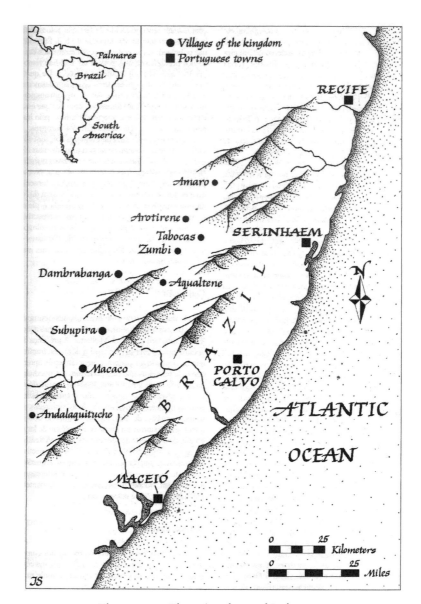

Figure 6.1. The Kingdom of Palmares.

kingdom's second city. The ruler of another town was the king's nephew, and that of another town, was his mother. Zumbi, the last great king of Palmares, was the king's nephew. Without question, kinship and power relations enacted as a series of interconnected dyads and triads helped to hold the kingdom together, even in the face of armed attack. This complex series of confederation and tributary relations helped to define Palmares both internally and externally (Anderson, 1996).

It would be relatively easy to argue that these relationships simply constitute cultural expression. All available evidence indicates that the Palmarinos busied themselves with building a new culture in the New World. But even this understanding allows for the presence of two effective scales: the individual villages and the kingdom itself. It is only when we combine a multiscalar perspective with a network approach that we can see other effective scales. For instance, within the kingdom itself existed a stark division between those Palmarinos who sought accommodation with the Portuguese and those who desired a constant, continual armed resistance. This conflict eventually caused Zumbi to murder his uncle the king, and to assume the reins of leadership. Similarly, a schism existed among the colonial Portuguese, because some Portuguese settlers living on the colonial frontier chose to support Palmares over their own colonial government. Thus, both in Palmares and outside on the frontier, power relations were constantly being enacted and redefined. Clearly, a full understanding of Palmares requires more than simple knowledge of the syncretic culture the fugitive men and women built among the palm trees of northeastern Brazil. A more complete understanding can be gained by adopting an explicit relational network model.

Further increasing the scale of analysis permits asking another question that otherwise may not be apparent: Why did the Dutch attack Palmares during their years in northeast Brazil? The answer to this question at first may seem too obvious to address. Caspar Barleus (1923: 315), a contemporary of Palmares, described the people who lived there as a "collection of robbers and fugitive slaves." Barleus was not alone in his perception of Palmares; most of its colonial enemies described it in the same terms. To them, the men and women of Palmares were simply thieves who robbed their coastal plantations. Knowing their perspective, it only makes sense that the colonial Dutch would seek to destroy the kingdom. But does this really make sense once we understand that the Dutch and the Portuguese were, in fact, deadly rivals in Brazil? Each superpower sought to control the native people and native riches of this part of South America. Keeping in mind the network model, we must ask why the colonial Dutch, enemies of the colonial Portuguese, did not create an alliance with Palmares, also enemies of the colonial Portuguese? Merely asking this question leads us to other questions: were the Dutch so appalled by the actions of the Palmarinos against another European nation that they sought to destroy it out of a sense of European solidarity? Or were the Dutch merely so racist that they simply sought to destroy a group of renegade Africans? Understanding a network model makes us wonder whether it was the connections the Palmarinos had made with Native Americans, with Portuguese settlers, and among themselves that really offended the Dutch (for details of these connections, see Orser, 1994b and 1996: 41–53). This multifaceted, interconnected web was a serious impediment to Dutch colonial expansion in the South American hinterland. Assuming that the Dutch believed they could wrest Brazil from the Portuguese, they may have decided to remove Palmares when the time seemed right. In any case, if the Dutch were simply racist, it would have made sense for them to unite with the Portuguese to destroy Palmares and, once this task was accomplished, to begin the quest for an empire against their former European allies.

The history and culture of Palmares was indeed complex, and it will take many more years of research before a new, truly meaningful reanalysis can be completed. Our initial archaeological research has only provided the briefest understanding of what is clearly an extremely deep and meaningful history. The application of a network perspective, however, permits archaeologists to ask new questions about Palmares and to approach an old topic in an entirely new way.

Conclusion

Network analysis opens up exciting opportunities for archaeologists, especially those studying modern history. The presence of written documentation and even oral testimony means that historical archaeologists have the potential to learn about the connections that held men and women together in ways that may not be readily apparent simply from archaeological deposits. The true advantages of using network analysis in historical archaeological research have yet to be demonstrated in a large-scale study. Network analysis, when combined with a multiscalar perspective, however, has the potential to permit archaeologists to ask new and interesting questions about the past, and to provide important new interpretations.

Acknowledgements

I would like to thank Pedro Funari for asking me to participate in the conference, and for his continued support and collaboration. I would also like to thank Jack Scott for drawing the figure.

References

Anderson, R. N., 1996, The *Quilombo* of Palmares: A New Overview of a Maroon State in Seventeenth-Century Brazil. *Journal of Latin American Studies* 28: 545–566.

Barleus, C., 1923, *Brazilie Onuder Het Bewind von Johan Maurits, Grave vau Nassau, 1637–1644*. Martinus Nijhoff, Gravenhage.

Barnes, A., 1954, Class and Committees in a Norwegian Island Parish. *Human Relations* 7: 39–54.

Carrithers, M., 1992, *Why Humans Have Cultures: Explaining Anthropology and Social Diversity*. Oxford University Press, Oxford.

Clarke, D. L., 1968, *Analytical Archaeology*. Methuen, London.

1977a, *Spatial Archaeology*. Academic Press, London.

1977b, Spatial Information in Archaeology. In *Spatial Archaeology*, edited by D. L. Clarke, pp. 1–32. Academic Press, London.

Crumley, C. L., 1979, Three Locational Models: An Epistemological Assessment for Anthropology and Archaeology. In *Advances in Archaeological Method and Theory*, volume 2., edited by M. B. Schiffer, pp. 141–173. Academic Press, New York.

De Cunzo, L. T., O'Malley, M., Lewis, J., Thomas, G. E., and Wilmanns-Wells, C., 1996, Father Rapp's Garden at Economy: Harmony Society Culture in Microcosm. In *Landscape Archaeology: Reading and Interpreting the American Historical Landscape*, edited by R. Yamin and K. B. Metheny, pp. 91–117. University of Tennessee Press, Knoxville.

Deetz, J., 1990, Landscapes as Cultural Statements. In *Earth Patterns: Essays in Landscape Archaeology*, edited by W. M. Kelso and R. Most, pp. 1–4. University Press of Virginia, Charlottesville.

——— 1991, Archaeological Evidence of Sixteenth- and Seventeenth–Century Encounters. In *Historical Archaeology in Global Perspective*, edited by L. Falk, pp. 1–9. Smithsonian Institution Press, Washington, D. C.

Drummond, C., 1859, Relação das guerras feitas aos Palmares de Pernambuco no tempo de Governador D. Pedro de Almeida de 1675 a 1678. *Revista do Instituto Histórico e Geográfico Brasileiro* 22: 303–329.

Durkheim, E., 1915, *The Elementary Forms of the Religious Life: A Study in Religious Sociology*, translated by J. W. Swain. Allen and Unwin, London.

Funari, P. P. A., 1995a, A cultura material de Palmares: o estudo das relações sociais de um quilombo pela arqueologia. *Idéias* :37–42.

——— 1995b, A Repblica de Palmares e a arqueologia da Serra da Barriga. *Revista USP* 28: 6–13.

——— 1996a, Novas perspectives abertas pela arqueologia na Serra da Barriga. In *Negras Imagens*, edited by L. M. Schwarcz and L. V. de Reis, pp. 139–230. Editora da Universidade de São Paulo, São Paulo.

——— 1996b, A arqueologia de Palmares: sua contribuiçáo para o conhecimento da história da cultura afro-americana. In *Liberdade por um fio: história dos quilombos no Brasil*, J. J. Reis and F. dos Santos Gomes, pp. 26–51. Editora Schwarcz, São Paulo.

Haggett, P., 1990, *The Geographer's Art*. Basil Blackwell, Oxford.

Haggett, P., and Chorley, R. J., 1969, *Network Analysis in Geography*. St. Martin's Press, New York.

Hassig, R., 1991, Roads, Routes, and Ties that Bind. In *Ancient Road Networks and Settlement Hierarchies in the New World*, edited by C. D. Trombold, pp. 17–27. Cambridge University Press, Cambridge.

Hillier, B., and Hanson, J., 1984, *The Social Logic of Space*. Cambridge University Press, Cambridge.

Hodder, I., and Orton, C., 1976, *Spatial Analysis in Archaeology*. Cambridge University Press, Cambridge.

Houseman, M., 1997, Comment on Thomas Schweizer's "Embeddedness of Ethnographic Cases: A Social Networks Perspective". *Current Anthropology* 38: 753–754.

Kelso, W. M., and Most, R., editors, 1990, *Earth Patterns: Essays in Landscape Archaeology*. University Press of Virginia, Charlottesville.

Kent, S., 1984, *Analyzing Activity Areas: An Ethnoarchaeological Study of the Use of Space*. University of New Mexico Press, Albuquerque.

Knoke, D., and Kuklinski, J. H., 1992, *Network Analysis*. Sage, Newberry Park, CA.

Leone, M. P., 1995, A Historical Archaeology of Capitalism. *American Anthropologist* 97: 251–268.

Leone, M. P., Stabler, J., and Burlaga, A-M., 1998, A Street Plan for Hierarchy in Annapolis: An Analysis of State Circle as a Geometric Form. In *Annapolis Pasts: Historical Archaeology in Annapolis. Maryland*, edited by P. A. Shackel. P. R. Mullins and M. S. Warner, pp. 291–306. University of Tennessee Press, Knoxville.

Lesser. A., 1961, Social Fields and the Evolution of Society. *Southwestern Journal of Anthropology* 17: 40–48.

Mander, J., 1996, Facing the Rising Tide. In *The Case Against the Global Economy and For a Turn Toward the Local*, edited by J. Mander and E. Goldsmith, pp. 3–19. Sierra Club Books, San Francisco.

Marquardt, W. H., 1985, Complexity and Scale in the Study of Fisher-Gatherer-Hunters: An Example from the Eastern United States. In *Prehistoric Hunter-Gatherers: The Emergence of Cultural Complexity*, edited by T. D. Price and J. A. Brown, pp. 59–98. Academic Press, Orlando.

1992, Dialectical Archaeology. In *Archaeological Method and Theory*, volume 4, edited by M. B. Schiffer, pp. 101–140, University of Arizona Press, Tucson.

Matthews, C. N., 1998, Part of a Polished Society: Style and Ideology in Annapolis's Georgian Architecture. In *Annapolis Pasts: Historical Archaeology in Annapolis, Maryland*, edited by P. A. Shackel, P. R. Mullins, and M. S. Warner, pp. 244–267. University of Tennessee Press, Knoxville.

Milanich, J. T., 1998, Case of the Missing Moat. *Archaeology* 51(5): 58.

Mitchell. J. C., 1974, Social Networks. *Annual Reviews of Anthropology* 3: 279–299.

Orser, C. E.. Jr., 1992, *In Search of Zumbi: Preliminary Archaeological Research at the Serra da Barriga, State of Alagoas, Brazil*. Report prepared for the National Geographic Society, Washington, D. C.

1993, *In Search of Zumbi: 1993 Season*. Report prepared for the National Geographic Society, Washington. D. C., and the Social Science Research Council, New York.

1994a, Searching for Palmares: the Serra da Barriga, Brazil. *National Geographic Research and Exploration* 10: 480–482.

1994b, Toward a Global Historical Archaeology: An Example from Brazil. *Historical Archaeology* 28: 1–18.

1996, *A Historical Archaeology of the Modern* World. Plenum, New York.

1998a, Archaeology of the African Diaspora. *Annual Reviews of Anthropology* 27: 63–82.

1998b, Epilogue: From Georgian Order to Social Relations at Annapolis and Beyond. In *Annapolis Pasts: Historical Archaeology in Annapolis, Maryland*, edited by P. A. Shackel, P. R. Mullins, and M. Warner, pp. 307–324. University of Tennessee Press, Knoxville.

1998c, Negotiating our 'Familiar Pasts'. In *The Familiar Past? Archaeologies of Britain, 1550–1950*, edited by S. Tarlow and S. West, pp. 273–285. Routledge, London.

2004, The Archaeologies of Recent History: Historical, Post-Medieval, and Modern-World. In *The Blackwell Companion to Archaeology*, edited by J. Bintliff, pp. 272–290. Blackwell, Oxford.

Orser, C. E. Jr., and Funari, P. P. A., 1992, Pesquisa arqueológica inicial em Palmares. *Estudos Ibero-americanos* 18: 53–69.

Rabinow, P., editor, 1994, *The Foucault Reader*. Pantheon, New York.

Radcliffe-Brown, A. R., 1940, On Social Structure. *Journal of the Royal Anthropological Society of Great Britain and Ireland* 70: 1–12.

Sanjek, R., 1996, Network Analysis. In *Encyclopedia of Social and Cultural Anthropology*, edited by A. Barnard and J. Spencer, pp. 396–397. Routledge, London.

Scott, A. J., 1998, *Regions and the World Economy: The Coming Shape of Global Production, Competition. and Political Order*. Oxford University Press, Oxford.

Schweizer, T., 1997, Embeddedness of Ethnographic Cases: A Social Networks Perspective. *Current Anthropology* 38: 739–760.

Shackel, P. A., Mullins, P. R., and Warner, M. S., editors, 1998, *Annapolis Pasts: Historical Archaeology in Annapolis, Maryland*. University of Tennessee Press, Knoxville.

Sheppard, E., and Barnes, T. J., 1990, *The Capitalist Space Economy: Geographical Analysis After Ricardo, Marx and Sraffa*. Unwin Hyman, London.

Soja, E. W., 1989, *Postmodern Geographies: The Reassertion of Space in Critical Social Theory*. Verso, London.

Struever, S., 1964, The Hopewell Interaction Sphere in Riverine-Western Great Lakes Culture History. In *Hopewellian Studies*, edited by J. R. Caldwell and R. L. Hall, pp. 85–106. Illinois State Museum, Springfield.

Struever, S., and Houart, G. L., 1972, An Analysis of the Hopewell Interaction Sphere. In *Social Exchange and Interaction*. E. N. Wilmsen, pp. Museum of Anthropology, University of Michigan, Ann Arbor.

Trombold, C. D., 1991, An Introduction to the Study of Ancient New World Road Networks. In *Ancient Road Networks and Settlement Hierarchies in the New World*, edited by C. D. Trombold, pp. 1–9. Cambridge University Press, Cambridge.

Warner, M. S., 1998, 'The Best There Is of Us': Ceramics and Status in African American Annapolis. In *Annapolis Pasts: Historical Archaeology in Annapolis, Maryland*, edited by P. A. Shackel, P. R. Mullins, and M. S. Warner, pp. 190–212. University of Tennessee Press, Knoxville.

Wasserman, S., and Faust, K., 1994, *Social Network Analysis: Methods and Applications*. Cambridge University Press, Cambridge.

Willey, G. R., 1953, *Prehistoric Settlement Patterns in the Viru Valley, Peru*. Smithsonian Institution, Bureau of American Ethnology Bulletin 153. Government Printing Office, Washington, D. C.

Wolf, E. R., 1982, *Europe and the People without History*. University of California Press, Berkeley.

1984, Culture: Panacea or Problem? *American Antiquity* 49: 393–400.

Yamin, R. and Metheny, K. B., editors., 1996, *Landscape Archaeology: Reading and Interpreting the American Historical Landscape*. University of Tennessee Press, Knoxville.

Zimmerman, L. J., 1977, *Prehistoric Locational Behavior: A Computer Simulation*. Report 10, Office of the State Archaeologist. University of Iowa, Iowa City.

7

The Comparative Method in Archaeology and the Study of Spanish and Portuguese South American Material Culture

Pedro Paulo A. Funari

The use of the comparative method in archaeology is still in its infancy in Latin America. This chapter explores differences in settlement patterns between the Hispanic and Portuguese worlds and tries to show how a comparative approach enables a better understanding of two contrasting ways of ordering the material world (Nassaney, 1998; Orser 1997). Furthermore, comparison, as a strategy in contextual archaeology, contributes to recognizing archaeological inquiry within its own historical and social context (Shanks, 1994: 32; Zarankin, 2000). Long ago archaeology was recognized as much more than ancillary to history (cf. Childe, 1956, first sentence of the book; contra Meneses, 1965: 22). To a global audience, it is probably amazing to discover that there are meaningful differences between Hispanic and Portuguese America from which a comparative archaeology can gain a lot.

Urban archaeology is an obvious field for comparative study, as urban development in South America has been very important and will continue to be so in the future. Diverse urban sites have been excavated, and even if in most cases it is not possible to try to reconstruct the urban setting as a whole and its changes over time, excavations have certainly produced archaeological evidence which can provide a better understanding of city life in South America. Furthermore, thanks to non-destructive techniques, such as field surveys and the study of ancient maps and other iconographic materials, it is possible to propose ways of understanding urban material culture in a variety of different historical and geographical contexts. In general terms, we should differentiate Hispanic cities, characterized by their planned location of streets and public building based on a checkered square-grid scheme, from Portuguese towns, first and foremost a medieval assemblage of houses, following curves and slopes (Hollanda, 1984; Marx, 1989). To explore the antecedents of practices in the New World, one must move not just in time but also in space, back across the Atlantic to Old World medieval origins (Johnson, 1999: 223).

The cultural importance of this difference can be judged by the subjective sense of being outsiders felt in the Americas by the Portuguese in Spanish cities and by Spaniards in Portuguese towns. Colonial documents often describe how these two different *Weltanschauungen* organized the perception of social life in the two parts of South America/Hispanic America had an orderly urban setting, where cities were regularly reproduced in different places, in flat areas where possible; Brazil, as the Portuguese colony soon became known, had a landscape which contributed to the scattering of houses around hills, with curved and narrow streets producing towns as varied as the topography of different areas. The Portuguese colonial land and streetscape were the result of human action framed by nature (Mrozowski and Beaudry, 1990: 205) and by a medieval outlook (Castro, 1996; Weckmann, 1993), so that still today "streets look like the Medieval Portuguese", as a recent newspaper piece stated (Martins, 2000). There was thus an official Portuguese policy to stress the Portuguese features of colonial towns, such that that the population identified themselves as Portuguese (Reis, 2000). Hispanic cities were built through the regular addition of *manzanas* ('apples'), or blocks of houses and squares felt to be as natural as apples. The Portuguese have no blocks; their town plan was conceptualized as an *arruamento*, a term which could be translated as "creases or wrinkles in the face of the land", as the term *rua* (street) itself connotes a "wrinkle" (from the Latin *ruga*, found also in the English "corrugation"). These differences are still important to this day, as there is a strong opposition to urban planning in Brazil and even the very few examples of planned cities desperately try to avoid right angles and squares, preferring curves and non-symmetric designs, as is noted in the case a the capital city, Brasìlia, founded in 1961. Hispanic Americans are still uncomfortable in Brazilian towns, always looking for a missing order in the chaotic 'wrinkles', while Brazilians cannot avoid deriding the lack of creativity in the reproduction of squares and blocks in Hispanic cities.

Hispanic America was grounded on cities, so that within the first one hundred years of colonization, there were already 225 Hispanic cities, reaching the impressive number of 330 cities by 1600. These cities obeyed the rules established by Spanish laws in relation to their features, most of them reproducing a checkered frame around central squares where the main legislative, administrative and religious buildings were located. The distribution of the population within the city was also regulated, so that *vecinos*, or citizens, and *habitantes*, or inhabitants, would settle in different areas. Downtown, around the main square or *plaza central* formed by the prestigious public buildings, were found the dwellings of the most important colonists, even though naturally their servants, Indians and African slaves, inhabited the same area. Most inhabitants in this hierarchical society, were classified as plebeian, and included a variety of 'races', as established by differences in status, skin color and general appearance, while ordinary people lived in peripheral blocks. The Spanish Crown wanted to keep Indians separate from Spaniards and enacted legislation towards this end, enforcing the segregation of Indians, black slaves and Spanish settlers. However, there were factors encouraging the breakdown of barriers, and colonists, blacks and Indians intermarried against the law (Wade, 1994: 60). A complete account of urban material life should include the parallel rise in vernacular buildings in the periphery, so that we could better understand the way in which the middle and lower orders expressed their view of the past and present through the layout and appearance of their own homes (Johnson, 1992: 54). A dialectical epistemology can reflect an interest in the lived experience of past people, their actions within fields of social relations and cultural meanings, and their roles as conscious creators and negotiators of culture (McGuire and Saitta, 1996: 198) so that ubiquitous domination and resistance can be studied by archaeology (Frazer, 1999: 5). The quarters occupied by ordinary people are often absent from historical documents and historians' discourses (cf. Skimore, 2000: 572).

Santa Fe la Vieja is probably the best example of an early Hispanic city in South America which has been the focus of archaeological research. It was the first city founded near the Río de La Plata in 1573, and its blueprint was reproduced by Buenos Aires when it was founded definitively in 1580, such that, in a way, studying Santa Fe la Vieja is like looking for a lost Buenos Aires. The checkered outline introduced to Hispanic America by Nicolás de Ovando in Santo Domingo in 1502 served as a model for most Spanish cities, including Santa Fe la Vieja, and was established as a statutory rule by Phillip the Second in the same year of 1573. Three main structures were established by law: the *Plaza Mayor*, or Main Square, the *Iglesia Mayor*, or Main Church, and the Cabildo, or Town Council House. Santa Fe la Vieja reached a peak of some five hundred inhabitants, but was affected by frequent floods and the town council decided in 1660 to move the whole town to a better site, subsequently reconstituting the original grid system, and thereby founding the modern Argentine city of Santa Fe (Zarankin, 1995).

Santa Fe la Vieja is thus a unique opportunity for archaeologists to study an abandoned town, in a way which would be impossible in a city which has been in normal use for hundreds of years, as is the case with most other Hispanic cities. As the city was abandoned, the buildings were gradually destroyed by the wind and the rain, but in the last

Table 7.1. Ceramic Distribution, Santa Fe la Vieja

	Local ware	Hispanic imports	Other imports
Central Blocks	48%	51%	1.2%
Periphery	100%	—	—

decades of the nineteenth century there were remains still visible at the old site. Later, the site was no longer identifiable and in 1948, the Provincial Assembly enacted a law ordering the identification of the old city, and Zapata Gollán found and excavated Santa Fe La Vieja in 1949. From then on, excavations have produced abundant archaeological material, including first and foremost human remains and pottery (Senatore, 1995).

The study of the spatial distribution of pottery shards enabled archaeologists to distinguish the central and peripheral quarters of the city as shown in Table 7.1. Fourteen different wares were found in the central blocks, but only three in the periphery, and apparently the local pottery was shared by people living downtown and at the periphery. The archaeologists who studied Santa Fe la Vieja have interpreted this as a result of a specific Hispanic colonial way of life, in opposition to a British colonial one, represented an Iberian tendency towards incorporation, characterized mostly by the inclusion of local women in elite houses, as servants, but also as wives. It is likely that natives, blacks and mixed *mestizos* were supposed to behave like good Spaniards, speak Castillian, make the bed, sew European clothes, prepare Spanish foods in a traditional Spanish fashion, and thus use European material culture. However, the study of pottery in Santa Fe la Vieja does not present us with clear enough evidence to the extent of this 'acculturation', and there is good reason to suggest that the ubiquitous use of local wares could indicate the importance of native material culture for urban dwellers in general. If the city itself was very much characterized by Spanish material culture, and the streetscape a grid framing the minds of every Hispanic town dweller, the local pottery could equally relate to a counter-discourse, produced by ordinary people, informing and expressing an overwhelming feeling of belonging to a colonial society, through the use of non-European pots to cook and eat different foods. Archaeology can thus shed much-needed light on the dispossessed, the downtrodden, and the disenfranchised (Orser, 1999: 143–145). Perhaps the most striking feature of archaeological inquiry in the recent past has been the way in which it has broken the association of subordination with stasis and passivity (Scott, 1988: 424), so that attention has been paid to the daily lives of ordinary people (Paynter and McGuire, 1991: 13; Trigger, 1998: 16).

Buenos Aires, from its conception, was a Hispanic city in a good position to become an important seat of the government, taking on initially the Governorship and later the Viceroyalty of La Plata, from 1776. The city grew continually, and during the 1880s, Buenos Aires experienced a building fever, in the course of which most the Spanish colonial architecture was replaced by Parisian style buildings, in the first decades of this century. The capital of Argentina underwent further interesting changes, such as the construction of one of the earliest underground metropolitan subway rail systems in the world. It is now one of the largest cities in the Southern Hemisphere, and although most urban archaeology must be restricted to limited excavations, there is still a lot that can be said about the historical features of Buenos Aires and the way it changed over time. As was already mentioned, it followed the grid pattern established by the Spanish authorities and even though it expanded significantly, it always respected the same checkered logic. Even small brooks, historically the main hindrances to the expansion of the city, were continually integrated into the planned streetscape.

The archaeological study of Buenos Aires has developed more so since the restoration of civilian rule in the 1980s, mostly as a result of interested architects, and therefore within a conceptual framework derived from architecture and urban studies (Schávelzon, 1992). From the start, then, "Urban Archaeology" was the term used to describe a growing interest in the material culture of the city and, even though it should include the study of smaller urban settlements, like *pueblos* ("towns" and "villages"), urban archaeology paid particular attention to large and complex cities, first and foremost to Buenos Aires, whose vitality has been impressive since the early days and whose architectural heritage is monumental, rightfully recognized as the most impressive city in South America. Furthermore, Buenos Aires has been for centuries the intellectual powerhouse of Latin America and its intelligentsia remains outstanding today. This goes a long way to explaining the conflation of historical archaeology with urban archaeology and the overwhelming importance of the search for historic Buenos Aires. Excavations of historical buildings and the publication of monographs focusing on typological studies of artifacts, like pottery and smoking pipes, were the main results of scholarly research, and several books were published on Buenos Aires, establishing urban archaeology as a very popular archaeological field in Argentina.

Buenos Aires has been considered a large, single city-site, studied mostly through limited rescue excavations, so that the excavation of a small area of 1469 *Defensa* Street, looking for early colonial remains, for instance, and the excavation of a nineteenth century publishing house, *Imprenta Coni*, are considered as part of the same overarching study of Buenos Aires. The general subject of interest remains Buenos Aires the results of which over the last fifteen years of archaeological research deal primarily with the character of the city and its changes over time. Probably the best way of assessing the advances in the field is to outline the study of pottery and its contribution to the understanding of the urban context. At *Imprenta Coni*, a well-known site in Buenos Aires, a specific archaeological survey produced the figures concerning sixteenth and seventeenth century ceramic styles shown in Table 7.2.

In other surveys, in the same area, Native style pottery could reach even higher percentages (i.e., 23.04%) and Schávelzon (1994: 41) has ordered differences in ware assemblages chronologically (see Table 7.3).

Table 7.2. 16th and 17th C.
Ceramic Styles at Imprenta
Conti

Ceramic style	%
Native South American	10.6
Mixed	25.7
Majolica	38.2
Cream and Pearlwares	16.5
Ordinary (form Spain?)	6.7

Table 7.3. Chronological
Sequence of Ceramic Ware
Assemblages

Native South American	1580–1800
Mixed Pottery	1590–1800
Majolica	1580–1800
Olive-oil vessels	1580–1850
Creamware	1750–1800
Pearlware	1800–1850
Stoneware	1830–1900
Whiteware	1890–1900

As such, the occupation of the area can be divided into four successive phases: the first with no clear architectonic remains (1580–1730), followed by the construction of a humble dwelling, the so-called *Casa Rodríguez* (1730–1822), whose destruction allowed for the building of the *Casa Goyena* (1822–1884); and subsequently the *Imprenta Coni*, established in 1884–5, all demonstrating the change in the use of the site from domestic to industrial. In the earliest period, Native South American pottery prevailed by and large, succeeded by cheap, locally made wares which exhibited mixed Indigenous and European features, with a few imported wares. The upper-class *Casa Goyena*, with nicely glazed tiles, produced fine Pearlware, while the factory is largely known for its architectural remains, particularly the construction of sanitary facilities in the late nineteenth century. There is a clear trend in the ceramic remains from Native to Mixed to European, from pre-modern to modern, from local to international, providing good material proof of the Europeanization preached by the ruling elites since the nineteenth century. However, it is also true that the area was continually enhancing contacts with the city center and so we should not read this change as a simple adoption of European traits, but as the result of a succession of occupations increasingly marked by upper class people (on the use of class in archaeology, see Saitta 1992: 889). It is symptomatic that the publishing house signals the heyday of European identification in Argentina as it was a national industry comparable with the most modern in the world at that time and printing itself was a symbol of modernity and intellectual strength. Schávelzon's emphasis on the changes brought about by the nineteenth century in this area could be extended to Buenos Aires as a whole, as Native South American and mixed peoples and cultures, who prevailed in the colonial period, were being subjected to a process of 'acculturation', sponsored by the new National State (for a criticism of 'acculturation', see Jones, 1997 and Carman, 1998: 135). Apparently the material remains seem to confirm that this policy was successful, but the continued use of oil jars from the beginning up to the mid nineteenth century could indicate that the negotiation process was more complex than presently envisaged, as ordinary people could have produced a syncretic culture. In this case, there could have been a mixed semiotic code in which Native, Mixed and European were indistinguishable as part of a continuum. The use of oil jars, from inception, could thus be interpreted as the maintenance of some mixed habits for a long period, uniting Natives and colonists, and their probable mixed offspring, into a specific pattern of cohabitation.

The archaeology of cities in Portuguese America has not developed as fast as one would expect for several reasons, not least because of two main prejudices: one against old things in general, and another against humble old things in particular. Cities are by definition powerful symbols and the history of Brazil in the last one hundred years or so has been dominated by a rush for so-called progress, so much so that the Republican flag carries the slogan "Order and Progress" (cf. Veríssimo and Bittar, 2001 for an architectural standpoint). If it is true that the country, since the proclamation of the Republic in 1889, has been mesmerized by modernity, this is particularly evident in the cities, as cities represent modern life *par excellence*. Any modern building is considered better than an old one, as a paved road is better than a dirt road. There were several reasons for transferring the capital from Rio de Janeiro to a newly constructed city, Brasília, in 1961, but whatever the economic, social or even geopolitical considerations, it would not have been possible without a mindset prone to constant movement towards modernity. The most appropriate image of Brazilian society could not be the historical buildings in Rio de Janeiro, nor even the natural landscape of Guanabara Bay and the Sugar Loaf, but a *most modern* city. Even the most humble rural dwellers in the backwoods would be able to look forward to Brasília, *a city with no past*.

The clearest example of this fight against material remembrance is the huge megalopolis, São Paulo, the economic capital of South America, a position established in less than forty years, having surpassed Rio de Janeiro in the sixties and Buenos Aires soon afterwards, in the 1970s. In this process, old remains suffered a constant ideological and physical degradation; new buildings were constructed to create a completely new city. The historical buildings are the Cathedral and a Modernist Park planned by Niemeyer, the renowned architect, both inaugurated in 1954. The main public buildings, like the Governor's Palace, or the State Assembly building, are also quite recent, and the most important avenue, Paulista Avenue, founded at the end of last century as a bastion of elite mansions, was completely remodeled as late as the 1970s to become the Latin American headquarter for multinationals, banks and business enterprises in general. In this context, interest in historical remains has been at best marginal, and traditionally restricted to important elite buildings, with high style architectural features, most of them of fairly recent date, as the city was very small and peripheral up to the end of the nineteenth century.

Historical Archaeology would thus develop very late and restricted itself to rescuing artifacts excavated by bulldozers in the process of constructing streets, avenues, underground train lines, buildings and other urban facilities, like sewage systems. In a recent paper (Araújo, 1994: 382) describing archaeology in São Paulo City, we are informed that even nowadays there are only five archaeologists in charge of all city archaeological research, prehistoric and historic alike, covering an area of 1,493 square km and ten million people in the state capital alone and rescuing what is possible. Even though there is no body of archaeological evidence comparable with that available for Buenos Aires or Colonia del Sacramento, the historical archaeologist can profit a lot from the study of maps and iconographic material, like paintings and photographs. São Paulo was originally a typical Portuguese town, as the streets adapted to the landscape. The last decades of the nineteenth century though saw the inception of the modernist resolve which would transform the urban setting. Nature should be tamed and so principal efforts were directed to constructing new river beds, as later would happen with the emphasis on tunnels and viaducts. "São Paulo is magnificent because it is an artifact, not at all natural" (Bresciani, 1999). This huge artifact awaits proper analysis by historical archaeologists.

Colonial towns are not, however, unknown in Brazil, and some of them are well known even abroad, as is the case with Ouro Preto, declared a World Heritage Monument (cf. Funari, 2001). The material culture of colonial towns in Minas Gerais has been studied first and foremost by architects and art historians (Machado, 1978). All of these colonial towns were established on the slopes of hills and the curves in the streets did not allow people to see much more than a few meters in any direction, so that the streetscape was not felt to be a distinguishable urban feature. The real town shape was given by the location of several church buildings, most of them used by white people, some of them used by black brotherhoods (Oliveira, 1990). The church buildings were composed of two basic structures: the rectangular chapel and the bell tower, the former with a ridge and two slopes of a roof, the latter being preferably two towers on the right and left of the main building (Arroyo, 1954). Society was ruled by the Church, in both senses, as the institution whose rules were overwhelmingly accepted as natural, and in its visible re-enactment in several Church buildings, shaping mental frameworks and physical landscapes at the same time (Machado, 1978; Pifano, 1996).

The comparative method, when applied to the Portuguese and Spanish settlement in South America, proves useful to contrast two different ways of ordering the material world (cf. Funari, 1999). Iberian colonists, considered by outsiders as very similar, built two different material culture settings, and archaeology can use a comparative approach to better understand the continent (cf. Funari, 1999b for a more comprehensive study). This study demonstrates the similarities and differences that characterize the various contexts of colonialism and testifies to the importance of a comparative framework which is at the same time attuned to the specificities of particular historical situations (Funari et al., 1999).

Acknowledgements

This is a revised version of a paper which I originally wrote for the conference "Greek archaeologists meet the world" (6th to 8th November, 1999, Athens, Greece), in a international forum held by the World Archaeological Congress and the Archaeological Society of Athens (22 Panepistimiou, 106 79 Athens, Greece). The author, who takes full responsibility for what is written in this paper, thanks Siân Jones for her useful comments and suggestions, and the following colleagues who forwarded papers (sometimes unpublished ones), exchanged ideas and helped in different ways: Maria Stella Martins Bresciani, Martin Hall, Matthew Johnson, Siân Jones, Randall McGuire, Charles E. Orser, Dean J. Saitta, Jr. Daniel Schávelzon, Michael Shanks, Thomas Skidmore, Bruce G. Trigger, Peter Wade, and Andrés Zarankin.

References

Araújo, A. G. M., 1994, Arqueologia urbana no município de São Paulo: considerações sobre algumas dificuldades de implantação. *Revista de Arqueologia* 8: 379–383.

Arroyo, L., 1954, *Igrejas de São Paulo*. Livraria José Olympio Editora, Rio de Janeiro.

Bresciani, M. S., 1999, Images of São Paulo: Aesthetics and Citizenship. In *Cultura Material e Arqueologia Histórica*, edited by P.P.A. Funari, pp. 35–68, IFCH/UNICAMP, Campinas.

Carman, J. C., 1998, Rethinking 'Resistance Accommodation': Toward an Archaeology of African-American Lives in Southern New England, 1638–1800. *International Journal of Historical Archaeology* 2(2): 133–160.

Castro, M. M., 1996, *Ex-votos Mineiros—As tábuas votivas no Ciclo do Ouro*. Editora Expressão e Cultura, Rio de Janeiro.

Childe, V. G., 1956, *A Short Introduction to Archaeology*. Penguin, London.

Frazer, B., 1999, Reconceptualizing Resistance in the Historical Archaeology of the British Isles: an Editorial. *International Journal of Historical Archaeology* 3(1): 1–35.

Funari, P. P. A., 1999a, Algumas contribuições do estudo da cultura material para a discussão da História da colonização da América do Sul. *Tempos Históricos* (Cascavel) 1: 11–44.

1999b, Historical Archaeology from a World Perspective. In *Historical Archaeology: Back from the Edge*, edited by P.P.A Funari, M. Hall and S. Jones, pp. 37–66. Routledge, London.

2001, Destruction and Conservation of Cultural Property in Brazil: Academic and Practical Challenges. In *Destruction and Conservation of Cultural Property*, edited by R. Layton, P. G. Stone and J. Thomas, pp. 93–101. Routledge, London and New York.

Hollanda, S. B. de, 1984, *Raízes do Brasil*. José Olympio, Rio de Janeiro.

Johnson, M., 1999, Historical, Archaeology, Capitalism. In *Historical Archaeology of Capitalism*, edited by M. P. Leone and P. Potter, Jr., pp. 219–232. Plenum, New York.

1992, Meanings of Polite Architecture in Sixteenth Century England. *Historical Archaeology* 26: 45–56.

Jones, S., 1997, *The Archaeology of Ethnicity: Constructing Identities in the Past and Present.* Routledge, London.

Machado, L. G., 1978, *Barroco Mineiro.* Editora Perspectiva, São Paulo.

Martins, N., 2000, Santos africanos e ruas parecem importadas de Portugal. *Estado de Minas*, March 26, p. 41.

Marx, M., 1989, *Nosso Chão: do Sagrado ao Profano.* Editora da Universidade de São Paulo, São Paulo.

McGuire, R. H., and Saitta, D. J., 1996, Although They Have Petty Captains, They Obey Them Badly: The Dialectics Of Prehistoric Western Pueblo Social Organization, *American Antiquity* 61(2): 197–216.

Mrozowski, S. A., and Beaudry, M. C., 1990, Archaeology and the Landscape of Corporate Ideology. In *Earth Pottery, Essays in Landscape Archaeology,* edited by W.M. Kelso and R. Most, pp. 189–208. University of Virginia Press, Charlottesville.

Nassaney, M. S., 1998, Taking the Pulse of Historical Archaeology. *Current Anthropology* 39: 579–581.

Oliveira, M. A. R., 1990, Elementos para o estudo do rococó religioso luso-brasileiro. *Revista de Ciências Históricas* 5: 213–217.

Orser, C. E., 1999, Archaeology and the Challenges of Capitalist Farm Tenancy in America. In *Historical Archaeology of Capitalism,* edited by M.P. Leone and P. Potter, Jr., pp. 143–167. Plenum, New York.

Paynter, R., and McGuire, R. H., 1991, The Archaeology Of Inequality: Material Culture, Domination, And Resistance. In *The Archaeology of Inequality,* edited by R. Paynter and R. H. McGuire, pp. 1–27. Blackwell, Oxford.

Pifano, R. Q., 1996, A concepção arquitetônica de Aleijadinho—Igreja São Francisco de Assis em Ouro Preto. Locus 2: 127–139.

Reis, N. G., 2000, *Imagens de vilas e cidades do Brasil colonial.* Edusp/Imprensa Oficial do Estado de São Paulo, São Paulo.

Saitta, D. J., 1992, Radical Archaeology and Middle-Range Methodology. *Antiquity* 66: 886–897.

Schávelzon, D., 1992, *La Arqueología Urbana en la Argentina.* Centro Editor de América Latina, Buenos Aires.

1994, *Arqueología e historia de la Imprenta Coni, Buenos Aires.* The University of South Carolina, Columbia.

Scott, R. J., 1988, Exploring the Meaning of Freedom: Post-emancipation Societies in a Comparative Perspective. *Hispanic American Historical Review* 68: 407–428.

Senatore, M. X., 1995, *Tecnologías Nativas y Estrategias de Ocupación Española en la Región del Río de La Plata* The University of South Carolina, Columbia.

Shanks, M., 1994, Archaeology: Theories, Themes, and Experience. In *Archaeological Theory: Progress Or Posture?,* edited by I. M. MacKenzie, pp. 19–39. Avebury, Aldershot.

Skidmore, T., 2000, Review of História da Vida Privada. *Hispanic American Historical Review* 80: 569–573.

Trigger, B. G., 1998, Archaeology and Epistemology: Dialoging Across the Darwinian Chasm. *American Journal of Archaeology* 102: 1–34.

Veríssimo, F. S., Bittar, W. S. M., and Alvarez, J. M., 2001, *Vida Urbana. A evolução do cotidiano da cidade brasileira.* Ediouro, Rio de Janeiro.

Wade, P., 1994, Representation and Power: Blacks in Colombia. In *Social Construction of the Past,* G.C. Bond and A. Gilliam, pp. 59–73. Routledge, London.

Weckmann, L., 1993, *La Herencia Medieval del Brasil.* Fondo de Cultura Económica, México.

Zarankin, A., 1995, *Arqueología Histórica Urbana en Santa Fe la Vieja: el final del principio.* The University of South Carolina, Columbia.

2000, El pensamiento moderno y el pensamiento posmoderno en Arqueología. In *Narrar o Passado, Repensar a História,* edited by M. Rago and R. A. O. Gimenes, pp. 341–360. IFCH UNICAMP, Campinas.

Bodies in Prehistory

Beyond the Sex/Gender Split

Benjamin Alberti

Introduction

My paper is about the theorizing of bodies in archaeology. Bodies are an important archaeological resource—from mortuary remains to figurative art, they reveal a great deal to us about people in past societies. In gender archaeology the visibility of bodies as archaeological evidence has lead to questions being asked of the very formulation of gender as a concept, of how gender is understood to operate through bodies and in society. The point I will argue in the course of this paper is that the sex/gender split naturalizes a binary division of bodies and hence naturalizes the exclusive division of bodies into male and female. Such a binary division may be a pertinent description of current ideals of the structure of bodies. Its establishment as a natural fact, however, is impeding the investigation of bodies in prehistory, preventing the questioning of how bodies gain significance, how bodies become sexed.

It is not my attention to do away with all the work that has been done to date using the sex/gender split in gender archaeology. Such work has been, and continues to be, invaluable because it frees gender from biological determinism. What I would like to demonstrate, rather, is that in some instances the formulation of gender as radically distinct from sex may be blocking potential interpretations of archaeological material.

This paper proceeds by firstly outlining how the concept 'gender' has been understood by gender archaeologists and what exactly the potential problems with that formulation are. Secondly, I will offer a critique of the sex/gender split based on the work of some so-called post-structuralist feminists. In particular, I will discuss Butler's (1993) critique of social constructivism and her understanding of how bodies gain significance through their materialization. Butler's work is useful for archaeology because she focuses on the surface of bodies; on the visible and mutually generative relationship between bodies, material culture, and coherent identities. She also offers insight into the relationship between sex and gender is in contemporary society.

Towards the end of the paper I will present a brief case study in order to demonstrate the possibilities of exploring sex, gender and bodies in a different way through archaeology. I will discuss the figurative imagery from the Palace site at Late Bronze Age Knossos in light of the arguments made in the first half of the paper. The Bronze Age Aegean may not seem particularly relevant to a conference on Latin American archaeology, but I believe the results have implications for archaeological interpretation in many areas. Nonetheless, the approach I adopt emphasizes the non-universal status and contextualised the production of bodies, and, as such, is not a universal theory.

Previous interpretations of the imagery from Knossos presented a rigid binary structure to gender. Such interpretations, however, are not fully substantiated by the evidence. It quickly becomes apparent on re-examination that the bodies are not rigidly divided into male and female. In fact, bodies are rarely shown with what we understand as physical sexual characteristics. Moreover, they are never differentiated from the opposite sex on the basis of such characteristics. It is apparent that sex, gender, and other means by which we categorize people are interpolated. In some cultural contexts particular aspects of bodies gain more significance than others. Sex—male and female—may not always be considered a natural means of categorizing bodies, nor may genitalia always be thought of as central to a body's identity.

Archaeologists Question the Sex/Gender Split

Archaeologists' understanding of gender as distinct from sex developed through contact with feminist research within anthropology (see di Leonardo, 1991; Moore, 1988; Strathern, 1988: 22–40). The crucial development was the splitting of gender into biological and cultural dimensions. Sex came to mean biological sex, whereas gender referred to the cultural component of women's and men's identity. Some archaeologists have pointed out the difficulties for archaeological interpretation in maintaining such a distinction between sex and gender. Their criticisms are based on two observations: firstly that the archaeological visibility of gender as opposed to sex is suspect (Claassen, 1992; Marshall, 1995; Sørensen, 1992) and, secondly, that sex is as much a cultural construction as gender (Claassen, 1992; Moore, 1994).

The first observation has lead to the question of whether an archaeology of gender is in fact dependent on an archaeology of sex. Marshall (1995: 5) has pointed out that the majority of remedial feminist research within archaeology has taken place in areas where there is greater access to biological sex, including burial studies, art, and human origins research which bases its models on primate societies. Similarly, Claassen (1992) has argued that many archaeologists assume that burials provide the best data for addressing questions of gender. However, she points out that if there has to be some unique combination of material for each gender, then those items will be attributed to the particular sex of the sexed skeleton with which they are found, and then to the gender attributed to that sex. Consequently, any possibility of identifying gender independently of sex is eliminated.

The second observation, that sex is as culturally constructed as gender, is a more fundamental challenge to gender archaeology. It broadens interpretative possibilities considerably, but it is also a lot harder for many archaeologists to accept. Much of this work stems from Foucault's (e.g., 1978, 1985, 1986) research into sex as a construct of discourse. The general assumption in presenting sex and gender as separate is that gender is social and sex is innate; gender is contingent, whereas sex is stable. A circularity in much gender archaeology has been to accept gender as cultural, yet explain it as the social elaboration of the supposedly obvious facts of biological sexual differences. There is a growing recognition—again, stemming from anthropological and feminist inquiry—that such differences may not in fact be so obvious. It will become clear in this paper that the first issue, one concerning methodology, loses its relevance once the second observation is properly addressed.

The Post-Structuralist Feminist Challenge to the Sex/Gender Split

The sex/gender split leaves bodies under-theorized. In such a formulation, gender is culturally and historically specific, subject to change and manipulation, while the body remains a transcultural, transhistorical common denominator—a blank slate onto which culture is inscribed. Cultural constructivism would appear to allow a freeing-up of gender from the constraints of "biology-is-destiny" type arguments. The substance of the blank slate, however, is not seen as subject to variability. Gender becomes a free-floating index, with no actual meaning other than the social embellishment of an androgynous body.

Butler (1993: 3–11) offers an incisive critique of the types of models of social construction that underlie such understandings of gender. Central to her critique is the observation that these models are based on the premise of a pre-social sex, of sex as somehow prior to cultural understanding and discourse. She argues that if sex were pre-social, then how would we have access to it? How would we know what sex was if it is always already gendered upon our entry into society?

Butler (1993: 5) argues that the distinction between sex and gender can be criticized for degrading the natural. The natural is cast as that which is before intelligibility, as that which is need of the mark of the social in order to gain meaning and value. The natural assumes its value at the same time as it assumes its social character. The social construction, and therefore transformation, of the natural presupposes the cancellation of the natural by the social.

The sex/gender split can be similarly criticized. If gender is the social significance that sex assumes within a given society, then what is left of sex once it has assumed its social character as gender? In other words, sex does not gain social meaning, but rather is replaced by the social meanings it takes on. Sex becomes replaced by gender—the only access to that sex is through gender. Sex, then, is a fantasy to which there is no direct access. In other words, how is it possible to know what sex is, if it is always already subsumed by gender? As a consequence, it makes no sense to search for such things as the 'origins' of gender (e.g., Whelan, 1991). Neither can we hope to know the 'true' sex of past peoples through their skeletal remains or artwork, yet believe we can determine their gender.

Butler (1993: 6) outlines the main positions in the debate over construction, in which either linguistic construction is understood to be deterministic (everything is produced by discourse); or, construction presupposes a subject who is doing the constructing, which leads to the question: 'If the subject is constructed, then who is constructing the subject?'. In the first case construction takes the place of a 'figure of God' type agency. In the second case a voluntaristic subject is presupposed who manipulates construction. In the first case, Butler (1993: 7) states that it is unclear whether there can be an 'I' or 'we' who has not been subjected to gender, and that the subject neither precedes nor follows the process of gendering but emerges as the matrix of gender relations themselves. Such a position, she claims, does not do away with the subject, but rather asks after the conditions of its emergence. She argues that such gendering cannot be an act of human agency as it is the matrix through which agency becomes possible, its 'enabling cultural condition'. Therefore, the matrix of gender relations is prior to the emergence of the human.

Furthermore, the existence of a matrix of gender relations does not mean to say that the matrix acts in a singular, deterministic way to produce genders as effects. That would be to install the matrix in the subject position, a simple reversal of the subject and discourse, a personification of such edifices as 'discourse', 'culture' or 'power'. In such a case, construction is still understood as a unilateral process initiated by a prior subject: it is an act which happens once and whose effects are firmly fixed.

Substantial Bodies

Rather than thinking of sex and gender as distinct and believing we know what one is and can reconstruct the other, it seems more useful to think of the way bodies become understood as substantial and significant in the first instance. What we understand as biological sexual characteristics may not be similarly understood in other cultural contexts. The distinction made between sex and gender has a particular place within Western discourse. Butler (1993: 5–6) argues that sex is a fiction, but a necessary fiction. Positing sex as pre-social hides the causality between sex and gender. Gender, therefore, is complicit in maintaining the ontological integrity of the categories male and female in contemporary thought. Again, Butler offers us a way to think about how such a process occurs. She urges us to return to the notion of matter and the idea of materialization; not matter as a surface, but rather, '. . . as a process of materialization that stabilizes over time to produce the effect of fixity and surface we call matter' (Butler, 1993: 9).

Butler (1990: 136) suggests that the gendered body has no ontological status apart from the acts and gestures which constitute its reality. The reality of the body, its naturalness, consists of the *stylization* of the body. Butler's thesis denies the possibility of a 'real' body, of a 'pure' body untouched by discourse or language. Her argument, however, does not entail that the body disappears altogether, that the body is entirely imaginary. Rather, the body sets limits to its conceptualization, but does not govern the system of meaning that it precipitates. The conceptualization of the body cannot be understood in relation to a 'real' body; it can only be understood in relation to another cultural idea of the body (Butler, 1990: 71). Butler does not deny biological differences, but questions the way they are thought of and how certain features become perceived as central to sex. For example, men's bodies cannot be impregnated and cannot produce children. However, positing impregnation as a foundational difference between men's and women's bodies ignores the fact that children, older women and other women for a variety of reasons also cannot be impregnated (Butler, 1994: 33–34). Rather, Butler asks why it is that certain biological differences become the salient characteristics of sex and not others.

A body in contemporary Western society, Butler (1990: 8) argues, is always already gendered—it gains intelligibility through that gendering. There is no recourse, therefore, to a natural, sexed body as distinct from a culturally elaborated gender. Through the workings of gender, sex and the body are established as immutable facts. The acts and gestures of gender hide the production of sex, therefore rendering it beyond culture. Furthermore, the constitutive link between sex and gender is hidden in this process; hence, Stoller (1964: 220–221, 225) was able to suggest a discontinuity between the two. That suggestion of discontinuity, however, works to reinforce the gendered production of sex by denying access to the body, by casting it beyond the social.

In order for gender to create the illusion of a substance, it must be continually repeated. Gender, therefore, is not an 'act', but rather a series of 'acts', a constant citation of prior practices. De Beauvoir (1988 [1953]: 295) argued that, 'One is not born, but rather becomes, a woman'. Butler (1990: 8; 1989) takes this formulation further by proposing that this becoming is a constant process, one that cannot be said to have a beginning or end. Gender has no teleology, but rather is 'an activity incessantly renewed' (Butler, 1989: 255). 'Man' and 'woman' cannot be thought of as nouns, as descriptions of a substantive being (Butler, 1990: 24). This constant imitative reiteration of acts, gestures and words Butler (1990: 34) describes as a 'ritualized repetition'. Gender reality is created through sustained social performances; the acts of gender are public and collective actions (1990: 140–141).

Moving beyond the sex/gender split means that what archaeologists are exploring, or have access to, is the materialization of a particular concept of sex through normative regulatory powers, rather than a cultural code placed onto an ontologically intact, 'natural' sexed body. Obviously, how bodies were understood as natural in past societies need not rely upon a distinction between sex and gender. However, recognizing that the stylization of bodies produces the effect of a particular form to those bodies can provide clues to how past societies conceived of and gave significance to their bodies. Whether male and female existed, or physical sexual characteristics were afforded the same weight in categorization, will be dependent upon each particular archaeological investigation.

The Figurative Art from Late Bronze Age Knossos

The particular archaeological context I will now discuss in relation to the production of bodies, is that from Late Bronze Age Knossos, on Crete. The type of figurative imagery from Knossos which has been used to substantiate arguments about gender include the well-known fresco material, relief sculpture, glyptic art, and several ornate figurines. Since soon after their discovery nearly one-hundred years ago, the figurative images have used as evidence of a rigid binary structure to gender relations in Minoan society (e.g., Cameron, 1975: 52–54; Castledon, 1990; Evans, 1928; Evasdaughter, 1997; Immerwahr, 1983) and, in fact, as evidence for a single gender regime based on the distinction between male and female throughout the Aegean Bronze Age and beyond (Immerwahr, 1990; Marinatos, 1993; Morgan, 1988).

More recent accounts have further strengthened the male and female dichotomy (e.g. Alexandri, 1994; Marinatos, 1987, 1993, 1995). Structuralist accounts of Minoan religion have resulted in men and women having opposing activities in most aspects of their lives. Binary oppositions such as sacred: profane, celestial: terrestrial, and reproduction and stasis versus virility and change proliferate in the literature. The resultant view of Minoan society is one in which sex is the most important means of differentiating between peoples; physical sexual characteristics and reproductive potential become the lynch-pins of Minoan social organization and social meaning.

In most cases the figurative imagery is the primary, and sometimes only, source of evidence for these interpretations. At first glance, the material does appear to offer a neat, easy division of bodies into male and female. It has been observed that the figures in the fresco art are divided into white and red. This would appear to follow on from a similar Egyptian color convention for gender-coding the people in the images, where red denotes men and white denotes women (Figure 8.1). Furthermore, a great deal has been made of supposedly sex-specific clothing in the art. Typically, loincloths and codpieces are considered the prototypes of male dress (Figure 8.2), whilst the 'flounced skirt' and open bodice are the equivalent women's attire (Figure 8.3).

Hence, according to previous interpretations one would expect the opposition of penis to breasts—of virility to reproductive capacity—to be a central feature of bodies in the art. That is not actually the case. In fact, the figurative imagery itself continuously presents evidence to the contrary. Such contradictory cases are well known to Minoan scholars and are most frequently referred to as ambiguous uses of the color convention. For example, the bull-leaper panels have both red and white figures with loin-clothing leaping bulls (Figure 8.4). The panels should challenge the binary oppositions used to describe gender in Minoan society. Instead, they are usually fitted into one scheme or another (e.g. Damiani-Indelicato, 1988; Evans, 1928: 35; 1930: 212; Immerwahr, 1983: 145; 1990: 91; Younger, 1995: 515). Furthermore, the appearance of a third color in the representations, such as the black figures in a fragmentary fresco from a fresco heap just outside the Palace confines (Figure 8.5), is

Figure 8.1. White and Red Figures, Great Tribune Fresco, Knossos (after Schachermeyer).

rarely discussed. These figures, however, challenge the basis of a clear-cut binary division of bodies based on sexual characteristics. Clearly, differences other than a simple male-female binary are being represented in the imagery.

I will argue that such ambiguous cases are only ambiguous if we assume an over-arching classification of bodies into a strict male–female binary division. The difficulty with the color convention stems not from its possible applicability, but in the attempt to see in it a clear binary division of bodies (see Alberti, 1997 for a more in-depth explanation of the arguments presented here).

Physical sexual characteristics are almost entirely absent from the imagery. The only bodies that can be comfortably sexed are those with

Figure 8.2. People with Kilts, Fragment from Knossos (after Evans).

Figure 8.3. People with Open Shirts, Great Tribune Fresco, Knossos.

Figure 8.4. Human Figure Playing with a Bull, with a Party of Red and White Figures with Kilts.

Figure 8.5. Fragment of a Fresco with Black Figures, from Knossos.

breasts. As a result, maleness has been assumed by the absence of breasts on particular figures. Yates (1993) has argued that a similar methodological mistake occurs in the interpretation of figures in rock carving from Göteborgs och Bohuslän in Sweden. The figures from Sweden include some with penises and a majority without. Those without have been assumed to be female because they lack penises, even though there are other variables that crosscut those two particular categories of figures. The juxtaposition of male identity to one of ambiguity has been assumed to be a methodological problem rather than a 'tangible aspect' of the carvings. Similarly, the ambiguous applications of the color code and the lack of depictions of genitalia in the Knossian imagery should be understood as an important part of the images, rather than a methodological problem of identification. Once a binary division of bodies into male and female is no longer an *a priori* for the Knossian imagery, then how can we understand their representation of bodies? What happens to sex and gender? To go back to the theory—What types of bodies are materialized, given form, substance, and value through the imagery? How are the features of biological sex understood in Knossian palatial art? Are such features a salient part of bodies in the imagery?

The most striking feature of these images is the consistency with which bodies are portrayed and not the distinction between figures on the basis of physical attributes of the body. There is a single body-shape that crosscuts all media and all recognizable sexual distinctions in the Knossian imagery. The body-shape is approximately hourglass in form—broad shoulders, very narrow waists and broad hips. Only rarely are the figures distinguished from one another by physical features. Rather, style of clothing, color, activity and body position are used to make a distinction between them. The larger groupings so established are then sub-divided by the detail on the figures—the patterns on clothing and ornamentation, such as jewelry. Such detail allows figures in the same composition to be individuated from one another.

The result of these means of distinguishing between figures is to set up a play between the universal body-shape and single figures. The larger groupings, such as color, do not automatically exclude particular types from representation. For example, a figure in the images will always adhere to the common body-shape, but within that template any number of ways of differentiation are possible. A white figure may have a particular style of clothing and body position; that does not, however, exclude a red figure from using the same clothing or body position (for example, see the figures from the bull-leaper panels).

Already it should be apparent that a binary division of bodies is not operating in these images. To illustrate the potentially different role that past societies attribute to physical sexual characteristics in the production of bodies, I will briefly contrast two groups of figurines found at the Palace site of Knossos. The first group consists of the remains of several ivory figurines. The one almost complete figure is white, but has always been considered to represent a male bull-leaper. The figure displays the typical hourglass body-shape, but no physical sexual characteristics at all (Figure 8.6). In contrast, the second group of figurines show an explicit depiction of breasts. The figures are faience with polychrome glaze. They are elaborately decorated with a great deal of detail, especially on their garments (Figure 8.7). The presence of this type of clothing on the figurines—the flounced skirt and bodice open at the front—is crucial. In fact, in the few instances where breasts are shown in the imagery they are always accompanied by this type of elaborate garment. In a way, breasts are a part of the clothing. Breasts and clothing in combination are mutually productive of a particular idea of the body.

The ivory figurines represent the normal body of the Knossians—unsexed, unclothed, with an hourglass shape. The clothing and breasts on the faience figurines are the cultural elaboration of that normal template. In our terminology, the Knossian idea of the 'natural' body is an unsexed body. Physical sexual characteristics only come out with what

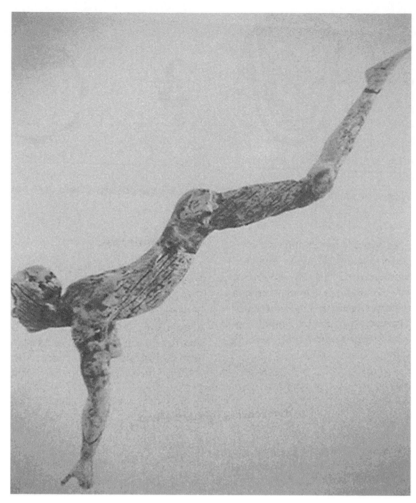

Figure 8.6. Ivory Figurine of a Bull Player, from Knossos.

we would understand as a cultural mark—the clothing. In other words, in the imagery breasts are the cultural elaboration of a cultural idea of a natural body.

In conclusion, it is apparent that in some cultural contexts particular aspects of bodies gain more significance than others. Sex—male and female—may not always be considered a 'natural' means of categorizing bodies, and genitalia may not always be thought of as central to a body's identity.

Acknowledgements

I am grateful to the organizers of the Primiera Reunião de Teoria Arque-ologíca da América Latina for inviting me to speak at the conference,

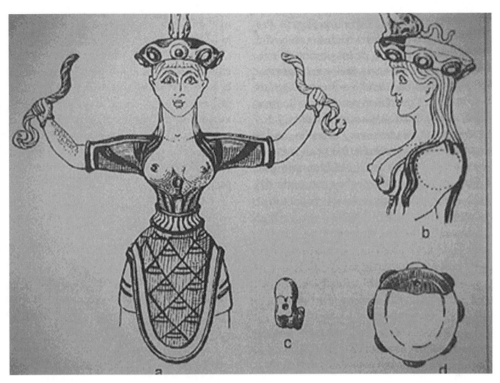

Figure 8.7. Human Figure, from a Votive Context, Knossos.

and to the World Archaeological Congress for financial assistance in attending.

References

Alberti, B., 1997, *Archaeology and Masculinity in Late Bronze Age Knossos*. Ph.D. dissertation, University of Southampton.

Alexandri, A., 1994, *Gender Symbolism in Late Bronze Age Aegean Glyptic Art*. Ph.D. dissertation, University of Cambridge.

Butler, J., 1989, Gendering the Body: Beauvoir's Philosophical Contribution. In *Women, Knowledge, and Reality: Explorations in Feminist Philosophy*, edited by A. Garry and M. Pearsall, pp. 253–262. Routledge, London.

1990, *Gender Trouble: Feminism and the Subversion of Identity*. Routledge, London.

1993, *Bodies that Matter: on the Discursive Limits of 'Sex'*. Routledge, London.

1994, Gender as Performance: an Interview with Judith Butler. *Radical Philosophy* 67: 32–39.

Cameron, M. A. S., 1975, *A General Study of Minoan Frescoes with Particular Reference to Unpublished Wall Paintings from Knossos*. Ph.D. dissertation, University of Newcastle-upon-Tyne.

Castleden, R., 1990, *Minoans: Life in Bronze-Age Crete*. Routledge, London.

Claassen, C., 1992, Questioning Gender: an Introduction. In *Exploring Gender Through Archaeology*, edited by C. Claassen, pp. 1–10. Monographs in World Archaeology 11. Prehistory Press, Madison.

Damiani-Indelicato, S., 1988, Were Cretan Girls Playing at Bull-Leaping? *Cretan Studies*, 1: 39–47.

de Beauvoir, S., 1988 [1953], *The Second Sex*. Picador, London.

di Leonardo, M., 1991, Introduction. In *Gender at the Crossroads of Knowledge: Feminist Anthropology in the Postmodern Era*, edited by M. di Leonardo, pp. 1–47. University of California Press, Berkley.

Evans, A. J., 1928, *The Palace of Minos at Knossos*. Volume 2. MacMillan and Co, London.

1930, *The Palace of Minos at Knossos*. Volume 3. MacMillan and Co, London.

Evasdaughter, S., 1997, A Sacred Island: a Feminist Perspective of Bronze Age Crete. *At the Edge* 6: 16–19.

Foucault, M., 1978, *The History of Sexuality, Volume 1: an Introduction*. Penguin, Harmondsworth.

1985, *The History of Sexuality, Volume 2: the Use of Pleasure*. Penguin, Harmondsworth.

1986, *The History of Sexuality, Volume 3: the Care of the Self*. Penguin, Harmondsworth.

Immerwahr, S. A., 1983, The People in the Frescoes. In *Minoan and Mycenaean Society*, edited by L. Nixon, pp. 143–153. Cambridge University, Cambridge.

1990, *Aegean Painting in the Bronze Age*. The Pennsylvania State University, Pittsburgh.

Marinatos, N., 1987, Role and Sex Division in Ritual Scenes of Aegean Art. *Journal of Prehistoric Religion* 6: 23–24.

1993, *Minoan Religion*. University of South Carolina Press, Charleston.

1995, Formalism and Gender Roles: a Comparison of Minoan and Egyptian Art. In *Politeia: Society and State in the Aegean Bronze Age*, edited by R. Laffineur and W.-D. Niemeier, pp. 577–587. Program in Aegean Scripts and Prehistory, Liège and Austin.

Marshall, Y., 1995, Why Do We Need Feminist Theory? Conference paper delivered at the Institute of Field Archaeologists, Bradford.

Moore, H., 1988, *Feminism and Anthropology*. Polity Press, London.

1994, *A Passion for Difference*. Polity Press, Cambridge.

Morgan, L., 1988, *The Miniature Wall-Paintings of Thera*. Cambridge University Press, Cambridge.

Sørensen, M. L. S., 1992, Gender Archaeology and Scandinavian Bronze Age Studies. *Norwegian Archaeological Review* 25: 31–49.

Strathern, M., 1988, *The Gender of the Gift*. University of California Press, Berkley.

Stoller, R. J., 1964, A Contribution to the Study of Gender Identity. *International Journal of Psychoanalysis* 45: 220–226.

Whelan, M.K., 1991, Gender and Archaeology: Mortuary Studies and the Search for Gender Differentiation. In *The Archaeology of Gender*, edited by D. Walde and N. Willows, pp. 358–365. Archaeological Association of the University of Calgary, Calgary.

Yates, T., 1993, Frameworks for an Archaeology of the Body. In *Interpretative Archaeology*, edited by C. Tilley, pp. 31–72. Berg, Oxford.

Younger, J. G., 1995, Bronze Age Representations of Aegean Bull-Games. In *Politeia: Society and State in the Aegean Bronze Age*, edited by R. Laffineur and W.-D. Niemeier, pp. 507–548. Program in Aegean Scripts and Prehistory, Liège and Austin.

9

Children's Activity in the Production of the Archaeological Record of Hunter-Gatherers
An Ethnoarchaeological Approach

Gustavo G. Politis

Introduction

Archaeological studies have generally considered populations as a whole; only in complex societies has attention been given to differences in class and/or status. In general, archaeologists have felt little attraction for studying "individuals" in particular, considering them methodologically inaccessible (Shennan, 1991). This archaeology "without people" has been criticized recently and the possibility of recovering individual lives throughout alleged "narrative windows" has been proposed (Hodder, 1999; Knapp and Meskell, 1997). Nonetheless, between the population and the individual exist factions and segments that are recognizable in the archaeological record: specialist groups (i.e., ceramists, workers in metals, etc.), elites, men, women, and so on. The recognition of the heterogeneous structure of society and of multiple social actors is founded to a certain extent in gender studies. Moreover, recent attention has also been paid to age groups, especially children, and their contribution to the archaeological record (Lillehammer, 1989; Sofaer Derevenski,

1994[1]). Explicit recognition has been given to something that is, in fact, entirely obvious: children are both producers as well as consumers of material culture.

In the interpretation of the archaeological record of hunter-gatherers, as well as that of other more complex societies, it has generally been assumed that all of the remains (artifacts, the debris and by-products of food processing and consumption) were generated by adults. Agents are adults by default. Many inferences about past behavior have been based on this almost universal assumption, and a variety of models related to technological organization, activity areas, sequences of lithic artifact production, and so on, have also been proposed. Within this framework, the shape, size and technology of a number of different artifacts (a typical example is projectile points) are considered to be idiosyncratic expressions. They are used for culture-historical reconstruction or to serve as a type of "unit of measure" in examining cultural distance and variability among different human groups. In these reconstructions, children have not been considered as social actors and their material production has only rarely been recognized (see, for example, Bodú et al., 1990; Dawe, 1997; Fisher, 1990; Park, 1998). In most cases, the origination of lithic clusters by children is distinguishable by the game-like and non-utilitarian character of poorly knapped pieces, displaying even less skill in their production than those created by novices (Finlay, 1997: 207). In other cases, children have been identified in mortuary contexts, where age has been treated as a variable and not a fundamental principle of social organization (Sofaer-Derevenski, 1994). In spite of these exceptions, however, little attempt has been made to develop a methodology that would allow for the recognition of children's contribution to the archaeological record of hunter-gatherer societies.

In South American archaeology the association of children with assemblages and objects is even rarer. An examination of the existing bibliography revealed only a few exceptions. For example, Gradín and Aguerre (1983) attribute black and white painted negatives of hands on the walls of several caves in the Área del Río Pinturas in Patagonia (Argentina) to children. Miniature clay figurines were found at Aconcagua sites on the central coast of Chile that were interpreted as children's toys (Rivas and Ocampo, 1997). At various sites in the Pampas Region of Argentina, some projectile points, *boleadoras* and rounded pieces of basalt may have been produced and/or used by children of the pre-Hispanic hunter-gatherer societies that inhabited the region (Politis, 1998). Finally, during the *Terceras Jornadas de la Arqueología de la Patagonia* ('Third Patagonean Archaeology Conference'), a round table entitled *Actores en escena: comportamiento social y registro arqueológico* ('Actors on stage: social behavior and the archaeological record') included a discussion on children's agency in the generation of archaeological sites (Mengoni Goñalons, 1999). Although there are assuredly more examples, these few serve to illustrate the scarcity of references that assign objects to children.

Moreover, in spite of these thorough studies, there has been even fewer systematic research programs directed toward building knowledge about child agents in past societies (i.e. Dawe, 1997; Park, 1998; Politis, 1998). Neither have attempts been made to identify children's activity in the creation of domestic spaces or in site formation. Some authors have drawn attention to the action of children on deposits, but from a narrow perspective where they are seen as distorting and disturbing agents of materials deposited by adults (Bonnichsen, 1973; Hammond and Hammond, 1981). In this approach, children are conceptualized in the same way as any other post-depositional, pre-burial biological agent; that is, as modifying a "normal" archaeological record produced by adults. This approach errs by assuming that children do not generate the archaeological record but only disturb it; they are considered to be neither producers nor consumers of material culture nor social actors.

As a consequence of the contributions of postprocessual archaeology, a vision of the past that is socially more inclusive and allows for the recovery of the internal variability of the archaeological record resulting from the participation of different genders and age groups is more and more common. This nascent archaeological interest in detecting children's activity is derived from considering children as significant social actors (James and Prout, 1990). Some recent work has even emphasized that: "... children contribute to the archaeological record, *whether or not we are competent in recognizing them*" (Chamberlain, 1997: 249, emphasis in the original). One way or another, this attempt at considering children as social actors and endowing them with archaeological visibility resembles the beginnings of gender archaeology which, more than fifteen years ago, sought to identify the protagonism of women in past societies and call attention to the androcentric bias in archaeological interpretation (Conkey and Spector, 1984; Conkey and Gero, 1991).

In the case of the archaeology of children, what I attempt in this chapter is not only to highlight children's activities in past societies, but also to introduce some methodological tools for adequately identifying them in the material record. This will be the first step toward future analysis and discussion of child agency in these societies and the exploration of the essential mechanisms of cultural transmission from a broad temporal perspective. For the remainder of this paper I will leave aside considerations related to the training for adulthood that games embody, as this fact is obvious. Neither will I tackle the participation of children in group subsistence. Both subjects, although of interest and related to the current material, exceed the objectives of this chapter.

In recent research it has been noted that gender is related to age. Sex is biologically determined, but gender is a social construction (Sofaer-Derevensky, 1997). As such, it has been observed that: "Ignoring the temporal of gender has led archaeologists to impose a static dualistic vision of gender onto the past through straightforward artifact association" (Sofaer-Derevenski, 1997: 877). The recognition of this temporal dimension in studies of gender has significantly changed the approach. Gender was no longer seen as a category or unit of analysis, rather as a process that evolves throughout a person's life (Lorber, 1994 in Sofaer-Derevenski, 1997). Currently, it is thought that learning gender is a continuous process strongly related to age.

The archaeology of childhood is new and has a short history. Some basic concepts related to children have already been discussed by Lillehammer (1989), based on a review of Scandinavian archaeology in a pioneer chapter on the subject. Interestingly, a series of studies have arrived at similar conclusions from different perspectives, such as a book edited by Moore and Scott (1997) on the theoretical and methodological ramifications of such a focus[1], and contributions by Dawe (1997) and Park (1998), which include original archaeological case studies from North American plains communities and the Inuit of Canada. The outcome of these studies indicates that the products of children's activities can be recognized if an appropriate methodology is developed. In this paper I attempt to develop methodological tools for recognizing children's production. I believe that the use of analogy must play a key role in this endeavor. Surviving traditional non-Western societies are a significant (although not the only) source of such analogies. Therefore, I will base the building of a methodological framework on analogy, using my own ethnoarchaeological data obtained among the Nukak as the main source, as well as including information from other South American foragers, such as the Guayakí from Eastern Paraguay, the Sirionó from Northern Bolivia, the Selknam and Yámanas from Tierra del Fuego and the Tehuelches from Patagonia (see Figure 9.1).

My own ethnoarchaeological data derive from the Nukak, a hunter-gatherer-fisher group affiliated with the Makú (Koch-Grünberg, 1906; Metraux, 1948; Reid, 1979; Silverwood-Cope, 1972) who live in the Colombian Amazon between the Guaviare and Inírida rivers. These data were collected between 1990 and 1996 during seven field seasons; summing 185 days in total (Cárdenas and Politis, 2000; Politis, 1992, 1996a, b, 1999; Politis et al., 1997) which enabled me to generate material expectations for children's activity and evaluate under which conditions one could expect, in analogous past societies, a similar context to occur.

When referring to "children" in this paper I include individuals who have begun to walk to just before puberty. For the Nukak, this means from between one or two years old to 12. Before they begin walking, babies depend entirely on their parents and produce no kind of material record, although some artifacts (like tooth beads) are produced for them. When they reach puberty, both girls and boys are economically and technologically similar to adults, even though they do not have full adult status as yet and are still in the later stages of their training period.

Children's Material Production

Children comprise almost half of the total current Nukak population. In a sample of 357 individuals, 135 (37.8 percent) were under 10 years old;

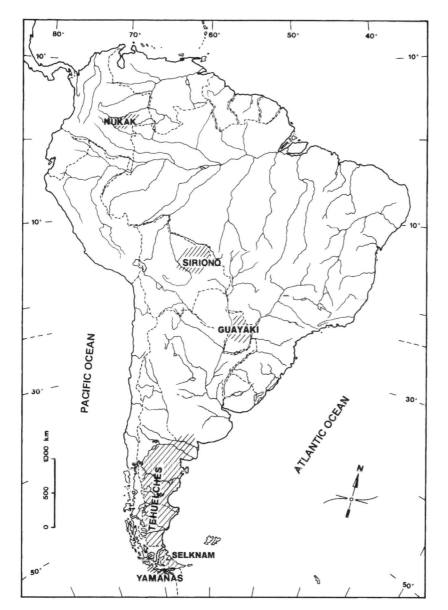

Figure 9.1. Map of Southamerica Showing the Location of the Indigenous Groups Mentioned in the Text.

this number increases to 175 (49 percent) if we consider all individuals below 15 years of age (Franky et al., 1995: 2). These children, especially those in the former age group, spend a great deal of the day within the camp or in its immediate environs (this is also common among other hunter-gatherer groups, such as the !Kung: Draper, 1976). A co-resident group usually consisting of four to five families with some degree of kinship inhabits each residential camp. Camps differ in the dry and rainy seasons. In the former, they lack roofs and their ground plan is amorphous (like the silhouette of an amoeba), while in the rainy season they are covered by leaf roofs and they have a geometrically shaped ground plan. Both types of camps are small and compact, with surface areas ranging between 32.5 m² and 178.9 m² (Politis, 1999). The maximum distance children are allowed to wander by themselves outside the camp is determined by the possibility of being heard by their parents. In the tropical rainforest, visual contact is lost quickly, thus verbal contact permits control over larger distances.

Three stages may be recognized in Nukak childhood. These are similar to those found among other hunter-gatherers such as the Guayakí (Clastres, 1998). The first stage is infancy, that is, from birth until walking with a degree of autonomy (approximately two years old). These babies depend entirely on adults and do not generate any type of artifact, although some objects are made for them (for example, monkey and feline tooth collars, etc.). Nor do they have a specific name yet, bearing the generic nomenclature *jim'bú or tóm'bú*, depending on their sex. The second stage is from two until seven or eight years old. During this period, learning is generalized and there is no marked difference between the sexes. In this second stage, children-both male and female-begin to be economically productive and collaborate in several food procurement tasks such as gathering or the hunting and capture of small animals (rodents, river crabs, palm grubs, etc.). In many cases, ludic activities are implicated in productive tasks, it being difficult to separate them or to assign greater importance to one or another. The third stage of childhood is from seven or eight years old until puberty. The boys who accompany their fathers on hunts and the girls who gather with their mothers and other adult women of the group are in this final stage of childhood. However, the participation of both in adult trips is a progressive process that begins when they are very young. As they grow, the frequency with which they accompany adults increases correspondingly. The only point of inflexion one can register tentatively is at seven or eight years old, because from this age onwards an accelerated process of preparation for adult life can be observed.

During this period, one notices that the learning process is not based on imitation or generalized teaching of children by their parents, but rather on teaching activities directed toward sex-specific tasks. For example, when boys are eight or nine years old, they go out with their fathers for long walks carrying darts and blowpipes, which allows them to try their marksmanship on birds and small animals. The boys are also encouraged to climb palms and collect fruit, and some time is invested in helping them to prepare blowpipes. At around 10 years of age, girls already frequently carry their younger sisters during gathering trips and almost always carry a basket full of gear. From this age, approximately, they begin to butcher monkeys (an exclusively female activity) or collaborate in this task with their mothers or older girls. They also partake in the fabrication of fiber bracelets *(kdn'yii)* (Figure 9.2), of baskets and *burup* (expedient bags).

Despite the fact that in the final stage of childhood boys and girls may spend part of the day at some distance from the esidential

Figure 9.2. Girl Making a Fiber Bracelet *(kdn'yii)* in a Rainy Season Residential Camp.

camp, they mainly stay within it or its immediate surroundings (Figure 9.3).

When children are younger than two years of age they always remain close to their mothers who carry them on trips outside the camp to gather food, tend their orchards, and fish. After they reach two or three years of age and are in the first stage of childhood they either remain in camp, watched by older children, or accompany their mothers. Older siblings play an important role in the care of the youngest and spend a great deal of time responsible for them. From six or seven years old children may travel short distances from the camp, accompanied by older children. They gather accessible fruit, fish and collect crabs in pools and streams in the surrounding area, or they simply play and enjoy themselves (Figure 9.4).

Despite these trips alone or with their mothers, children spend most of the twelve daytime and all the nocturnal hours inside or around the residential camp, where they produce and use three classes of artifacts:

Class 1

Artifacts designed specifically for play (toys). Typical toys are bark hammocks, rounded stones, fruit spinning tops, large rings made of

Figure 9.3. Children Playing Inside a Rainy Season Residential Camp.

Figure 9.4. Boy Practicing with a Blowpipe in the Surrounding of a Camp.

vines, etc. These artifacts do not have homologues among the adult's tools.

Class 2

Artifacts that replicate adult objects, but are smaller and poorly made. They are used for the same function or for play. Examples include bows, harpoons, blowpipes, darts, baskets, pottery vessels, gourd vessels and spears (Figure 9.5).

Class 3

Adult artifacts, complete or broken, that are used for play. Examples include any adult artifact that can potentially be used in play. The most frequent are metal axes (Figure 9.6), machetes, vessels (Figure 9.7) and pestles.

Class 1 artifacts are generally made by the children themselves (at times with the help of their parents), with minor modifications, or even with no shaping at all (such as the case of the rounded stones). Within this class, it is of interest to mention the stones that Nukak children on some occasions bring from the "Blowpipe Hills" when the entire band approach these hills in order to gather canes for blowpipes (Politis, 1996b:284). These rounded pebbles are carried from one place to another for weeks or months until they are finally abandoned or lost at the camps or in their surroundings. They are used principally by children for play; no other function has been observed.

Class 2 contains far more artifacts and includes practically all the tools made by adults, but smaller. An important distinction must be made in this second class. On the one hand, adults make smaller versions of artifacts so they may be used by children, fulfilling a function similar to that of the full-sized objects. The only difference between adult and children's artifacts is their size, which is appropriate for the age and size of the child, but the quality of fabrication and the function are identical (e.g., gourd and pottery vessels). On the other hand, there are replicas of adult tools, made by the children themselves or their parents for play or practice. Children do not used them for the same functions as adults do, although their use can be similar, and they are of a lower quality. This lower quality is due to two reasons: a) When they are made by adults the technology has an expedient character-due to the ludic goal of the artifacts they are not made with the same care; b) when children make them the lower quality is due to limitations in technique.

The size of these artifacts occurs in relation to the size of the child. Virtually any size possible may be produced within a particular range. In the case of blowpipes, for example, the smallest we recorded was 0.82m long. From there on, they gradually increase in size until the adult

Figure 9.5. Boy Playing with an Expedient Spear.

tools reach 3.2m. The difference between adult and child blowpipes is determined by the relationship that exists between the length of the tool and the stature and ability of the user.

The third class is made up of unmodified adults' artifacts; the activity of the children only influences their spatial distribution. This class is the most utilized by the youngest children who pick up any object close by to use as a toy.

Children's artifacts are also differentiated from adult ones by their discard loci. Children discard the vast majority of their objects within the residential camp or its immediate vicinity, while adults tend to do

Figure 9.6. Boy Cutting Plants around the Camp with a Metal Axe.

so far from the camp where many activities are carried out (hunting, gathering, butchering of peccary, etc.). One of the most interesting cases is that of darts, as children play with blowpipes frequently and conduct target practice within the camps (Figure 9.8), although these darts do not have *curare* (poison). As a consequence, small darts-sometimes whole—are left on the floors of abandoned camps as a result of this activity.

Further, inside the residential camps or on their periphery, there are two types of constructions made by children. The first are small, open areas where children hang hammocks and light a fire during

Figure 9.7. Baby Playing with a Metal Bowl inside the Camp.

the day. Generally speaking, these consist of a few flimsy posts and crossbeams, although plantain leaves are also occasionally involved. These camps are not used to sleep in and their function is to replicate the residential camps in miniature and mimic similar activities within them. In these little camps, a series of small, generally poor-quality objects are left, as well as one or two small hearths. The second type of construction are replicas of single shelters, on a smaller scale, built by children inside the camps. This second type might also have an as yet unidentified socio-ideational meaning, since heavily

Figure 9.8. Children Making Darts to Play inside a Rainy Season Residential Camp.

painted children on occasion remain inside them quietly for some time.

Children's Material Production In Other American Hunter-Gatherer Groups

The generation of several classes of artifact made by or for children is a universal behavior, recorded among all hunter-gatherer groups studied from an anthropological perspective. Interesting data have been obtained from both chronicles and historical documents and from ethnographic studies. A rapid summary of some examples facilitates a picture of general tendencies, which serves to contextualise the Nukak case. Furthermore, some examples refer directly to objects that are common in the archaeological sites of South America, such as projectile points and *boleadoras*.

In the case of projectile points, the references inventoried by Dawe (1997) for North America are of particular interest. Among these, the following stand out: Grinnell (1923) observed that as soon as a Cheyenne child "was able to run easily, a small bow and some arrows were made for him"; Schoolcraft noted that: "Boys were always furnished with small arrow-points" (1923 in Dawe, 1997:307); and the commentaries of Wallace and Hoebel (1952:16) indicate that among the historic Comanche, parents began to teach their male children to make hunting equipment (including projectile points) at five years of age. Dawe (1997) has demonstrated that among diverse indigenous groups of the North American plains the production of small projectile points was frequent, ensuring that children played and acquired the ability to hunt. These references coincide with observations among the Nukak as far as the smaller size of the equipment and the existence of homologues among the adult gear is concerned. There are further similarities—including Grinnell's remark above—such as points being made for children by adults (as are some Nukak artifacts) and that there is a relationship between the size of the artifact and the stature and age of the child. Among the groups of the Lower Basin of the Mississippi river, Swanson mentioned that when children ". . . approach 12 years, a bow and arrow are made for them, proportioned to their strength (Swanson, 1911 in Dawe, 1997:307). In this sense it has been observed that bows and arrows were constructed based on the height of the archer (Bourke, 1891). In the archaeological record, then, one would expect to find a continuum of projectile point sizes. The range could vary from "small points enough to fit a two years old boy's arrow, to those having the optimum dimensions of those for adult weaponry" (Dawe, 1997).

Among the Yámanas of the channels of Tierra del Fuego, Gusinde (1987) relates in great detail the activities of children and the objects they utilize. In one quote, he mentions that there are no toys really for boys (those that would be included in the aforementioned Class 1), rather emphasizing the manufacture of objects that can clearly be included within Class 2: "Games do not exist, strictly speaking, for boys. An adult, generally the father, constructs reproductions for them of weapons and utensils that serve the men in the hunt . . . Naturally, the pieces are quickly ruined or lost, but the adults indefatigably make substitutes, and the larger the child grows the larger these utensils are" (Gusinde, 1987: 729). The same author states that these reproductions of weapons are not particularly effective and that "they barely serve as toys" because the child is not given the entire weapon—it lacks the bone point—because it would be too valuable. As an alternative, "straight sticks cut to a point or useless harpoon shafts are used" (Gusinde, 1987: 729).

The example of the Yámanas girls is more complex, as real toys do exist, such as simple dolls made from a cylindrical stone and a fragment of wood (Gusinde, 1987). The girls, however, appear to be more active economically than the boys. From an early age they make graters, weave baskets, weave cord for adornments, and so on. Moreover, as paddling canoes is a female responsibility, from a young age girls are trained in this task through the construction of small canoes, in accordance with their size and age: "the father constructs a small reproduction of this canoe for his semi-adolescent daughter. It agrees in all its details with a larger canoe and its dimensions are such that a single girl is able to sit in it and go for a paddle" (Gusinde, 1987: 733).

There is also a rich literature on the Selknam that describes children's games and the objects that children use. Gallardo (1910) mentions small projectile points as children's toys, used only for diversion and training. Gusinde (1982: 373) describes the intense activity of the girls within the camps: "The young girls practice with anything that falls into their hands. There is a continuous touching and throwing of every class of object, grabbing of insects and small plants, throwing of straps, hitting of wood, throwing of pieces of skin, picking at the wool of their own little clothing, bumping into erect objects". This author also describes the careful and complicated elaboration of dolls that requires a great deal of work and dedication. One of the most interesting quotes refers to the production of bows for children: "The father prepares them already for the suckling child in the simplest way: a rough stick is slowly bent and maintained at this curvature with sinew, a superficially smoothed stick serves as an arrow. Although the young boy for the moment is only capable of shaking it and throwing it away, the parents have to see it in his hands, as if he would be missing something otherwise. I have seen such bows only 12cm long. As the child grows, so too do his toys. In his fourth or fifth year these are no longer mere pastimes, and in the future the father makes them with extreme care. From that time on they are an actual imitation of the hunting bow" (Gusinde, 1982: 376–377). A similar situation arises with the *hondas*, which "in spite of its smaller size resembles exactly the men's" (Gusinde, 1982: 378).

At the end of the nineteenth century Musters described in several passages of his book some artifacts used by children among the Southern Tehuelches of Patagonia. One such passage narrates that: "The youngsters had several nandú (*Rhea*) young for diversion; they often let them go in order to hunt them with diminutive *boleadoras*, which generally ended in the death (of the birds)" (Musters, 1997: 176). Another paragraph clearly explains the children's' activities, which are similar to those recorded among the Nukak: "The youngsters generally entertain themselves by imitating the older people: the boys play with diminutive *boleadoras* and hunt dogs with small spears, while the girls construct small shelters to sit inside of, with which they are all absorbed and hence avoid being reprimanded, which seems to everyone highly convenient" (Musters, 1997: 205). Another quote refers to a boys' game involving pebbles, similar to the contemporary child's game known as "knucklebones". The objects described in these references are identifiable as belonging to the three classes already discussed in this paper. Musters also explains that it was rare for sons to go hunting with their fathers before they were 10 or 12 years old, and that they only participated in combat at the age of 16. The girls helped at domestic chores and in the production of objects at nine or 10 years old, and by 16 they were already considered suitable for marriage (Musters, 1997: 210).

Clastres (1998) has recorded interesting data on children's behavior among hunter-gatherers from the Guayakí of Eastern Paraguay. To begin, he recognizes three stages to childhood. The first lasts until three years old, during which time the infants are being breast-fed and spend almost all their time at their mothers' sides. The second stage lasts until they are seven, and the third until they are approximately 15. In this last stage, which is called *Kybuchu*, the boys already own a set of bows and arrows that were given as a gift to them by an adult (not always their father). Within this age group ". . . boys were already well trained in handling their weapon; without going far away from the camp, they could spend hours alone in the woods stalking prey suitable to the power of their bows (which was not negligible)" (Clastres, 1998: 96).

Holmberg (1978) has also recorded a similar pattern to the Nukak among the Sirionó of eastern Bolivia in reference to child weapons. He states that before a boy reaches three years old, his father has already made him a miniature bow and arrows, and although the child cannot use them for several years, they symbolize his role as a hunter. From the age of three onwards, boys are already using a kind of bow, and spend many hours playing and shooting arrows at any inert target. When a little older they shoot at butterflies and birds; by eight years old they have already successfully hunted a small animal. In the case of girls, before they reach three, their parents have made them a small distaff in order that they may later on practice the art of spinning. In general, the majority of the games fall within Class 2, as they replicate adult tools: "In a somewhat surprising way, the boys' miniature bows and arrows and the girls' distaffs are the only toys the Sirionó make for their sons and daughters" (Holmberg, 1978: 186).

In summary, observations of indigenous groups from the North American Plains and South America enable one to identify the same three classes of children's artifacts as those seen among the Nukak. One may also identify the two variants of Class 2, that is, those made by the children themselves and those made for them by adults, generally their parents, that are usually of better quality. Furthermore, the similarity in the correlation between the size of the artifact and that of the user is notable. In the North American cases and among the Yámanas, Selknam and Sirionó, this correlation is noticeable in the case of bows and arrows. In the Nukak example, the relationship is found between hunting and fishing weapons, such as blowpipes, darts, spears and bows.

Archaeological Expectations

If we compare the cluster generated by children with those produced by adults (Table 9.1), some clear-cut differences arise. These differences allow us to generate some archaeological expectations in order to identify material Classes 1 and 2. Class 3 is virtually impossible to identify because children's activities do not generate diagnostic characteristics in these artifacts.

The other form of identification that must be analyzed in conjuncture with the preceding characteristics is 'discard location'. While Class

Table 9.1. Differences between Children and Adults'
Artifacts

	Homologous?	Size	Quality
CLASS 1	No	Variable medium or small	Low or Unmodified
CLASS 2	Yes	Smaller	Lower

1 artifacts are discarded exclusively where they were used in play, objects from Class 2 are also thrown away where they were used as toys, which, in many cases, is different from the place where their adult homologues are abandoned. This is notable in the case of darts, arrows and other male adult objects that are abandoned (usually broken) in places outside and a certain distance away from the residential camps, i.e., where hunting takes place. Artifacts such as containers and wicker baskets, both those belonging to adults and to children, are discarded in the residential camp. Obviously, in all cases, the discard location may change due to cleaning activities within the camp (Politis, 2000).

In particular contexts some adult artifacts could be confused with children's tools. These are: a) small design elements; b) elements that wear through use; and c) miniatures or replicas at a smaller scale. In principle, there are indicators for the three cases that enable them to be discriminated from children's artifacts. In the first case, small adult artifacts (e.g., projectile points) are good quality products and are found in discard loci related to their function (for example, hunting loci). Furthermore, the entire archaeological assemblage would need to be analyzed and in most cases larger homologues would not be found (which would be the case for children's artifacts).

In the second context, it is also possible to distinguish between the small size of children's artifacts and use wear. In general, reduction in size through use is accompanied by other traits that enable the intensity of use to be identified (for example, rough edges on lithic material, or the reduction in blowpipe length). An interesting example is that of the *porotadí*, long wooden artifacts with beveled ends that are used by the eastern Ayoreo to scrape the pulp of an edible root (Bórmida, 1973). As this artifact is gradually worn away, the point is renewed; the piece therefore loses length until reaching two thirds of its original size. Due to its mythic connotations (it is also usually decorated with clan signs), when it is worn down to this degree it is said to have "aged" and only old people may use it, while the young must be careful not to transport it in the bags they carry on their backs (Bórmida, 1973: 50–60). This example enables us to anticipate that the *porotadí* would not be identified, according to the proposed methodology, as a child's artifact, in spite of examples of varied sizes existing within the same context. On the one hand, it is only one dimension that is reduced—the length—while the other two remain constant. In this sense, the "aged" *porotadí* are not smaller, but rather only shorter. On the other hand, the good quality of the most used examples, including the existence of incisions that have clanic connotations, allow them to be separated from Class 2 children's artifacts.

The third case is perhaps the most difficult to identify. A good example is that of the miniatures that some Inuit adults use. Initially, it was proposed that many of the Inuit miniatures were children's artifacts and that these objects represented the status of children as "little adults" (Park, 1998). Distinguishing children's miniatures from those placed in the burials of certain people and those used by Shamans is still problematic, due, above all, to the high quality of the former. Nonetheless, the distinction is possible because this type of miniatures has different discard loci, and in one case (the adult burials) this is sufficiently informative, in the context of Inuit culture, to judge them not to be children's artifacts.

Conclusion

In this chapter I have sought to contribute to the generation of a methodology that allows children's activities to be identified in archaeological deposits. This is the first step towards a more ambitious objective: to explore child agency in past hunter-gatherers. Children represent a significant percentage of human populations and they spend a great deal of time in residential camps. This has several significant implications for archaeology. Analyzing the data gathered among the Nukak and comparing them to other South American foragers and North American Plains Indians enables several common patterns to emerge, allowing the following expectations to be put forward:

First, it should be anticipated that a high proportion of archaeological remains from hunter-gatherer residential camps will be children's artifacts and by-products.

Second, some of the artifacts produced and/or used by children can be identified by bearing in mind that they *do exist*, as well as by using the archaeological expectation stated above. It should also be possible to identify, in a given context, to which class an artifact belongs.

Third, adult and children's artifacts do not separate into discrete clusters. There is a full range of variation in size and quality depending on the age of the user, her/his stature, her/his ability and the situation. At one end of this range are the smaller, poorly made artifacts; at the opposite end are the larger and better quality objects. In between, there are infinite possible combinations of these qualities.

Fourth, the recognition of a variety of clusters generated by children is a further, independent indicator that can be used to confirm the function of the site as a residential camp.

Bearing in mind the first point, one should expect the remains of children's activities to include a wide range of residues that are not the function of a *chaîne opératoire* aimed at the production of artifacts to be used in techno-economic tasks or as items of symbolic value. These artifacts and their residues will have different trajectories that fall outside the expectations generated by the more usual models of the optimization of raw materials.

Based on ethnographic information from hunter-gatherers, one can anticipate that sites generated by this type of society in the past, when residential camps are in evidence, will contain significant percentages of artifacts produced by children. These will range from those produced by practicing the reduction of nodules to training with primary and secondary flakes, as well as the fabrication of various generally poor-quality artifacts. The same can be expected for pottery, with training in the decoration and practicing the manufacture of vessels. Consequently, one should expect quantities of clay and small recipients molded by children who were together with the adults during the production process to be present at ceramic production locus.

The normative perspective within archaeology relies on the reasoning that the ethnic or cultural distance between different populations in the past can be measured in terms of the degree of similarity between archaeological assemblages (Jones, 1997: 25). Processual archaeology signaled differences in site function, modes of resource exploitation and technological strategies as sources of archaeological variation within a single society (see Binford, 1977, 1978, 1979 among many others). However, this latter perspective has resulted in a degree of "technocentrism", as it has considered artifacts to be simple tools used for strictly practical and functional purposes without addressing other dimensions of material culture such as its social and symbolic content. Ethnography has demonstrated how objects are included within a symbolic system that affects their use, reuse and abandonment (see Bórmida, 1973; Politis 1996b; Toth et al., 1992; among many other examples). The consideration of age groups in the formation of the archaeological record generates novel perspectives as they constitute a significant source of artifactual variation whose utilitarian dimension varies according to the age group that the user belongs to.

Technological activities are not only the consequence of planned tasks, consciously directed toward the obtainment of functionally efficient artifacts. They are also the result of learning and teaching processes. Among the old, the production of objects in particular ways also signifies a means of maintaining status and prestige. The technological ability of older people has its particularities that should be reflected in the trends of the archaeological record. Bearing in mind such considerations opens a new perspective in the study of hunter-gatherer material culture, as it is clear that the record produced is multi-dimensional and responds to a variety of causes, among which are included teaching and learning, diversions and games, and the management of objects in order to maintain social prestige. What percentage of residue did a linear process in the production of a set of utilitarian artifacts produce? How much of this derives from the recurrent and constant action of children playing and practicing within the camps? Aside from a few exceptions (e.g., Bodú et al., 1990; Nami, 1994), this postulate has not been advanced in past hunter-gatherer lithic technology studies. Undoubtedly, the answer is complex and different for each case study. In principle however, the best way of approaching the analysis is from a perspective that gives space to multiple agents, not all of whom attempt to use raw material optimally. Neither may they be sufficiently trained and skilled or worried about obtaining useful and efficient artifacts in techno-economic terms.

The range of variation in size and quality of some artifacts (especially hunting weapons) according to the age and the stature of the user also bears important implications for archaeological analysis and interpretation. Firstly, it indicates that adult and children's artifacts are not separated into discrete groups, but rather should be visualized as a continuum in size and quality. Along this continuum there are infinite combinations depending, among other factors, on the stature, age and ability of the maker and user. Therefore, it is expected that some artifacts frequently used diagnostically in archaeological interpretation may vary in the form and function of these three properties. Variation in the design of projectile points, for example, has been widely used as an indicator of a distinct point type in the archaeology of hunter-gatherers (taken to indicate, for example, ethnicity, idiosyncrasy, social hierarchy, function, etc.). I do not deny that this and other reasons are causes of stylistic and technical variation in projectile points and other artifacts (i.e., Wiessner, 1983). However, I argue that artifactual variability is also a consequence of age groups and that this must be considered not as a contingent element but as a recurrent factor in the generation of the variability of archaeological deposits.

A further important point that needs to be explored is the participation of children in the reproduction of material culture. In several ethnographic examples (see, for example, Gusinde, 1982) and the Nukak case it has been observed that some elements that are no longer used by adults remain active as children's toys. This is the case of bows and arrows among the Nukak that are used by children after adults have abandoned them. This theme, therefore, would allow discussion of children's agency within society, as some material elements that in the face of intense cultural contact are no longer used by adults, survive with the children. In this way, children are transformed into a type of artifactual "reservoir", maintaining objects in circulation that would otherwise disappear from society.

Old people as well as children make artifacts in a distinct fashion and with purposes beyond the strictly utilitarian. Adolescents also fabricate specific objects, generally related to rites of passage. As such, it is fairly clear that different age groups within hunter-gatherer societies generate a variety of utensils that do not function solely within the techno-economic sphere, but rather embody multiple dimensions of meaning related to learning, entertainment, status, teaching, ritual, and so on. With an appropriate methodology it will be possible to see how material culture transforms itself over the lifetime of individuals and how this generates different trends in archaeological deposits. In the case with which this chapter is concerned, the expectations generated from ethnoarchaeological, ethnohistoric and ethnographic information should not be used as recipes for universal application. Rather they should be considered as guides or reference points pertinent to archaeological landscapes formed by societies in which children are active producers and consumers of material culture and, consequently, important protagonists in the generation of the archaeological record.

Acknowledgements

I am extremely grateful to Benjamin Alberti for his translation and helpful comments and suggestions. Fieldwork among the Nukak was financed though two subsidies (numbers 5389 and 5701) from the Wenner Gren Foundation for Anthropological Research; and by the Instituto Amazónico de Investigaciones Científicas (SINCHI), Colombia between 1995 and 1996.

This research forms part of the projects administered by INCUAPA (*Núcleo de Investigaciones Arqueológicas y Paleontológicas del Cuaternario Pampeano*) of the Universidad Nacional del Centro de la Provincia de Buenos Aires, Argentina. This program receives subsidies from the Universidad Nacional del Centro de la Provincia de Buenos Aires, the Agencia Nacional de Promoción Científica and CONICET (Consejo Nacional de Investigaciones Científicas y Técnicas), Republic of Argentina.

Notes

[1] A recent book edited by Sofaer-Derevensky (2000) is also a significant contribution. Unfortunately, I could not comment and discuss this body of work as it was published after I sent this paper for publication.

References

Binford, L., 1977, Forty-seven Trips: A Case study in the Character of Archaeological Formation Process. In *Stone Tools as Cultural Markers,* edited by R. V. S. Wright, pp. 24–36. Australian Institute of Aboriginal Studies, Canberra.

1978, *Nunamiut Ethnoarchaeology.* Academic Press, New York.

1979, Organization and Formation Processes: Looking at Curated Technologies. *Journal of Anthropological Research* 35(3):255–273.

Bodú, P., Karlin, C., and Ploux, S., 1990, Who is Who? The Magdalenian Flintkanppers of Pincevent. In *The Big Puzzle,* edited by C. Cziesla, S. Eichoff, N. Arts, and D. Winter, pp. 143–163. Holos, Bonn.

Bonnichsen, R., 1973, Millie's Camp: an Experiment in Archaeology. *World Archaeology* 4: 277–291.

Bórmida, M., 1973, Ergon y mito: Una hermenéutica de la cultura material de los Ayoreo del Chaco *Boreal. Scripta Ethnologica* 1(1):9–68.

Bourke, J., 1891, Arrows and Arrow-makers: Remarks. *American Anthropology* 4: 71–74.

Cárdenas, D., and Politis, G., 2000, *Territorio, movilidad, etnobotánica y manejo del bosque de los Nukak Orientales (Amazonía Colombiana)*. Informes Antropológicos 3. Universidad de los Andes-Instituto Sinchi, Santafé de Bogotá.

Chamberlain, A., 1997, Commentary: Missing Stages of Life—Towards the Perception of Children in Archaeology. In *Invisible People and Processes: Writing Gender and Childhood into European Archaeology*, edited by J. Moore and E. Scott, pp. 248–250. Leicester University Press, London.

Clastres, P., 1998, *Chronicle of the Guayaki Indians*. Faber and Faber, New York.

Conkey, M., and Spector, C., 1984, Archaeology and the Study of Gender. In *Method Advances in Archaeological and Theory* 7: 1–38.

Conkey, M. and Gero, J., 1991, Tension, Pluralities, and the Engendering Archaeology: An Introduction to Women and Prehistory. In *Engendering Archaeology. Women and Prehistory*, edited by J. Gero and M. Conkey, pp. 3–30. Blakwell, Oxford.

Draper, P., 1976, Social and Economic Constraints on Child Life Among the !Kung. In *Kalahari Hunter-Gatherers*, edited by R. Lee and I. de Vore, pp. 199–217. Harvard University Press, Cambridge.

Finlay, N., 1997, Kid-knapping: the Missing Children in Lithic Analysis. In *Invisible People and Processes. Writing Gender and Childhood into European Archaeology*, edited by J. Moore and E. Scott, pp. 203–212. Leicester University Press, London.

Fisher, A., 1990, On Being a Pupil Flinknapper of 11,000 Years Ago. In *The Big Puzzle*, edited by E. Cziesla, S. Eichoff, N. Arts and D. Winters, pp. 447–464. Holos, Bonn.

Gallardo, C. B., 1910, *Tierra del Fuego: Los Onas*. Buenos Aires.

Gradín, C., and Aguerre, A., 1983, Arte rupestre del Area la Martita: Sección A del Departamento Magallanes, Provincia de Santa Cruz. *Relaciones* 15 (N.S.): 195–223.

Grinnell, G., 1923, *The Cheyenne Indians: Their History and Ways of Life*. Yale University Press, New Haven.

Gusinde, M., 1982, *Los Indios de Tierra del Fuego: Los Selknam*. Centro Argentino de Etnología Americana, Buenos Aires.

1987, *Los Indios de Tierra del Fuego: Los Yámanas*, Centro Argentino de Etnología Americana, Buenos Aires.

Hammond, G., and Hammond, N., 1981, Child's Play: A Distorting Factor in Archaeological Distribution. *American Antiquity* 64: 634–636.

Holmberg, A., 1978, *Nómadas del arco largo: Los Sirionó del Oriente boliviano*. Instituto Indigenista Interamericano, Ediciones Especiales 77.

Hodder, I., 1999, *The Archaeological Process*. Blakwell Publishers, Oxford.

James, A., and Prout, A., 1990, *Constructing and Reconstructing Childhood*. The Farmel Press, Basingstoke.

Jones, S., 1997, *The Archaeology of Ethnicity: Constructing Identities in the Past and Present*. Routledge, New York.

Koch-Grünberg, T., 1906, Die Makú. *Anthropos* 1:877–906.

Knapp, B., and Meskell, L., 1997, Bodies of Evidence in Cypriotic Prehistory. *Cambridge Archaeological Journal* 7(2): 183–204.

Lillehammer, G., 1989, A Child is Born: The Child's World in an Archaeological Perspective. *Norwigian Archaeological Review* 22(2): 89–105.

Mengoni Goñalons, G., 2000, Mesa Redonda: Actores en escena: comportamiento social y el registro arqueológico. *Soplando en el viento: Actas de la Terceras Jornadas de Arqueología de la Patagonia*. Universidad del Comahue e INALP.

Metraux, A., 1948, The Hunting and Gathering People of the Rio Negro Basin. In *Handbook of Southamerican Indians,* volume 3, edited by J. Steward, pp. 861–867. Smithsonian, Washington.

Moore, J. and Scott, E., editors, 1997, *Invisible People and Processes: Writing Gender and Childhood into European Archaeology*. Leicester University Press, London.

Musters, G., 1997, *Vida entre los Patagones*. Elefante Blanco, Buenos Aires.

Park, R., 1998, Size Counts: the Miniature Archaeology of Childhood in Inuit Societies. *Antiquity* 72 (276):269–281.

Politis, G., 2000, Patrones de descarte entre cazadores-recolectores amazónicos. *Arqueología del Area Intermedia* 2. Santafé de Bogotá. Colombia.

1999, Plant Exploitation among the Nukak (Hunter-gatherers of Amazonia: Between Ecology and Ideology. In C. Gosden and J. Hather, *The Prehistory of Food*, edited by, pp. 99–126, London: Routledge.

1998, Arqueología de la infancia. Una perspectiva etnoarqueológica. *Trabajos de Prehistoria* (Madrid) 55(2): 5–19.

1996a, Moving to Produce: Nukak Mobility and Settlements Patterns in Amazonia. *World Archaeology* 27(3): 492–510.

1996b, *Nukak*. Instituto Amazónico de Investigaciones Científicas SINCHI, Santafé de Bogotá.

1992, La Arquitectura del Nomadismo en la Amazonía Colombiana. *Proa* 412: 11–20.

Politis, G., Martínez, G. and Rodríguez, J., 1997, Caza, recolección y pesca como estrategia de explotación de recursos en forestas tropicales lluviosas: los Nukak de la amazonía colombiana. *Revista Española de Antropología Americana* 27:167–197.

Reid, H., 1979, *Some Aspects of Movement, Growth, and Change Among the Hupdu Makú Indians of Brazil*. Ph.D. dissertation, Cambridge University.

Rivas, P., and Ocampo, C., 1997, Dinámica sociocultural de las poblaciones asentadas en el ecosistema Litoral Santa Augusta de Quintay, Proyecciones regionales e interregionales y el Período Medio de Chile Central. Paper presented at the *XIV Congreso Nacional de Arqueología Chilena*, October 13–18, 1997, Copiapó.

Shennan, S., 1991, Tradition, Rationality, and Cultural Transmission. In *Processual and Postprocessual Archaeologies: Multiples Ways of Knowing the Past*, edited by R. Preucel, pp. 197–208. University of Carbondale, Illinois.

Sofaer-Derevenski, J., 1994, Where are the Children? Accesing Children in the Past. *Archaeological Review from Cambridge* 13 (2):7–20.

1997, Age and Gender at the Site of Tiszapolgár-Basatanya, Hungary. *Antiquity* 71 (274):875–879.

Sofaer-Derevenski, J., editor, 2000, *Children and Material Culture*. Routledge, London.

Silverwood-Cope, P., 1972, *A Contribution to the Ethnography of the Colombian Makú*. Ph.D.dissertation, Cambridge University.

Toth, N., Clark, D. and Ligabue, G., 1992, Los últimos fabricantes de hachas de piedra. *Investigación y Ciencia* Septiembre: 6–11.

Wiessner, P., 1983, Style and Ethnicity in the Kalahari San Projectile Point. *American Antiquity* 50:253–276.

10

The Archaeology of Identity Construction

Ceramic Evidence from Northern Chile

Emily M. Stovel

Introduction

Although ethnicity has a long history in archaeology (e.g., Aldenderfer, 1993; Athens, 1992; Auger et al., 1987; Cordell and Yannie, 1991; Kelly and Kelly, 1980; Oakland Rodman, 1992; Penner, 1997; Pollard, 1994; Sackett, 1977, 1986, 1990; Shennan, 1989), its study as a shifting, contextual phenomenon in conjunction with the idea of *identity construction* is relatively new and represents an interesting manifestation of postmodern archaeological variants that attempt to import modern models into the past (e.g., Bowser, 2000; Emberling, 1997, 1999; Hill, 1998; Jones, 1996, 1997; MacEachern, 1998, 2001; McGuire, 1982; Terrell, 2001; Wells, 1998). New understandings of identity construction stem from a modern interest in subverting imposed identities and examining the contextual and historical conditions for the strategic homogeneous construction of group identity. This perspective presumes that group formation and definition, or the construction of difference, is intimately related to the exercise or rejection of power (i.e., Comaroff, 1985, 1996). In this vein, archaeologists interested in power relations in the past have recently explored two modes of ethnic identity construction: identification and attribution (Brumfiel, 1994). Ethnic identification[1] implies members of an inferior faction or community actively (re)define ethnic categories as a mechanism of unification and of negotiating for

145

economic or political resources. We find this perspective in several of Ian Hodder's (1979, 1982) early texts. Ethnic attribution implies the imposition of ethnic categories or qualities and traits on certain communities by dominant groups. As such, ethnic identity construction does not usually involve the development of new ethnic categories, but rather the struggle for the right to define extant categories, usually using essential and value-laden characteristics. This process suggests that cultural homogeneity is a product of intercultural communication and interaction instead of isolation.

What does this mean to the archaeologists working in prehistory? Part of postprocessual archaeology has involved questioning old normative cultural categories by demonstrating diversity within them or the lack of spatial and temporal correspondence of cultural attributes (e.g., Blom, 1999; MacEachern, 1998, 2001; Sharpe, 1986; Speth, 1988; Stahl, 1991). Cultural or ethnic categories are seen as potentially misleading because of their presumption of internal homogeneity and mutual exclusivity, and their role in serving modern nationalistic and ethnic goals (Díaz Andreu and Champion, 1996; Kohl and Fawcett, 1995). The archaeological organization of the past into a mirror of present cultural and ethnic differences is particularly dangerous in that it offers valuable historical longevity to modern groups according to which they can justify claims of authenticity and superiority. Obviously, this same mechanism can help subaltern communities in their struggle for power as well, but this leaves archaeologists to decide which modern community they will choose to promote through their research, or worse, to be caught by the demands of several groups seeking the same historic authentification.

These ethical dilemmas will not be the focus of the present paper. Here I will instead offer some empirical and methodological reflections on the use of such post-modern visions of ethnogenesis in archaeology. The breaking down of archaeological cultural categories is part of exploring the historical, contextual, and active nature of social relations in the present and the past. Such categories, in other words, are not passive products of innate differences between groups, impervious to political and economic developments. They are conditioned by time and place, such that cultural or ethnic difference is seen as the result of the active positioning of people inside and outside each community. An explicitly homogeneous and discrete material entity excavated in the present, then, is considered the result of a potentially politicized community in the past and constitutes a form of prehistoric 'strategic essentialism' (viz. Spivak, 1988). The archaeological development of models that share this perspective is found in the work of Siân Jones (1996, 1997) and Geoff Emberling (1997, 1999).

The development of an ethnic identity in the past, presumably represented by salient homogeneous material symbols, requires additional study not only to weigh the philosophical ramifications of imputing such complex social mechanisms and ethnic consciousness into the past, but also to test appropriate analytical tools for its study. This paper argues that the study of ethnic identity construction involves a diachronic and power-based consideration of the development of material (read community) homogeneity. In other words, one must look for three elements: 1) increased homogeneity over time, 2) the concurrent evidence of economic or political tension leading to a need for ethnic differentiation, and 3) the evidence of intentionality on the part of ancient producers. This approach avoids the chronic archaeological pitfall of equating pots with people because it looks for the development of a distinctive style; that is, it looks for temporal evidence of community representation rather than assuming all material culture reflects innate cultural difference; and it requires evidence of intentional self-representation. Toward these ends, I provide diachronic data from the development of the highly homogenous and distinctive *Negro Pulido* ceramic tradition of San Pedro de Atacama, northern Chile (Figure 10.1). These data then provide the basis for the comparison of statistical measures of vessel standardization over time. It is hoped that the perceived homogeneity of this material style is mirrored by high metric standardization and that the temporal enhancement of these qualities can be tied to coeval political and economic changes in the region.

Figure 10.1. Map of the South-Central Andes.

Identity Construction

Because of the extreme difficulty of discriminating between ethnic identification and attribution in prehistory where we have no explicit mandates or documents delineating 'appropriate' ethnic dress or behavior (as in the case of the Inca, Blom 1999), we must presume that increasing homogeneity in one or more emblematic material realms is a product of both mechanisms. In less complex social situations such as that of San Pedro de Atacama in northern Chile, explicit ethnic affiliation may be more of a contributing factor because limits to power asymmetries constrain the ability of groups to impose identities on others. Thus, as is found in previous case studies (Emberling, 1997, 1999), the focus here will be on ethnic identity construction internal to the community under study, or prehistoric 'strategic essentialism'.

Strategic Essentialism

Essentialism implies the exaggeration and promotion of presumed fundamental and defining characteristics of groups. This process can occur 'from above' or 'from below'. In other words, certain essential traits are assigned to discrete groups as a mechanism of control or as a reflection of prejudice, while some subaltern communities project essential traits to emphasize desired values or qualities. This latter process has been described as 'strategic essentialism' in that such projects are usually employed strategically to negotiate for key political or economic resources. Modern strategic essentialism (Spivak, 1988; also Azoulay, 1997), whereby marginalized groups promote reified and deterministic categories of themselves, is due in part to the institutionalization of difference that links distinctiveness to special treatment on the part of the state (Collier et al., 1995), and in part to the power of unification found in a sense of a common past and belonging.

The use of essentializing categories is dangerous for it serves to unify and strengthen the subaltern at the same time as it reifies identity-based mechanisms of controling them used by dominant groups. Revealing the temporary and constructed nature of identities should not be seen as undermining political aspirations, nor should it suggest we can discard the emphasis of essentials for political power. Deconstruction should highlight how dangerous this process is; it should be a precarious "acknowledgement of something one cannot not use." (Spivak, 1993: 5). This is because, despite its potential benefit to the disenfranchised, strategic essentialism still endorses the mechanism of oppression. For this reason, subaltern identity construction should not be romanticized by those who question power relations and who privilege certain types of representation (i.e. subaltern) over others (i.e., nation-states; Spivak, 1988).

How can we presume this same process occurred in the past? To begin, it is clear that this process occurred in Republican, colonial and peri-colonial Latin America. Part of Inca imperialism involved assigning appropriate ethnic dress and labels to subject communities

(Blom, 1999: 100–107). Spanish colonial administration imposed elaborate racial and ethnic categories—*castas*—for both political and economic reasons (e.g., Cahill, 1994; Cope, 1994). Newly independent Latin American Republics grappled with the different definitions and constituent rights and responsibilities of the various categories of citizens, Indians and *mestizos* (Adorno, 1991; de la Cadena, 1991, 1996; Gootenberg, 1991; Harris, 1995; Méndez, 1991, 1996). Marginalized groups throughout fought for the right to be defined according to different categories or different qualities (e.g., Combés, 1991).

New models that articulate identity construction, power and self-determination are a product of an academic interest in the use of identity to justify modern violence and in the new shifting definitions of nations, indigenous people, and ethnic groups in a globalized, post-modern context. This does not mean, however, that they should only be used in investigations of the modern world. If this were so, such analyses would falsely oppose a stable, accessible and reliable past, devoid of power struggles and violence, to a fragmented and unreliable present. This opposition cannot be supported; nor can we assume the exact same quality and quantity of identity construction in the past. As such, we must continue exploring the application of this model in prehistoric archaeology.

Archaeological Identification of Identities and Ethnicities

Although there is a general lack of clear methods available for the study of identities and ethnicities in the past, there is agreement regarding the political nature of these entities although this differs significantly from earlier understandings of the same concepts. Despite slight differences, the general characterization of ethnic groups and ethnogenesis proposed by Jones (1996, 1997) and Emberling (1997, 1999) can be summarized as follows:

1. Ethnicity represents shifting, situational, and subjective identifications of self and others rooted in daily praxis and historical experience.
2. Ethnic groups are also rooted in lineage, kingship, and ancestry metaphors and a sense of a common, even at times utopian, future and/or past.
3. They exist or become fixed within asymmetrical power relations with other, usually more dominant, groups.
4. Ethnic representation (i.e., emblematics, viz. Wiessner, 1983, 1984) is built from pre-existing cultural symbols into a *salient political entity*.

In a general archaeological sense, then, we must look for the diachronic waxing and waning of distinctive and homogeneous expressions of group unity using objects or symbols from previous daily material culture.

Emberling (1997) has argued more specifically that ethnicity can be recognized archaeologically in the generalized consumption (i.e., throughout the entire community) of key materials or styles that were previously used as objects of prestige. Brumfiel (1994) looked for emblematic elements first in historical documents and then in archaeological contexts. It seems necessary to determine further ways of identifying this process of community unification in the past, particularly for the prehistoric period. If we accept that ethnic identity is political in nature and linked to the negotiation of power, then we must look for the temporal development of emblematic essentialism in a context of asymmetrical power relations. It follows that such an approach demands diachronic evidence of material or stylistic homogenization in one or more emblematic material realms. Of course, it is difficult to assign an emblematic function to certain material styles or objects. Here, and within a postprocessual interpretive context, it seems clear that the production of a distinctive and highly standardized material style can no longer be considered a reflection of unquestioned aesthetic norms, but a quasi-intentional decision to represent group unity in specific contexts of power negotiation. The present study explores this juncture in the Middle Period (c. AD 300–1000) ceramic production of northern Chile.

San Pedro de Atacama and the Rise of Tiwanaku

San Pedro de Atacama is a small town of colonial origin found in the second region of Chile on the western slope of the Andean cordillera (see Figure 10.1). It is located in an oasis at the eastern limit of the Atacama desert and has been a locus of human settlement for over 10,000 years. It is one of the premier archaeological areas of Chile and has provided important theoretical and empirical contributions to Andean archaeology and ethnohistory (e.g., Berenguer, 1993, 1998; Martínez, 1998; Núñez and Dillehay, 1995). This stems primarily from the role San Pedro played in extensive regional interaction networks throughout the south-central Andes, evinced by the varied non-local objects of material culture deposited in local graves (Bravo, 1991; Tarragó, 1977, 1984, 1989, 1994). Long-distance relationships articulated San Pedro inhabitants with communities from across southern Bolivia and northwestern Argentina (Fernández, 1978; Llagostera, 1996; Núñez, 1992, 1996; Núñez et al., 1975), including Aguada (Berenguer, 1984; Llagostera, 1995) and even perhaps northern Peru (Berenguer, 1986).

In particular, research has focused on the relationship between San Pedro inhabitants and the highland polity of Tiwanaku (see Figure 10.1). Tiwanaku, whose urban center was located in western Bolivia near Lake Titicaca, became a pivotal source of economic, religious and political power in the south-central Andes between approximately 500 and 1000 AD (Berenguer and Dauelsberg, 1989; Goldstein, 1993a, b; Kolata 1993). Along with evidence from other areas, the distribution and nature of Tiwanaku goods in San Pedro graves has contributed to the recent redefinition of this polity from a state to a complex multiethnic federation (Albarracín-Jordán, 1996a, b, c; Berenguer, 1993, 1998; Browman, 1995–96, 1996, 1997; Mujica, 1996), although there remains some debate concerning the specific character of San Pedro-Tiwanaku relations.

There is a general agreement that Tiwanaku had an indirect impact on local affairs, probably functioning as a source of prestige goods and power for local elite (Berenguer, 1993, 1998; Berenguer and Dauelsberg, 1989; Berenguer et al., 1980; Llagostera, 1996), or as one client of many with whom San Pedro inhabitants communicated through Bolivian llama caravans (Orellana, 1984, 1985, 1986; Serrancino, 1980). Interpretations range from the consumption of goods and beliefs linked to, but not acquired directly from, the altiplano centre (Torres and Conklin, 1995; Uribe, n.d.) to images of direct management by altiplano leaders living locally (Benavente et al., 1986; Oakland Rodman, 1992; Kolata, 1993; Varela and Cocilovo, 2000). There is a general preference for a prestige economy model (Berenguer, 1998; Berenguer and Dauelsberg, 1989) because recovered Tiwanaku goods are extremely elaborate and found only (so far) in mortuary contexts (Stovel 1997). The use of political models of ethnic identity construction can contribute further to this important shift in recent research by providing another measure of the local response to increasing regional political and economic pressure from this complex society.

This is achieved here through the study of local mortuary ceramic production and consumption. Interestingly, despite active participation in regional trade networks and regular burial consumption of diverse, occasionally polychrome, non-local ceramic styles, local San Pedro potters produced a distinctive homogenous monochrome ceramic style—*Negro Pulido*—between A.D. 300 and 700. In previous processual or diffusionist frameworks, the existence of a persistent homogenous distinctive ceramic style in conjunction with an active and complex range of long-distance relationships seems counterintuitive in that local styles would be subject to influence from outside. San Pedro potters, however, never painted their pots. They maintained a monochromatic mortuary style throughout the growth of both regional trade and Tiwanaku influence.

The first three mortuary ceramic types produced in San Pedro are, in chronological order, *Rojo Pulido* (300 BC–AD 100), *Negro Pulido* (0 BC–AD 700) and *Gris Grueso Pulido* (AD 500–1000) (Burnished Red, Black and Greywares;[2] Berenguer et al., 1986; Berenguer et al., 1988; Montané, 1963; Tarragó, 1976, 1989; Thomas et al., 1984). *Rojo Pulido* is characterized by a reduced range of forms in which short-necked, globular jars with everted rims predominate. *Negro Pulido* is found in 13 or 14 different shapes, including smaller versions of the globular jars. The most popular forms are illustrated in Figure 10.2. The subsequent *Gris Grueso Pulido* displays fewer forms (i.e., 4 or 5 shape classes) and a significant reduction in the quality of surface burnishing, color homogeneity, and thinness of the walls and rims when compared with *Negro Pulido*. In sum, however, all of these wares lack decoration except for

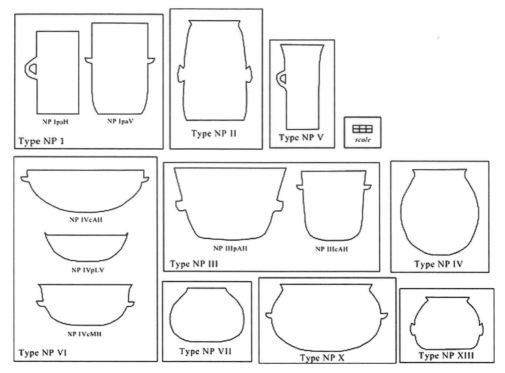

Figure 10.2. Popular *Negro Pulido* Ceramic Forms.

incised anthropomorphic designs on bottle necks (see Figure 10.4) or the geometric incisions of later Red and Black Incised wares (i.e., post-AD 400, Munizaga, 1963; Tarragó, 1989).

It is suggested here that the homogeneity and standardization of *Negro Pulido* ceramics, although a pre-existing stylistic tradition, may have been accentuated through political and economic negotiation with Tiwanaku, which may or may not have been related to San Pedro's incorporation into a peer polity or prestige economy (cf. Berenguer et al., 1980; Llagostera, 1996) with the highland community. Support for this supposition would be provided by the temporal coincidence of increasing *Negro Pulido* standardization with increasing consumption of Tiwanaku goods in local graves. The pinnacle of Tiwanaku presence in San Pedro occurred between AD 700 and 1000 (i.e., the Coyo Phase; Berenguer and Dauelsberg, 1989:158–159), during the transformation of *Negro Pulido* to *Gris Grueso Pulido* (Berenguer, n.d.:9). Nonetheless, the development of the *Negro Pulido* style may have been related to the *initial* phases of Tiwanaku influence, and a more empirical examination of this issue from a local perspective may offer valuable insights to changing understandings of highland-San Pedro interaction and the structure of the Tiwanaku polity. The present study employs statistical measures of vessel standardization in maximum width and height, and base and mouth diameter (see Figure 10.3) through early, middle and late *Negro Pulido* production phases (see Figure 10.4) as an index of intentional

stylistic homogenization which serves, in turn, as a possible material
manifestation of identity construction and community unification.

153
IDENTITY
CONSTRUCTION

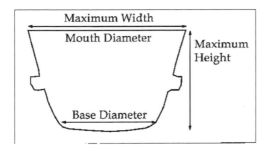

Figure 10.3. Metric Dimensions.

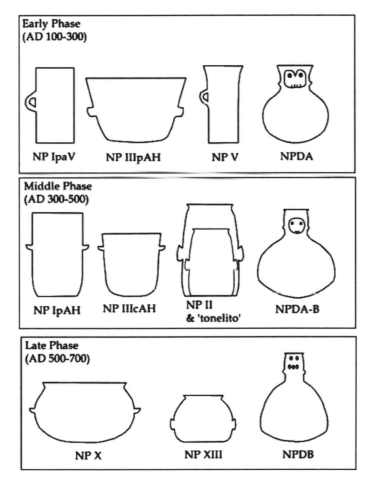

Figure 10.4. Early, Middle and Late *Negro Pulido* Production Phases.

Measures of Standardization

The statistical measure chosen to gauge vessel standardization was the coefficient of variation (CV). This coefficient usually serves the study of ceramic production levels and/or social complexity in that it is assumed that less complex societies or less formal (i.e., household vs. highly specialized) ceramic production generate more variable vessels (e.g., Blackman et al., 1993; Costin, 1991; Costin and Hagstrum, 1995; Feinman et al., 1984; Rice, 1981, 1989, 1991, 1996; Stark, 1995; Underhill, 1991). Variation in ceramic standardization is generally presumed to reflect different degrees of centralization in production, although this is also subject to debate (Arnold, 1991; Rice, 1991; Stark, 1995). The CV is the standard deviation expressed as a percentage of the mean. The higher the variation within the sample, the closer the standard deviation is to the mean, and the closer the CV is to 100%. Visually, this would appear as a graph as wide (SD) as it is tall (X). A high coefficient, then, implies low standardization and that potters are not ensuring or needing to ensure the regular replication of exact vessel metric dimensions such as base and rim diameter.

When used in ceramic analysis, the CV gives a general index of how regularly the dimensions of one ceramic type or style are reproduced. This is one of the more common measures of standardisation (Allen, 1992; Arnold and Nieves, 1992; Benco, 1988; Blackman et al., 1993; Costin and Hagstrum, 1995; Crown, 1995; Longacre et al., 1988; Mills, 1995), although there are others.[3] The CV has been rejected on occasion because of the presumed inability of testing the significance of differences between coefficients (Arnold and Nieves, 1992; Blackman et al., 1993; Stark, 1995) and because it is a relative measure. In other words, until recently, there were no universal limits to standardization; the importance of each coefficient was only revealed in comparison with another coefficients from the same historical and cultural context (Rice, 1991; Stark, 1995). Obviously, the inability to test the difference between coefficients, then, prevents researchers from making more powerful statements about changes in standards and standardization.

Both of these supposed limitations are unfounded, however. Although Eerkens and Bettinger (2001) suggest a formula from Feltz and Millcr (1996) which compares numerous sample CVs and follows an X^2 distribution, Lande (1977) and Lewontin (1966), argue that in samples with CVs smaller than 20%, a test for significance can be conducted by performing an F-test with two CVs. This is the procedure employed in the present study. Eerkens and Bettinger (2001) also provide universal limits to the perception of variation, that suggest that variation between approximately 5% and 60% is appreciable to the human eye, and therefore standardization measures between these parameters is probably relatively *intentional*.

Metric standardization is typically considered an *unintentional* measure of production levels or social organization. Archaeologists have seen the reproduction of exact vessel dimensions (e.g., mouth and base diameter) as a by-product of potter skill level, indicative of the amount of time potters devote to their craft and the level of organization of production (i.e., household vs. workshop). The level of ceramic production is then used to argue for various types of social organization (state vs. chiefdom). Stylistic or decorative uniformity, however, is not simply an unconscious by-product of productive organization or technique (cf. Costin and Hagstrum, 1995), but a sought-after indication of skill and potentially a conscious element applied (or not) according to the intentions of the potter and social circumstances (Longacre, 1999). Thus, any variation in the vessel dimensions is presumed here to reflect a certain degree of intention on the part of the potter, and perhaps an increasing or decreasing interest in the reproduction of a standardized (read homogeneous), potentially emblematic, material form.

Standardization Levels

The present study sought to trace the development of the highly distinctive *Negro Pulido* style and assess its homogenization/standardization over time. Toward this end, a database for 1190 whole vessels, including shape class, catalogue number, and millimeter dimensions for Maximum Width, Maximum Height, Mouth Diameter and Base Diameter was compiled.[4] These data provided the quantitative basis for the calculation of metric standardization indices. Values for the various metric dimensions were pooled to give an index of standardization for each vessel shape (see Table 10.1), while values for the different shape classes were pooled to provide and index for different chronological periods (see Table 10.2).

Table 10.1. Coefficient of Variation by Ceramic Type and Chronological Period

Ceramic type	CV	TL Dates	Phase	Period
RP	19.26		Toconao	300 BC–AD 100
NP V	5.27		Toconao	
NP IpaV	15.72	AD 90 + 200	Toconao	
NP IIIpAH	9.07	AD 140–325 + 190	Sequitor	AD 100–400
NPDA	14.33	AD 160 + 180	Sequitor	
NP IpAH	17.01	AD 230 + 160	Sequitor	
NPDA-B	10.90	AD 310 + 160	Sequitor	
NP I/III[a]	15.90		Sequitor	
NP IIIc	17.02	AD 560 + 145	Sequitor	
NP II	11.96	AD 720 + 95[b]	Sequitor-Quitor	
NP II (tonelito)	16.12		Sequitor-Quitor	
NP X	18.20		Quitor	AD 400–700
NP XIII	19.19	AD 620 + 199[b]	Quitor	
NPDB	11.24	AD 720 + 95	Quitor	

[a]Type NP I/II was established to accommodate ambiguous vessels that could been late variants of either class (Tarragó, 1989).
[b]TL dates (Berenguer et al., 1986) for individual tombs, not for entire type classes.

Table 10.2. Coefficients of Variation by
Chronological Period

	Early	Middle	Late
HEIGHT	12.31	14.19	15.15
WIDTH	11.85	15.30	14.75
MOUTH DIAMETER	13.28	17.34	19.75
BASE DIAMETER	14.76	15.91	18.97

Table 10.3. Significant Differences between Production Phase
Coefficients by Metric Attributes (F-Ratios: $CVmax^2/CVmin^2$)

Metric attribute	Periods	Ratio	F Distribution[a]
HEIGHT	Middle/Early	1.328767	*0.032164*
	Late/Early	1.514639	**0.005319**
	Late/Middle	1.139884	0.098643
WIDTH	Middle/Early	1.667041	**0.000434**
	Late/Early	1.549342	**0.003076**
	Middle/Late	1.075967	0.240953
MOUTH DIAMETER	Middle/Early	1.704912	**0.000459**
	Late/Early	2.21176	**1.89E-06**
	Late/Middle	1.297287	**0.005887**
BASE DIAMETER	Middle/Early	1.161897	0.161593
	Late/Early	1.651817	**0.000968**
	Late/Middle	1.421655	**0.000262**

[a] *Italic* result: significant at 0.05, **Bold** result: significant at 0.01

These values were then compared between periods to see whether any change in standardization levels was significant through time (see Table 10.3).

Interpretation

Variation in Standardization Levels

The general trends evident in this analysis are as follows:

1. Standardization levels in *Negro Pulido* are very different from those of *Rojo Pulido*.
2. These standardization levels are at their highest at the inception of *Negro Pulido*.
3. Levels decrease through time, eventually resulting in the transformation of the *Negro Pulido* style into *Gris Grueso Pulido*.
4. Significant differences are found primarily between early and late *Negro Pulido* production phases.

Ethnographic studies of ceramic production have produced CVs between 3% and 10% for specialized ceramicists and between 10% and 15% for non-specialists (Arnold, 1991; Arnold and Nieves, 1992; Longacre et al., 1988; Stark, 1995). These studies, however, are able to ask producers about their size categories, thus provide standardization measures within emic classification systems. Archaeological studies tend to lump emic vessel classes (Longacre et al., 1988) because they are not able to speak directly with producers, and as a result, supply slightly inflated CVs between 15% and 30% for both specialized and non-specialized producers (Allen, 1992; Blackman et al., 1993; Crown, 1995; Longacre et al., 1988). A few have even obtained CVs between 20% and 50% (Costin and Hagstrum, 1995).

In comparison with these values, Table 10.1 reveals that throughout the history of its production *Negro Pulido* metric standardization is relatively high across all types. This is only to be expected considering the aesthetic homogeneity and exclusive mortuary use of this style. Specifically, CVs fall between 10% and 20% with slightly more variation in base and mouth diameters than in maximum heights and widths. This difference in the variation of metric attributes has been identified in other studies too (Crown, 1995; Mills, 1995) and would suggest that more variation is tolerated in base and mouth diameters, and that height and width are more important defining attributes of vessels.

Table 10.1 shows that the earliest *Negro Pulido* shapes are the most standardized (CV = 5. 27%–15.72%), even though immediately preceding and at times contemporary *Rojo Pulido* ceramics show a high level of variability (CV = 19.26%). Through time, we can see the CVs rise, reflecting a relaxation of dimensional standards over time until the later *Negro Pulido* types are produced with variation levels similar to that of *Rojo Pulido* (CVs = 18.20% and 19.19%, NP X and NP XIII respectively). Table 10.2 also illustrates this increase through successive *Negro Pulido* production phases: the early phase shows CVs from 12% to 15%, and the late phase shows values from 15% to 20%. Even so, Table 10.3 confirms that this increase is never abrupt. Differences are only highly and regularly significant between the early and late phases.

The decline in metric homogeneity of the *Negro Pulido* ceramic tradition terminates in the production of a *Gris Grueso Pulido* tradition which is characterized by fewer shape classes, thicker vessel walls, more variable color treatment and less careful surface polishing (see Berenguer, n.d.:9). In fact, *Gris Grueso Pulido* attributes appear to be degraded from or derivative of *Negro Pulido* norms. A gradual trend away from initially high standards of *Negro Pulido* production slowly over time may have 'devolved' into a simpler, less homogeneous, more variable *Gris Grueso Pulido* tradition. In consulting diachronic tables and graphs, then, we can see that *Negro Pulido* ceramic began, AD 100, more standardized than ever. Standardization did not develop over time as potters became more skilled and efficient, as suggested by previous studies, but became less important. And more important to the present paper, this process began *before* the rise of Tiwanaku influence in the area.

Link to Asymmetrical Power Relations

There is the possibility that the standardization of this material culture is tied to changing political relationships on a regional level due to the early rise in regional prominence of the Tiwanaku federation around 200 AD. Tiwanaku material culture, however, does not gain prominence in local graves until the middle to late phases of *Negro Pulido* production when there is a decline in aesthetic standards as a whole, eventually resulting in the production of *Gris Grueso Pulido*. It could be that material homogeneity in San Pedro is not a product of identity construction, or that *Negro Pulido* ceramics were not 'emblematic' of a community identity. Although *Negro Pulido* is used predominantly as a mortuary ceramic, this does not entirely explain its high standardization nor its decline. Both *Rojo Pulido* and *Gris Grueso Pulido* were used as grave goods and display much lower stylistic and metric standardization levels. Moreover, it is difficult to ascertain the true 'meaning' or symbolic function of these vessels, and stylistic differences probably had several functions in the past. That *Negro Pulido* was traded in much the same manner as other ceramic traditions throughout the regions—in small quantities to very specific centers (Llagostera, Costa and Téllez, 1988; Núñez and Dillehay, 1995; Stovel, 2002)—suggests, however, that vessels from these traditions represented special links between individuals and specific communities and in this way served an 'emblematic' function. We are still confronted with explaining high *Negro Pulido* standards in comparison with other local wares, their decline through time, and the maintenance of a discrete and distinctive San Pedro aesthetic through so many years of regular and abundant interaction.

It may be that Tiwanaku influence did not take the form of ethnic attribution (i.e., an imposed, state-defined San Pedro identity), nor did it engender salient ethnic affiliation. This would support the conclusion that Tiwanaku did not have a significant impact on local political and economic behavior. It is more likely that a unified communal identity, encapsulated in *Negro Pulido* homogeneity, developed before Tiwanaku influence, during the expansion of regional trade relationships where self-differentiation was an important tool in the negotiation of exchange. Identity was subsequently overtaken by metallurgy and other manufacturing activities in the face of intensifying trade relationships, including those with Tiwanaku, which were no longer antagonistic but collaborative (Martínez, 1998; Núñez and Dillehay, 1995; Stovel, 2002). In particular, it would appear that that competition, requiring the development of a salient group identity, was more significant before the peak of Tiwanaku influence, giving more support to the suggestion that interaction with the highland state was relatively innocuous.

Conclusions

The current study explored the production of a salient material style during a period of intense regional interaction and the rise of potentially asymmetrical power relations between local inhabitants and members of a highly influential religious and economic highland center. It presumed to link production of this homogeneous style with the political and economic power negotiation in order to 1) provide further evidence of ethnic identity construction in prehistory and 2) test the regional impact of Tiwanaku from a local perspective. There is no clear-cut support for any aggressive local impact on the part of Tiwanaku elite, which may require a re-examination of the peer polity or prestige economy models currently in use (e.g., Berenguer and Dauelsberg, 1989). Evidence provided here, however, concurs with the current literature (e.g., Berenguer, 1998) that relations with Tiwanaku were not antagonistic and that the polity may have promoted economic activity in the area (Núñez and Dillehay, 1995), thus refocusing local production from ceramics to other realms.

Certainly, we need to enhance our understanding of the period immediately prior to the introduction of interaction with Tiwanaku to explain the development of such a homogeneous stylistic tradition. Current models of identity construction are excessively focused on competitive or antagonistic causes of differentiation (e.g., Comaroff, 1998; Hill, 1998; Hodder, 1982). An extremely valuable future avenue of research would involve exploring alternative explanations for the persistence of a distinctive and homogeneous material style within contexts of trade and exchange. I would argue that *Negro Pulido* still represents the intentional production, maintenance, and negotiation of unified community identity, but we may find that such a discrete and intentionally distinctive identity develops in non-competitive contexts (e.g., Filer, 1990; Martínez, 1990, 1996, 1998; Terrell, 2001; Terrell et al., 1997; Terrell and Welsch, 1990; Welsch and Terrell, 1998). It bchooves us now to consider other catalysts of *Negro Pulido* homogeneity after perhaps excessive concentration on Tiwanaku.

Acknowledgements

The author would like to thank the staff and directors of the Instituto de Investigación Arqueológica y Museo "R.P. Gustavo Le Paige S.J." (IIAM) de la Universidad Católica del Norte of San Pedro of Atacama, Chile, for their inestimable support and aid. In particular, thanks is given to Lautaro Núñez, Francisco Téllcz, and those unnamed assistants who measured so many vessels in the museum during the 1980s. Willam Isbell warrants recognition of his support and advise and I would also thank Pedro Funari and Andrés Zarankin for the opportunity to participate in this volume.

Notes

[1] The terms used here will be ethnic *affiliation* and ethnic *attribution*.

[2] The literal translation of '*pulido*' is 'polished', but these vessels are actually highly burnished, so that is the translation provided here. The original Spanish terminology will be preserved throughout the rest of this paper.

[3]Such as the Brown-Forsythe test (Kvamme et al., 1996), the Krushkall-Wallis test, (Mills, 1995; Sinopoli, 1988), the F-ratio (Blackman et al., 1993; Longacre et al., 1988), and the Q distribution (Stark, 1995).

[4]The measurements used here were provided by San Pedro Museum staff (see acknowledgements). The database developed for this study involved classifying all available *Negro Pulido* vessels in the museum collection according to shape. This classification was then combined with the available measurements using vessel catalogue numbers.

References

Adorno, R., 1991, Images of *indios ladinos* in early colonial Peru. In *Transatlantic Encounters: Europeans and Andeans in the Sixteenth Century*, edited by, pp. 232–270. University of California Press, Berkeley.

Albarracín-Jordán, J., 1996a, De Tiwanaku a Uma-Pacajes: Continuidad y Cambio Cultural, *Beitrage zur allegeminen und vergleichenden Archaologie* 16:301–329.

    1996b, *Tiwanaku, arqueología regional y dinámica segmentaria*. Plural Editores, La Paz.

    1996c, Tiwanaku Settlement System: the Integration of Nested Hierarchies in the Lower Tiwanaku Valley. *Latin American Antiquity* 7(3):183–210.

Aldenderfer, M., editor, 1993, *Domestic Architecture, Ethnicity, and Complementarity in the South-Central Andes*. University of Iowa Press, Iowa City.

Allen, K., 1992, Iroquois Ceramic Production: A Case Study of Household Level Organization. In *Ceramic Production and Distribution: An Integrated Approach*, edited by G. Bey and C.A. Pool, pp. 133–154. Westview Press, Boulder.

Arnold, P. J., 1991, Dimensional Standardization and Production Scale in Mesoamerican Ceramics. *Latin American Antiquity* 2:363–370.

Arnold, D., and Nieves, A., 1992, Factors Affecting Ceramic Standardization. In *Ceramic Production and Distribution*, edited by G. Bey and C. Pool, pp. 93–113. Westview Press, Boulder.

Athens, J. S., 1992, Ethnicity and Adaptation: The Late Period-Cara Occupation in Northern Highland Ecuador. In *Resources, Power, and Interregional Interaction*, edited by E.M. Schortman and P.A. Urban, pp. 193–220. Plenum Press, New York.

Auger, R., Glass., M. F., MacEachern, S., and McCartney, P. H., editors, 1987, *Ethnicity and Culture*. Proceedings of the 18th Annual Conference of the Archaeological Association of the University of Calgary. University of Calgary Archaeological Association, Calgary.

Azoulay, K. G., 1997, Experience, Empathy, and Strategic Essentialism. *Cultural Studies* 11(1):89–110.

Benavente, M. A., Massone, C., and Winter, C. T., 1986, Larrache, evidencias atípicas ¿Tiwanaku en San Pedro de Atacama? *Revista Chungará* 16–17:67–73.

Benco, N., 1988, Morphological Standardization: An Approach to the Study of Craft Production. In *A Pot for all Reasons: Ceramic Ecology Revisited*, edited by C.C. Kolb and L.M. Lackey, pp. 57–71. Laboratory of Anthropology, Temple University, Philadelphia.

Berenguer, J., n.d., El norte grande en la prehistoria: donde el agua es oro, http://www.precolumbino.cl/inves/invest16.html, retrieved 5/13/02

    1984, Hallazgos La Aguada en San Pedro de Atacama, norte de Chile. *Gaceta Arqueológica Andina* 12.

    1986, Relaciones iconográficas de larga distancia en los Andes: nuevos ejemplos para un viejo problema. *Boletín del Museo de Arte Precolombino* 1:55–78.

    1993, Gorros, identidad e interacción en el desierto chileno antes y después del colapso de Tiwanaku. In *Identidad y prestigio en los Andes: gorros, turbantes y diademas*, edited by, pp. 41–64. Museo Chileno de Arte Precolumbino, Santiago de Chile.

    1998, La iconografía del poder en Tiwanaku y su rol en la integración de zonas de frontera. *Boletín del Museo Chileno de Arte Precolombino* 7: 19–37.

Berenguer, J., Castro, V., and Silva, C., 1980, Reflexiones acerca de la presencia Tiwanaku en el norte de Chile *Estudios Arqueológicos* 5:81–93.

Berenguer, J., and Dauelsberg, P., 1989, El Norte Grande en la órbita de Tiwanaku (400 a 1200 d. C.). In *Culturas de Chile: Prehistoria desde sus orígenes hasta los albores de la conquista*, edited by J. Hidalgo et al., pp. 129–180. Editorial Andrés Bello, Santiago de Chile.

Berenguer, J., Deza, A., Román, A., and Llagostera, A., 1986, La secuencia de Myriam Tarragó para San Pedro de Atacama: un test por termoluminiscencia, *Revista Chilena de Antropología* 5:17–54.

Berenguer, J. and Plaza, F., 1977, Revisión y critica de la terminología relacionada con la Cultura Tiwanaku en el ámbito Andino. *Sarance* 4:15–27.

Berenguer, J., Román, A., Deza, A., and Llagostera, A., 1988, Testing a Cultural Sequence for the Atacama Desert, *Current Anthropology* 29(2):341–346.

Blackman, M. J., Stein, G. J., and Vandiver, P. B., 1993, Standardization Hypothesis and Ceramic Mass Production: Technological, Compositional, and Metric Indexes of Craft Specialization at Tell Leilan, Syria, *American Antiquity* 58(1):60–80.

Blom, D., 1999, *Tiwanaku Regional Interaction and Social Identity: A Bioarchaeological Approach*, Ph. D. dissertation, University of Chicago.

Bowser, B., 2000, From Pottery to Politics: An Ethnoarchaeological Study of Political Factionalism, Ethnicity, and Domestic Pottery Style in the Ecuadorian Amazon, *Journal of Archaeological Method and Theory* 7(3): 219–248.

Bravo, L., 1991, Las evidencias puneñas en el oasis de San Pedro. In *Actas del XI Congreso de Arqueologia Chilena, Santiago, 1988*, pp. 115–120. Museo Nacional de Historia Natural, Sociedad Chilena de Arqueología, Santiago de Chile.

Browman, D., 1995–1996, Pragmatic Politics: Bolivian-Chilean Central Altiplanic Connections. *Diálogo Andino* 14/15:291–304.

1996, South Andean Federation and the Origins of Tiwanaku. In *Debating Complexity*, edited by D. A. Meyer, P.C. Dawson, and D. T. Hanna, pp. 607–613. Proceedings of the 26th Annual Conference of the Archaeological Association of the University of Calgary, Calgary.

1997, Political Institutional Factors Contributing to the Integration of the Tiwanaku State. In *Emergence and Change in Early Urban Societies*, edited by L. Manzanilla, pp. 229–241. Plenum Press, New York.

Brumfiel, E., 1994, Ethnic Groups and Political Development in Ancient Mexico. In *Factional Competition and Political Development In The New World*, edited by E. M. Brumfiel and J. W. Fox, pp. 89–102. Cambridge University Press, Cambridge.

Cahill, D., 1994, Color by Numbers: Racial and Ethnic Categories in the Viceroyalty of Peru, 1532–1824. *Journal of Latin American Studies* 26(2):325–346.

Collier, Jane F., Maurer, B., and Suárez-Navaz, L., 1995, Sanctioned Identities: Legal Constructions of Modern Personhood. *Identities* 2(1–2):1–27.

Comaroff, J. L., 1985, Of Totemism and Ethnicity: Consciousness, Practice and the Signs of Inequality. *Ethnos* 52(3–4):301–323.

1996, Ethnicity, Nationalism, and the Politics of Difference in an Age of Revolution. In *The Politics of Difference: Ethnic Premises in a World of Power*, edited by E. N. Wilmsen and P. McAllister, pp. 162–184. The University of Chicago Press, Chicago.

Combés, I., 1991, El Testamento Chiriguano: Una política desconocida del post 1892, *Bulletin de l'Institute Francaise des Etudes andines* 20(1):237–251.

Cope, R. D., 1994, *The Limits of Racial Domination: Plebian Society in Colonial Mexico City, 1660–1720*. University of Wisconsin Press, Madison.

Cordell, L. S., and Yannie, V. J., 1991, Ethnicity, Ethnogenesis, and the Individuals: A Processual Approach Toward Dialogue. In *Processual and Postprocessual Archaeologies: Multiple Ways of Knowing the Past*, edited by R. Preucel, pp. 96–107. Center for Archaeological Investigations, Occasional Paper No. 10. Southern Illinois University, Carbondale.

Costin, C., 1991, Craft Specialization: Issues in Defining, Documenting, and Explaining the Organization of Production. In *Archaeological Method and Theory*, edited by M.B. Schiffer, pp. 1–56. University of Arizona Press, Tucson.

Costin, C., and Hagstrum, M. B., 1995, Standardization, Labor Investment, Skill, and the Organization of Ceramic Production in Late Prehispanic Highland Peru. *American Antiquity* 60(4):619–639.

Crown, P. L., 1995, Changing Patterns of Pottery Manufacture and Trade in the Northern Rio Grande Region. In *Ceramic Production in the American Southwest*, edited by B. J Mills and P. L. Crown, pp. University of Arizona Press, Tucson.

de La Cadena, M., 1991, Las mujeres son más indias: etnicidad y género en una comunidad del Cusco. *Revista Andina* 9(1):7–29.

1996, The Political Tensions of Representations and Misrepresentations: Intellectuals and Mestizas in Cuzco (1919–1990). *Journal of Latin American Anthropology* 2(1):112–147.

Díaz-Andreu, M., and Champion, T., editors, 1996, *Nationalism and Archaeology in Europe*. Westview Press, Boulder.

Eerkens, J. W., and Bettinger, R. L., 2001, Techniques for Assessing Standardization in Artifact Assemblages: Can We Scale Material Variability? *American Antiquity* 66(3):493–504.

Emberling, G., 1997, Ethnicity in Complex Societies: Archaeological Perspectives. *Journal of Archaeological Research* 5(4):295–344.

1999, The Value of Tradition: The Development of Social Identities in Early Mesopotamian States. In *Material Symbols: Culture and Economy in Prehistory*, edited by J. E. Robb, pp. 277–301. Occasional Paper 26, Center for Archaeological Investigations. Southern Illinois University, Carbondale.

Feinman, G., Kowaleski, S., and Blanton, R., 1984, Modeling Ceramic Production and Organizational Change in the Pre- Hispanic Valley of Oaxaca, Mexico. In *The Many Dimensions of Pottery: Ceramics in Archaeology and Anthropology*, edited by S.E. van der Leeuw and A. Pritchard, pp. 295–338. Albert Esses can Giffen Instituut Voor Prae-en Protohistorie, Vol. 7. University of Amsterdam, Amsterdam.

Feltz, C. J. and Miller, G. E., 1996, Asymptotic Test for the Equality of Coefficients of Variation from K Populations. *Statistics in Medicine* 15 (6):647–658.

Fernández, J., 1978, Los chicas, los lipes y un posible enclave de la cultura de San Pedro de Atacama en la Puna limítrofe argentino-boliviana. *Estudios Atacameños* 6: 19–35.

Filer, C., 1990, Diversity of Cultures or Culture of Diversity? In *Sepik Heritage: Tradition and Change in Papua New Guinea*, edited by N. Lutkehaus, C. Kaufmann, W. E. Mitchell, D. Newton, L. Osmundsen, M. Schuster, pp. 116–128. Carolina Academic Press, Durham.

Goldstein, P., 1993a, House, Community and State in the Earliest Tiwanaku Colony: Domestic Patterns and State Integration at Omo M12, Moquegua. In *Domestic Architecture, Ethnicity and Comlementarity in the South Central Andes*, edited by M. S. Aldenderfer and C. Stanish, pp. 25–41. Iowa Press, Iowa City.

1993b, Tiwanaku Temples and State Expansion; A Tiwanaku Sunken-Court Temple in Moquegua, Peru. *Latin American Antiquity* 4(1):22–47.

Gootenberg, P., 1991, Population and Ethnicity in Early Republican Peru: Some Revisions. *Latin American Research Review* 26(3):109–157.

Harris, O., 1995, Ethnic Identity and Market Relations: Indians and Mestizos in the Andes. In *Ethnicity, Markets and Migration in the Andes*, edited by B. Larson and O. Harris, pp. 351–390. Duke University Press, Durham.

Hill, J. D., 1998, Violent Encounters: Ethnogenesis and Ethnocide in Long-Term Contact Situations. In *Studies in Culture Contact: Interaction, Culture Change and Archaeology*, edited by J. Cusick, pp. 146–171. Occasional Paper 25, Center for Archaeological Investigations. Southern Illinois University, Carbondale.

Hodder, I., 1979, Economic and Social Stress and Material Culture Patterning. *American Antiquity* 44(3):446–454.

1982, *Symbols in Action: Ethnoarchaeological Studies of Material Culture*. Cambridge University Press, Cambridge.

Jones, S., 1996, Discourses of Identity in the Interpretation of the Past. In *Cultural Identity and Archaeology: the Construction of European Communities*, edited by P. Graves-Brown, S. Jones, and C. Gamble, pp. 62–80. Routledge, London.

1997, *The Archaeology of Ethnicity: Constructing Identities in the Past and Present*, Routledge, London.

Kelly, M. and Kelly, R., 1980, Approaches to Ethnic Identification in Historical Archaeology. In *Archaeological Perspectives on Ethnicity in America: Afro-American and Asian American Culture History*, edited by R. Schuyler, pp. 133–143. Baywood Publishing Company Inc., New York.

Kohl, P. L., and Fawcett, C., editors, 1995, *Nationalism, Politics, and the Practice of Archaeology*. Cambridge University Press, Cambridge.

Kolata, A. L., 1993, *The Tiwanaku: Portrait of an Andean Civilization*. Blackwell, Cambridge, USA.

Kvamme, K. L., Stark, M. T., and Longacre, W. A., 1996, Alternative Procedures for Assessing Standardization in Ceramic Assemblages. *American Antiquity* 61(1):116–126.

Lande, R., 1977, On Comparing Coefficients of Variation. *Systematic Zoology* 26:214–217.

Lewontin, R. C., 1966, On the Measurement of Relative Variability. *Systematic Zoology* 15:141–142.

Llagostera, A., 1995, El componente cultural Aguada en San Pedro de Atacama. *Boletín del Museo Chileno de Arte Precolumbino* 6:9–34.

1996, San Pedro de Atacama: Nodo de complementariedad reticular. In *La integración surandina: cinco siglos después*, edited by J. Albó et al., pp. 17–42. Centro de Estudios Andinos Bartolomé de las Casas, Corporación Norte Grande Taller de Estudios Andinos. Universidad Católica del Norte, Antofagasta.

Llagostera M., A., Costa J., M., and Tellez C., F., 1988, *Interacciones transandinas en la formación y consolidación de la Cultura San Pedro*, unpublished manuscript, FONDECYT project 86/1016, Santiago de Chile.

Longacre, W., 1999, Standardization and Specialization: What's the Link? In *Pottery and People: A Dynamic Interaction*, edited by J. M. Skibo and G. M. Feinman, pp. 44–58. The University of Utah Press, Salt Lake City.

Longacre, W. A., Kvamme, K. L., and Kobayashi, M., 1988, Southwestern Pottery Standardization: An Ethnoarchaeological View from the Philippines. *The Kiva* 53:101–112.

MacEachern, S., 2001, Setting the Boundaries: Linguistics, Ethnicity, Colonialism, and Archaeology South of Lake Chad. In *Archaeology, Language and History: Essays on Culture and Ethnicity*, edited by J. Terrell, pp. 79–101. Bergin & Garvey, Westport.

1998, Scale, Style and Cultural Variation: Technological Traditions in the Northern Mandara Mountains. In *The Archaeology of Social Boundaries*, edited by M. T. Stark, pp. 107–131. Smithsonian Institution, Washington.

Martínez, J. L., 1990, Interetnicidad y complementariedad en el altiplano meridional: el caso Atacameño. *Andes, Antropología e Historia* 1:11–30.

1996, Papeles distantes, palabras quebradas: las informaciones sobre Lipes en el siglo XVI. In *La integración surandina: cinco siglos después*, edited by J. Albó et al., pp. 229–257. Centro de Estudios Andinos Bartolomé de las Casas, Corporación Norte Grande Taller de Estudios Andinos, Universidad Católica del Norte, Antofagasta.

1998, *Pueblos del Chañar y el Algarrobo: los Atacameños en el siglo XVII*. DIBAM, Santiago de Chile.

McGuire, R., 1982, The Study of Ethnicity in Historical Archaeology. *Journal of Anthropological Archaeology* 1:159–178.

Méndez, C., 1991, Los campesinos, la independencia y la iniciación de la Republica: el caso de los quichanos realistas: Ayacucho 1825–1828. In *Poder y Violencia en los Andes*, edited by H. Urbano. Centro de Estudios Regionales Andinos Bartolomé de las Casas, Cusco.

1996, *Incas sí, Indios no*: Notes on Peruvian Creole Nationalism and its Contemporary Crisis. *Journal of Latin American Studies* 28:197–225.

Mills, B. J., 1995, Problems in the Analysis of Standardization and Specialization. In *Ceramic Production in the American Southwest*, B. J. Mills and P. L. Crown. University of Arizona Press, Tucson.

Montané, J., 1963, La alfarería negra pulida. Congreso Internacional de Arqueología de San Pedro de Atacama. *Anales de la Universidad del Norte* 2: 43–46.

Mujica, E., 1996, La integración surandina durante el período Tiwanaku. In *La integración surandina: cinco siglos después*, edited by J. Albó et al., pp. 81–116. Centro de

Estudios Andinos Bartolomé de las Casas, Corporación Norte Grande Taller de Estudios Andinos. Universidad Católica del Norte, Antofagasta.

Munizaga, C., 1963, Tipos cerámicos del sitio de Coyo en la región de San Pedro de Atacama. Congreso Internacional de Arqueología de San Pedro de Atacama. *Anales de la Universidad del Norte* 2: 99–131.

Núñez Atencio, L., 1992, *Cultural y Conflicto en los Oasis de San Pedro de Atacama*, Editorial Universitaria, Santiago de Chile.

1996, Movilidad caravánica en el área centro sur andina: reflexiones y expectativas. In *La integración surandina: cinco siglos después*, edited by J. Albó et al., pp. 43–62. Centro de Estudios Andinos Bartolomé de las Casas, Corporación Norte Grande Taller de Estudios Andinos. Universidad Católica del Norte, Antofagasta.

Núñez Atencio, L. and Dillehay, T. S., 1995, *Movilidad giratoria, armonía social y desarrollo en los andes meridonales: patrones de tráfico e interacción económica*. Universidad Católica del Norte, Antofagasta.

Núñez Atencio, L., Zlatar, V. and Núñez H., P., 1975, Un circuito trashumantico entre la costa de pisagua y el borde occidental de la Pampa del Tamarugal, *Estudios Atacameños* 3:49–52.

Oakland Rodman, A., 1992, Textiles and Ethnicity: Tiwanaku in San Pedro de Atacama, North Chile. *Latin American Antiquity* 3(4):316–340.

Orellana, M., 1984, Influencias altiplánicas en San Pedro de Atacama. Primer Simposio de Arqueología Atacameña, San Pedro de Atacama,1983. *Estudios Atacameños* 7:197–208.

1985, Relaciones culturales entre Tiwanaku y San Pedro de Atacama. *Diálogo Andino* 4: 247–257.

1986, La cultura San Pedro de Atacama y sus relaciones con la civilización de Tiwanaku. *Prehistóricas* 1:29–38.

Penner, B. R., 1997, Old World Traditions, New World Landscapes: Ethnicity and Archaeology of Swiss-Appenzellers in the Colonial South Carolina Backcountry. *International Journal of Historical Archaeological* 1(4):257–251.

Pollard, H. P., 1994, Ethnicity and Political Control in a Complex Society: the Tarascan State of Prehispanic Mexico. In *Factional Competition and Political Development In The New World*, edited by E. Brumfiel and J. Fox, pp. 79–88. Cambridge University Press, Cambridge.

Rice, P., 1981, Evolution of Specialized Pottery Production: A Trial Model. *Current Anthropology* 22:219–240.

1989, Ceramic Diversity, Production, and Use. In *Quantifying Diversity in Archaeology*, edited by R.D. Leonard and G.T. Jones, pp. 109–117. Cambridge University Press, Cambridge.

1991, Specialization, Standardization, and Diversity: A Retrospective. In *The Ceramic Legacy of Anna O. Shepard*, edited by R. Bishop and F.W. Lange, pp. 257–279. University of Colorado Press, Niwot.

1996, Recent Ceramic Analysis 2: Composition, Production, and Theory, *Journal of Archaeological Research* 4(3):165–201.

Sackett, J. R., 1990, Style and Ethnicity in Archaeology: the Case for Isochrestism. In *Uses of Style in Archaeology*, edited by M. Conkey, pp. 32–43. Cambridge University Press, Cambridge.

1986, Isochrestism and Style: A Clarification. *Journal Of Anthropological Archaeology* 5(3):266–277.

1977, The Meaning of Style in Archaeology: a General Model. *American Antiquity* 42(3):369–380.

Serrancino, G., 1980, Tiwanaku desde San Pedro de Atacama. *Estudios Arqueologicos* 5:95–106.

Sharpe, B., 1986, Ethnography of a Regional System: Mental Maps and the Myth of States and Tribes in North-Central Nigeria. *Critique of Anthropology* 6(3):33–65.

Shennan, S. J., 1989, Introduction: Archaeological Approaches to Cultural Identity. In *Archaeological Approaches to Cultural Identity*, edited by S. J. Shennan, pp. 1–32. Unwin Hyman, London.

Sinopoli, C. M., 1988, The Organization of Craft Production at Vijayanagara, South India. *American Anthropologist* 90:580–597.

Smith, C. A., 1996, Myths. Intellectuals, and Race/Class/Gender Distinguished in the Formation of Latin American Nations. *Journal of Latin American Anthropology* 2(1):148–169.

Speth, J. D., 1988, Do We Need Concepts Like 'Mogollon', 'Anasazi', and 'Hohokam' Today? A Cultural Anthropological Perspective. *The Kiva* 53:201–204.

Spivak, G. C., 1988, Subaltern Studies: Deconstructing Historiography. In *Selected Subaltern Studies*, edited by R. Guha and G. C. Spivak, pp. 3–32. Oxford University Press, New York.

1993, *Outside in the Teaching Machine*. Routledge, New York.

Stahl, A. B., 1991, Ethnic Style and Ethnic Boundaries: A Diachronic Case Study from West-Central Ghana. *Ethnohistory* 38(3):250–275.

Stark, B. L., 1995, Problems in Analysis of Standardization and Specialization in Pottery. In *Ceramic Production in the American Southwest*, edited by B.J. Mills and P.L. Crow, pp. 231–267. University of Arizona Press, Tucson.

Stovel, E. M., 1997, *Habitational Analysis and Cultural Contact at Coyo Aldea, Northern Chile: the Surface Deposits*. Master's thesis, State University of New York at Binghamton.

2002, *The Importance Of Being Atacameño: Political Identity And Mortuary Ceramics In Northern Chile*. Ph.D. dissertation, State University of New York at Binghamton.

Tarragó, M., 1976, Alfarería típica de San Pedro de Atacama. *Estudios Atacameños* 4:37–64.

1977, Relaciones prehisp·nicas entre San Pedro de Atacama (Norte de Chile, y regiones aldeañas: la Quebrada de Humahuaca. *Estudios Atacameños* 5:50–60.

1984, La historia de los pueblos circumpuneños en relación con el altiplano y los Andes meridionales. *Estudios Atacameños* 7:116–132.

1989, *Contribución al conocimiento arqueológico de las poblaciones de los oasis de San Pedro de Atacama en relación con los otros pueblos puneños, en especial, el sector septentrional del valle Calchaquí*, Ph.D. dissertation, Universidad de Rosario, Rosario, Argentina.

1994, Intercambio entre Atacama y el Borde de Puna. In *Taller 'De Costa a Selva': Producción e Intercambio entre los Pueblos Agroalfareros de los Andes Centro Sur*, edited by M. E. Albeck, pp. 199–209, Instituto Interdisciplinario Tilcara, Facultad de Filosofía y Letras, Universidad de Buenos Aires, Buenos Aires

Terrell, J., 2001, Ethnolinguistic Groups, Language, Boundaries and Culture History: A Sociolinguistic Model. In *Archaeology, Language and History: Essays on Culture and Ethnicity*, edited by J. Terrell, pp. 199–221. Bergin & Garvey, Westport.

Terrell, J., Hunt, T. L., Gosden, C., 1997, Dimensions of Social Life in the Pacific: Human Diversity and the Myth of the Primitive Isolate. *Current Anthropology* 38(2):155–195.

Terrell, J., and Welsch, R. L., 1990, Trade, Networks, Areal Integration, and Diversity Along the North Coast of New Guinea. *Asian Perspectives* 29(2):155–165.

Thomas, C., Massone, C., Benavente, A., 1984, Sistematización de la alfarería del área de San Pedro de Atacama. *Revista Chilena de Antropología* 4: 49–120.

Torres, C. M. and Conklin, W., 1995, Exploring the San Pedro de Atacama/Tiwanaku Relationship. In *Andean Art: Visual Expression and its Relation to Andean Beliefs and Values*, edited by P. Dransart, pp. 78–108. Avebury, Aldershot.

Underhill, A., 1991, Pottery Production in Chiefdoms: the Longshan Period in northern China. *World Archaeology* 23(1):12–27.

Uribe, M., n.d., *La alfafería Tiwanaku desde su periferia*. Unpublished report, FONDECYT Project 1970073, 1997.

Varela, H. H., and Cocilovo, J. A., 2000, Structure of the Prehistoric Population of San Pedro de Atacama. *Current Anthropology* 41(1):125–132.

Wells, P., 1998, Culture Contact, Identity and Change in the European Provinces of the Roman Empire. In *Studies in Culture Contact: Interaction, Culture Change and Archaeology*, edited by J. Cusick, pp. 316–334. Occasional Paper 25, Center for Archaeological Investigations. Southern Illinois University: Carbondale.

Welsch, R. L. and Terrell, J., 1998, Material Culture, Social Fields, and Social Boundaries on the Sepik Coast of New Guinea. In *The Archaeology of Social Boundaries*, edited by Miriam T. Stark, pp. 50–77. Smithsonian Institution Press, Washington, D.C.

Wiessner, P., 1984, Reconsidering the Behavioral Basis for Style: A Case Study among the Kalahari San. *Journal of Anthropological Archaeology* 3(3): 190–234.

1983, Style and Social Information in Kalahari San Projectile Points. *American Antiquity* 48(2):253–276.

Rethinking Stereotypes and the History of Research on Jê Populations in South Brazil

11

An Interdisciplinary Point of View

Francisco Silva Noelli

Introduction

During the last 120 years, many researchers have tried to define the human populations that inhabited southern Brazil and neighboring areas, including the state of São Paulo in Brazil and the Province of Misiones in Argentina. Certain archaeological assemblages were tied to hunter-gatherers (i.e., Umbu and Humaitá traditions; Dias, 1994; Hoeltz, 1997) and generalized hunter-gatherers and ceramists (i.e., Vieira tradition; Brochado, 1984; González, 1998) as well as Jê-speaking (Taquara, Casa de Pedra and Itararé traditions; Brochado, 1984; González, 1998) and Tupi-Guarani speaking (Guarani groups; Brochado, 1984, 1989; Noelli, 1993, 1996a, 1998) tropical agriculturalists and ceramists. In the last 35 years, data were coherently tabulated, synthesized and ordered into sets called archaeological traditions (Terminologia, 1976), strictly defined according to cultural-historic, diffusionist, cultural and ecological determinism. This program was coordinated by Betty Meggers and Clifford Evans for South and Central America (see critical analysis

167

in Barreto, 1998; Faria, 1989; Funari, 1989, 1991, 1994, 1995, 1998; Lathrap, 1970a, 1973; E. Neves, 1995, 1998; W. Neves, 1988; Noelli, 1993, 1996a, b, 1998; Roosevelt, 1991a, b, 1995).

The Brazilian version of Meggers and Evans's synopsis has been called The National Program of Archaeological Research or PRON-APA developed by 11 archeologists in 9 states between 1965 and 1970 (Dias, 1995; Meggers, 1985, 1992; Meggers and Evans, 1978; PRONAPA, 1970). As a rule, the PRONAPA approach involved a pre-supposition suggested by Meggers (1955: 129) in the 50s, which "deals with culture artificially separated from human beings". Such a premise justified a closed and refractory interpretation of ideas and facts from the Americanist scene and adopted a strategy of data selection that set aside preexisting information and results obtained by researchers employing other ideas. Its application caused the formulation of water-tight models and hypotheses set apart from those developed in other disciplines. Archaeological research was thus dissociated from Anthropology and the other social sciences whose development in Brazil hailed from the 19th century. The PRONAPA intervention caused an artificial picture of the past based on "few and often irrelevant attributes" (Barreto, 1998: 577) of pottery and lithic samples collected at the surface or in test pits.

Fieldwork developed at a terrific speed (with only one or two days on each site), such that Evans and Meggers' (1965) program of activities in the *Guia para prospecção arqueológica no Brasil* (Guide to Archaeological Prospecting in Brazil) could be complied with, with evidence collected from the surface or in small test pits. However, PRONAPA archeologists did not endeavor to understand regional contexts, incorporate environmental adaptation/management studies and physical anthropology, research material culture or face sociological and politically directed questions within the different possibilities of interdisciplinary archaeological research. Roosevelt (1991a: 107) writes that "their methods of excavation and analysis combined material of different periods and artificially composed the archaeological sequence". They thereby built a set of events interpreted "under the aegis of a non-historic ecological determinism" (Funari, 1998), followed by publications merely concerned with transforming scanty evidence into facts and numbers. The result of this prevailing academic context, still at large and under-discussed at present, is an approach which does not contribute to the study of material specifics and the possible historical and sociological realities lived by the populations in the area classified as "southern Brazil and neighboring areas."

As no strict study of collections and archaeological sites at local and regional levels exists, an alternative and interdisciplinary approach is needed that would take into account the uniformity of morphological attributes of pottery and lithic from approximately 1,350 archaeological sites (Figure 11.1) (Noelli, in press). It would also establish a generic association among elements of the "Taquara, Itararé and Cada de Pedra traditions" and material culture of southern Jê populations. At the same time, the material assemblages of hunter-gatherering Umbu and

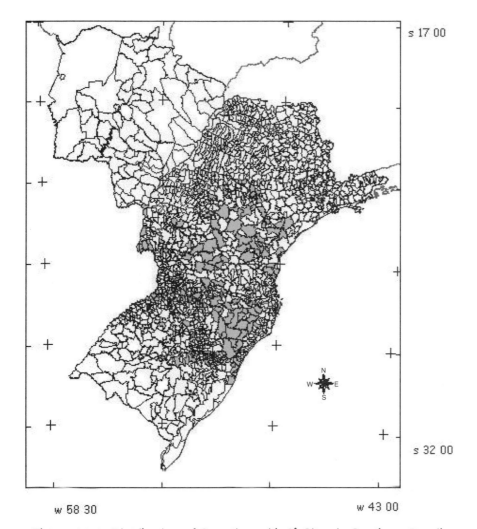

Figure 11.1. Distribution of Counties with Jê Sites in Southern Brazil.

Humaitá populations and the ceramic producing Minuano, Charrua and Guarani populations are distinct from those of southern Jê populations, except where there is archaeological or historical evidence of contact.

When one looks beyond the archaeological literature and deviates from the PRONAPA perspective, one can see that information on the Kaingang and Xokleng populations comes from different sources. These include scientific studies undertaken since the 19th century, and official and personal documents dating from the 16th century to the present, written by military and religious people, and civilians. Data are available from over 1,100 published titles for the Kaingangs (Noelli et al., 1998) and over 600 for the Xokleng (Noelli et al., m.s.), notwithstanding innumerous unpublished documents in various public and private archives found in Brazil and abroad. Unfortunately, and because of the predominance of PRONAPA procedures, this information has not been consistently used by archeologists who have always enhanced poor compilations and distorted analogies with historical and ethnographical data (e.g., Becker, 1975a, b, 1985, 1991; Chmyz, 1981; E. Miller, 1971; Schmitz and Becker, 1991).

With this situation in mind, the aim of this paper is twofold. The first deals with the chief PRONAPA formulations and conclusions concerning the "Itararé, Taquara and Casa de Pedra archaeological traditions". This would highlight the water-tight scenery of the last four decades on their origin and definition. The second comprises my interpretation of the entire set of information on the southern Jê populations, while providing observations about their history, origin and expansion in southern Brazil, Misiones Province and surrounding area of Itaipu dam in Paraguay. At the same time, I will also describe the manner by which various ideas and facts previous to and contemporary with the PRONAPA activities have been neglected or indirectly employed from second or third hand usage.

My endeavor is to avoid falling into the constant reproduction of the PRONAPA environment and to contribute towards an alternative interpretation that would see the Kaingang and the Xokleng peoples as integrating parts of the multicultural complex that defines the Jê populations of central Brazil. I would also like to enhance a fundamental premise for the basis of my suggestion: pains must be taken to establish the correlations between the archaeological past and the ethnographic present according to the strict approach employed by Wüst (1998) in the Bororo case. The reanalysis and reinterpretation of archaeological collections lying in museums and laboratories should be undertaken; likewise, permanent regional research should be maintained, while ethno-archaeological research, physical anthropology and the critical integration of existing historical and ethnographical information all should be undertaken.

Pronapa, Its Followers in Southern Brazil, and the Establishment of Archaeological Traditions

Following PRONAPA conventions, Eurico Th. Miller, José Proenza Brochado, Wilson F. Piazza, Igor Chmyz, José W. Rauth and Sílvia Maranca found several archaeological sites and substantially enlarged the archaeological map of the south of Brazil and of São Paulo. They included areas which had not been researched until the mid-1960s, including the interior of the states of Paraná and Santa Catarina. In the 1960s and 1970s, in the states of Rio Grande do Sul, Paraná and Santa Catarina, other researchers adopted the PRONAPA methodology and ideas. Pedro I. Schmitz, Ítala B. Becker, Guilherme Naue, Fernando La Salvia, Pedro Mentz Ribeiro, João A. Rohr, Alroino Eble, Oldemar Blasi may all be considered "pronapians" (Meggers, 1985: 369–370). The next generation of archaeologists may be also included to a certain extent, especially researchers of the 70s and 80s who perpetuated PRONAPA ideas and aims. This same generation of archeologists was inserted within the interests of the political and "feudal" academic complex dominated by PRONAPA archeologists and their followers (Funari, 1989, 1994, 1995, 1998; Roosevelt, 1991a, b, 1995).

Although they mention archaeological works published since the 19th century, the PRONAPA archeologists take into consideration exclusively the results of their own activities derived from their central aim of"defin(ing) routes of pottery diffusion" (Dias, 1994, 1995). They were successful in defining for the first time the archaeological assemblages of Jê populations which, until then, had only been mentioned occasionally and which did not appear in the few syntheses related to southern Brazil and neighboring areas published by professional archeologists up to the early 60s (Howard, 1948; Silva and Meggers, 1963; Willey, 1949). The exceptions, restricted to relatively small areas, consisted of research by Serrano (1936, 1937) in the coastal area and within the Kaingang territory in the northeastern part of Rio Grande do Sul (the latter was based on second-hand information), and work published by Menghin (1957) on northeastern Argentina. Compounding the research work undertaken in the 60s and that of the late 50s, the PRONAPA archeologists and their followers were able to collect sufficient material to give a general panorama of the existence of what they initially defined as "non-Guarani pottery". Besides these scanty studies, the greatest impediment to regional syntheses that would allow the identification of southern Jê archaeological assemblages was the absence of comparative results and scientific training.

By the late 1960s, the PRONAPA interpretation suggested three archaeological traditions for south Brazil and the state of São Paulo. They were called Itararé, Casa de Pedra and Taquara, defined during 1968 when the first systematic comparisons between data from south Brazil and those of Misiones, Argentina, were undertaken. According to the PRONAPA methodology, cultural traditions were defined by traits found in earthenware and/or ceramic fragments, such as the temper, color, surface treatment, sometimes pottery forms, or even the different environments where archaeological sites were located (for methods, see Meggers and Evans, [1967] 1970; for a detailed description of the archaeological record, see Brochado, 1984; 109–138).

In the Second Symposium of Archeology in the Plata Region Igor Chmyz (1968) suggested the definition of two archaeological traditions. He based his study chiefly on the characteristics of earthenware vessels and, at a lower key, on the types of sites occupied and on the lithic material found in the southeastern part of the state of São Paulo, in the states of Paraná and Santa Catarina, and in Misiones, Argentina. These traditions were called Itararé and Casa de Pedra.

In the same symposium, Pedro I. Schmitz (1968: 128) included evidence from the state of Rio Grande do Sul and thus also contributed toward a synthesis of pottery traditions in south Brazil. In fact, he enlarged the area of occurrence of archaeological record of the Itararé and Casa de Pedra traditions. Without using the PRONAPA terminology, Schmitz (1968: 128) qualified the nomenclature of the three "great ceramic native complexes" in the south of Brazil as of "highly short-lived validity" and "an attempt subjected to many revisions". He himself mentioned them in a highly vague manner:"Tupi-Guarani complex", "Cerritos and Vieira phases"; "southern Gê."

A few months thence, official PRONAPA members met in Belém, state of Pará, to compare their data (Meggers, 1985, 1992; PRONAPA, 1970) and ratified Chmyz's suggestions. Revising their general data on south Brazil, they suggested a third archaeological tradition, called "Taquara" by Eurico Th. Miller (Meggers and Evans, 1978; PRONAPA, 1970: 6–9). Following the PRONAPA tradition with regard to the notion of tradition and employing what was established in Belém for the traditions under analysis, Schmitz never attempted to establish a relationships between the archaeological record and the "southern Gê" populations mentioned in his 1968 research work.

It should be emphasized that it was during this period that the material distinctions between the archaeological assemblages of the various ceramist populations of south Brazil were defined. When he compared evidences for the Guarani, southern Jê and Charrua/Minuano populations, Schmitz (1968: 138) concluded that "up to now no single type common to two or three of the great pottery traditions of southern Brazil has been discovered. This shows that their development was independent".

Although these general conclusions were of a passing nature and might be revised, they have been repeated and accepted to the present day even by researchers that have employed different approaches (Barreto, 1988; Blasi 1973; Blasis, 1988; Brochado, 1984; Caggiano, 1984; Chmyz, 1968, 1971, 1976; González, 1998; Kern, 1981, 1994; Meggers and Evans, 1978; Neves, 1984; Noelli, 1993, 1996a and c, 1998; Poujade, 1992; Prous, 1992; Reis, 1980; Ribeiro, 1991; Robhran, 1988; Schmitz, 1968, 1972, 1973, 1977, [1979] 1981, 1988, 1991; Schmitz and Brochado, [1972] 1981a, [1974] 1981b)

In 1988, although no new material evidence was shown (except more archaeological sites), and no reevaluation of the problem from other points of view had been attempted, Schmitz substantially altered his preliminary conclusions in another synthesis of the same "three traditions" according to data available till that year:

> In spite of commonly using such nomenclature identifying the three pottery traditions, not all researchers agree which differences in the production technique, in the form and in the decoration of earthenware would be sufficiently distinct to form a tradition... For the time being it is clear that the complex forms a technological and cultural tradition. (Schmitz, 1988: 75)

Some time afterwards, in another synthesis of southern Brazil, Schmitz (1991: 9), again without new data or presuppositions, totally metamorphosed his preliminary conclusions on the "three ceramic traditions" in southern Brazil:

> The area shows dense Neolithic occupation which archeologists identified as three regional (ceramic) traditions: Taquara tradition in the south, Casa de Pedra tradition in the middle and Itararé tradition in the north. Externally

differences are so slight that it would be more correct to speak of a tradition
with three subtraditions.

173
RETHINKING
STEREOTYPES

Such an interpretative shift with regard to the nature of these populations, chiefly based on the same differences and similarities of pottery, indicates the limitations of a hermetic and refractory approach towards a set of facts and ideas in the broader scene of eastern South American ethnology. It reveals the instability of a model without sufficient data to uphold the differences among the three archaeological traditions. Brochado (personal communication, 1998), a former PRONAPA member, says that the establishment of these "three traditions" was a preposterous act and not the result of scientific investigation. Some of his colleagues working on the program were more interested in naming new "archaeological traditions" in a vast territory researched for the first time. According to Brochado, during the first PRONAPA meeting in Belém, there was no agreement on the definition of the three traditions. Meggers, the mastermind of the program and manager of the financial support, was followed without question. It was she who decided on the establishment of the Itararé, Casa de Pedra and Taquara traditions.

The PRONAPA Idea of the Geographic Origin of the Itararé, Taquara, and Casa de Pedra Traditions

Another idea adopted and developed by PRONAPA members which reflected the deep isolation of the Americanist context deals with the autochthonous origin of these three traditions of southern Brazil from evolutionist and diffusionist principles. It is based on Osvaldo Menghin's hypothesis (1957) about the continuity in "Alto Paraná" and "Eldorado" populations of the Argentine province of Misiones as deduced from the similarity existing in some lithic objects common to the two traditions. In PRONAPA terms, this means the continuity between hunter-gatherer populations of the Humaitá tradition and farmer populations of the Taquara, Casa de Pedra and Itararé traditions. The chief premises of this hypothesis is that the "Alto Paraná IV" populations which occupied the region since 8,000 B.P. went through 'neolithization' after 2,000 B.P. Through diffusion they adopted the technology of (unpolished) gravel smoothing and later turned to agriculture and to pottery manufacture (Menghin 1957). Such ideas were already known by future PRONAPA members as Schmitz (1959) and they soon appeared in the first PRONAPA reports (Chmyz, 1969: 114; Miller, 1967: 19; 1969: 46) and in later publications. In the late 70s, Schmitz (1981) analyzed Menghin's research and established correlations with archaeological results after the 50s. He considered the German archeologist's synthesis as "sufficiently worthwhile".

On the other hand, Menghin seemed to have based his ideas and interpretative model on the hypotheses of Canals Frau (1940, 1954: 294) with regard to the historical continuity between the Kaingang and

Pampean populations. In spite of the warning of Herbert Baldus (1941; 1954: 250; 1955; 1968: 296), an important Americanist, who proved that Canals Frau's was a speculative interpretation ("mere fantasy!") without any of the necessary foundations, PRONAPA members forged ahead. They gave little attention to catalogue work on material, sociological and anthropological data which showed abundant cultural relationships between the Kaingang/Xokleng and the other Jê populations. Syntheses by Ploetz and Métraux (1930; Métraux, [1946] 1963), Haekel (1952, 1953), Hicks (1966, 1971), and more recently by Khne (1979, 1980), have also shown the flimsiness of Menghin's and Canals Frau's hypotheses and conclusions.

Antonio Serrano's suggestions also derived from Canals Frau and Menghin. After 40 years of research in northeastern Argentina, he constructed a model of occupation in the area and suggested three general periods based on his interpretation of stratigraphic sequences and on a classification of the archaeological record: 1) "pre-ceramic"; 2) "early ceramist"; 3) late ceramist" (Serrano, 1972). To Menghin, the nomenclature "early" and "late" confirmed the continuity between the periods "Alto Paraná IV" and "Eldorado". Other important works that synthesized human occupation in northeastern Argentina reproduced these ideas without any criticism or discussions (Caggiano, 1984; Lafon, 1971, 1972; Poujade, 1992).

Willey's interpretation (1971: 459) given in his well-known book on the pre-history of the Americas, may also be considered a reproduction of Canals Frau's ideas, albeit indirectly. Writing from a detached position with regard to research in southern Brazil, Willey suggested that Taquara pottery would have originated from Vieira pottery. Several studies showed that this development is impossible since these populations had distinct cultural traditions (Brochado, 1984).

In spite of the factual results agreed upon or under discussion by Americanists, Menghin's hypothesis is still accepted by many researchers that study southern Brazil. Ribeiro (1991: 106) shares Miller's presupposition (1967: 1971) and considers that, with the exception of semi-subterranean houses and ceramic style, there is no difference in the archaeological register of the Humaitá and Taquara traditions. Kern (1981: 193–194), González (1998: 622) and Schmitz and Becker (1991: 275–276; Schmitz 1991: 9) share the same opinion too. These last two writers suggest the Rio Grande do Sul as the center of the Taquara tradition's origin. Later, Kern (1994: 78–79) would change his interpretation and follow the "Jê populations migration" model proposed by Brochado (1984). These populations would be the source of several "neolithic innovations" in the south.

Well-known researchers of other disciplines in the Social Sciences accepted these ideas without any reservations and brought them outside the boundaries of PRONAPA and South American archeology. Susnik (1975: 58; 1994: 44–46) considers Kaingang populations "pre-ceramic proto-colonisers" of south Brazil and Misiones. She bases her interpretation on the already obsolete notion of "marginal peoples" used by Lowie (1946, 1949) in his *Handbook of South American Indians*.

Although modifying Menghin's original hypothesis and in spite of taking into account the obvious relationship between the "three traditions" with the other Jê populations, archeologists have continued to reproduce, even if only partially, evolutionist and diffusionist ideas. *Arqueologia Brasileira* (Brazilian Archeology), the great Brazilian archaeological synthesis published by André Prous in 1992, suggests that "Taquara-Itararé" pottery would be related to a "(migratory) wave that goes beyond southern Brazil and northern Argentina and extends itself to central Brazil where it associates itself with distinct cultural patterns " (Prous, 1992: 329). Although the author's doubts prevent him from "accepting any evolutionary hypothesis "(1992: 331), he shows several similarities in the archaeological assemblages of the Humaitá and Taquara-Itararé traditions. With regard to the geographic origins of the "Taquara-Itararé" from the archaeological point of view, Prous concludes that "there are no hypotheses on this issue ... Someday it would probably be possible to associate this great 'wave' to an ancient dispersal of Jê populations: southern Jê (Taquara-Itararé) and central Jê (Una tradition and related forms)" (Prous, 1992: 329). Finally, Prous (1992: 330) suggests that "if we have to accept the chronological priority usually accepted in scientific nomenclature, the entire complex described up to now should be called Eldorado", as it was formerly by Menghin (1957).

After publicly repudiating PRONAPA conventions, José Brochado (1984, 1991) showed that the general distribution of historical populations "coincided exactly with the distribution of archaeological materials", chiefly in the plateau regions of the steppes of northern São Paulo state and in the Araucarian forests and grasslands of southern Brazil, including Misiones Province (Brochado, 1984: 1–3). The author says that people would be related in their remotest origins (Macro-Jê origins) to the Pedra do Caboclo tradition. The latter is said to be one of the original places where South American pottery developed and whose most ancient variants are the simple globular forms of Mina and Taperinha in the lower Amazon basin dated to more than 8,000 years B.P in the lower Amazon (Roosevelt et al., 1991). Brochado based his hypothesis on evidence from pottery and, to a smaller degree, other material evidence and the geographic position of sites, comparing the Mina (lower Amazon) and Pedra do Caboclo (Northeast) traditions. His hypothesis explains the origin and the expansion of peoples that would be the ancestors of the Macro-Jê populations. Thus Brochado begins to work in a context that had been, until then, devoid of any archaeologically based explanation. Such evidence would correspond to the most ancient ancestors of the Macro-Jê branch which Brochado (Lathrap, 1970b) qualifies as representatives of the languages of "Ancient East Brazilian" whose relationships "to each other or to Gê has not been demonstrated" (Brochado, 1984: 3). Since these pottery traditions, considered the oldest, show scanty evidence owing to insufficient research, they cannot be associated to known historical peoples. The only exception is that of the Una tradition in the states of Bahia, Minas Gerais, Espírito Santo and Rio de Janeiro, which is related to speakers of the Puri family of the Macro-Jê branch. Albeit without any analysis of correlations with historical populations, the same may be said of the Periperi (Bahia) and Jataí (Goiás) styles, both lying, according to Brochado, in an intermediate region between the Amazon basin and south Brazil.

From archaeological and linguistic evidence, Brochado (1984) suggests that at first the Jê populations would have expanded towards the south and later adopted pottery by diffusion. The premise would be that the Jê populations had already been culturally defined and established in their territories in eastern and southern Brazil when pottery from the Amazon lower basin began to be diffused into their area. Although based on scanty information, according to Brochado (personal communication, 1990), the 1984 archaeological model does not diverge sufficiently from the linguistic ones (Davis, 1966, 1968; Rodrigues, 1986; Urban, 1992). Brochado (personal communication, 1992) says that the model needs adjustments and continuous trials as new data arrive. In this manner, the definition of prehistoric peoples may be fine-tuned and, when necessary, either related to historical populations or disposed of altogether.

PRONAPA Ideas on the Historical Continuity of Jê Populations

Coupled to the problems with defining archaeological traditions and geographical origin, there is still another unsolved discussion caused by PRONAPA hermetic attitudes concerning the definition of the historical continuity of indigenous populations of southern Brazil. Since PRONAPA adepts following Meggers statement of that "culture (is) artificially separated from human beings", they have not established the means by which historical populations could be related to archaeological evidence. As may be verified in much of the archaeological bibliography of southern Brazil, the sole criterion employed to establish such correlations was the oversimplified geographical superimposition of the archaeological record over historically known populations. Table 11.1 gives some examples of correlations between archaeological traditions and Kaingang and Xokleng populations.

Table 11.1. Archaeological Correlations with Kaingang and Xokleng Populations

Authors	Kaingang	Xokleng
La Salvia, Schmitz and Becker (1970)	Taquara	
E. Miller (1971: 54)	Taquara	
T. Miller (1978: 30, 33)	Itararé/Casa de Pedra	
Chmyz (1967: 35, 1981: 95)	Casa de Pedra	Itararé
Brochado (1984: 109)	Itararé/Case de Pedra	Taquara/Taquaruçu
Schmitz and Becker (1991: 252)	Taquara	
Prous (1992: 329)	Jês meridionais = Taquara-Itararé	

An interpretative archeology should be more restrained, respecting the past and never seeking the final word. (Barret, 1996: 578)

In spite of several problems with historical continuity, it is the present author's opinion that the discussion on the Jê populations in southern Brazil has been adequately redefined. Although existing data have been obtained from superficial archaeological studies and interpreted solely by unicausal determinist and diffusionist presuppositions, it may be stated that the general sequence of ceramist populations in southern Brazil are no longer hypothetical. Although archaeological assemblages have not revealed significant differences that would question distinguishing elements of the Guarani, Charrua, Minuano, Kaingang and Xokleng populations, it may be possible in the future to detect material evidence that would disclose distinct ethnicities. This has happened in the many cultural variations verified historically at the linguistic, biological, anthropological and sociological levels.

Contrary to hermetic PRONAPA dogmas, which interpreted archaeological evidence according to its own presuppositions, regardless of and unconnected to the development of international archeology and other Social Sciences in the Americanist context, data should be analyzed in a comparative way within a wider cultural environment; or rather, within the Macro-Jê linguistic branch and Jê culture and thus reflect the positions and discussions of both ethnologists and linguists. Without discarding the innumerable traps that such a model may contain, as Jones (1997), Sims-Williams (1998), and other Indo-European researchers have warned, I am of the opinion that there are enough data to start the building of a non-diffusionist model of the origin and expansion of Jê populations in southern Brazil. Needless to say, we are dealing with populations with sufficient linguistic, biological, ethnographic, historical, geographical and archaeological information. We are not in the world of ancient peoples or populations that need analogical juggling for analysis and interpretation.

Nor do I intend to reproduce Gustaf Kossinna's diffusionist models nor Nazi manipulations to prove the origin of the German peoples, as Funari (1997: 91) ambiguously commented on my analysis of Tupi expansion (Noelli, 1996a, 1998). This investigation is in its initial stages and its problems, dimensions and complexities have not yet been fully evaluated. Various theoretical and methodological possibilities from archeology and related sciences remain open to us (Noelli, 1996b).

To begin, what is the evidence that would explain the presence of the Kaingang and Xokleng populations in south Brazil? The first synthesis that included populations in the Macro-Jê branch was undertaken by Martius some 140 years ago. At that time he suggested the Jê denomination (Martius, 1867). Afterwards, von den Steinen (1894) employed the linguistic and comparative methods in use by the European academy in the late 19th century and revised Martius's research. He thus widened the Jê language set. Throughout the 20th century, comparative linguistics among Jêgroups was developed by Loukotka (1939, 1968), Mason (1950) and Davis (1966, 1968) and the Macro-Jê branch was defined. Thus the internal relationship between languages and populations has been established. It is clear that these internal relationships suggest evidence of contact among languages in general, and those of distinct branches or families. An approach that takes into account multivariate aspects of biological, sociological and anthropological aspects becomes necessary.

Present day ethnological, linguistic, biological and archaeological data support the hypothesis that Kaingang and Xokleng populations did not originate nor expand from southern Brazil. Their true, yet still-to-be-determined origin point probably lies in central Brazil somewhere above the 16° parallel where the great majority of Macro-Jê populations is concentrated (Davis, 1966, 1968; Jacques, 1988: 35–7; Rodrigues, 1986; Salzano and Callegari-Urban, 1992). This hypothesis finally obviates Menghin's, Canals Frau's and PRONAPA ideas about the autochthonous origin of "Itararé, Casa de Pedra and Taquara traditions" in south Brazil.

The relationships among Jê languages within the Macro-Jê branch show that the Kaingang language belongs to a complex that includes the languages of the Akwen groups (Xakriabá, Xavante and Xerente) and that of the Apinaye in the states of Minas Gerais, Mato Grosso and Goiás (Davis, 1966; Rodrigues, 1986). When a map of language distribution (Nimuendajú, 1981) is observed, one can see that these languages lie predominantly in central Brazil, centered in the basins of Tocantins (Xerente) and Araguaia (Xavante) rivers and in their lower courses (Apinayé), and in the area comprising the Tocantins, São Francisco and Paraná (Xakriabá) river basins. On the other hand, the Xokleng are also related to Jê groups outside southern Brazil found in the Kayapó, Timbira, Kren-Akarore, and Suyá complexes (Davis, 1966, 1968; Rodrigues, 1986). In Nimuendajú's, map the Kayapó lie along the Xingu and Paraná river basins, in the eastern part of the lower Tocantin river (Timbira), in the upper part of the Xingu river (Suyá), and in the middle sector of the São Manoel river (Kren-akarore).

From the above linguistic data, Urban (1992: 90–91) suggested a Macro-Jê genealogical tree and marked the process of separation and differentiation among the various languages. The first separation would have occurred among the southern Jê populations (Kaingang and Xokleng), which began their displacement towards the south of Brazil through the Brazilian Plateau territories (Figure 11.2). Although Urban (1992: 90) recognizes that migration causes are still unknown, Lathrap's (1970b) and Brochado's (1984; Brochado and Lathrap, 1980) hypotheses may be recalled. The movements of these populations out of the Amazon basin may have been caused by an important demographic increase which would have pushed them out of original areas. The separation process has not been sufficiently studied from an archaeological point of view and remains totally open to future reports in the

Figure 11.2. Map of Jê Routes.

archaeological record of central Brazil which might be associated to the Jê populations (with an exception made to Brochado's hypotheses mentioned above).

Besides showing that the Kaingang and Xokleng populations are not indigenous to southern Brazil, a set of important conclusions obtained in the mid-60s and not employed by archeologists lay down the parameters that differentiate the Kaingang and the Xokleng populations: 1) Kaingang and Xokleng are two distinct languages (Davis, 1966, 1968; whose research was updated in the 1970s by Wiesemann, 1978); 2) they are two biologically distinct populations (Salzano and Freire-Maia, 1967; Salzano and Sutton, 1965); 3) they are culturally distinct (Hicks, 1966, 1971; Schaden, 1958; Urban, 1992). Ironically, while revealing sharp distinctions between the Kaingang and Xokleng populations, studies still produce this information through unifying elements, according to comparative studies of social systems as suggested by Maybury-Lewis and others (1979). This means that when one is talking about archaeological populations, linguistic, biological or cultural information may also be referred to.

Nonetheless, in spite of evident biological, linguistic and cultural differences mentioned above, the archaeological record itself still does not shown marked differences and contrasts which might be employed to distinguish the Kaingang and the Xokleng populations in a material. Differences in sites seem to indicate distinct indices of adaptability and functionality, since all types are represented in different environments in southern Brazil and neighboring areas (Brochado, 1984). According to some researchers (Hicks, 1966, 1971; Métraux, 1963; Ploetz and Métraux, 1930), differences in other cultural aspects (material or symbolic) are still not taken into account, especially because of the absence of correlations with archaeological record.

Aware of the context surrounding the southern Jê populations, some researchers try to show that there are no significant differences between the pottery found in the archaeological record and that made by ethnographic populations or by populations mentioned by historical sources.

Taking into consideration the archaeological information known until the 1970s, Tom Miller Jr. (1978: 31) suggested in his conclusion to the ethnographic research on the Kaingang pottery of the state of São Paulo that

> ...for (1) technical, (2) form and (3) space- time distribution reasons, we are inclined to think that all the non-Tupi-Guarani regional traditions from the Rio Grande plateau ... to the Tietê basin should be considered as a single pottery tradition.

Miller argues that the temper, the color and the surface treatment are not sufficient elements to separate the two archaeological traditions analyzed (Itararé and Casa de Pedra), since the first two elements may have derived from the local supply of raw materials according to the geological characteristics of each region (Miller Jr., 1978: 32–33). Although he has presented a vast quantity of ethnographic information on raw materials, form, manufacture, functionality and nomenclature, Miller Jr. restricted himself to the material aspects of pottery from the archaeological perspective to support his hypothesis. He thus lost the opportunity of showing in an incisive and definite manner an alternative to the PRONAPA model.

On the other hand, there are several 19th and early 20th Century publications that document the southern Jê populations in their every day life and other interesting aspects important to archaeological interpretation. Since the PRONAPA methodology discarded these sources, another opportunity was lost to make headway in the construction of Kaingang and Xokleng history. These publications described either in a general or in a specific way the Kaingang and the Xokleng peoples have manufactured pottery since the 18th century, while recording other elements of material culture, their use in daily life and other sociologically useful information. A critical review of these sources and of ethnographic data would have avoided the beating around the bush attitude begun in the 1960s, even prior to the advent of PRONAPA. Archeologists could have seen Kaingang and Xokleng populations manufacturing and using their pottery.

In her employment of historical documents and ethnographic work which describe Kaingang and Xokleng pottery and in her preparations for future archaeological and ethnoarchaeological research, Fabìola Silva (1999) identified the following items organized chronologically from eldest sources for comparative purposes: 1) selection processes; 2) extraction and treatment of raw materials; 3) building techniques; 4) drying process; 5) baking process; 6) surface smoothing. She tried to identify general aspects of Kaingang and Xokleng technological systems to determine "operational sequences" in pottery production according to suggestions by Lemmonier (1992: 26). The researcher also prepared a preliminary characterization of southern Jê populations' technological styles from the Reedy and Reedy's point of view (1994). Her aim was to identify technological elements that could show the historical continuity between Kaingang and Xokleng populations and their precolonial ancestors. Silva systematized data found by Ambrosetti (1895), Barbosa (1916), Fernandes (1941), Kempf (1947), Keller (in Lovato, 1974), Mabilde (1896), Maniser (1930), MÈtraux (1963), T. Miller (1978), Moura (1905), Paula (1924), Piza (1938), Santos (1973), Serrano (1957), Simonian (1975) and Sullivan and Moore (1990). She concluded that the technological production styles of the Kaingang and the Xokleng peoples "are very similar, especially in the manufacturing process and, in particular, pottery making".

Kaingang and Xokleng pottery thus has a common technology and likeness determined by the same cultural matrix with the Jê populations. Silva (1999) thinks that cultural reasons may have influenced the uniformity of choice of certain elements (raw material, temper, surface smoothing etc). She exhorts researchers to abandon the PRONAPA point of view with regard to the three distinct traditions. At the same time, she emphasizes that pottery is not an absolute parameter for detecting differences between the Kaingang and Xokleng populations. Other indicators must be discovered.

Employing historical and archaeological data to define direct relationships between historical continuity and the several rubrics give to local and regional groups by chroniclers for over 400 years, José Reis (1997a, 1997b) concluded that there is a set of necessary information to establish the continuity between the Kaingang and Xokleng with the populations that occupied archaeological sites. This important research involving settlement patterns contains the basis for the development of further regional studies with the aim of establishing definitively (or not) the archaeological territories and historical correlates of the "Guianá, Gualacho, Cabelludos, Mbiazá, Caaguá, Ibiraiara, Botocudo, Coroado" and others.

Conclusions

An alternative, interdisciplinary, model of Jê populations in southern Brazil, beyond the hierarchical environment of Brazilian archeology, will make clear that the PRONAPA interpretation is now obsolete. Moreover, if the ideas and facts produced and collected within the Americanist environment since the 19th century are taken into account, we are forced to admit that PRONAPA presuppositions, hypotheses and interpretations concocted a false and self-contained scenery of South America. It amounts to what Funari (1998) called "anti-historical, positivist and ingenious empiricism". This means that while Americanists of different disciplines and distinct theoretical orientations debated and constructed a model for the Jê and Macro-Jê populations, the PRONAPA members tried to "rediscover the wheel", giving no heed to the discoveries of other scientists such as ethnologists, linguists, geneticists, and historians.

The striking characteristic of PRONAPA is its isolation from the larger research field which gives cohesion to the Americanist community. In spite of the relationships that may be easily established between the archaeological past, the historical past and the ethnographic present of the southern Jê populations, the predominant mentality of the archeologists who work in south Brazil and the type of scientific product they have built hinders the establishments of such relationships. Wholesome disconnection is the result of the monopolization of south Brazilian archeology's scientific production around its power, interests, political and academic struggles and success in the form of prestige. It constitutes a classical example of what Bourdieu (1976) defined as the "*champ scientifique*". Survival has been possible through patronage even up to the present, especially among archeologists, as Funari (1989, 1994, 1998) and Roosevelt (1991a, 1995) have showed. Any researcher who analyzes the scientific production of the PRONAPA members, their allies and disciples will perceive that they maintain no continuous dialogue with other disciplines, such as History and Ethnology, towards a holistic and diachronic approach (Lightfoot, 1995). Some tried an incipient dialogue, as was the case of Eble (1973), but were not successful.

If we discard the PRONAPA monopolistic content and if we interpret from an Americanist perspective the archaeological evidence attributed to the "Itararé, Casa de Pedra and Taquara" traditions as belonging to southern Jê populations, the history of the Kaingang and the Xokleng peoples will truly be built. Recent work in historical and anthropological studies based in oral information and documents has proved to be of paramount importance (Lavina, 1994; Mota, 1994, 1998; Reis, 1997a; Tommasino, 1995; Urban, 1978; Veiga, 1994).

If one takes into account that PRONAPA data are extremely unreliable and that little useful information is available, such as the geographical localization of sites, archaeological collections in museums and laboratories and, with extreme care, radiocarbon dating, we must realize that the sites should be excavated once more, collections reanalyzed and dating redone. Thus, a study must be undertaken aiming at the unification and critical analysis of historical, geographical, ethnographical, linguistic and archaeological information collected in the last 460 years. With these results, the archaeological community would begin comparative analyses to identify relationships of continuity and cultural and biological change in the past and, at the same time, to determine the successive boundaries of geographic spaces occupied during the entire period.

This also means that Kaingang and Xeklong peoples may be sometimes studied apart and sometimes comparatively, since cultural, linguistic and biological evidence discloses marked differences, whilst archaeological traits show a high degree of similarity. With the origin points and the cultural matrix of the Jê and Macro-Jê populations in mind, comparisons ought to be made between Kaingang peoples and their linguistic neighbors, such as Akwén (Xakriabá, Xavante and Xerente) and Apinayé groups. At the same time, comparisons should be made among Xokleng peoples and Kayapó, Timbira, Kren-akarôre and Suya populations. Comparison has to be carefully undertaken from the linguistic, genetic, and cultural point of view to determine similarities and differences, and the retention and loss of elements from the Macro-Jê cultural matrix. Genetic studies are necessary among the Jê populations as a whole so that affinities between present and past populations can be evaluated.

The most important problem concerns the definition of material similarities among the Kaingang and Xokleng archaeological record since no marked differences have been found. In the comparisons of Hicks (1966, 1971) and Schaden (1958), many items are not related to cultural material, whilst the common archaeological markers in southern Brazil are not mentioned. For example, how can one rely on the knowledge that the Xokleng cremated their dead if all data on this item was recorded during intense contact in the state of Santa Catarina (Santos, 1973) after the second half of the 19th century? Was cremation among the Xokleng traditional or the result of great pressure which hindered them from having a fixed territory and which forced them towards constant displacements as a distancing strategy? On the other hand, until some decades ago, Kaingang populations built earth mounds to bury their dead since they were only in recently colonized areas in the states of Paraná, Santa Catarina and São Paulo. Many archaeological sites with mounds have been found (Drumond and Philipson, 1947; MÈtraux, 1963; Schaden, 1958). Such a difference may be considered an important marker of material difference to be taken into account.

How can these limitations be eliminated except through further archaeological research? Roosevelt's warning (1991a: 105–106) about erroneous interpretations of Amazon populations should be heeded. Nineteenth century and early twentieth century sources would not be interpreted ingeniously. Xokleng populations of the past cannot be imagined like their descendants at the time of contact. Contacts with the Guarani populations which occurred over one thousand years before the arrival of Europeans should be thought of likewise. The example of the Bororo (included among the Macro-Jê peoples) genesis is a warning to the development of research. In an interdisciplinary study Irmi Wüst (1990, 1992, 1998) disclosed that present day Bororo populations "would be the product of a process of incorporation of ethnic and cultural distinct groups". Archeologists must be concerned about such a problem, whether to accept or to refute it.

A new approach to the history, culture, politics and the process of territorial expansions of Jê populations in southern Brazil needs all existing information since its aim will be the consideration of several possibilities in the individual historical processes of each Kaingang and Xokleng group. Probably most research problems have still to be rethought and redefined. The archeology of southern Jê populations should follow international archaeological approaches and challenges so that the "pseudo-scientific procedures of PRONAPA" (Brochado, 1984: 29) can be superceded and substituted.

Acknowledgements

I began this research work and innumerable discussions with Fabíola Andréa Silva in 1993. Joint and single publications ensued, as the bibliography testifies. Most of what is written above is due to her as a quasi co-author of this paper. I would like to thank my friends José Brochado, Kimiye Tommasino and Lúcio Tadeu Mota who contributed decisively in the discussions and who greatly collaborated in my university career. I would also like to thank Eduardo Góes Neves and Pedro Paulo Funari for their support, challenges, divergent ideas and debates which we had and which certainly will continue to have. Needless to say the responsibility of the above paper is entirely mine.

References

Ambrosetti, J. B., 1895, Kaingangues, San Pedro (Misiones). *Revista del Jardín Zoológico de Buenos Aires* 2(10):305–387.

Baldus, H., 1941, Salvador Canals Frau: Paleoamericanos (Láguidos) en la mesopotamia argentina en laépoca colonial. *Revista do Arquivo Municipal* 75:245–246.

1954, *Bibliografia Crítica da Etnologia Brasileira*. Comissão do IV Centenário da Cidade de São Paulo, São Paulo.

1955, Salvador Canals Frau: Las poblaciones indígenas de la Argentina, su origen, su pasado, su presente, Revista do Museu Paulista 9:321–323.

1968, *Bibliografia Crítica da Etnologia Brasileira*, volumen 2. Kommissionsverlag Mnstermann-Druck GMBH, Hannover.

Barbosa, L. B.H., 1918, *A pacificação dos Caingang paulistas (hábitos, costumes e instituições desses índios*. Conferência no Salão da Biblioteca Nacional em 19 de novembro, Rio de Janeiro.

Barret, J. C., 1996, Post-processual theory. In *The Oxford Companion to Archaeology*, edited by B. Fagan, pp. 576–578. Oxford University Press, New York.

Barreto, C., 1988, *A ocupação pré-colonial do vale do Ribeira de Iguape, SP: os sítios concheiros do médio curso*. Master's thesis, FFLCH-USP, São Paulo.

1998, Brazilian Archaeology from a Brazilian Perspective. *Antiquity* 72(277):573–581.

Becker, I. I. B., 1975a, Dados sobre o abastecimento entre os índios Kaingang do Rio Grande do Sul conforme a Bibliografia dos séculos XVI, a XX. In *Estudos sobre o abastecimento indígena* (Publicações avulsas 2) Instituto Anchietano de Pesquisas (São Leopoldo):39–59.

1975b, O índio Kaingang no Rio Grande do Su. *Pesquisas* 29:1–264.

1985, O índio Kaingang no Rio Grande do Sul e a exploração dos recursos naturais. *Boletim do Marsul* 3:77–85.

1991, Alimentação dos índios Kaingang no Rio Grande do Sul. *Revista de Arqueologia* 6:107–119.

Blasi, O., 1973, A pesquisa arqueológica no Estado do Paraná. *Dédalo* 9(17–18): 41–47.

Blasis, P. A. D. de, 1988, *A ocupaçà pré-colonial do vale do Ribeira de Iguape, SP: os grupos pré-ceramistas do médio curso*. Master's thesis, FFLCH-USP, São Paulo.

Bourdieu, P., 1976, Le champ scientifique. *Actes de la recherche en Sciences Sociales* 2–3:88–104.

Brochado, J. P., 1984, *An Ecological Model of the Spread of Pottery and Agriculture into Eastern South America*. Ph.D. dissertation, University of Illinois at Urbana-Champaign.

1989, A expansão dos Tupi e da cerâmica da tradição policrômica amazônica. *Dédalo* 27:65–82.

1991, Um modelo de difusão da cerâmica e da agricultura no leste da América do Sul. Anais do I Simpósio de Pré-História do Nordeste Brasileiro. *CLIO* (série arqueológica) 4: 85–88.

Brochado, J. P., and Lathrap, D., 1980, *Amazonia*, manuscript.

Brochado, J. P. et al., 1969, *Arqueologia Brasileira em 1968*. Museu Paraense Emílio Goeldi, Belém.

Caggiano, M. A., 1984, Prehistória del N.E. Argentino y sus vinculaciones con la Republica Oriental del Uruguay y sur de Brasil. *Pesquisas* (antropología) 38:1–109.

Canals-Frau, S., 1940, Paleoamericanos Láguidos, en la mesopotamia argentina en la época colonial. *Anales del Instituto de Etnografía Argentina* 1:129–153.

1953, *Las poblaciones indígenas de la Argentina: su origen, su pasado, su presente*. Editorial Sudamericana, Buenos Aires.

Chmyz, I., 1967, O sítio arqueológico PR UV 1 (abrigo sob-rocha Casa de Pedra). *Arqueologia* (Curitiba, CEPA-UFPR), 3:1–42.

1968, Considerações sobre duas novas tradições ceramistas arqueológicas no Estado do Paraná. *Pesquisas* (antropología) 18:115–125.

1969, Dados parciais sobre a arqueologia do vale do rio Ivaí, PRONAPA, volumen 2. *Publicações Avulsas do Museu Parense Emílio Goeldi*. 10:95–118.

1971, Contatos interétnicos verificados em sítios arqueológicos no Estado do Paraná/Brasil. *Prevista do Instituto de Biologia e Pesquisas Tecnológicas* (Curitiba) 16:11–14.

1976, A ocupação do litoral dos Estados do Paraná e Santa Catarina por povos ceramistas. *Estudos Brasileiros* (Curitiba)1:7–43.

1981, *Relatório das pesquisas arqueológicas realizadas na área da usina hidrelétrica de Salto Santiago (1979–1980)*. ELETROSUL/ IPHAN, Florianópolis/Curitiba.

Davis, I., 1966, Proto Jê Phonology. *Estudos lingüísticos. Revista Brasileira de Lingüística Teórica e Aplicada* 1(2):10–24.

1968, Some Macro-Jê Relationships. *International Journal of American Linguistics* 34:42–47.

Dias, A. S., 1994, *Repensando a tradição Umbu a partir de um estudo de caso*. Master's thesis, IFCH-PUCRS, Porto Alegre.

1995, Um projeto para a arqueologia brasileira: breve histórico da implementação do PRONAPA. *Revista do CEPA* 19(22):25–39.

Drummond, C., and Philipson, J., 1947, Os túmulos Kaingang de Parapuã. *Sociologia* 9(4):386–393.

Eble, A. B., 1973, Problemas arqueológicos da Região do Alto Vale do Itajaí. *Anais do Museu de Antropologia* 6:41–50.

Evans, C., and Meggers, B., 1965, *Guia para prospecção arqueológica no Brasil*. Museu Paraense Emílio Goeldi, Belém.

Faria, L. de C., 1989, Domínios e fronteiras do saber: a identidade da arqueologia. *Dédalo* 1(1):26–39.

Fernandes, J. L., 1931, Os Caingangues de Palmas. *Arquivos do Museu Paranaense*, 1:161–209.

Funari, P. P. A., 1989, Brazilian Archaeology and World Archaeology: Some Remarks. *World Archaeology Bulletin* 3:60–68.

1991, Archaeology in Brazil: Politics and Scholarship at the Crossroads. *World Archaeology Bulletin* 5:122–132.

1994, Arqueologia brasileira—visão geral e reavaliação. *Revista de História da Arte e Arqueologia* 1: 23–41.

1995, Mixed Features of Archaeological Theory in Brazil. In *Theory in Archaeology*, edited by P. J. Ucko, pp. 236–250. Routledge, London.

1997, Cidadania, erudição e pesquisas sobre a Antigüidade Clássica no Brasil *Boletim do CPA* (ano II) 3:83–97.

nd, *A importância da teoria arqueológica internacional para a Arqueologia Sul-Americana: o caso brasileiro*.

González, E. M. R., 1998, Regional Pottery-making Groups in Southern Brazil. *Antiquity* 72(277):616–624.

Haekel, J., 1952, Neue Beiträge zur Kulturschichtung Brasiliens. *Anthropos* 47:963–991.

1953, Neue Beiträge zur Kulturschichtung Brasiliens. *Anthropos* 48:105–157.

Hicks, D., 1966, The Kaingang and Aweikoma: a Cultural Contrast. *Anthropos* 61:839–846.

1971, The Comparative Analysis of the Kaingang and Aweikoma Relationships Terminologies (Brazil). *Anthropos* 66:931–935.

Hoeltz, S. E., 1997, *Artesãos e artifatos pré-históricos do vale do rio Pardo*. EDUNISC, Santa Cruz do Sul.

Howard, G. D., 1948, Northeast Argentina. In *Lowland Argentine Archaeology,* edited by G. D. Howard and G. R. Willey, pp. 9–24. Publications in Archaeology, 39. Yale University, New Haven.

Jones, S., 1997, *The Archaeology of Ethnicity: Constructing Identities in the Past and Present*. Routledge, London.

Kempf, V. G., 1947, Notas sobre um grupo indígena de Santa Catarina. *Revista do Arquivo Municipal* 113:25–34.

Kern, A. A., 1981, *Le précéramique du plateau sud-brésilien*. Ph.D. dissertation, EHESS, Paris.

1994, *Antecedentes indígenas*. Mercado Aberto, Porto Alegre.

Kühne, H., 1979, Der Bodenbau der Kaingang—und Lakranó—Indianer und dessen Stellung im Rahmen de Gê-Völker. Der Bodenbau in Wechselwirkung zum geistigen Leben, zur Gesellung und zur Umwelt. *Archiv für Völkerkunde* 33:61–84.

1980, Sammelwirtschaft, Fischfang und Tierhaltung der Kaingang und Lakranó—Indianer. Ihre Stellung im Rahmen der Gê-Völker. *Archiv für Völkerkunde* 34:101–122

Lafon, C. R., 1971, Introducción a la Arqueología del Nordeste Argentino. *Relaciones* (N.S.) 20(2):119–152.

1972, El replanteo de la Arqueología del Nordeste Argentino. *Antiquitas* 14:1–16.

Lightfoot, K., 1995, Culture Contact Studies: Redefining the Relationship Between Prehistoric and Historical Archaeology. *American Antiquity* 60(2):199–217.

La Salvia, F., Schmitz, P.I., and Becker, Í. I. B., 1970, Cerâmica Caingang—fase Vacaria. In *Estudos de Pré-História geral e brasileira*, pp. 493–497. Instituto de Pré-História—USP, São Paulo.

Lathrap, D., 1970a, Archäologische Untersuchungen am Mittleren Amazonas, Peter Paul Hilbert (book review). *American Antiquity* 35(4):499–501.

1970b, *The Upper Amazon*. Thames and Hudson, London.

1973, Amazonia, Man and Culture in a Counterfeit Paradise, Betty J. Meggers (book review) *American Anthropologist* 75(4):988.

Lavina, R., 1994, *Os Xokleng de Santa Catarina: uma etnohistória e sugestões para os arqueólogos*. Master's thesis, IAP/UNISINOS, São Leopoldo.

Lemonnier, P., 1992, *Elements for an Anthropology of Technology*. Museum of Anthropological Research—University of Michigan, Michigan.

Loukotka, C., 1939, Línguas indígenas brasileiras. *Revista do Arquivo Municipal* 54:147–174.

1968, *Classification of South American Indian Languages*. University of California Press, Los Angeles.

Lovato, L. A., 1974, A contribuição de Franz Keller à etnografia do Paraná. *Boletim do Museu do Índio* (antropologia) (1):3–44.

Lowie, R., 1946, Eastern Brazil: an Introduction. In The *Handbook of South American Indians,* volume 1, edited by J. Steward, pp. 381–398. Smithsonian Institution, Washington.

1949, Social and Political Organization of the Tropical Forest and Marginal Tribes. In The *Handbook of South American Indians,* volume 5, edited by J. Steward, pp. 313–350. Smithsonian Institution, Washington.

Mabilde, A. P. T., 1896, Apontamentos sobre os indígenas selvagens da nação Coroados que habitam os sertões do Rio Grande do Sul. *Annuario do Estado do Rio Grande do Sul* Anno XIII:125–151.

Maniser, H. H., 1930, Les Kaingang de São Paulo. *Proceedings of the 23rd International Congress of Americanists*, New York.

Martius, C. P., 1867, *Beiträge zur Ethnographie uns Sprachenkunde Südamerika's, zumals Brasiliens*. Friedrich Fischer, Leipzig.

Mason, J., 1950, The Languages of South American Indians. In *The Handbook of South American Indians*, volume 6, edited by J. Steward, pp. 157–317. Smithsonian Institution, Washington.

Maybury-Lewis, D., editor, 1979, *Dialetical Societies: the Gê and Bororo of Central Brazil*. Harvard University Press, Cambridge.

Meggers, B., 1955, The Coming of Age of American Archaeology. In *New Interpretations on Aboriginal American Culture History*, edited by M. T. Newman, pp. 116–129. Anthropological Society of Washington, Washington D.C.

1985, Advances in Brazilian Archaeology, 1935–1985. *American Antiquity* 50(2):364–373.

1992, Cuarenta años de colaboración. In *Préhistoria sudamericana: nuevas perspectivas*, edited by B. Meggers, pp.13–26. Taraxacum, Washington D.C.

Meggers, B., and Evans, C., 1970, *Como interpretar a linguagem da cerâmica: guia para arqueólogos*. Smithsonian Institution, Washington D.C.

1978, Lowland South America and the Antilles. In *Ancient Native Americans*, edited by J. D. Jennings, pp.13–26. W.H. Freeman and Co., San Francisco.

Menghín, O. F. A., 1957, El poblamiento prehistórico de Misiones. *Anales de Arqueología y Etnología* 12:19–40.

Mentz Ribeiro, P. A., 1991, Arqueologia do vale do rio Pardo, Rio Grande do Sul, Brasil, *Revista do CEPA* 18(21):1–184.

Métraux, A., 1963, The Caingang. In *The Handbook of South American Indians*, volume 1, edited by J. Steward, pp. 445–475. Cooper Square Publ. Inc., New York.

Miller, E. Th., 1967, Pesquisas arqueológicas efetuadas no nordeste do Rio Grande do Sul, PRONAPA, 1. *Publicações Avulsas do Museu Paraense Emílio Goeldi* 6:15–38.

1969, Pesquisas arqueológicas efetuadas no Noroeste do Rio Grande do Sul (Alto Uruguai), PRONAPA, 2. *Publicações Avulsas do Museu Paraense Emílio Goeldi* 10:33–54.

1971, Pesquisas arqueológicas efetuadas no planalto meridional Rio Grande do Sul, PRONAPA, 4. *Publicações Avulsas do Museu Paraense Emílio Goeldi* 15:37–60.

Miller Jr., T., 1978, Tecnologia cerâmica dos Caingang paulistas. *Arquivos do Museu Paranaense* (nova série, etnologia) 2:1–51.

Mota, L. T., 1994, *As guerras dos índios Kaingang: a história épica dos índios Kaingang no Paraná (1769–1924)*. EDUEM, Maringá.

1998, *O aço, a cruz e a terra: índios e brancos no Paraná Provincial (1853–1889)*. Ph.D. dissertation, UNESP, Assis.

Neves, E. G., 1995, Village Fissioning in Amazonia: A Critique of Monocausal Determinism. *Revista do Museu de Arqueologia e Etnologia* 5:195–209.

1998, Twenty Years of Amazonian Archaeology in Brazil (1977–1997). *Antiquity* 72(277):625–632.

Neves, W. A., 1984, *Paleogenética dos grupos Pré-Históricos do litoral sul do Brasil (Paraná e Santa Catarina)*. Ph.D. dissertation, FFLCH-USP, São Paulo.

1988, Arqueologia brasileira—algumas considerações. *Boletim do Museu Paraense Emílio Goeldi* (antropologia) 4(2): 200–205.

Nimuendajú, C., 1981, *Mapa Etno-Histórico*. IBGE, Rio de Janeiro.

Noelli, F. S., in press, *Catálogo de sítios arqueológicos de povos ceramistas do Brasil Meridional, Uruguai, Nordeste da Argentina e do Paraguai Oriental*.

1993, *Sem Tekohá não há Tekó (em busca de um modelo etnoarqueológico da subsistência e da aldeia Guarani aplicado a uma área de domínio no delta do Jacuí-RS)*. Master's thesis, IFCH-PUCRS, Porto Alegre.

1996a, As hipóteses sobre o centro de origem e as rotas de expansão dos Tupi. *Revista de Antropologia* 39(2):7–53.

1996b, Resposta Eduardo Viveiros de Castro e Greg Urban. *Revista de Antropologia* 39(2):100–118.

1996c, Os Jê do Brasil meridional e a antigüidade da agricultura: elementos da lingüística, arqueologia e etnografia. *Estudos Ibero-Americanos* 22(1):13–26.

1998, The Tupi: Explaining Origin and Expansion in Terms of Archaeology and Historical Linguistics. *Antiquity* 72(277):648–663.

Noelli, F. S., Silva, F., Veiga, J., Tommasino, K., Mota, L. T., and D'Angelis, W. da R., 1998, *Bibliografia Kaingang: referências sobre um povo Jê do sul do Brasil*. Editora da Universidade Estadual de Londrina, Londrina.

Noelli, F. S., Silva, F. and Mota, L. T., n.d., *Bibliografia Xokleng: referê ncias sobre um povo Jê do sul do Brasil,*manuscript.

Paula, J. M. de., 1924, Memória sobre os Botocudos do Paraná e Santa Catarina organizado pelo Serviço de Proteção aos Índios sob a inspeção do Dr. José M. de Paula. *Annaes do XX Congresso Internacional de Americanistas* 1:117–137.

Piza, M., 1938, Notas sobre os Caingangs. *Revista do Instituto Histórico e Geográfico de São Paulo* 35:199–209.

Ploetz, H., and Métraux, A., 1930, La civilisation matérielle et la vie sociele et religieuse des indiens Zé du Brésil méridional et oriental. *Revista del Instituto de Etnología de la Universidad Nacional de Tucumán* 1:107–238.

Poujade, R., 1992, Poblamiento préhistorico y colonial de Misiones. *Estudos Ibero-Americanos* 18(1):29–70.

PRONAPA, 1970, Brazilian archeology in 1968: An Interim Report on the National Program of Archeology Research—PRONAPA. *American Antiquity* 35(1): 1–23.

Prous, A., 1992, *Arqueologia Brasileira*. Editora Universidade de Brasília, Brasília.

Reedy, C., and Reedy, T., 1994, Relating Visual and Technological Styles in Tibetan Sculpture Analysis. *World Archaeology* 25(3):304–320.

Reis, J. A., 1997a, *Para uma Arqueologia dos buracos de bugre: do sintetizar, do problematizar, do propor*. Master's thesis, IFCH-PUCRS, Porto Alegre.

1997b,... Guaianá, buraco de bugre, Kaingang/Xokleng:... qual ancestralidade ?... qual analogia?... de que campo pode-se falar?... *Revista do CEPA* 21(26):35–90.

Reis, M. J. *A problemática arqueológica das estruturas subterrâneas no Planalto catarinense*. Master's thesis, FFLCH-USP, São Paulo.

Robrahn, É. M., 1988, *A ocupação pré-colonial do vale do Ribeira de Iguape, SP: os grupos ceramistas do médio curso*. Master's thesis, FFLCH-USP, São Paulo.

Rodrigues, A. D., 1986, *Línguas Brasileiras. Para o conhecimento das línguas indígenas*. Loyola, São Paulo.

Roosevelt, A. C., 1991a, Determinismo ecolóico na interpretação do desenvolvimento social indígena da Amazônia. In *Origens, adaptações e diversidade biológica do homem nativo da Amazônia*, edited by W. A. Neves, pp. 103–141. SCT/CNPq/Museu Paraense Emílio Goeli, Belém.

1991b, *Moundbuilders of Amazon*. Academic Press, New York.

1995, Early Pottery in the Amazon: Twenty Years of Scholarly Obscurity. In *The Emergence of Pottery: Technology and Innovation in Ancient Societies*, edited by W. K. Barnett and J. Hoopes, pp. 115–131. Smithsonian Institution, Washington D.C.

Roosevelt, A.C. et al., 1991, Eighth Millennium Pottery from a Prehistoric Shell hidden in Brazilian Amazon. *Science* 254:1621–1624.

Salzano, F. M., and Callegari-Jacques, S., 1988, *South American Indians: a Case Study in Evolution*. Clarendon Press, Oxford.

Salzano, F. M., and Freire-Maia, N. 1967 *Populações brasileiras: aspectos demográficos, genéticos e 0antropológicos*. Cia Editora Nacional, São Paulo.

Salzano, F. M., and Sutton, H. E., 1985, Haptoglobin and Transferring Types of Indians from Santa Catarina. *American Journal of Human Genetics*17(3):280–289.

Santos, S. C., 1973, *Índios e Brancos no Sul do Brasil—a dramática experiência dos Xokléng*. Edeme, Florianópolis.

Schaden, F., 1958, Xokléng e Kaingang. *Revista de Antropologia* 6(2):105–112.

Schmitz, P. I., 1959, A cerâmica guarani da ilha de Santa Catarina e a cerâmica da Base Aérea. *Pesquisas* (antropologia) 3:267–325.

1968, Grandes complexos de cerâmica indígena no sul do Brasil. *Pesquisas* (antropologia) 18:127–140.

1972, Cronologia de las culturas del sudeste de Rio Grande do Sul, Brasil. *Antecedentes y Anales del I Congreso Nacional de Arqueología. II Encuentro de Arqueología del Interior*, pp.105–117, Fray Bentos.

1973, A pesquisa arqueológica no Estado do Rio Grande do Sul. *Dédalo* 17–18:67–86.

1977, Os primitivos habitantes do Rio Grande do Sul. *Anais do II Simpósio Nacional de Estudos Missioneiros*, pp. 50–60.

1981, La arqueología del nordeste argentino y del sur de Brasil en la visión del Dr. Osvaldo Menghín y de los arqueólogos posteriores. *Estudos Leopoldenses* 18(64):207–224.

1988, As tradições ceramistas do planalto sul-brasileiro. *Arqueologia do Rio Grande do Sul, Documentos* 02:74–130.

1991, Áreas arqueológicas do litoral e do planalto do Brasil. *Revista do Museu de Arqueologia e Etnologia* 1:3–20.

Schmitz, P. I., and Becker,í. I. B., 1991, Os primitivos engenheiros do planalto e suas estruturas subterrâneas: a tradição Taquara. In A. Kern (ed., *Arqueologia Pré-Histórica do Rio Grande do Sul*, edited by, pp. 251–289, Porto Alegre: Mercado Aberto.

Schmitz, P. I. and Brochado, J. P., 1981a, Datos para una secuencia cultural del Estado de Rio Grande do Sul, Brasil. *Estudos Leopoldenses* 18(64):131–160.

1981b, Arqueología de Rio Grande do Sul, Brasil. *Estudos Leopoldenses* 18(64):161–184.

Serrano, A., 1936, *Etnografia de la Antigua Província del Uruguay*. Melchior, Paraná.

1937, Arqueologia brasileira: Subsídios para a arqueologia do Brasil meridional. *Revista do Arquivo Municipal* 36:3–42.

1957, Los Kaingang de Rio Grande do Sul a mediados del siglo XIX. Según un Manuscrito del Ten. Cel. A. Mabilde. *Revista do Museu Júlio de Castilhos e Arquivo Histórico do Rio Grande do Sul* 7:164–182.

1972, *Líneas fundamentales de la Arqueología del Litoral (una tentativa de periodizacíion*. Universidad Nacional de Córdoba, Córdoba.

Silva, F. A., 1999, As cerâmicas dos Jê do sul do Brasil e os seus estilos tecnológicos: elementos para uma etnoarqueologia Kaingang e Xokleng. *Revista do Cepa* 23(30):57–74.

Silva, F. A., and Noelli, F. S., 1996, Para uma síntese dos Jê do Sul: igualdades, diferenças e dúvidas para a etnografia, etno-História e arqueologia. *Estudos Ibero-Americanos* 22(1):5–13.

Silva, F. A., and Meggers, B. J., 1963, Cultural Development in Brazil. In *Aboriginal Cultural Development in Latin America: An Interpretative Review*, edited by B. J. Meggers and C. Evans, pp. 119–129, Smithsonian Institution, Washington D.C.

Simonian, L. T. I.., 1975, *Cultura Material Xokléng*. Museu Antropológico Diretor Pestana/FIDENE, Ijuí.

Sims-Williams, P., 1998, Genetics, Linguistics and Prehistory: Thinking Big and Thinking Straight. *Antiquity* 72(277):505–527.

Sullivan, E., and Moore, S., 1990, *The Schokleng of Brazil*. Saint Augustin.

Susnik, B., 1975, *Dispersión tupí-guaraní prehistórica*. Ensayo analítico. Museo Etnográfico Andrés Barbedo, Asunción.

1994, *Interpretución etnocultural de la complejidad sudamericana antigua. Formación y disperción étnica*. Museo Etnográfico Andrés Barbedo, Asunción.

Tommasino, K., 1995, *A História Kaingáng da bacia do Tibagi: uma sociedade Jê meridional em movimento*. Ph.D. dissertation, FFLCH-USP, São Paulo.

TERMINOLOGIA, 1976, Terminologia arqueológica brasileira para a cerâmica. *Cadernos de Arqueologia* 1(1):119–148.

Urban, G., 1992, A História da cultura brasileira segundo as línguas nativas. In *História dos índios no Brasil*, edited by M. Carneiro da Cunha, pp. 87–102. São Cia das Letras/FAPESP/SMC, Paulo.

Veiga, J., 1994, *Organização social e cosmovisão Kaingang: uma introdução ao parentesco, casamento e nominação em uma sociedade Jê meridional*. IFCH-UNICAMP, Campinas.

Von Den Steinen, K., 1894, *Unter den Naturvölkern Central Brasiliens*. Dietrich Reimer Verlag, Berlin.

Wiesemann, Ú., 1978, Os dialetos da língua Kaingáng e Xokléng. *Arquivos de Anatomia e Antropologia* 3:197–217.

190
FRANCISCO SILVA
NOELLI

Willey, G., 1949, Ceramics. In *The Handbook of South American Indians,* volume 5, edited by J. Steward, pp. 139–204. Smithsonian Institution, Washington.

1971, *An Introduction to American Archaeology: South America,* volume 2. :Prentice-Hall, Englewood Cliffs.

Wüst, I., 1990, *Continuidade e mudança: para uma interpretação grupos pré-coloniais na bacia do rio Vermelho, Mato Grosso.* Ph.D. dissertation, FFLCH-USP, São Paulo.

1992, Contribuições arqueológicas, etnoarqueológicas e etno-históricas para o estudo dos grupos tribais do Brasi Central: o caso Bororo. *Revista do Museu de Arqueologia e Etnologia* 2:13–26.

1998, Continuities and Discontinuities: Archaeology and Ethnoarchaeology in the Heart of the Eastern Bororo Territory, Mato Grosso, Brazil. *Antiquity* 72(277):663–675.

Traveling Objects and Spatial Images

12

Exchange Relationships and the Production of Social Space

Marisa Lazzari

The anthropological concern about gift exchange drew attention to the fact that people exchange things that are not necessary from the point of view of basic subsistence (Mauss, 1925; Strathern, 1992:169). Consequently, from the beginning of the 20th century, the exploration of the principles by which people need to exchange at all has been a subject of central importance. Quite often this search ended with the answer that people need to build a socially integrated life, and that these transactions help towards that integration (Strathern, 1992). However, exchange theory has been lately reconfigured in anthropology, focusing the debate on the ambiguities and heterogeneities in exchanges more than in normative or homogeneous aspects (Weiner, 1992:17). Following this line, understanding the roots of exchange relationships requires the re-evaluation of some concepts, such as space, value and reciprocity.

It has been argued that societies can rarely be reduced to a single spatial structure (Gregory, 1989). Human beings build their personal networks of social relationships, and material culture is a powerful medium of negotiation of both personal and social values. As a consequence of this, a variety of flexible networks can be expected, some related to the legitimization of power relationships, others to the construction of personal identities, others to resistance. These networks create a series of spatial images that are of central importance in the reproduction of personal and communal values. Space, then, cannot be reduced either to the physical or the cognitive domain. Space is the result of both domains, giving form to and structuring them in turn. As active participants in the structuring process of social life rather than mere reflections of it, spatial dimensions are not neutral but rather they are embedded in and constitutive of power relations. Central to this paper is the assumption about the intimate connection between exchange relationships and the creation of spatial images, a concept I will discuss in this section.

The exchange of goods is more than an economic process. It is a social practice constituted by many layers in which labor, social reproduction and the construction of personal and group identities can meld. Moreover, through exchange relationships, individuals and societies frequently build enormous spatial dimensions. The exchange of goods reconfigures one's perspective on space and physical distance, not as an abyss that is necessary to overcome or minimize, but as something intentionally manipulated and created which also recursively structures societies and individuals. Space is built through the circulation of material culture, while at the same time having an active role in the formation of these circulation networks. Therefore, we could ask: What happens when people establish long distance connections? Which types of images of itself does a society build through the manipulation of these spatial images? Is it possible to see the distribution of material culture as a spatial language of power?

Value Creation, Social Reproduction, and Space

What makes something worth exchanging? Archaeologists have usually assumed that geographical distance is the source of value for an exchanged object. The more distant its origin, the more exotic the object or resource is considered to be. This often implies the assumption that the exchange-value of the good is also higher, as a consequence of the possible high-status role that the object or resource can have inside a group. Energy invested in producing or obtaining the objects or resources is usually another measure, since the more energy invested to obtain or produce a certain good, the higher its cost and therefore, the higher its supposed value (e.g., Earle and Ericson, 1977; Earle, 1982; Ericson, 1982; Renfrew and Shennan, 1982; Torrence, 1986, 1989). Marxist perspectives sometimes follow this approach, where the labor used in the production of the goods is seen as what make objects exchangeable. Nevertheless, Marxist perspectives oppose the approaches mentioned above by considering all economic terms as embedded in social relationships of production (Miller and Tilley, 1984).

Through the movement of objects or resources that labor creates, by means of the objects or knowledge obtained through their exchange, labor is intertwined with other social landscapes beyond the local area.

Even in strict ceremonial exchanges, the labor process is present, since material objects are often exhibited as the objectification of the natural yield of the manpower of the different sectors involved (Battaglia, 1990). Although in non-capitalist economies the abstract equivalence of labor is not transformed into money, general labor processes -much more than just the division of tasks[1]—are involved in the generation of value. However, we should remember that what is usually considered an "equivalent" quantity of used manpower it is not easily reducible to the investment of time or energy. The equivalence of the exchanged objects can imply a consideration of the work involved to create and obtain them as the minimum possible rate of exchange. But as most ethnographic cases show, it is social necessity that defines "rarity" and plays a central role in determining the value of a certain object (Godelier, 1977:149, 1981).

Exotic objects are usually considered as the containers of power and symbols of the distant regions controlled only by those that know them. Politico-religious specialists tend to be interested in and better informed about these worlds beyond their places of origin, and they usually look for tangible evidence of these associations (Helms, 1988:164). This tangible evidence can include crafts, animals, or even human beings, technical skills, manufacturing styles or any other form of knowledge. Many problems arise from these assumptions about distance and value: Can distance always be considered as a measure of power? Can we assume every time that we find "exotic" objects that these had that role in the past? Did all exotic objects mean the same thing in the daily life of a past society? Besides the problems that arise from the definition of what is exotic (Gamble, 1993), there are others regarding the supposition that physical distance is a cost to minimize through exchange networks, either in a strict economic sense, or to maximize political benefits. The point is not to deny these aspects, but to take them as one among many possibilities, being open to the fact that exotic objects can be used to negotiate a diverse array of relationships in different social interaction networks (Gamble, 1995, 1998).

Taking this into account, what is the role of space in social reproduction? Social relationships have a double dimension: they create spaces and at the same time they depend on the same for their reproduction. Societies, or rather, the social relationships between people, are the creative agents of their own spatial images. This process is at the heart of the creation of social values, and central to the tensions caused by social values in competition. In this way, physical distance is very important not because it gives a source of "objective" value for the goods circulating among people. As with all spatial dimensions, physical distance is a created dimension that is not an abyss to overcome, a mere cost to minimize, but a resource of authority created to be disputed (Gregory, 1989).

The value of an object or resource is not an objective and universal measure, but rather value is built in relation to processes of social reproduction. In anthropological studies the reproduction of a community has been considered when framing the exchange of gifts and commodities in a wider set of exchanges: of food, alliances, marriages, and even of life and death (Battaglia, 1990, 1994; Godelier, 1977; Helms, 1988; Humphrey and Hugh-Jones, 1989; Munn, 1986, 1992; Thomas, 1991; Strathern, 1992; Weiner, 1992). Communities create the values that then become essential for their social reproduction. Since this is a dialectical process, it supposes both a positive aspect of value creation (of those values seen as "positive"), and the intention of controlling what the community thinks that undermines this value or defines how it could not be carried out (negative values; Munn, 1986). Consequently, within each relationship is the reminder of what could ruin it, how it could effectively cease. The circulation of gifts is embedded in an intricate time-space-person system which is recursively structured (Munn, 1986: 3). This perspective implies adding a new dimension to the analysis of the exchange of objects and resources: material exchanges should not be seen as separated from other types of exchanges. Although different social practices—in this case material exchanges- can be part of the same symbolic system, the tension that can exist among them in terms of the demands that they establish on labor processes, allows us to imagine the coexistence of different social networks in competition. Social tensions can be resolved by means of the construction of a "symbolic whole", however, we can use the archaeological time perspective to understand the changes in these symbolic resolutions of the social tensions and their legitimacy. Both material and symbolic[2] exchanges should be seen as fundamental parts both of the constitution of people as of societies, since they participate in the creation of the social values (embodied by objects) that communities consider essential for their social reproduction. In the dialectics of value creation, each established relationship involving the circulation of objects also involves the awareness of its failure, since it implies a series of assumptions about its appropriate operation and significance, which are shared by those that participate in the exchange (Munn, 1986; Battaglia, 1990).

Any act has a certain social value, which is manifested through its essential capacities or possible consequences in the social realm. Value, then, can be measured as the relative capacity of an act to expand the space-time of a relationship "self-other" formed in and through social practices (the intersubjective[3] space-time). As a consequence, each act or practice has a level of *potentiality*, since the space-time that forms has relatively expandable capacities (Munn, 1986: 6–9). This implies the capacity to develop spatio-temporal relationships that go beyond the self and thus expand the actor's capacity to control space and time. Potentiality then refers to the capacity of certain practices to create a present that is experienced as implying a desired act or later return (Munn, 1986: 11)

Long distance exchanges create an intricate time-space-person system, because they constitute practices with a high level of potentiality and consequently of central importance for the production of social values (Munn, 1986: 3). These exchanges create wider personal extensions than intra-community exchanges. In this context, the circulation of material culture creates paths or routes that expand space and personal and social time, but also objects become especially unique devices, developing historical properties (memorability) that make them easy to remember even long after having stopped circulating (Munn, 1986: 12; Weiner, 1992). Material culture in these exchanges embodies a series of qualities that are considered signifiers of the time-space extension. Through exchanges, an actor produces a spatiotemporal extension of the self, and this way, she/he produces her/his own value. An individual's value, in terms of the potentially reciprocal returns that she/he may obtain in the future, is expressed in terms of a *value product*, such as fame, prestige or any other form of social recognition. In this process, the community or social group also acquires value—and possesses a role in the regional circulation of goods—through its renowned or noted members (Munn, 1986). Through the capacity of being remembered (memorability), and the material objects within which memorability is embodied, time-space extension is possible and the presence of other people and places becomes available. Other worlds, other values, become entangled in daily life and in consequence, routinize any claim that they might help to sustain, whether communal, singular or sectarian. One could say then that material culture can help to draw space representations, mental maps of the universe to which a person belongs or from which she/he is excluded.

Within these maps of the universe, physical distance turns out to be another dimension of space and its construction and perception is directly related to the construction of spaces on a smaller, daily scale. Daily spaces are related to routine practices, and it is in these daily spaces, in daily interaction, where most exchanges happen (Barrett, 1989). One could argue then that exchanges are entangled with labor practices. The form and place of the exchanges, especially of those ordinary, non-ceremonial exchanges, will depend on different agents' routine routes and paths shaped by daily activities.

The symbolic and material dimensions of exchange are intimately entangled with the experience of spatiality, or the socially created spaces that structure social life (in the sense of Soja, 1989, 1997). The symbolic dimensions of space are not separable from the material spatial practices that concretize the social relations of production (buildings, structures, roads, landscapes and the labor they involve), but neither they are mere reflections of them (Soja, 1996, 1997). Space is constituted by a "trialectics": the physical, the mental or cognitive, and the social. As Soja puts it (1996: 65), these three dimensions "...are simultaneously real and imagined, concrete and abstract, material and metaphorical". More specifically, social space in itself is constituted by three dimensions that overcome the traditional cognitive/material binary opposition: perceived space (spatial practice), representations of space (conceived space), and spaces of representation (lived space) (Soja, 1996: 65). All these aspects of spatiality help to build the time-space extensions of social life (Gregory, 1989: 206; Soja, 1989). Spatiality, in a general sense, is constituted as much through the small practices of daily life as it is through the broader political strategies. As a consequence of this, spatiality can develop different shapes and layers (Gregory, 1989). In material terms, this means that the demands that are established upon the labor processes of a society can come from diverse places or chains of authority and that this process will be manifested in the many overlapping layers of socially structured space, which recursively acts upon those demands. The social networks created through the circulation of material culture draw a particular kind of spatiality, a wider landscape (a spatial image) of social relations that has both a symbolic and a material dimension. This wider social landscape is intimately connected to the local landscape of daily activities and to the creation of value through space-time extensions of both the self and the community (Munn, 1990, and see Gamble, 1995, 1998 for a discussion of social landscapes in Palaeolithic societies).

The development of different spatiotemporal extensions implies different levels of space-time control, and these levels are in their nature relative categories. The space-time control that an actor can exercise can always be hierarchically ranked when compared to the control another person can exercise (Munn, 1986). Thus, the process of expansion of the intersubjective space-time implies a hierarchization process. Exchanges, and the intersubjective space-times that are constructed through them, attempt to mediate the tensions created by antithetic principles such as individual autonomy and social encompassment. In relation to this, different practices possess positive or negative values, according to social assumptions about the type of power relationships that are possible and/or acceptable for the society (Munn, 1986: 19–20). This can be considered as a particular set of networks, resulting in a specific mode of domination[4] (in the sense of Bourdieu, 1974: 57). Another class of antithetic principles, or contradiction axis, could be hierarchy/equality (Giddens, 1984). Besides being structural contradictions of a society, these antithetical principles can be the point around which social conflict takes place.[5] Each interaction network, with the chain of authority associated with each of them, and each set of contradictory principles, can also be described as a *field* (in the sense of Bourdieu, 1974: 55) or social space that restricts people's capacity to negotiate yet it is contingent upon each agent's means and objectives. In these fields the control of spatio-temporal extensions constitutes a powerful resource to negotiate personal and group positions.

Returning to the initial point of this section, we could say that all exchanges have characteristics traditionally assigned only to gift exchanges.[6] In other words all exchanges, whether of prestige or of ordinary items, have a "gift dimension" since value only occurs in a context of social meaning (Appadurai, 1991; Strathern, 1992). There is no possible way to establish the exchange value of something outside of the social relationship involved in its circulation. The evaluation, the consideration of the value of an object or resource, is more qualitative than quantitative and absolute. The cause of exchange lies in the previously established debt, and political life consists of people forcing others to be the cause of their own action (Strathern, 1992: 180). In this process, both things and people are created, since a person becomes socially visible through the effects that she/he causes in other people (Strathern, 1992). In barter the apparent equality of the partners is no more than the formal agreement of exchanging (Humphrey and Hugh-Jones, 1989; Liep, 1990; Strathern, 1992), where the coercion exercised in order to engage the other person in the exchange is a constituent part of the ongoing process. Conversely, all exchanges also have a "commodity" dimension, because many times personal interest in the political game is what makes these relationships continual (Bourdieu, 1974, 1977; Appadurai, 1991). Commodity exchanges, because they have specific properties that distinguish them from gifts, become by these very properties the privileged conveyors of particular social values and appropriation practices (see Taussig, 1980; Miller, 1987; Weiss, 1996; Burke, 1999).

What gives value to an object, product or service, is neither only the amount of labor invested in its production or acquisition, nor physical distance involved in its procurement. Rather, being acquired through certain exchange channels—of any nature—confers value. As mentioned at the beginning of this section, this is supported by the well-documented habit of seeking goods through exchange relationships that are already available locally (Godelier, 1977; McBryde, 1989; Taçon, 1991). The imported exotic object is valued because it is placed in a transactional mode (be it barter, gift exchange, or any other type) which is valued positively within the society, and in this way it gives value to the involved goods (Gell, 1992: 148). Objects do not have social value until they enter in strategies of social reproduction (Barrett, 1989). Moreover, as Bourdieu (1977: 64) highlighted, "the homogeneity of the production of *habitus*[7] produces a homogenization of dispositions and interests that, far from excluding competition, engenders it by inclining those who are the product of the same conditions of production to pursue the same goods, *whose rarity may arise entirely from their competition*" (my emphasis).

In both archaeological and anthropological exchange studies, the measure of an object's value in absence of money is usually inferred from abstract considerations of the work or time invested in the production or procurement of an object or resource, whereas reciprocity is usually taken as the natural rule that orders all non-commodity exchanges. In response to this and based on what has been discussed up to now, we could assert that: 1) the existence of an objective measure—at least seemingly—of value is a historical product characteristic of particular societies such as capitalist (although not restricted to this). Consequently, in the absence of money, we should not limit ourselves to "natural currencies" (such as time, distance, energy invested) when considering the value of things in non-market societies, and 2) reciprocity is not a rule in the sense of a consciously followed plan for action, and neither should it be seen as a universal template that gives form and cohesion to human societies, like a kind of social glue. Following Weiner (1992: 41), reciprocity is "...an unbounded arena where combative forces are subtly or aggressively engaged." The exchange of goods of any nature is better understood as being composed by different levels, a labyrinth of games and strategies, which must be constantly built through time by the actors, who must not loose sight of its steps and changes in order to stay in the game. More than promoting "equality" and "cohesion", the structuring principles of exchange networks are more often "hierarchy" and "difference". Material exchanges are embodied denials of social stability since the risk of their failure is always present (Battaglia, 1994:641; Bourdieu, 1977; Strathern, 1992; Weiner, 1992).

One might propose that the circulation of material culture can create very wide *spatial images* of a society, which I define *as the structuring of a social landscape of exclusion and/or belonging, a relational universe that it is learned through the direct experience with that material culture that circulates and has the property of creating space-time extensions.* The spatial images drawn by material culture can be seen as any other spatiality; a series of multiple, intersecting and overlapping socio-spatial networks of power (Gregory, 1989), which should be analyzed in terms of what Battaglia (1994) has called the "discourse and representation of power relationships". This dimension should also be integrated with the material aspects of the relationships of power; namely the labor processes and their material outcomes. It thus becomes possible to argue that the circulation of different classes of materials creates different spatial images, which may be contradictory in terms of the demands they can establish upon the labor processes of a society.

Social Interaction and Exchange in Northwestern Argentina: The Formative Period

Considerations of geography and ecology have always been fundamental to Andean archaeological and anthropological studies. Certainly, the mountainous region demands a particular economic rationality (Golte, 1980; Salomon, 1985). Andean communities in the present typically use different ecological environments in different altitudes or *pisos* by means of dispersed residence. This "vertical" approach to economic livelihood affords the advantage of being able to supplement the productive cycles of diverse basic products and resources with an overall increase of productivity in the long run (Golte, 1980). This model of economic system in which communities directly and independently exploit ecologically diverse microenvironments has also been used to interpret a variety of cases in the past (Murra, 1972; but see Salomon, 1980 for a nuanced approach). It is widely accepted that these efforts seek communal self-sufficiency, which is though of as the "Andean ideal" *par excellence* in common literature and is commonly presented as something overarching and supra-regional, a particular worldview intimately linked to the nature of the physical landscape. This ideal is thought to be responsible for the long stability observed in the economic and social strategies of the Andean area. Even when political and symbolic aspects are considered in the interpretations of past Andean societies, they are usually seen as cohesive entities adapting to ecological *pisos* as a way to benefit the community as a whole. Yet as critics of this model have pointed out, the establishing of *vertical archipiélagos* to exploit resources located in distant regions was often the result of factional interests of elite groups (Van Buren, 1996).

Particularly in the south Andean region, it is believed that this vertical, economic self-sufficiency was achieved by a combination of two strategies: direct control of different ecological *pisos*, and exchange by means of llama caravans. The variations in the emphasis between these strategies are usually attributed to time and changes in the social organization (e.g., Albeck, 1994). As for llama caravans, it is generally assumed that they were formed by pastoral societies that circulated and communicated along routes connecting the subtropical forest, the temperate valleys, the Puna (dry highlands) and the Pacific coast (Dillehay and Núñez, 1988: 611). This caravan system is considered to have guaranteed economic integration and political harmony, as it effectively mobilized the productive resources between different areas (Dillehay and Núñez, 1988: 604, 620). From this perspective, "social harmony" is understood as the absence of violent conflicts or war in the archaeological record (Dillehay and Núñez, 1988). Social conflict and power relationships in the sense discussed in the previous section are clearly absent in these explanations, as the reciprocity norm is seen as a kind of glue that provides groups with social cohesion.

The Formative period in the Argentinean Northwest (600 BC–AD 1000)[8] is generally characterized as a period when segmentary groups lived in small agricultural-herding sedentary or semi-sedentary villages, with little social hierarchy. These communities are generally seen as having maintained dynamic social interactions that were symmetrical and oriented towards the procurement of exotic goods and to supplement subsistence, which nevertheless, is seen as basically self-sufficient (Núñez Regueiro, 1974; Raffino, 1977, 1991; Berberián and Nielsen, 1988; Olivera, 1988; Scattolin, 1990; Núñez Regueiro and Tartusi, 1993; Tarragó, 1993; but see Gero and Scattolin, 1995). While this characterization has gained wide spread popularity, I would like to suggest an alternative way of considering social interaction and the exchange of goods in this period, especially for the Early Formative (600 BC–AD 500).

There is clear evidence of the circulation of different classes of objects and resources between the diverse ecological areas of NWA[9] from even the earliest moments of human occupation in the area. For example, specific products of the subtropical rainforest such as woods, feathers, drugs, and animals among other things have been found in archaeological sites of the pre-Formative Periods in both the temperate valleys and in the Puna (Fernández Dístel, 1974; Aschero, 1979; Aschero and Yacobaccio, 1994), as well as in Chile, particularly in San Pedro of Atacama and the Loa Valley (Berenguer and Dauelsberg, 1993; Muñoz, 1993). In addition, Formative ceramic and metalwork styles, usually considered as having geographically bounded production areas that do not overlap (Núñez Regueiro and Tartusi, 1993), have been found in distant places, including localities in Chile. Despite the fact that researchers have long acknowledged the dispersal of these items across the south Andean region, the apparent differences in their distributions gave rise to the designation of mutually exclusive stylistic spheres and cultural areas (but see Ventura, 1991; Pérez Gollán, 1994; Quiroga, 1995). In these designations, lithic materials, like obsidian, have never been considered in terms of their possible role in social interaction (but see Escola et al., 1997). The consideration of materials different from pottery or metal crafts has been limited to some organic goods whose origin can be easily traced.

Researchers may recognize that demand for the objects and resources mentioned above could have come from a community's symbolic life, and that social factors did play a central part in the definition and redefinition of social reproduction strategies (Pérez Gollán, 1994: 36; Tarragó, 1994). It is still common to read that exchange relationships were structured by the complementarity stemming from the differential distribution of resources across the environment. In many explanations, this distribution of resources is the primary cause of social demand. Economic complementarity is seen as something that enables the political exchanges at the superstructural level, which in turn can only be carried out when a certain level of communal economic self-sufficiency is assured. This gives the idea that economic life is somehow independent from power and symbolism, which seem to be considered as by-products of subsistence activities. Similarly problematic is the notion that space seems to be merely the backdrop, as well as a restrictive factor, for human action. While space is central to the discussion, it is only seen as a passive dimension, an abyss to be overcome when objects of prestige are not locally available. Physical distance is the source of value of the objects but only in terms of the costs that the communities have to minimize in order to acquire the goods. Space here arises as an ordering principle, since ecological diversity is seen as imposing the necessity of economic complementarity. Exchange then, is seen as a regulative mechanism that balances subsistence needs and feeds ritual activities. As a consequence, the differences observed in the material culture of Formative period societies are explained in terms of adaptations to ecological differences and in terms of specialization. Similarities observed in material culture, on the other hand, such as the widely distributed pottery and metalwork styles throughout the south Andean area, are usually interpreted as the consequence of the search of prestige items and of locally non-available subsistence goods.

The differential availability of resources certainly influences the necessity of special mechanisms for their procurement. Yet, if we consider social life as more than a mere reflection of the "order" imposed by nature, the consideration of local histories in the context of the south Andean area becomes even more complex. To see through this complexity we need to consider power relationships in the past as both actively reproduced and challenged.

The inclusion of other materials, for example, could illuminate different aspects of exchange relationships in the NWA Formative period. Recent research shows that the pattern of obsidian procurement and circulation could have been extremely complicated. While different areas of NWA used obsidian from at least four different sources; in some cases groups did not use obsidian from the nearest source (Yacobaccio et al., 1999). Obsidian distributions suggest a distinct Formative Period, one that is different from the one we already know from the study of ceramic styles and metalwork. Such a diversity of "Formatives" can give us a more complex image of the period in its entirety.

Recent studies show that the distribution of ceramic styles could have been quite more flexible and mixed than what was thought until now. In Yutopián (Cajón Valley), for example, distinct pottery styles appear together in contexts usually considered as part of different cultural areas, together with evidence of metalwork and obsidian (not local) all of them in a domestic compound that appears separated from the rest (Gero and Scattolin, 1994, 1995). This provides an alternative image to those which stem from the analysis of the evidence of other areas, where obsidian, seashell beads, metalwork and different ceramic styles occur in separate contexts, or are not present at all, for example in the cases of Loma Alta (W skirt of the Aconquija), Alamito (Campo del Pucará), Hualfin valley, Laguna Blanca (Puna) (Figure 12.1).

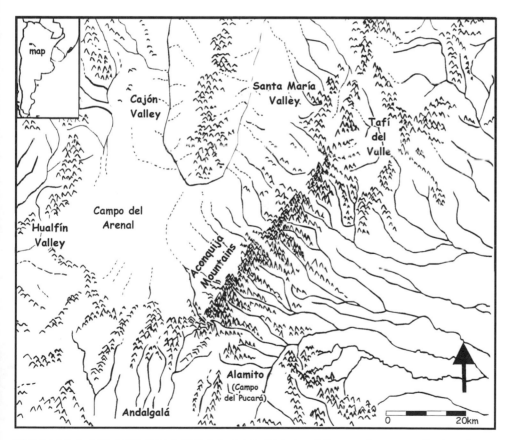

Figure 12.1. Western slope of the Aconquija mountains and surrounding archaeological areas.

In the particular case of Loma Alta, while the settlement pattern indicates similarities with the eastern humid valleys, while the pottery shows similarities with sites from the Hualfín valley (Scattolin, 1990), obsidian and seashell beads show connections to a wider spatial scale towards the west, the Puna and the Pacific (Lazzari, 1998). These relationships with the Puna did not obey an underlying necessity of camelid herding, since the Aconquija mountains, which offer acceptable conditions for herding at the higher altitudes, are closer to the actual settlement areas.[10]

It is therefore interesting to look at the varied use and depositional contexts of the different types of materials in each site. For instance, while in Yutopián (Cajón valley) these different classes of evidence appear in one context—a domestic compound separated from the rest of the site—(Gero and Scattolin, 1994, 1995), in Loma Alta they appear in different contexts: Obsidian appears only in domestic spaces, while seashell beads appear in some rooms and in certain tombs. Not all these categories of objects are present in all the sites of this period. For example, at archaeological sites with different types of ceremonial architecture, as in Alamito (Campo del Pucará) or Tafí (Figure 12.1), non-local objects, particularly obsidian, are underrepresented (Berberián and Nielsen, 1988; Cremonte, 1996; González and Núñez Regueiro, 1960; Núñez Regueiro, 1971; Núñez Regueiro and Tartusi, 1993;). This could demonstrate a tendency to privilege control over the contexts where public action occurred, rather than the control over the objects themselves[11] (see Scattolin, 1999). If we add to this picture the ubiquity of high quality ceramic styles associated with caravan traffic, such as Vaquerías or Polychrome Condorhuasi styles, both with seemingly specific contexts of occurrence (González and Baldini, 1989; Korstanje, 1995; Núñez Regueiro and Tartusi, 1993), the pattern becomes even more complex. Finally, it has been noticed that Formative Period settlements which did not share the same pottery styles were engaged in the use of the same obsidian sources over long periods of time (Scattolin and Lazzari, 1998). This contradicts the traditional idea that archaeological sites with different stylistic universes did not participate in the same social interaction networks (see for example Núñez Regueiro and Tartusi, 1993).

These cases allow us to think of circulation networks in the NWA Formative Period as more flexible and complicated and as reflections of the constitution and reproduction of different social bonds. When we look at the evidence from this period, the time-space scale of each site was extended in each possible direction by means of the circulation of material culture. The spatial patterns that this circulation reflects, that is, the paths that the traveling objects marked, seem to have created multiple intersecting and overlapping networks, which bring us back to the ideas about social interaction and circulation of objects previously exposed in this chapter.

The observed pattern in NWA of the circulation of goods is sufficiently complex as to suggest a great variety of interaction relationships and networks that coexisted and created demands on the local labor processes. It is possible then to think that these demands, which were bound to different social relations and different forms of authority, could have created conflict or at least, raised tensions in everyday life. The relationship between the circulation of non local goods and labor processes should be explored in each case, in order to assess whether these goods were part of the same interaction network or whether they were wrapped in different, competing networks that would have created conflict between themselves. This in turn, could take us to the identification of contradictory forces and perhaps, to the identification of social conflict (in any of its versions) and the possibilities of resistance, if they existed. A bottom-up approach can also be proposed (Saitta, 1994; Thomas, 1993) which focuses upon aspects of daily life, such as habits and daily tasks, in order to trace the construction of domination, resistance, difference, and identity. We could obtain a better vision of the different ways in which power was manifested, thus gaining a more encompassing understanding of social practices in this period. In fact, many of our objects of study seem to be for daily use, (for example obsidian, Lazzari, 1998). These ordinary objects which often come from distant areas, while possibly lacking a special role or high level of investment in their manufacture, created a conceptual as well as a material map of wider spatial dimensions, wider than those spaces immediately experienced in everyday tasks. This map in turn constituted a lived experience that was learned in a non discursive way (or rather, as a material discourse), and served as a kind of window to a world in which agents belonged or from which they were excluded, depending on how they participated in the interaction networks.

Exchanges of objects, resources, services, knowledge, etc. are not mechanisms for homeostatic regulation (*contra* Halstead, 1989). Rather, they are social practices that build particular social landscapes. The maps of these social landscapes, the respective position of the agents, are learned by the members of each society through their participation in the networks of circulation of material culture. In this way, these social landscapes are at the same time the outcome and the precondition and means for social action.

Architectural spaces are "books to be read with the body" (Bourdieu, 1977: 90). In a similar manner, social landscapes built by means of the objects that circulated and the social relationships that were enacted through them could also be considered as "books" to be read with the body, with usage and interaction, in an experiential way. People learned social values and roles from these social landscapes by participating in these circulation networks and the daily use of the objects acquired through exchange. The local landscape of everyday tasks was embedded in a wider landscape of social connections that in this way were always present. Moreover, if we consider the multiple and overlapping nature of these social networks, then the demands that these networks might have placed upon the local labor processes are of central importance. One might propose that the spatial images that these networks created should be studied as *fields* where social contradictions were reflected as a consequence of the struggles over both meaning and labor allocation, and where diverse forms of social conflict were manifested in either overt or subtle ways (see Barrett, 1988).

Instead of considering "The Formative" as a point of ancestral origin of the pristine version of the "Andean Ideal", we might identify several Formatives, thus rendering a picture where cohesion and harmony are far from being the norm. This, in turn, would allow for a better understanding of the later processes of complexity and social inequality. It is not my intention to entirely contradict the idea of a specific economic rationality related to some extent with south Andean ecology and physical geography. Instead, my hope is to include in the dialogue the notion that history is a much more fragmented process in which economic rationality and its applications vary according to power relationships and processes of self and group identity. Societies do not solve their economic problems first, reach their self-sufficiency level second, and then, in their remaining free time, devote time to rituals and social reproduction. As we have seen previously, seemingly purely economic exchanges may fuel other types of exchanges, for example ceremonial exchanges, but they also have a social meaning of their own. This symbolic dimension of apparently "practical" exchanges should be acknowledged in archaeological studies, since they imply the presence of a chain of socially accepted values and a legitimate way of reproducing them.

Final Considerations

Ecological complementarity and physical distance are material dimensions of diverse significance. Even at the intra-community level where they outline more than a relationship beyond the social realm. They are not mere external features that are used and in this way give form to social life. In fact, both are maps of the world whose meaning and importance could very well have been different according to different groups or even according to different agents. The symbolic dimension of ecological complemetarity has already been recognized (Núñez and Dillehay, 1979; Pérez Gollán, 1994; Salomon, 1985), however it does persist as a superficial expression of the distribution of resources in Andean societies, which are thought to be ordered following the logic of nature. In the search to reveal all the possible manifestations of power, nature and society cannot be separated. The explanations should not stop at the conditions given by the natural environment or the organization of subsistence activities. In such a case, we would fall into the trap of writing recurrent histories where a single explanatory variable, in growing influence and complexity, would determine the course of history.

We could say that neither reciprocity as a norm or rule, nor physical distances and the economic complementarity that stems from a particular ecology, organizes all aspects of social life. Rather, rules, re-sources, and strategies can have different histories, as both the out-come of and the condition for different habituses (Bourdieu, 1977). These intertwined histories can involve the reproduction of different so-cial values and authorities, as different competing networks are created in this process. Different networks, related to different social practices, material objects and social values, all give build very different geogra-phies. These spatialities are created both through the movement of ob-jects and the allocation of labor. Just as any other society, NW Argentina Formative societies cannot be reduced to a single spatial structure. Un-derstanding that these spatial images in the Formative were both the outcome and the means by which power relationships, resistances, dif-ferences and identities could be constructed, depends on recognizing the fundamental role of daily life in the reproduction, the tension and the subversions of established social relationships.

As we have seen, exploring the spaces of social organization and production can help to uncover the social relationships that are so much inscribed therein, as well as constituted through its varied forms and pro-ductions (Soja, 1997). When we speak of relationships that appear as strictly economic, such as the complementarity among different ecolog-ical areas, we are speaking of both a construction of past societies and of our own. Such a spatial distribution of labor and consumption could have been in the past as much a cognitive space as a material structur-ing of the space; and still, to what extent both were related to each other and with the physical space should be evaluated before assumed. The naturalization of social relationships by discourses and practices is a property of power relationships in whose complexities we are certainly trapped (Yanagisako and Delaney, 1995). In this way we create pristine pasts where there were more "rational" ways of living. Nevertheless, tak-ing this into account should not imply that this naturalizing property of social power be erased from past communities. We should explore the diverse configurations of power relationships and certainly, the material discourses (in this case, the material landscapes of ecological comple-mentarity) by which societies dealt with nature are a rich arena for this exploration.

Acknowledgements

I would like to thank the organizers of the "I Encontro de Teoria Arque-ologica na America do Sul", Pedro P. Funari and Eduardo G. Neves, for their hospitality. I am grateful to L. Meskell, C. Gifford and K. Olson for the careful reading and editing of this paper and their insightful com-ments. I would also like to thank J. Thomas and C. Gamble, whose guidance and insights were invaluable during my stay in Southampton, thanks to a Fundación Antorchas Fellowship. Finally, my special thanks to M. Cristina Scattolin for her constant support and guidance in this complex process of understanding NWA Formative Period archaeology.

Needless to say, all the ideas and mistakes in this paper are of my entire responsibility.

Notes

[1] The general labor process has two aspects: one involving surplus production and appropriation, the other one not involving surplus of any kind and being basically of communal interest. Both aspects co-exist in every society (Saitta, 1989).

[2] Meaningfulness exists in every action. As Munn (1986:7) says, significance comes from a relational process between practices of any kind. "Symbolic" as a term does not only refer to rituals but includes " ... the practices by means of which actors construct their social world, and simultaneously their own selves and modes of being in the world are thought to be symbolically constituted and themselves symbolic processes."

[3] "Intersubjetive" is used in the sense of the mutual creation of actors through their interaction and the mutual evaluation involved in the relationship (Munn, 1992).

[4] For Bourdieu (1994:57), domination is the indirect effect of a complex group of actions which are engendered by the crossed restrictions of the dominants, who find themselves limited by the field through which domination is exercised. This can be complemented by Gidden's (1984:50) concept of domination as structured asymmetries in the distribution of resources, both allocative and of authority, used and reconstituted in power relationships.

[5] See Giddens (1979, 1984: 232–233) for the difference between *contradiction* and *social conflict.*

[6] Gregory (1982: 8–9) has defined gift exchange as the exchange of inalienable goods between non-strangers that establishes *qualitative* personal relationships between the *persons* involved in the transaction. On the contrary, commodities exchange is the exchange of alienable goods between strangers, establishing *quantitative* relationships between the *objects* that take part in the transaction.

[7] Bourdieu (1977: 86) defined habitus as " ... a subjective but not individual system of internalized structures, schemes of perception, conception, and action, common to all members of the same group or class and constituting the precondition for all objectification and apperception..." See also p. 95 for the limits of the concept.

[8] In NW Argentina, the Formative Period occurred after the Archaic (a period of experimental domestication, ca. 8000–1800 BC), and before the Regional Development period (characterized by highly hierarchical chiefdoms with clear-cut territorial boundaries maintained through the political control of other ecological areas, agglomerated settlements and warfare, ca. 1000–1436 AD). Subsequently, the Inkas conquered the area, interrupting local social developments (Núñez Regueiro, 1974).

[9] NW Argentina is segmented in three geographical sub-areas: Puna or dry highlands, "valliserrana" (temperate valleys and sierra), and the subtropical rainforests (on the eastern skirts of the Andes). They include the provinces of Jujuy, Salta, Catamarca, Tucumán and La Rioja. When we refer to south-central Andes, we include northern Chile, north western Argentina and the south of Bolivia (González, 1979).

[10] It should be noticed that salt may have been a common staple brought from the Puna by the caravans (see Lecoq, 1987, for an ethnographic example of the exchange of salt).

[11] Scattolin (1999) proposed a similar idea to the one presented here. Looking at the spatial structuration of settlements, Scattolin proposes that during the first Millenium AD in NW Argentina there where two modes of spatial differentiation based on the use of distinct resources: one founded on the control and manipulation of symbolic (sacred) resources and the other based on the control and manipulation of socio-political (secular) resources.

References

Albeck, M. E., editor, 1994, *Taller "De Costa a Selva": producción e intercambio entre los pueblos agroalfareros de los Andes Centro Sur*. Instituto Interdisciplinario Tilcara, FFyL, UBA, Buenos Aires.

Appadurai, A., 1991, Introducción: las mercancías y la política del valor. In *La vida social de las cosas: perspectiva cultural de las mercancías*, edited by A. Appadurai, pp. 17–87. Cambridge University Press, Cambridge.

Aschero, C., 1979, Un asentamiento acerámico en la Quebrada de Inca Cueva (Jujuy). Inorme preliminar sobre el sitio ICc4. In *Actas de las Jornadas de Arqueología del NOA*, pp. 62–71. Universidad del Salvador, Buenos Aires.

Aschero, C., and Yacobaccio H., 1994, 20 años después: Inca Cueva 7 revisitado. Actas y Memorias del XI Congreso de Arqueología. *Revista del Museo de Historia Natural de San Rafael* (Mendoza) 13(1/4): 116–119.

Barrett, J., 1989, Food, Gender and Metal: Questions of Social Reproduction. In *The Bronze Age-Iron Age Transition in Europe. Aspects of Continuity and Change in European Societies ca. 1200 to 500 B.C.*, edited by M. L. S. Sorensen and R. Thomas, pp. 304–320. British Archaeological Reports, Oxford.

1988, Fields of Discourse: Reconstituting a Social Archaeology. *Critique of Social Anthropology* 7 (3): 5–16.

Battaglia, D., 1990, *On the Bones of the Serpent: Person, Memory and Mortality in Sabarl Island Society*. The University of Chicago Press, Chicago.

1994, Retaining Reality: some Practical Problems with Objects as Property. *Man* 29:631–644.

Berberián, E., and Nielsen., A., 1988, Sistemas de asentamiento prehisánico en la etapa Formativa del valle de Tafí (Pcia. de Tucumán, República Argentina). In *Sistemas de asentamiento prehispánico en el Valle de Tafí*, edited by E. Berberián, A. Nielsen, E. de Dorsch, B. Bixio, J. Salazar, and E. Pillado, pp. 21–53. Editorial Comechingonia, Córdoba.

Berenguer R., J., and Dauelsberg H., P., 1993, El Norte grande en la órbita de Tiwanaku (400 a 1200 d.C.). In *Culturas de Chile: Prehistoria, desde sus orígenes hasta los albores de la conquista*, edited by J. Hidalgo L., V. Schiappacasse F., H. Niemeyer F., C. Aldunate del S., and I. Solimano R., pp. 129–180. Editorial Andrés Bello, Santiago de Chile.

Bourdieu, P., 1994(1974), *Raisons pratiques: Sur la théorie de l'action*. Seuil, Paris

1997(1977), *Outline of a Theory of Practice*. Cambridge University Press, Cambridge.

Burke, T., 1999, *Lifebuoy men, Lux women: Commodification, Consumption and Cleanliness in modern Zimbabwe*. Duke University Press, Durham and London.

Cremonte, B., 1996, *Investigaciones arqueológicas en la Quebrada de la Ciénaga (Depto. de Tafí, Tucumán)*. Ph.D. dissertation, Universidad Nacional de Jujuy, San Salvador de Jujuy.

Dillehay, T., and Nuñez., L., 1988, Camelids, Caravans, and Complex Societies in the South-Central Andes. In *Recent Studies in Pre-columbian archaeology*, edited by N. Saunders and O. de Montmollin, pp. 603–634. BAR International Series 421 (ii), Oxford.

Earle, T.K., 1982, Prehistoric Economics and the Archaeology of Exchange. In *Contexts for Prehistoric Exchange*, edited by J.E. Ericson and T.K. Earle, pp. 1–12. Academic Press, New York.

Earle, T.K., and Ericson, J.E., 1977, Exchange Systems in Archaeological Perspective. In *Exchange Systems in Prehistory*, edited by T.K. Earle and J.E. Ericson, pp. 3–12. Academic Press, New York.

Ericson, J.E., 1982, Production for Obsidian Exchange in California. In *Contexts for Prehistoric Exchange*, edited by J.E. Ericson and T.K. Earle, pp. 129–148. Academic Press, New York.

Escola, P.S., Vázquez, C., and Momo, F., 1997, Análisis de procedencia de artifactos de obsidiana: vías metodológicas de acercamiento al intercambio. *Arqueología Contemporánea* 6. In press.

Fernández Distel, A., 1974. Excavaciones arqueológicas en la Cueva de Huachichocana. Departamento Tumbaya, Pcia. de Jujuy. *Relaciones de la Sociedad Argentina de Antropología* (N.S.) 8(1):101–127.

Gamble, C., 1993, Exchange, Foraging and Local Hominid Networks. In *Trade and Exchange in Prehistoric Europe*, edited by C. Scarre and F. Healy, pp. 35–44. Oxbow Monograph 33. Oxbow Books, Oxford.

1995, Making Tracks, Hominid Networks and the Evolution, of the Social Landscape. In *The Archaeology of Human Ancestry. Power, Sex and Tradition*, edited by J. Steele and S. Shennan, pp. 253–276. Routledge, London.

1998, Palaeolithic Society and the Release from Proximity: a Network Approach to Intimate Relations. *World Archaeology* 29(3):426–449.

Gell, A., 1992, Inter-Tribal Commodity Barter and Reproductive Gift-Exchange in Old Melanesia. In *Barter, Exchange and Value: An Anthropological Approach*, edited by C. Humphrey and S. Hugh-Jones, pp. 143–168. Cambridge University Press, Cambridge.

Gero, J., and Scattolin., C., 1994, Hacia la comprensión de la jerarquización: un estudio desde Yutopián, Valle del Cajón. In *Actas del XI Congreso Nacional de Arqueologúa Argentina*. San Rafael, Mendoza. *In press*.

1995, *Household Production as Glue: Insights from the Early Formative of Northwest Argentina*. Paper presented to "Re-examining Theoretical and Methodological Approaches to Production and Specialization: Where do we go from here?" Society for American Archaeology 60th Annual Meeting, Minneapolis, Minnesota.

Giddens, A., 1979, *Central Problems in Social Theory. Action, Structure and Contradiction in Social Analysis*. Macmillan, London.

1984, *A Contemporary Critique of Historical Materialism*. Macmillan, London.

Godelier, M., 1977, *Perspectives in Marxist Anthropology*. Cambridge University Press, Cambridge.

1981, *Instituciones económicas*. Editorial Anagrama, Barcelona.

Golte, J., 1980, *La racionalidad en la organización andina*. IEP, Lima.

González, A., 1979, Pre-Columbian Metallurgy of NW Argentina: Historical Sequence and Cultural Process. In *Metallurgy of Central and South America*, edited by E. Benson, pp. 133–202. Dumbarton Oaks, Washington DC.

González, A., and Baldini, M., 1989, Vaquerías: la más antigua alfarería polícroma del noroeste argentino. *Más allá del objeto Revista Artinf* Edición 78–79, Año 14:8–12.

González, A., and Núñez Regueiro, V., 1960. Preliminary Report on Archaeological Research in Tafí del Valle, NW Argentina. *Akten des 34 C.I.A.*: 485–496.

Gregory, C., 1982,*Gifts and Commodities*. Academic Press, London.

Gregory, D., 1989, Presences and Absences: Time-Space Relations and Structuration Theory. In *Social Theory of Modern Societies: Anthony Giddens and his Critics*, edited by D. Held and J. Thompson, pp. 185–214. Cambridge University Press, Cambridge.

Halstead, P., 1989, The Economy has a Normal Surplus. In *Bad Year Economics: Cultural Responses to Risk and Uncertainty*, edited by P. Halstead and J. O'Shea, pp. 68–80. Cambridge University Press, Cambridge.

Helms, M., 1988, *Ulysses' Sail: An Ethnographic Odyssey of Power, Knowledge and Geographical Distance*. Princeton University Press, New Jersey.

Humphrey, C., and Hugh-Jones, S., editors, 1992, *Barter, Exchange and Value: An Anthropological Approach*. Cambridge University Press, Cambridge.

Korstanje, A., 1995, Nuevas reflexiones en torno a Vaquerías: un estilo cerámico polémico. *Cuadernos* (San Salvador de Jujuy) 5:169–179.

Lazzari, M., 1998. La economía más allá de la subsistencia: intercambio y producción lítica en el Aconquija. *Arqueología* (Buenos Aires) 7:9–50.

Lecoq, P., 1987, Caravanes de Lamas, sel et echanges dans une communauté de Potosi, en Bolivie. *Bulletin de l'Institute Français des Etudes Andines* 16(3–4):1–38.

Liep, J., 1990, Gift Exchange and the Construction of Identity. In *Culture and History in the Pacific*, edited by J. Siikala, pp. 164–181. The Finnish Anthropological Society, Helsinki.

Mauss, M., 1990(1925), *The Gift: The Form and Reason for Exchange in Archaic Societies*. Routledge, London.

Miller, D., 1987, *Material Culture and Mass Consumption*. Blackwell, London.

Miller, D., and Tilley, C., 1984, Ideology, Power and Prehistory: an Introduction. In *Ideology, Power and Prehistory*, edited by D. Miller and C. Tilley, pp. 1–15. Cambridge University Press, Cambridge.

Munn, N. D., 1986, *The Fame of Gawa. A Symbolic Study of Value Transformation in a Massim (Papua New Guinea) Society.* Duke University Press, Durham and London.

1990, Constructing Regional Worlds in Experience: Kula Exchange, Witchcraft and Gawan Local Events. *Man* 25:1–17.

Muñoz O., I., 1993, El período Formativo en el Norte Grande (1000 a.C. a 500 d.C.). In *Culturas de Chile: Prehistoria, desde sus orígenes hasta los albores de la conquista*, edited by J. Hidalgo L., V. Schiappacasse F., H. Niemeyer F., C. Aldunate del S. and I. Solimano R., pp. 107–128. Editorial Andrés Bello, Santiago de Chile.

Murra, J., 1972, *Formaciones económicas y políticas del mundo andino.* IEP, Lima.

1995, Did Tribute and Markets Prevail in the Andes before the European Invasion? In *Ethnicity, Markets and Migration in the Andes: At the Crossroads of History and Anthropology*, edited by B. Larson, O. Harris, and E. Tandeter, pp. 57–72. Duke University Press, Durham and London.

Núñez, L., and Dillehay, T., 1979, *Movilidad giratoria, armonía social y desarrollo en los Andes meridionales: patrones de tráfico e interacción económica (ensayo).* Edición numerada, 22. Universidad del Norte, Antofagasta.

Núñez Regueiro, V., 1971, La Cultura Alamito de la Subárea Valliserrana del N.O. argentino. *Journal de la Societé des Américanistes* 60:7–65.

1974, Conceptos instrumentales y marco teórico en relación al análisis del desarrollo cultural del Noroeste argentino. *Revista del Instituto de Antropología* (Córdoba) 5:169–190.

Núñez Regueiro, V., and Tartusi, M., 1993, Los centros ceremoniales del N.O.A. *Publicaciones* (Tucumán) 5: 1–49.

Olivera, D., 1988, La opción productiva: apuntes para el análisis de sistemas adaptativos de tipo formativo en el Noroeste Argentino. *Precirculados del IX Congreso Nacional de Arqueología Argentina, Buenos Aires*: 83–101.

Pérez Gollán, J., 1994, El proceso de integración en el Valle de Ambato: complejidad social y sistemas simbólicos. *Rumitacama* (Catamarca) 1(1):33–41.

Quiroga, L., 1995, *El contacto Hispano-indígena en Yocavil.* Honors thesis, FFy L, UBA, Buenos Aires.

Raffino, R., 1977, Las aldeas del Formativo Inferior de la Quebrada del Toro (Provincia de Salta; Argentina). *Obra Homenaje al Centenario del Museo de La Plata*, volume 2 (Sección Antropología): 253–299.

1991, *Las poblaciones indígenas en Argentina.* Editorial TEA, Buenos Aires.

Renfrew, C., and Shennan, S., editors, 1982, *Ranking, Resource and Exchange: Aspects of the Archaeology of Early European Society.* Cambridge University Press, Cambridge.

Saitta, D., 1994, Agency, Class and Interpretation. *Journal of Anthropological Archaeology* 13:201–227.

Salomon, F., 1985, The Dynamic Potential of the Complementarity Concept. In *Andean Ecology and Civilization*, edited by S. Masuda, M. Shimada, and C. Morris, pp. 511–531. University of Tokyo Press, Tokyo.

Scattolin, M., 1990, Dos asentamientos formativos al pie del Aconquija: el sitio Loma Alta (Catamarca, Argentina). *Gaceta Arqueológica Andina* 5(17): 85–100.

1999, Organización residencial y arquitectura en el Aconquija durante el primer milenio A.D. In *Actas del XIII Congreso Nacional de Arqueología Argentina.* Córdoba, Argentina. *In press.*

Scattolin, M., and Korstanje, A., 1994, Tránsito y frontera en los Nevados del Aconquija. *Arqueología* (Buenos Aires) 4: 165–197.

Scattolin, M., and Lazzari, M., 1998, Tramando redes: Obsidianas al Oeste del Aconquija. In Taller de investigación Binacional. Interacciones socio-económicas entre el Noroeste Argentino y el Norte de Chile en épocas prehispánicas. *Estudios Atacameños* 14:189–209.

Soja, E., 1989, The Spatiality of Social Life: Towards a Transformative Re-theorization. In *Social Relations and Spatial Structures*, edited by D. Gregory and J. Urry, pp. 90–127. Macmillan, London.

1996, *Thirdspace. Journeys to Los Angeles and Other Real and Imagined Places.* Blackwell, Oxford.

1997, The Socio-Spatial Dialectic. In *Reading Human Geography. The Poetics and Politics of Inquiry,* edited by T. Barnes and D. Gregory, pp. 244–255. Arnold, London.

Strathern, M., 1992, Qualified Value: The Perspective of Gift Exchange. In *Barter, Exchange and Value: An Anthropological Approach,* edited by C. Humphrey and S. Hugh-Jones, pp. 169–191. Cambridge University Press, Cambridge.

Taçon, P., 1991, The Power of Stone: Symbolic Aspects of Stone Use and Tool Development in Western Arnhem Land, Australia. *Antiquity* 65:195–207.

Tarragó, M. N., 1993, *Contribución al conocimiento arqueológico de las poblaciones de los Oasis de San Pedro de Atacama en relación con los otros pueblos puneños en especial, el sector septentrional del Valle Calchaquí.* Ph.D. dissertation. Facultad de Humanidades y Artes, UNR, Argentina.

1994, Intercambio entre Atacama y el borde de Puna. In *Taller "De Costa a Selva". Producción e intercambio entre los pueblos agroalfareros de los Andes Centro Sur,* edited by M.T. Albeck, pp. 199–213. Instituto Interdisciplinario de Tilcara, Universidad de Buenos Aires, Buenos Aires.

Taussig, M., 1980, *The Devil and Commodity Fetishism in South America.* University of North Carolina Press, Chapel Hill.

Torrence, R., 1986, *Production and Exchange of Obsidian Tools: Prehistoric Obsidian in the Aegean.* Cambridge University Press, Cambridge.

1989, Tools as Optimal Solutions. In *Time, Energy and Stone Tools,* edited by R. Torrence, pp.1–6. Cambridge University Press, Cambridge.

Thomas, J., 1993, Discourse, Totalization and "The Neolithic". In *Interpretative Archaeology,* edited by C. Tilley, pp. 357–394. Berg, Oxford.

Thomas, N., 1991, *Entangled Objects: Exchange, Material Culture and Colonialism in the Pacific.* Harvard University Press, Cambridge.

Van Buren, M., 1996, Rethinking the Vertical Archipelago. Ethnicity, Exchange and History in the South Central Andes. *American Anthropologist* 98(2):338–351.

Ventura, B., 1991, Síntesis de las investigaciones arqueológicas en el sector norte de las selvas occidentales. Arqueología (Buenos Aires) 1: 51–73.

Weiner, A., 1992, *Inalienable Possessions: The Paradox of Keeping-While-Giving.* University of California Press, Berkeley.

Weiss, B., 1996, *The Making and Unmaking of the Haya Lived World: Consumption, Commoditization and Everyday Practice.* Duke University Press, Durham and London.

Yacobaccio, H., Escola, P.S., Pereyra, F.X., Glascock, M.D., and Lazzari, M., 1999, *Quest for Ancient Routes. Obsidian Sourcing Research in NW Argentina.* Paper presented at XIII Congreso Nacional de Arqueología Argentina, Córdoba, Argentina.

Yanagisako, S., and Delaney, C., 1995, Naturalizing Power. In *Naturalizing Power: Essays in Feminist Cultural Analysis,* edited by S. Yanagisako and C. Delaney, pp.1–22. Routledge, London.

The Materiality of Inka Domination

13

Landscape, Spectacle, Memory, and Ancestors

Félix A. Acuto

Introduction

As Julian Thomas (1996, 1999) has claimed, modern western thought has tended to separate the world of social actions and relations from the world of objects. According to Thomas, since the Enlightenment material culture has been considered an inert or passive aspect in the constitution of social life. This perspective was also adopted in the social sciences. In some sense, the social sciences have analyzed social processes as disconnected from material culture, as if instruments, clothes and the buildings that people use in daily interactions do not participate significantly beyond their existence as functional and external devices of social actions.

On the other hand, this is not to suggest that the only solution to this passive vision of material life is to view objects as merely active (Glassie, 1999; Miller, 1987, 1998), because in some sense this would still portray or position material culture as external and separate from us. What I want to emphasize here is that material culture is a pivotal part of our social being, and as such, human beings are actually materially composed. As beings-in-the-world our subjectivity is a historical product, and is also shaped by the materiality and spatiality of the world (Thomas, 1996). We cannot understand nor think about the world appropriately

211

without taking objects into account. Material culture is inserted into our cognition of the world. Although perhaps we are not always conscious that our social world is constructed through objects, or that our social relations are constantly objectified, we cannot deny that women, men and societies as a whole would not exist without the world of things. Material culture is part of us; it is in our actions, in our bodily movements, in our relations, and also in our ideas about the world. Social actions and material culture form a dialectically constituted unity (McGuire, 1992).

Space is certainly a clear example of this. Spatiality (or socially produced space) is not simply a container where social relationships are established, but rather represents a fundamental part of these relations, a key dimension where social actions and relations are produced and reproduced (Giddens, 1979, 1984; Gregory and Urry, 1985; Lefebvre, 1974; Soja, 1989). In this way, there exists a dialectical relation between social space and social actions. Spatialities are created by social actions, but at the same time these actions are constituted and built by the same spatialities they produce. Spatial structure is therefore not only the arena where social relations are expressed but also the domain where, and through which, these relations are constituted (Parker Pearson and Richards, 1994). Social space is not a dimension that individuals experience externally, such as the place they inhabit; rather, space exists within social beings, and it is embodied through experience, practice and routine (Gregory, 1989; Thomas, 1993). Moreover, through the use of space and architectural structures, social principles are created and transmitted (Locock, 1994).

Spatiality is a social product and an integral part of the material constitution and structuration of social life (Soja, 1989). We must distinguish spatiality from physical space (the space of nature), and mental space (the space of cognition and representation), because the former is materially constituted. This material aspect of spatiality is represented by the material culture socially built in space, including both fixed physical infrastructure (such as architecture) and moveable objects, and also by natural features socially incorporated and loaded with meanings.

Archaeology and anthropology have recently demonstrated that several non-western societies do not understand or conceive material culture, as we do, as something external and passive, but rather they view things as if they were living beings that, as human beings, have their own biographies and powerfully participate in social life (Appadurai, 1986; Gillespie, 2000; Kopytoff, 1986; Thomas, 1999). In this paper I will try to show how landscape, buildings, objects and nature were constitutive aspects of Inka society. For the Inka, the material world was a fundamental dimension in their domination over other Andean societies, the legitimization of Inka social structure, and their understanding and explanation of the world.

In general, Inka processes of domination have been described from the perspective of how the Empire controlled and subjugated local societies at two levels; economic and political (see, for example, D'Altroy, 1992; Hyslop, 1979, 1993; Morris, 1982; Morris and Thompson, 1985; Pease, 1982, 1989; among many others). In the first case, the main focus was on the study of the imperial political economy and its influence on ruled societies' economies, especially concerning relations of production and the reorganization of local labor, the system of land holding, social relationships of exchange between the state and the subordinate populations, and the financing policies that the Inka Empire generated in order to obtain the necessary resources to sustain and reproduce the state machinery. On the other hand, with regards to the political level, a favorite topic of study has been the alteration of provincial societies' power structures, principally through the re-structuration of settlement systems and the forced mobilization of ethnic groups (or part of them) from their regions of origin to other locations to serve the interests of the Inka State, either as soldiers, artisans or officials representing the Empire in some of its multiple provinces.

I consider this quite a narrow view of domination. Domination in the Inka case not only involved political and economic aspects, but symbolic aspects as well. Domination was not simply the imposition of new political and economic structures on other societies, and its justification through ideological mechanisms. The relation between Inka and local societies did not simply concern political control and resistance. On the contrary, a more complex dialectical relation was involved (in the sense of McGuire, 1992 and Ollman, 1993) that, as I will show, incorporated ritual, traditions, landscapes, ancestors, and nature. In this sense, and in agreement with Sayer (1987: 139), we have to be aware that when analyzing non-western, non-capitalist societies, "(W)e are dealing, in fine, with entirely different relations, which take different phenomenal forms, and demand appropriate and specific historical categories for their analysis."

In this paper, I will attempt an alternative interpretation of Inka domination. My hypothesis is that the Inka sought to transform Andean cosmology and social order, and impose their own worldview and ideology, locating themselves at the pinnacle of the new social order, but also representing the Inka as the true carriers of Andean traditions and the past, as the original people and ancestors of the world. Material culture was an integral part in the development of this symbolic aspect of Inka domination, especially in terms of the construction and reconstruction of new landscapes. With these ideas in mind, I will explore Inka spatiality or how the Inka re-organized the social space in the areas they conquered. I intend to demonstrate how the Inka sought to impose their worldview and legitimize their domination using the re-organization of the landscape and the appropriation of ritual spaces.

Cusco's Landscape and Inka Social Order

Specific cultural spatialities are meaningfully constituted and help to fix social order (Lawrence and Low, 1990; Parker Pearson and Richards, 1994). Through their materiality they communicate meanings and transmit messages about the characteristics of social structure, and about which social actions and relations are allowed and which are not. Experience and routine allow any social actor to know her or his role in this context, the actions that he or she can and cannot perform, and the class of relationships he or she should and could establish with other agents (Giddens, 1984). Spatial design and mobile objects help to fix all these aspects, acting in certain sense as 'memory aid' (Kchler, 1993).

A key aspect of the production and reproduction of spatialities is that social conflict is involved. This internal antagonism entails social struggle as spatialities produce and reproduce relations of domination, therefore functioning as an instrument of power and a way to create social inequalities (Acuto, 1999a; Lefebvre, 1974). In this sense, space is loaded with meaning and ideological connotations. The production and reproduction of spatialities implies a profound struggle for the imposition of social meanings and a specific type of symbolic and material discourse and representation about how social order should be. The imposition of these factors logically produces the domination of one group (the one that produces them) on another (the one that recognizes this as the legitimated order). On the other hand, the production and reproduction of spatialities not only implies domination, or the control of one group over others, but negotiations and resistance of the imposed order as well (Miller et al., 1989; Paynter and McGuire, 1991). Although an "official" and "legitimate" narrative exists, there are competitive meanings and alternative discourses simultaneously built and superimposed on the same space and material culture (Bourdieu, 1985; Hebdige, 1979). As such, the elaboration of new spatial orderings is never a simple nor quick matter. In fact, in the capital of the Inka Empire, Cuzco, the landscape was never a direct metaphor or one-dimensional representation of social structure. Inka cosmology, ideology, social order and history are all encapsulated in the Cuzco landscape. Yet, it was at once a product of and a participant in the repeated interactions among its inhabitants as they actualized social relations. Cuzco's landscape and social structure were dialectically constituted. They were parts of the same whole.

To begin, it is important to clarify that this city was not like contemporary European cities. The core was a stage where rituals were regularly performed. There were no residential areas in this sector, and people only congregated there for special occasions (Agurto Calvo, 1987; Niles, 1992; Rowe, 1967). The city core was a sacred place composed of ritual plazas and temples. Royal families or *panacas*, non-royal lineages or *ayllus*, and representatives from all conquered lands inhabited the area around this core. Between the core and this residential area there was a ring of unoccupied land that separated sacred from mundane space.

Inka society of Cuzco was divided according to the principles of bi, tri and quadripartition that marked hierarchal relationships among people, groups, and royal and non-royal lineages. These divisions were not only reified through discourses, but also through landscape layout. They instituted or regulated differences in power, practices (especially ceremonies and religious rituals), and access to resources (such as land and water, Bauer, 1999; Zuidema, 1983, 1990, 1995). Ascription to one of these social groups determined the rank of each individual, defining at the same time his or her identity, the relations he or she were allowed to establish with individuals of other social segments (marriage is one of the most cited examples), and the roles he or she would carry out in different social activities (Bauer, 1999; Zuidema, 1990, 1995).

Bipartition was one of the main principles underlying Inka society that was inscribed in the landscape of Cuzco. Cuzco's population was divided in two halves, Hanan (upper Cuzco) and Hurin (lower Cuzco). The groups belonging to Hanan were considered more important than those of Hurin, who were contemplated as poor Inka or as the illegitimate children of the Inka king. Even in the symbolic battles enacted in Cuzco during certain religious ceremonies, Hanan always defeated Hurin Cuzco (Pärssinen, 1992). Although some Spanish chroniclers characterized this hierarchical relationship as similar to that found between older and younger brothers, relations between these two groups were nevertheless characterized by subjugation and control. Moreover, people of Hanan or hanansayas had the first degree of nobility and they served as soldiers in every war, while hurinsayas were only assistants and performed tasks such as transporting provision and weapons (Bauer, 1992). These facts marked the subjugation of Hurin by Hanan. The division between Hanan and Hurin was also used to structure social relations. Royal lineage kinship rules stated that the Inka ruler's primary or legitimate children were distinguished from secondary ones because they had been conceived with the ruler's primary wife, who should also be his sister or cousin. As such, primary children belonged to Hanan Cuzco and secondary to Hurin (Zuidema, 1995: 167).

Inka relations with non-Inka populations were also defined in terms of the Hanan-Hurin division. For example, Hurin Cuzco was the moiety related to the non-Inka population that inhabited Cuzco before the arrival of the Inka. Once the Inka controlled and displaced the original inhabitants of the city they established themselves as the dominant and most prestigious half. Hanan thus represented Inka conquerors (or in the case of the provincial centers, their officers and administrators), and Hurin the subjected, non-Inka population.

Each of these two socially distinct halves were divided themselves into two parts, forming the basic quadripartition of the whole Empire or *Tawantinsuyu* (quechua, translated "as reign of the four parts"). Hanan Cuzco was divided into Chinchaysuyu and Antisuyu, and Hurin Cuzco into Collasuyu and Cuntisuyu. This principle marked the distribution of sociopolitical prestige among the Inka of the Cuzco, according to the following descendent ranking order; Chinchaysuyu (considered Hanan of Hanan), then Antisuyu (the Hurin of Hanan), Collasuyu (Hanan of Hurin) and Cuntisuyu (Hurin of Hurin; Pärssinen, 1992; Zuidema, 1995).

As in the case of bipartition, quadripartition, or what is also called the Second Representation of the Cuzco, not only established hierarchical relations between different groups, but also defined the social practices each group was allowed to participate in. The rulers of the Cuzco belonged to Chinchaysuyu. The inhabitants and workers of those areas surrounding the sacred city were classified as Antisuyu. The entire priestly hierarchy belonged to Collasuyu. Collasuyu and Cuntisuyu also represented those non-Inka individuals that resided outside Cuzco but were included in the class of 'Inka of Privilege' (Zuidema, 1995: 222).[1] According to Hyslop (1990), this Second Representation was principally an imperial vision, since it included non-Inka populations, emphasized in the four suyus, and articulated the power relations between Inka and non-Inka.

A further principle of social organization divided society and space into three parts. This division defined social hierarchy and roles between the groups that inhabited the Inka capital, and also those in the provinces. Tripartition, or the First Representation, was the most important principle of Inka hierarchical sociopolitical organization (Zuidema, 1995). According to this principle, groups and people were divided in Collana, Payan and Callao, representing (depending on the social context) kinship, sociopolitical or power relations. In terms of sociopolitical relationships, the connection among these three social segments was characterized as the relations between aristocratic rulers (Collana), their assistants and allies (Payan), and the general non-aristocratic population (Cayao).

In Cuzo, the emperor and his attendants or nobles comprised Collana, Payan the other royal lineages or *panacas*, and Callao the non-royal *ayllus*. In general, Collana were also the elite rulers, Payan the original owners of the land and Callao the priests. This last perspective was closely associated with the Inka origin myth (Zuidema, 1995). In the provinces, Payan referred to local populations that resided in Inka towns, Collana were Inka rulers and Cayao, the groups that inhabited the outskirts of these towns. In conditions of imperial conquest, then, Collana represented the conquerors and Payan the conquered.

In addition to the levels of partition previously mentioned two further levels of social division and organization functioned. As these systems are little understood and do not appear to be dominant ordering principles, they will not be considered here. It becomes obvious, however, that social relations of power and control between elite and commoner, clerical and secular, and conqueror and conquered were tightly defined by a complex system of overlapping 'factions' or groups in reference to which each actor would position him or herself in response to certain context and interpersonal relations. The complex segregation of people in *Tawantinsuyu* was elaborated in the construction and experience of the built and natural landscape of the Late Horizon Andes.

The Ceque System and the Organization of Space in Cuzco

Within the city, and in the neighboring areas, there were several locations, such as rock outcrops, springs, mountains, houses, natural or carved stones, etc. that were considered sacred places or *wak'as*[2] (Bauer, 1999). These important locales were organized into groups of

intangible lines or *ceques* that radiated from the Temple of the Sun or *Korikancha*, at the center of the city. These lines were of central im-
portance to Inka rituals, sociopolitical organization, and astronomic and calendric practices and divinations (Pärssinen, 1992). *Koricancha* was Cuzco's *axis mundi* around which ritual cycles and spatial structuration were organized (Farrington, 1992: 370). Each of the ten panacas and *ayllus* that lived in Cuzco had to guard, care for, and worship one of these lines and the sacred places associated with it (Bauer, 1999). These lines were also ranked hierarchically and the most important segments of Cuzco society were in charge of the most important *wak'as*.

As with social stratification, the ceque system divided Cuzco's space in two parts (Hanan to the north and Hurin to the south), four quarters (Chinchasuyu, Collasuyu, Antisuyu, Cuntisuyu), and each of these in three sections (Collana, Paya and Cayao). Two quarters and six sections respectively belonged to Hanan and Hurin Cuzco (Zuidema, 1983). Each quarter had nine ceque lines (except Cuntinsuyu that had fourteen) divided in three groups or sections (Collana, Payan, Callao) of three lines each (Collana, Payan, Callao). Chinchaysuyu was located to the northwest, in Hanan, while Antisuyu was found to the northeast, also in the Hanan portion of the city. Collasuyu and Cuntinsuyu were in Hurin Cuzco, the former in the southeast corner and the latter in the southwest (Farrington, 1992; Hyslop, 1990).

Furthermore, key ceremonies and legends confirmed the limits of these social spaces and the relation between the core of the Empire and surrounding areas (Farrington, 1992). The ceque system established over Cuzco a network of daily ritual practices that radiated from the *Korikancha*, and stated the rights of each social group to land and water (Bauer, 1999; Farrington, 1992).

At the same time, the principle of quadripartition was extended beyond Cuzco and employed to divide the whole Empire. As such, Cuzco became the Empire writ small. People and lords from all conquered provinces came to reside in the city, occupying the district or quarter of the capital that coincided with the place in the Empire they came from (Hyslop, 1990; Rowe, 1967).

Cuzco also embodied Inka history. In Cuzco's landscape Inka memory was materialized and history was made visible, rendering the past into the present (Bengtsson, 1999; McEwan and van de Guchte, 1992; Niles, 1999). Mythical and real history were recreated through monuments, shrines and objects principally oriented to remember, glorify and diffuse Inka ancestors' achievements, gods, emperors and victorious battles. Cuzco had thus a commemorative side that empowered material culture to celebrate the emergence and glory of *Tawantinsuyu*. I agree with Niles (1999: xvii) in her statement that Inka architecture and landscape were not as some scholars have seen them; "historically anonymous and directed to administrative needs of the state." She also claims that the Cuzco landscape was a propagandistic tool that emperors used to assert their power and the centrality of the Inka, to depict ancestors in a flattering light, and to inscribe their names in history. Niles states that

...the remembrance of history was central to Inca royal politics and that events believed to be historical were commemorated in the built and imagined landscape of Cuzco and reenacted in the ritual that took place in these spaces. Because members of the Inca royal families saw themselves as active participants in the creation of their histories, we can view their handiwork as testimonies to those histories (Niles, 1999: 4).

Many of the sacred places or *wak'as* that composed the ceque system commemorated the life of a mythical ancestor or emperor, a battle or a myth. For instance, buildings where an emperor lived, slept, drank, etc., were preserved and worshipped, and became loci of rituals. The same occurred in the location of the war against the Chankas, after which the Inka imposed their hegemony in the region of Cuzco. In the same light, Bauer (1992) has showed that the Inka constructed in the area of Paruro, beyond the outskirts of Cuzco, a religious landscape composed of a series of sites (Maukallaqta and Puma Orco) especially installed to commemorate the Inka origin myth during important religious ceremonies. In one of these sites, an elaborate building with a secret passage was built in order to recreate the moment during which the founding ancestors of the royal Inka lineage emerged from their original mythical cave or *pacarina*. But aside from built environments, other objects and even human bodies or parts of them, were recruited to remember Inka history and victorious battles. These objects were exhibited in special locations, such as houses, which served as little museums. Objects of war were particularly important, such as weapons, insignias, the decapitated heads of captured enemies or drums made with their skin, etc. Battlefields were also used as mnemonic devices. Sometimes dead bodies and weapons were intentionally left *in situ*. For example Niles (1999) describes a case where bodies were left, half buried upside down, with their legs in the air, literally sowing the field with the dead of the vanquished.

But, why was Cuzco itself so imbued with meanings, history, and material mnemonics? To whom were the Inka trying to communicate their narrative and propaganda? Certainly both Cuzco's landscape and the multiple rituals performed in the area were oriented to produce and reproduce social organization within Inka society itself. But the Inka were not the only recipients of these narratives. Cuzco's landscape and the rituals developed in the area were also oriented to transmit Inka cosmology, history and ideas about the places that every group occupied to non-Inka visitors or prisoners.

Non-Inka inhabitants of Cuzco were engaged in two principal ways of facilitating the quasi-indoctrination of newly incorporated groups into the Empire. First, non-local nobles and elite were required to reside periodically in Cuzco and educate their sons there. In conjunction with their servants, these 'ambassadors' represented an important community of non-Inka inhabitants. Second, many non-local people traveled to Cuzco to participate in important rituals that essentially sought to reaffirm the ceque line system and the integration of provinces into the Empire (Rowe, 1967).

In this way, the landscape of this sacred city not only structured Cuzco society, but was also employed to communicate the Inka ideology to provincial elites that seasonally resided there and to visitors that came to the city for many different reasons. For example, people from every corner of *Tawantinsuyu* went on a pilgrimage to Cuzco at special occasions (such as the death of the emperor or the coronation of a new one) to participate in a complex ritual called *Capacocha* (Duviouls, 1976). It is said that the *Capacocha* served to unify the empire and to convince provincial groups of the greatness and benevolence of *Tawantinsuyu* (Farrington, 1998; McEwan and van de Guchte, 1992). The *Capacocha* was the extension of the ceque lines throughout the rest of the Empire (Bauer, 1999). It included the enactment of rituals of pilgrimage that would have originated in the provinces, progressed to Cuzco, and then moved back to the province again, where the final part of the ritual would have been performed at a *wak'a*, or sacred location in the landscape. During the *Capacocha* people from all over the Empire went to Cuzco carrying gifts for the emperor. In this city, after having participated in several rituals, they returned to their homelands with sanctified objects directly obtained from the emperor himself, which were later sacrificed to local *wak'as* (Duviols, 1976; McEwan and van de Guchte, 1992). Children were also sacrificed to special powerful *wak'as* during the *Capacocha*. Cuzco thus became the center of religious activity for the entire Empire. *Capacocha* ritual was also a strong statement of Inka hegemony over the Andean world (McEwan and van de Guchte, 1992).

Cuzco, thus, was not a final and static product generated in the mind of an Inka elite and materialized in the layout and buildings of the city. It was also shaped by the presence of non-Inka population. Nor was Cuzco a finished product in the heads of homogenous Inka society that was translated into a material product to be sold to non-Inka people residing or visiting the city. Cuzco was made through the establishment of social relations between Inka and non-Inka realms. Non-Inka societies contributed to the creation of the Inka world. The Inka worldview, ideology, rituals and capital were constantly transformed and reshaped as a consequence of the dialectic of domination between rulers and subordinates. Important provincial *wak'as*, representatives form all corners of the Empire, and important local chiefs were brought to the Inka capital, and would have had great influence in the daily life of the city, both in terms of the activities carried out there and its spatial organization.

In sum, the ceque system formed a spatiality whose materiality and meanings metaphorically represented Inka social stratification and worldview, and actively produced and reproduced them. In the Cuzco area this spatiality was a strong mnemonic device that helped Inka and non-Inka remember who was who and what his or her location was in the imperial hierarchy. In this landscape, past and present were experienced at the same time, and history, ancestors, myths and gods were present in all daily interactions. It is possible to conclude then that in this particular case social space vigorously acted to produce and reproduce the hierarchical social structure of the Inka. Belonging to a division of

Cuzco implied certain privileges, and defined specific roles and access to resources (Bauer, 1999; Zuidema, 1964). Moreover, material culture was actively used to transmit Inka ideology, cosmology and culture to non-Inka peoples that for various reasons attended to this amazing Andean theater.

Provincial Landscapes: New Cuzcos, Mountains, and Ancestors

In this section I explore the nature of Inka spatiality and objects outside Cuzco in the provincial territories, and the role they played in the domination of other Andean societies. Archaeologists have often used Inka material culture to determine Inka presence in different regions (Hyslop, 1993; Morris, 1988). The unique attributes of Inka material culture, especially in the realm of architecture and ceramics, have allowed archaeologists to define the Late Horizon Period and the degree of influence *Tawantinsuyu* had on different areas of the Andes. As such, Inka material culture has usually been considered in general terms of style and function. For example, studies of Inka architectural features and settlement patterns have centered on characterizing typical Inka buildings and their construction techniques. Furthermore, imperial sites are usually classified according to their function, such as administrative centers, military fortresses, ritual centers, *tambos* or way stations, production enclaves, etc. (González, 1980; Kendall, 1985; La Lone and La Lone, 1987; Raffino, 1978, 1981; Raffino et al., 1979–82).

Contrary to these perspectives, and following Hyslop (1987, 1990) and Morris (1987), I claim here that provincial Inka sites were not exclusively oriented toward economic, administrative or military purposes. As in the case of Cuzco, I think that the Inka sought to communicate and impose their cosmology and social order through their settlements. In the following I consider not only the ways they constructed and diffused their discourse and narrative in conquered regions, but I also explore and discuss the meanings they sought to communicate. I define this aspect of the relationship between Inka and subjected societies as a process of cultural domination.

There appears to have existed a lack of attention to the Inka modification or control of cultural practices of subjugated non-Inka groups. There are three reasons that explain this situation. First, many feel the Inka were not interested in this aspect of their relations with provincial societies because their main goal was to extract tribute labor (called *mita*) from dominated populations, while impacting only minimally on the social organization and self-sufficiency (an Andean 'ideal') of these societies (Murra, 1978). Second, it was always thought that Inka domination in most imperial territories lasted a very short period of time (in some regions only slightly more than 50 years) and as such, it could not have had a deeper impact on the more intimate social aspects of provincial societies (Rowe, 1946). Contrary to this idea, new radiocarbon dates are showing that the development of the Inka Empire lasted at least 150 years, depending on the region. Finally, it was generally thought that many of the territories outside Central Andes were too distant and marginal from Empire's core and therefore the Inka did not fully apply all their mechanisms of domination (González, 1980, 1982). In this way, all the possible changes at cultural level suffered by ruled societies were considered secondary effects of the Inka conquest, rather than fundamental social aspects that the Inka sought to change.

Here I will show how Inka domination went beyond political and economic realms. Specifically, I explore the way the Inka sought to communicate and impose their cosmology and diffuse their ideology in provincial territories through three mechanisms: 1) the re-structuration of local landscapes, 2) the construction of "New Cuzcos" and 3) the appropriation of local ritual spaces and the transformation of local beliefs and history.

The Re-Structuration of Local Landscapes

Many scholars have focused on Inka settlement patterns in provincial contexts. It has been proposed that Inka administrative sites were established to take advantage of natural resources, human labor, and strategic locations either near the Inka road which facilitated connection with Cuzco or other major Inka sites, in places that facilitate the administration of provincial communities, or in defensive locations. It has also been said that the Inka constructed principal settlements in areas that previously lacked a centralized or hierarchical political organization, or where they met with serious resistance to imperial domination. In the cases where local communities had complex political structures or did not resist the Inka presence, the Inka employed local political structures, replacing the principal stratums with Inka personnel, and erecting few administrative buildings, generally in one or two of the main local centers (Hyslop, 1990; Menzel, 1959; Morris, 1988). It is not my goal to discuss these propositions here. Certainly political and economic goals influenced decisions about where to settle imperial sites. Nevertheless, I consider that other factors, beyond the need to control resources, labor or roads, connected to Inka ritual and ideology, were also involved in the making of the Inka landscape.

Why and where did the Inka establish their main centers? I have proposed elsewhere (Acuto, 1999a, b) that the construction of Inka landscape was meaningful and sought to impact the experience of both Inka and non-Inka populations alike (Gifford and Acuto, 2002). In many cases the Inka settled their main provincial centers or concentration of second level administrative sites (Williams and D'Altroy, 1998) in depopulated areas, away from local towns, not directly related to resources, and sometimes at the very margins of the territory of local communities (Acuto, 1999a; D'Altroy, Williams and Lorandi, 1998; González, 1980: 77; Hyslop, 1990; Raffino, 1988: 238; Von Hagen and Morris, 1998).[3] According to Morris (1972), Inka sites appear to be artificial, imposed on the local landscape, without following the local settlement pattern logic. Rather, they appear to be the product of centralized state planning, reflecting interests that went beyond each particular region. Morris labeled this strategy as compulsory urbanism, in which "the nature and growth of substantial settlements are understandable only in reference to a larger system and to politically based direction coming from far away" (Morris, 1972: 393).

Along with Morris, I have also wondered why the Inka chose to settle in such exclusionary conditions, away from local political, economic and cultural centers, in areas that local agents experienced as peripheral, marginal, and even dangerous. I have discounted some possible explanations. To begin, the Inka obviously did not seek direct control over natural resources or human labor by settling their sites in such marginal areas, since these present low amounts of potentially exploitable resources (such as mines of highly valued minerals or rich lands for agricultural and grazing), or lack them all together. On the other hand, although some routes that allowed interregional connections could have been controlled from these sites, there were many other that were not possible to supervise, some of which, in many cases, were the roads used by local populations.[4]

I believe that the Inka were interested in marginal areas because they saw them as a kind of empty stage, or a blank canvas upon which they could create a distinct and new Inka landscape full of Inka-related designed symbols and meanings (Gifford and Acuto, 2002). The Inka transformed former marginal areas into new regional centers of power and of political, economic, cultural and ritual activities. These areas were selected because they were less associated with pre-existing local meanings, traditions and structures of power. By constructing a new landscape embedded into the imperial ideology, the Inka re-signified the sense of place that these marginal regions had for local communities. People who experienced the imposition of this imperial landscape (i.e., local agents working in imperial activities, visiting groups participating in special ceremonies, or mitimaes brought from other regions of the Empires) confronted not only a differently built environment, but also a set of new meanings to be learned that would help them to become competent actors in this new context of domination.

The Inka thus developed a novel landscape of its own, with different materialities and meanings attached to it. In order to do this, it seems that they preferred to occupy areas that local agents did not perceive as extant regional centers of power. In this sense, the Inka not only moved the location of power, but also changed local ideas of how power and social order were exhibited and materialized in the region. The mental maps of local agents were thus radically modified. The centers of power and domination in each region were no longer established where they used to be; rather they appeared in areas that were seldom used previously. Center became periphery and periphery became centers. The Inka thereby re-signified the social landscape of many conquered regions, deeply modifying residents' mental space images and even the perception of their own local spatiality. In this sense, the area that once was marginal became a center with the arrival of the Empire, a center where much of the political power was concentrated, where local society should pay tribute, and where local elites began to negotiate their position in the new power structure.

The Inka created a landscape where their principal sites were concentrated apart from local settlements. Both landscapes, that of the Inka and of the local, were markedly different in terms of material culture, meanings and power. The Inka actively differentiated the civilized Inka world form the uncivilized world beyond. "What lay within the Inca domain was ordered and defined: every element or being found its place within a tightly structured social hierarchy. All that lay outside Inca territory and the Inca social universe belonged to the wild, unordered, and uncontrollable world that was at once ambivalent and potentially threatening" (McEwan and van de Guchte, 1992: 368). Inka architecture and sites followed in some ways this idea of order since they were structured according to principles of symmetry, opposition and repetition (Agurto Calvo, 1987). Inka architecture was erected by using fixed ratios and the same architectural unit or *kancha*, which gave a sense of mathematical and repetitive order (Agurto Calvo, 1987; Lee, 1997).

Aside from transforming local power structures and marking their differences with local societies, what other ideas did the Inka wish to communicate? What were the meanings local agents experienced in Inka landscape? The analysis of one particular type of site installed in almost every region of *Tawantinsuyu* might help to answer this question.

New Cuzcos, Social Stratification, and the Diffusion of Inka Ideology

In each conquered region the Inka installed several sites oriented to fulfill different goals (administrative, military, ceremonial, logistical, economic, etc.). In general, the principal settled site symbolically replicated Cuzco. These sites, that many early Spanish chroniclers (e.g., Guaman Poma, Cieza de León, and Garcilaso de la Vega) described as "new Cuzcos" or "other Cuzcos", copied the Inka capital in terms of its spatial organization, buildings, names, and meanings. According to some scholars (Agurto Calvo, 1987; Farrington, 1998) these cities, although presenting physical similarities with Cuzco, were not necessarily exact copies of it. They were really conceptual and symbolic replicas. These settlements were thus sanctioned as centers created in the image of Cuzco,

> as a place to worship the gods, in particular the Sun (Punchao), the Inka as the Son of the Sun, and the creator gods—Payachachic, Inti Illapa and Ticsi Viracocha; as an ancestral place which linked the worlds past of Viracocha and the foundation myths of the Inka with the contemporary world (kay pacha); as a place of communication of the contemporary world with the world above (hanan pacha) and the world below (uku pacha); and as a place surrounded by a series of other sacred places or wakas whose attributes were to enhance those connections with the worlds of the gods and the origins of the Inka, their ancestors and their neighbors were duplicated. (Farrington 1998: 53)

Although I agree with Farrington, I consider that the physical similarities between these "new Cuzcos" and the main imperial capital were significant as well, since these physical characteristics promoted the fixing of meanings and made them more recognizable to every imperial subject. Traveling through the Empire, it was possible to see in the most important Inka sites the same buildings, names, functions, and spatial structuration, and to experience the same meanings. This certainly consolidated the unity of *Tawantinsuyu* and reinforced Inka discourse about world order.

All these secondary Cuzcos presented a similar spatial design, orthogonal or radial pattern (Hyslop, 1990), and buildings of particular architectural styles, such as: walled plazas with a central platform or *ushnu*, one or more *kanllanka* placed next to the plaza, fortified towers, *kancha*, storage facilities or *qollcas*, channels and drainages near or in ceremonial areas, carved rocks, etc.[5] Moreover, and like Cuzco, these places presented axes based on astronomical models and some standard measures (Farrington, 1998; Hyslop, 1990; Lee, 1997; Raffino, 1981; Von Hagen and Morris, 1998; Zuidema, 1982). Furthermore, the same names given to Cuzco's plazas, buildings and sectors were used in its provincial copies. Even the natural landscape was named after that of Cuzco (Hyslop, 1987). It was further said that soil from Cuzco was taken to the other Cuzcos to certify their identification with the sacred capital (Pease, 1989: 52). It seems also that some of these sites were settled in locations where similar natural features of Cuzco region were present (Farrington, 1998).

But most important of all was the fact that these new Cuzcos replicated the Inka capital spatial design and meanings. In other words, the system of ceques, with its social connotations, might have been used to organize and stratified both people and space **within** these provincial centers (Bauer, 1999; Niles, 1992). For example, and according to the Spanish chronicler Bernabé Cobo; "They made in all their Kingdom the same division in which the city of Cuzco was distributed, of Hanan Cuzco and Hurin Cuzco; dividing each town and chiefdom in two parts or sides, hanansaya and hurinsaya, or the high and low neighborhoods, or the superior part or side and the inferior side" (cited in Bauer, 1992: 125).[6]

As in Cuzco, the organization of spacc in these provincial centers intended to classify, stratify, and physically separate individuals and groups, dividing them into foreign conquerors/local conquered, rulers/subjects, elite/commoners, Inka/non-Inka (Morris, 1987; Pärssinen, 1992). Each of the known New Cuzcos became after Inka conquest the new local center of power, and indigenous social life became strongly attached to them. Moreover, local elites had to negotiate their new positions with representatives of *Tawantinsuyu* that resided there. Local agents were forced to work in these places periodically, while elite participated in new ceremonies and rituals. Some people from other regions of the Empire, and even in some cases local people (Acuto, 1999b), were removed from their original land and towns and permanently settled here. All these individuals, in different circumstances, experienced a novel built environment, new social practices, and new meanings. They would have learned how to use, move and decode the spatiality of these new settlements in order to become competent agents in this new social environment.

The Inka built thus sites that were stages where everyone had fixed roles, and through these sites, and the rituals performed there, they taught everyone the script they would have to play. According to some scholars, many of the most important Inka sites were sites for ritual and spectacle rather than for habitation or productive activities (von Hagen and Morris, 1998). For example, and according to Morris (1982; Morris and Thompson, 1985), intensive studies in Huánuco Pampa, a main Inka provincial center that historical accounts have designated a "New Cuzco," the principal tasks developed in this site were ritual and diplomatic more than activities related to the military or production. According to von Hagen and Morris (1998), the great size of Inka plazas in general seems to confirm the key importance of their public activities. Contrary to what happened in previous important sites (such as those of Huari), Inka plazas were geared toward gathering a large body of people.

Experiencing Inka centers implied the realization of the existence of deep inequalities and differences in power between groups that did not belong together. Those who resided in or visited Inka sites faced a landscape that promoted social separation and stratification, and that located the Inka at the top of this new social structure.

The Appropriation of Local Ritual Spaces and the Inka as Ancestors

I propose here that one of the most important mechanisms used by the Inka to spread and impose their cosmology and ideology, and to transform vernacular beliefs, was the appropriation or "conquest" of ritual spaces and facilities. The most important pilgrimage centers and oracles of the Andean world were eventually captured and occupied by the Inka (i.e., Tiwanaku, Isle of the Sun, Pachacamac, Samipata, Puma Punku, among some of the most important; Bauer and Stanish, 2001; Farrington, 1998; Meyers and Ulbert, 1997; Niles, 1992, 1999; Rostworowski, 1992). In each of these religious centers, the Inka presence is witnessed by their imperial buildings. The Inka, however, not only controlled the best known religious centers, but there is some evidence that they also managed to take over and rebuild the public and ceremonial spaces of important local settlements (see for example, Acuto, 2002; Cornejo, 1995; Heffernan, 1996; Nielsen and Walker, 1999; Wallace, 1998;). Why was there such a concern for local ritual practices? What role did ritual play in Inka domination?

Rituals are formalized and repetitive social practices closely associated to the communication and reproduction of religious and cosmological ideas and meanings, that beyond promoting unity and social balance (like a Rousseauian 'Social Contract'), act ideologically to legitimate the social order and naturalize inequality and dominance (Godelier, 1986). They make social order appear fixed by relating it to a superior sacred order. Through rituals, the elite justify their privileged position, demonstrating that supernatural forces positively sanction social inequality. Rituals have been generally described as practices that promote social reproduction and defend social order and homogeneity. Rituals not only distinguish what it is permitted from what it is prohibited, but they also allow some transgressions to the rules, although limiting them. Through rituals, society controls the risk of change (García Canclini, 1995).

Ritual practices not only involve 'ideas', but also objects, structures, monuments and the people that use them. Control over these practices, the associated material culture and meanings, or what has been denominated 'Ritual Conquest' (Nielsen and Walker, 1999), by external conquerors is a form of symbolic violence that aims to promote and legitimate a new social order and domination.

It is known that under the Inka Empire, subject societies' religious objects could be violently destroyed, in the case of resistance, and in the case of 'voluntary' subjection local *wak'as* or deities could be incorporated into the imperial vault (Silverblatt, 1988; Nielsen and Walker, 1999). Nevertheless, as Nielsen and Walker (1999: 154; my translation) point out:

> ... it is possible that the active manipulation of objects and ritual behaviors have also played a central role in the Inka expansion. In some cases, ritual conquest could have constituted the main strategy used by the Empire to dominate or 'promote obedience' of rivals groups, using in this way violence in a more limited but more effective way.

In brief, Inka domination implied the appropriation of important pan-regional religious pilgrimage centers, key local ceremonial spaces, and local gods or *wak'as* (Silverblatt, 1988). In the latter case, transportable objects that were considered *wak'as* in provincial cults, were subtly taken to Cuzco. According to Rowe's (1967: 63) ethnohistorical research,

> Each province of the empire was required to send one of its principal cult objects to Cuzco every year. The provincial cult objects were installed in all honor in the chief temple of the state religion, where they served at the same time as hostages for the good behavior of their worshippers and as remainders that Cuzco was a religious center for the entire empire. Each year when new cult objects were brought the provincials were allowed to take back the ones that had remained in Cuzco the previous year.

The control of *wak'as* implies the control of their worshippers. When a community was defeated, it was said that their *wak'as* were defeated by the *wak'as* of the victorious community.

During the Capacocha all the *wak'as* incorporated into Inka religion received sacrifices, depending on their relative importance and the relationship of their worshippers with the Inka. All the objects or people sacrificed to a *wak'as* were previously legitimated in ceremonies carried out in Cuzco by the emperor himself (Duviols, 1976). In this way, the Inka gained the monopoly of every cult and thus had the power to destroy or promote provincial *wak'as*. Through the type and amount of tribute granted, they decided the importance of these local sacred places, and even created new *wak'as* to impose on the provinces. In fact, during the *Capacocha*, children from the provinces (generally sons or daughters of principal chiefs) were taken to Cuzco to participate in different rituals. In these ceremonies they were sanctified as sons of the Sun (Farrington, 1998), like the emperor himself, and after returning to their homeland they were sacrificed to and buried on the summit of important mountains. These children became "made-in-Cuzco" *wak'as* that were subsequently worshiped by provincial populations (Reinhard, 1985; Farrington, 1998). Broadly speaking, these children were created as *wak'as* in the imperial center and imposed on the provinces, possibly as reminders of Cuzco's centrality and power. As Silverblatt (1988: 97) states: "As conquered groups worshiped these imperial creations, they were honoring the very symbols of their subordination."

Local pacarinas were among the most common *wak'as* appropriated by the Inka (Albornoz, 1984 [c. 1584]; Heffernan, 1996; van de Guchte, 1999). Pacarinas were natural places (such as caves, islands, water springs, and mountains, for example) that were considered as places of origin of a community or *ayllu*, where their mythical ancestors came from. The Inka constructed their own sites in these places and claimed the very origin points of conquered groups. As Niles (1999: 84) says: "For the Incas, architecture was a way to give form to claims of mythical or legendary history. It could legitimate claims to kingship, to ownership, and to victory; it could validate claims to mythical descent or justify the usurpation of a mythical history, as at Titicaca, Tiahanaco, and Pachacamac." In this way, the Inka sought to usurp those features of local landscapes that represented "memory of origins" and means of communication with the supernatural world and the past to local communities (van de Guchte, 1999).

What did the Inka actually do with mountains? On the peak of the highest mountains, generally above 5,000 meters, the Inka constructed impressive ceremonial complexes, where rituals and human sacrifices were carried out (Besom, 2000). Mountains were central participants in daily Andean life. Mountain worship seems to be, and have been, a Pan-Andean phenomena (Albornoz, 1984 [c. 1584]; Martínez, 1983). Some mountains have particular imposing features that still draw our attention, including their outstanding height, their permanent snowcaps, which contrasts starkly with the Andean desert landscape, and their generosity in supplying water to valley rivers year-round. It is well known that mountains were and are meaningful for Andean societies and participated actively in daily life (Cornejo, 1995; Bastien, 1978; Martínez, 1976, 1983; Meddens, 1994, 1997; Reinhard, 1985). It is possible, therefore, to claim that for many Andean societies nature was not external or something alienated from culture. Rather some natural features were constitutive aspects of social life. For instance, Cuzco, as a meaningful unit, as a concept and as a sacred space, included not only the city itself but the surrounding natural landscape (Agurto Calvo, 1987; Farrington,

1998; Niles, 1999). The Inka domesticated, materially and symbolically, the natural landscape of Cuzco Valley; and it seems they did the same in each of the conquered territories (van Hagen and Morris, 1998). This still happen in many parts of the Andes, where local communities humanized the natural environment by giving and loading the landscape with names and meanings (see for example Martínez, 1976).

Some mountains were (and still are) considered as ancestors, places of ancestor origin, transformed ancestors, gods that controlled water and weather and agricultural activities, givers of protection, fertility, keepers of the social order, and places to communicate with supernatural levels (Bastien, 1978; Bauer, 1999; Bengtsson, 1999; Heffernan, 1996; Martínez, 1983; Meddens, 1994, 1997). Mountain peaks were in many cases considered pacarinas (Albornoz, 1984 [c. 1584]): the place where ancestors emerged and where they returned after dying. They were also conceived of as ancestors themselves. Today, in several parts of the Andes, the same quechua or aymara words employed to name the gods of the mountains, also mean grandfather and ancestor (Martínez, 1983: 88). For example, in a contemporary ethnographic research on the topic, Martínez found that the way people name mountains is connected to the role they consider mountains play in their life. When mountains are seen as *wak'as*, they usually give them (quechua or aymara) names that also mean father or grandfather, reckoning mountains, in this way, as procreators or as the head of the family (Martínez, 1983: 100). While there is evidence that pre-Inka groups worshipped mountaintops (Cornejo, 1995; Heffernan, 1996; Meddens, 1994; Reinhard, 1985), the Inka were the first to introduce permanent structures on even the highest mountaintops. Nowadays, few are the opportunities when people climb mountains to perform rituals at their summit (Martínez, 1976: 272, 1983). Even in these rare occasions, the activities developed in these places do not, of course, reach the formality and magnificence of Inka rituals. In general, few people, little material culture, and sparse constructions are involved in contemporary mountain worshiping. In the Inka case, this activity included architectural complexes built at the top of the mountains, pilgrimages to the summit, human sacrifices, and even permanent workers the Inka assigned to assist the mountain (Albornoz, 1984 [c. 1584]: 198; Reinhard, 1985).

Through the formal conquest of these sacred mountains, the Inka claimed a monopoly over the connection with the supernatural world, they appropriated local gods and mythic history, and claimed a direct association with local ancestors. Now the Inka themselves directed ceremonies to and worshipped the mountains, and their connection with these places was even better than that established by local groups. The Inka could reach the sacred summits, materially formalize their rituals, and feed the mountains with the greatest offering possible, children of the Sun. The ancestors and the mountain gods belonged now to the Inka. Furthermore the Inka became the ancestors themselves, they now lived and emerged from the same places as the ancestors and gods. I would say that through the symbolic and material appropriation of these sacred places, mythical histories and pacarinas, the Inka claimed they had always been there, that they were part of the natural order of things, part of nature and the supernatural order. They positioned themselves as the natural continuum between the past and the present, seeking to transform local beliefs and history.

There is interesting evidence that supports the idea that the Inka sought to position themselves as the ancestors of subject communities. For example, in the northern part of Chile, local communities still identified the Inka as *mallkus* or deities from the mountains, as mountains themselves, and as ancestors or grandfather (Martínez, 1976). In the same vein, Irene Silverblatt (1988) claims that the Inka intentionally attempted to rewrite local histories and to create a common past between the Empire and their subjects.

> The Incas would attempt to accomplish such historical reconstruction by capturing their subordinates' ideologies of descent, the ideologies that voiced social time and gave human significance to the past. Selecting and reworking those histories—along with the widespread custom of deifying ancestors—Cusco was intent on transforming the familiar into a flattering, novel, imperial fantasy in which kings became kin of those they ruled (Silverblatt, 1988: 85).

In this truly accomplished chapter, Silverblatt gives several examples of how the Inka attempted to make themselves relatives of their subjects, and in many cases, the very ancestors of local communities and local chiefs. She explains that inside the most important temple in Cuzco, the Coricancha or Temple of the Sun—which the Inka continued to reproduce in their most important provincial centers—, the Inka presented, during different ceremonies, their idea of the correct social and cosmological order. These ideas, of course, had political motives. In this scheme, Viracocha the creator, occupied the highest position. He was the origin and source of a series of masculine and feminine deities. On the masculine line, arranged in hierarchical order, were the Sun, Viracocha's first descendant, the planet Venus in its morning apparition, the Lord Earth, and finally men. Within the female sequence we find the Moon, Venus of the evening, Mother Sea, and women (Silverblatt, 1988: 88). The Inka emperor claimed to be the son of the Sun. Provincial chiefs where placed within Coricancha's organization as the children of Venus. Venus occupied the same position as the Inka, as both were considered children of the Sun. From the union of Venus and the Inka came the local chiefs who were positioned as the fathers of the commoners. "Thus imperial descent ideologies contended that the Inca was the 'father' of local chiefs..." (Silverblatt, 1988: 89). We might assume, hence, that in rituals and ceremonies performed in Inka provincial sites, local leaders played the role of the son of the Inka, which implied that the whole community descended from their imperial rulers. Here again, the Inka became the ancestors of local people.

Silverblatt (1988) also states that the Inka sought to create actual descent groups. The Inka selected special women from each community to become *aqlla*, the 'wives of the Sun' or the 'wives of the Inka'. These women were taken to Cuzco and other imperial centers where the Inka controlled both their labor and social reproduction. Eventually, the Inka emperor took one of these women for himself or gave them to other important lords. Since the *aqlla* were separated from their native communities, and belonged exclusively to the Sun and the Inka, their offspring were considered of pure imperial descent. Again we see how the Inka positioned themselves as ancestors thereby linking different communties' identity directly to *Tawantinsuyu*.

Finally, Silverblatt (1988: 97) presents an interesting example of how the Inka introduced an imperial deity into a provincial vault. This god (who belonged, after all, to the group that had defeated local communities and gods) reflected power and support from Cuzco that could transform her into a figure worshipped and revered by local people. This goddess eventually married, according to local traditions, the most important local god, whom the local community considered its ancestor. Thus, this particular Inka deity became the ancestor of this local group.

To conclude, I believe that in order to naturalize their domination, the Inka sought to represent their presence within the provincial context as something essential, as an integral part of the natural landscape. In this particular Andean world, nature was incorporated as a fundamental part of social life. Natural features were esteemed as *wak'as*, pacarinas, ancestors, places of origin, etc. Inka architecture was itself part of nature. Inka sites are not imposed on the natural landscape, but rather were seen as a continuation of nature. According to Agurto Calvo (1987), Inka sites acted in communion with nature. They adapted their settlements to natural topography and if any natural feature was in their way, instead of eliminating it, the Inka incorporated it into architectural design (Niles, 1999; van de Guchte, 1999). "[Inka] architects harmonized architecture and sacred geography, framing views of nearby mountains in doorways and windows and even carving some stones to echo the mountains' shapes" (van Hagen and Morris, 1998: 183). Thereby, I would say this reinforces the idea that the Inka positioned themselves as ancestors, originating in the past. Inka sites were thus nature itself, considered a natural continuum of nature, and not something that was imposed on, or built in spite of topography.

Conclusions

The complexity of the relationship between Inka and provincial societies allow us only to grasp some aspects of this process of domination. Many variables were involved in this process, but it seems ritual, landscape, memory, nature and material culture all played central roles. In Inka society, landscape and social structure were part of the same dialectically constituted whole. Material culture thus not only played an active part in people's everyday life, but was embedded in their understanding of the world and their social nature themselves. The materiality of nature, ancestors, social relations and history was an essential aspect of being-in-the-world and a fundamental and integral part of Inka processes of domination.

Cuzco was a very meaningful setting that regulated the social practices and relations within Inka society. Moreover, the city was an overwhelming propaganda device used to insinuate itself onto non-Inka visitors' perception of the world.

The concepts and materiality of the core were used as well to promote Inka cosmology in provincial contexts. The Inka construction of the landscape here was twofold. In the first instance, they sought to distinguish themselves from prior structures of power and set themselves apart as something different and something greater. In the second instance, however, the Inka did not position themselves as entirely new. In contrast, and through the conquest of the mountains, the Inka claimed to be closely linked to the local past through their natural relation with the ancient landscape. In this sense they established two interrelated narratives; one that said that they were bearers of a new world order (in which they were at the pinnacle) and the second which said that that power was as old as time itself and came from their intimate relationship with the ancestors, gods, and nature.

This is, of course, but a partial view of this story. Although I have addressed Inka strategies of domination without exploring the reaction of ruled populations, I do not pretend to say that all these communities, or even a part of them, bought *en toto* or passively accepted Inka power and ideology. Moreover, we must start exploring how the Inka remade themselves through interaction with provincial societies. Despite this general view of the Inka Empire, I am conscious that by considering specific cases we might better comprehend the dynamic relationship between rulers and subordinates, and understand how the Inka adapted their strategies of domination in each situation.

Acknowledgements

The graduate studies I am conducting in SUNY-Binghamton are developed thanks to the support of Fundación Antorchas (Argentina). This paper benefited from the useful comments made by Randy McGuire, Ann Stahl, Tom Beason, Emily Stovel, Reinhard Bernbeck, and Bill Isbell. I would especially like to thank Emily Stovel for helping me with the editing of the paper. Errors remain the responsibility of the author.

Notes

[1] These groups did not belong to Inka lineages and lived in the vicinity of the Cuzco. They formed a class or segment located between the Inka and non-Inka populations (Zuidema, 1983). Inka of privilege had access to hierarchical positions in the administrative and military structure of the Empire.

[2] *Wak'as* have multiple meanings and significations for Andean people such as the power of their ancestors, their gods, place of origins, and places of rituals.

[3]It is impossible to enumerate all the cases of Inka sites in marginal and depopulated areas. For a more detailed description of this see Acuto (1999a).

[4]In my study of the Calchaquí Valley (Argentina), the Inka did not control the access to the Puna directly from where important mineral, obsidian and salt resources could be obtained. On the contrary, local populations privileged their connection with this region by settling in and controlling the routes that connected Calchaquí Valley with the Puna.

[5]*Ushnus* can be characterized as thrones, places for rituals, libations and sacrifices, and as stone altars. Cuzco's *ushnu* was a representation of the Sun. Provincial *ushnus*, on the other hand, were the place where the Inka emperor, as the Sun's representative, sat during special ceremonies (Meddens, 1997). *Kallankas* were big rectangular buildings, without interior divisions, that were used for administrative functions and to lodge high state officials (Hyslop, 1984; Raffino, 1988). *Kanchas* were a basic Inka architectural unit, constituted by rectangular buildings around a central patio and surrounded by a wall. There was a great variation in their size and the number of structures they contained. Some represented residential units, other temples and palaces, and even others of production (Hyslop, 1990).

[6]Salomon (1986) claims that during Inka domination in Ecuador, the local population and space was divided into two parts, Hanan and Hurin, and that this structure was completely novel to the region. On the other hand, some archaeologists have suggested that the spatial organization of some of the main Inka provincial centers followed principles of bipartition and quadripartition (see Morris, 1987 regarding Huánuco Pampa, and Matos, 1994 in the case of Pumpu).

References

Acuto, F., 1999a, Paisaje y dominación: La constitución del espacio social en el Imperio Inka. In *Sed Non Satiata: Teoría social en la arqueología latinoamericana contemporónea*, edited by A. Zarankin and F. Acuto, pp. 33–75. Ediciones Del Tridente, Buenos Aires.

1999b, Paisajes cambiantes: La dominación Inka en el valle Calchaquì Norte (Argentina). In *Teoría Arqueologica na América do Sul*, edited by P. P .A. Funari, E. G. Neves and I. Podgorny, pp. 143–157. Museu de Arqueología e Etnología da Universidade de Sao Paulo, Sao Paulo.

2002, *Landscapes of Spectacle and Dominance: Inka Conquest of the North Calchaquí Valley*. Master's thesis, State University of New York, Binghamton.

Agurto Calvo, S., 1980, *Cusco: La traza urbana de la ciudad Inca*. UNESCO and Instituto Nacional de Cultura del Perú, Cusco.

Albornoz, C. de, 1984[c. 1582], Instrucción para descubrir todas las guacas del Pirú y sus camayos y haziendas. In *Albornoz y el espacio ritual andino prehispánico*, edited by P. Duviols. *Revista Andina* 2(1):169–222.

Appadurai, A, 1986, Introduction: commodities and the politics of value. In *The Social Life of Things*, edited by A. Appadurai, pp. 3–63. Cambridge University Press, Cambridge.

Bastien, J., 1978, *Mountain of the Condor: Metaphor and Ritual in an Andean Ayllu*. Waveland Press Inc., Prospect Heights, Illinois.

Bauer, B., 1992, *The Development of the Inca State*. University of Texas Press, Austin.

1999, *The Sacred Landscape of the Inca*. University of Texas Press, Austin.

Bauer, B., and Stanish, C., 2001, *Ritual and Pilgrimage in the Ancient Andes: The Islands of the Sun and the Moon*. University of Texas Press, Austin.

Bengtsson, L., 1999, The Concept of Time/Space in Quechua: Some Considerations. *Etnologiska Studier* 42:119–127.

Besom, J. T., 2000, *Mummies, Mountains, and Immolations: Strategies for Unifying the Inka Empire's Southern Quarters*. Ph.D. dissertation, State University of New York at Binghamton.

Bourdieu, P., 1985, *¿Qué significa hablar?* Akal, Madrid.

Cornejo, M., 1995, Arqueología de santuarios de altura en la Guaranga de Sisicaya, valle de Lurín. *Tawantinsuyu* 1:18–28.

D'Altroy, T., 1992, *Provincial Power in the Inka Empire*. Smithsonian Institution Press, Washington D.C.

D'Altroy, T., Williams, V., and Lorandi, A. M., 1998, *The Inka in the Southlands*. Dumbarton Oaks, Washington D.C.

Duviols, P., 1976, La Capacocha. *Allpanchis* 9:11–57.

Farrington, I., 1992, Ritual Geography, Settlement Patterns and the Characterization of the Provinces of the Inka Heartland. *World Archaeology* 23(3):368–385.

1998, The Concept of Cusco. *Tawantinsuyu* 5:53–59.

García Canclini, N., 1995, *Hybrid Cultures: Strategies for Entering and Leaving Modernity*. University of Minnesota Press, Minneapolis.

Giddens, A., 1979, *Central Problems in Social Theory*. MacMillan, London.

1984, *The Constitution of Society: Outline of the Theory of Structuration*. Polity Press, Cambridge.

Gifford, C., and Acuto, F., 2002, Space, Place and Inka Domination in Northwest Argentina. In *Experimental Archaeology: Replicating Past Objects, Behaviors, and Processes*, edited by James R. Mathieu, pp. 95–110. British Archaeological Report. International Series 1035, Oxford.

Gillespie, S., 2000, Maya 'Nested Houses': The Ritual Construction of Place. In *Beyond Kinship: Social and Material Reproduction in House Societies*, edited by R. Joyce and S. Gillespie, pp. 53–72. University of Pennsylvania Press, Philadelphia.

Glassie, H., 1999, *Material Culture*. Indiana University Press, Bloomington.

Godelier, M., 1986, *The Mental and the Material: Thought, Economy and Society*. Verso, London.

González, A. R., 1980, Patrones de asentamiento incaico en una provincia marginal del Imperio: implicaciones socioculturales. *Relaciones de la Sociedad Argentina de Antropología* 14(1):63–82.

1982, Las provincias Inca del antiguo Tucumán. *Revista del Museo Nacional* 46:317–380.

Gregory, D., 1989, Presences and Absences: Time-Space Relations and Structuration Theory. In *Social Theory of Modern Societies: Anthony Giddens and his Critics*, edited by D. Held and J. B. Thompson, pp. 185–214. Cambridge University Press, Cambridge.

Gregory, D., and Urry, J., editors, 1985, *Social Relations and Spatial Structures*. MacMillan, London.

Hebdige, D., 1979, *Subculture: the Meaning of Style*. Methuen, London.

Heffernan, K., 1996, The Mitimaes of Tilka and the Inka Incorporation of Chinchaysuyu. *Tawantinsuyu* 2:23–36.

Hyslop, J., 1979, El área Lupaca bajo el dominio incaico: Un reconocimiento arqueológico. *Histórica* (Pontificia Universidad Católica del Perú) 3(1):53–82.

1984, *The Inka Road System*. Academic Press, New York.

1987, Inkawasi, el mundo en microcosmos. *Cuadernos del Instituto Nacional de Antropología* (Argentina) 12:47–71.

1990, *Inka Settlement Planning*. University of Texas Press, Austin.

1993, Factors Influencing the Transmission and Distribution of Inka Cultural Materials throughout Tawantinsuyu. In *Latin American Horizons*, edited by D. Rice, pp. 337–356. Dumbarton Oaks Research Library and Collection, Washington, D.C.

Julien, C., 1982, Inca Decimal Administration in the Lake Titicaca Region. In *The Inca and Aztec States: 1400–1800*, edited by G. Collier, R. Rosaldo, and J. Wirth, pp.119–152. Academic Press, New York.

Kendall, A., 1985, *Aspects of Inca Architecture: Description, Function, and Chronology*. B.A.R. International Series 242, Oxford.

Kopytoff, I., 1986, The Cultural Biography of Things: Commoditization as Process. In *The Social Life of Things*, edited by A. Appadurai, pp. 64–91. Cambridge University Press, Cambridge.

Küchler, S., 1993, Landscape as Memory: The Mapping of Process and its Representation in a Melanesian society. In *Landscapes: Politics and Perspectives*, edited by B. Bender, pp. 85–106. Berg Publisherds Ltd., Oxford.

La Lone, M., and La Lone, D., 1987, The Inka State in the Southern Highlands: State Administrative and Production Enclaves. *Ethnohistory* 34(1):47–62.

Lawrence, D., and Low, S., 1990, The Built Environment and Spatial Form. *Annual Review of Anthropology*, 19:453–505.

Lee, V., 1997, Design by Numbers: Architectural Order among the Incas. *Tawantinsuyu* 3:103–118.

Lefebvre, H., 1974, *La production de l'espace*. Anthropos, Paris.

Locock, M., 1994, Meaningful Architecture. In *Meaningful Architecture: Social Interpretations of Buildings*, edited by M. Locock, pp. 1–13. World Wide Archaeology Series, Avebury.

Martínez, G., 1976, El sistema de los uywiris en Isluga. In *Homenaje al Dr. Gustavo Le Paige, SJ*, edited by H. Niemeyer, pp. 255–328. Universidad del Norte, Antofagasta.

1983, Los dioses de los cerros en los Andes. *Journal de la Societé des Americanistes* 85:85–115.

Matos, R., 1994, *Pumpu: Centro administrativo Inka de la Puna de Junín*. Editorial Horizonte, Lima.

McEwan, C., and van de Guchte, M., 1992, Ancestral Time and Sacred Space in the Inca State Ritual. In *The Ancient Americas: Art from Sacred Landscapes*, edited by R. Townsend, pp. 359–371. The Art Institute of Chicago, Chicago.

McGuire, R. H., 1992, *A Marxist Archaeology*. Academic Press, New York.

Meddens, F., 1994, Mountains, Miniatures, Ancestors, and Fertility: The Meaning of Late Horizon Offerings in a Middle Horizon Structure in Peru. *Bulletin of the Institute of Archaeology* 31:127–150.

1997, Function and Meaning of the Usnu in Late Horizon Peru. *Tawantinsuyu* 3:5–14.

Menzel, D., 1959, The Inca Occupation of the South Coast of Peru. *Southwestern Journal of Anthropology* 15(2):125–42.

Meyers, A., and Ulbert, C., 1997. Inka Archaeology in the Eastern Bolivia: Some Aspects of the Samaipata Project. *Tawantinsuyu* 3:80–85.

Miller, D., Rowlands, M., and Tilley, C., editors, 1989, *Domination and Resistance*. Routledge, London.

Miller, D., 1987, *Material Culture and Mass Consumption*. Basil Blackwell, Oxford.

1998, Why Some Things Matter. In *Material Cultures: Why Some Things Matter*, edited by D. Miller, pp. 3–21. University of Chicago Press, Chicago.

Morris, C., 1972, State Settlements in Tawantinsuyu: A Strategy of Compulsory Urbanism. In *Contemporary Archaeology*, edited by M. Leone, pp. 393–401. Southern Illinois University Press and Simons Inc., Carbondale.

1973, Establecimientos estatales en el Tawantinsuyu: una estrategia de urbanismo obligado. *Revista del Museo Nacional* (Lima) 39:127–141.

1982, The Infrastructure of Inka Control in the Central Highlands. In *The Inca and Aztec States: 1400–1800*, edited by G. Collier, R. Rosaldo and J. Wirth, pp. 153–170. Academic Press, New York.

1987, Arquitectura y estructura del espacio en Huánuco Pampa. *Cuadernos Instituto Nacional de Antropología* (Buenos Aires) 12:27–45.

1988, Progress and Prospect in the Archaeology of the Inca. In *Peruvian Prehistory: An Overview of Pre-Inca and Inca Society*, edited by R. W. Keating, pp. 233–256. Cambridge University Press, Cambridge.

Morris, C., and Thompson, D., 1985, *Huánuco Pampa: An Inca City and Its Hinterland*. Thames and Hudson, London.

Murra, J., 1978, *La organización económica del Estado Inca*. Editorial Siglo XXI, Buenos Aires.

Nielsen, A., and Walker, R., 1999, Conquista ritual y dominación política en el Tawantinsuyu: El caso de Los Amarillos (Jujuy, Argentina). In *Sed non Satiata: Teoría social en la arqueología latinoamericana contemporánea*, edited by A. Zarankin and F. Acuto, pp. 153–169. Ediciones Del Tridente, Buenos Aires.

Niles, S., 1992. Inca Architecture and Sacred Landscape. In *The Ancient Americas: Art from Sacred Landscapes*, edited by R. Townsend, pp. 346–357. The Art Institute of Chicago, Chicago.

1999, *The Shape of Inca History: Narrative and Architecture in an Andean Empire*. University of Iowa Press, Iowa City.

Ollman, B., 1993, *Dialectical Investigation*. Routledge, New York.

Parker Pearson, M., and Richards, C., 1994, Ordering the World: Perceptions of Architecture, Space and Time. In *Architecture and Order*, edited by M. Parker Pearson and C. Richards, pp. 1–37. Routledge, New York.

Pärssinen, M., 1992, *Tawantinsuyu: The Inca State and its Political Organization*. Kirkkokatu 14, 00170. Suomen Historiallinen Seura, Helsinki, Finlandia.

Pease, F., 1982, The Formation of Tawantinsuyu: Mechanisms of Colonization and Relationships with Ethnic Groups. In *The Inca and Aztec States: 1400–1800*, edited by G. Collier, R. Rosaldo and J. Wirth, pp. 173–198. Academic Press, New York.

1989, *Del Tawantinsuyu a la Historia del Perú*. IEP, Lima.

Raffino, R., 1978, La ocupación Inka en el N.O.A.: Actualización y perspectivas. *Relaciones de la Sociedad Argentina de Antropología* (Buenos Aires) 12.

1981, *Los Inka del Kollasuyu*. Ramos Americana Editora, La Plata.

1988, *Poblaciones indìgenas de la Argentina*. Editorial TEA, Buenos Aires.

Raffino, R., Raviña, G., Iacona, L., Olivera, D., and Albornoz, A., 1979–82, Aplicaciones de la teoría de sistemas y propuesta taxonómica de los vestigios Inka en los Andes meridionales. *Cuadernos del Instituto Nacional de Antropología* (Buenos Aires) 9:59–76.

Reinhard, J., 1985, Sacred Mountains: An Ethnoarchaeological Study of High Andean Ruins. *Mountain Research and Development* 5(4):299–317.

Rostworowski, M., 1992, *Pachacamac y el Señor de los Milagros: Una trayectoria milenaria*. Instituto de Estudios Peruanos, Lima.

Rowe, J., 1946. Inca Culture at the Time of the Spanish Conquest. In *Handbook of South American Indians*, volume 2, Bulletin 143, edited by J. Steward, pp. 183–330. Bureau of American Ethnology, Washington, D.C.

1967, What Kind of Settlement was Inca Cuzco? *Ñawpa Pacha* 5:59–75.

1982, Políticas e instituciones Inka relativas a la unificación del Imperio. In *The Inca and Aztec States: 1400–1800*, edited by G. Collier, R. Rosaldo and J. Wirth, pp. 23–39. Academic Press, New York.

Salomon, F., 1986, *Native Lords of Quito in the Age of the Incas*. Cambridge University Press, Cambridge.

Sayer, D., 1987, *The Violence of Abstraction*. Basil Blackwell, Oxford.

Silverblatt, I., 1988, Imperial Dilemmas, the Politics of Kinship, and Inca Reconstruction of History. *Comparative Studies in Society and History* 30:83–102.

Soja, E., 1989, *Postmodern Geographies: The Reassertion of Space in Critical Social Theory*. Verso, London and New York.

Thomas, J., 1993, The Hermeneutics of Megalithic Space. In *Interpretative Archaeology*, edited by C. Tilley, pp. 73–98. Berg Publishers Ltd., Oxford.

1996, *Time, Culture, and Identity*. Routledge, London.

1999, An Economy of Substances in Earlier Neolithic Britain. In *Material Symbols: Culture and Economy in Prehistory*, edited by J. E. Robb, pp. 70–89. Occasional Paper no. 26, Center for Archaeological Investigations. Southern Illinois University, Carbondale.

Thomas, N., 1991, *Entangled Objects: Exchange, Material Culture, and Colonialism in the Pacific*. Harvard University Press, Cambridge MA.

van de Guchte, M., 1999, The Inca Cognition of Landscape: Archaeology, Ethnohistory, and the Aesthetic of Alterity. In *The Archaeologies of Landscapes: Contemporary Perspectives*, edited by W. Ashmore and B. Knapp, pp. 149–168. Blackwell, Oxford.

von Hagen, A., and Morris, C., 1998, *The Cities of the Ancient Andes*. Thames and Hudson, London.

Williams, V., and D'Altroy, T., 1998, El sur del Tawantinsuyu: un dominio selectivamente intensivo. *Tawantinsuyu* 5:170–178.

Zuidema, T., 1983, Hierarchy and Space in Incaic Social Organization. *Ethnohistory* 30 (2):49–75.

1990, *Inca Civilization in Cuzco*. University of Texas Press, Austin.

1995, *El sistema de ceques del Cuzco*. Fondo Editorial de la Pontificia Universidad Católica del Perú, Lima.

Walls of Domestication— 14
Archaeology of the
Architecture of Capitalist
Elementary Public Schools

The Case of Buenos Aires

Andrés Zarankin

Introduction

One of the characteristics of the modern world is the concentration of social life in big cities. These artificial landscapes created by man have replaced natural landscapes radically. Architecture, as part of that new world, occupies a central place in our life. As inhabitants of these big cities, consciously or not, we spend almost our entire life circulating inside buildings. We are born, grow up, eat, reproduce ourselves, rest, seek protection, die and we are also buried inside them. This situation makes natural things become exotic, making in turn artificial things appear more natural. For example, living inside small apartments; walking along streets where the sky is generally only a tiny blue line above our heads; or working in closed, controlled and watched spaces—generally engaged in bureaucratic activities—is usual for us. Cities that lack green spaces and wallow below contaminating fog amidst only mechanical sounds have become more natural to us than mountains or a lake— which have become exotic objects. But in opposition to oceans, valleys or mountains, architectural structures are thought, designed and built by humans (so are a cultural product full of meaning).

Then, why not use architecture to study the social world? This question is the starting for this paper. Here, I am specifically interested in the function of architecture to the foundation process of the modern world (Orser, 1996). In order to explore this, following Foucault (1976), I understand architecture as a "technology of power", that is to say, as a strategy employed by the System to produce disciplined individuals who will contribute to its reproduction. Because of its inherent characteristics, architecture becomes a central tool in this process.

There are many ways to face this issue. In our case, followig Johnson's proposals (1996), I chose a twofold archaeological approach first using archaeology in its traditional sense, as the study of the social world through material culture, and at the same time, following Foucault (1970), thereby using archaeology as the search for the specificity of speech:

> In short archaeology doesn't try to restore what may have been thought, faced, experienced or wanted by men in a very moment they generated speech (. . .) it is only a re-writing, that is to say (in the maintained form of exteriority), an average transformation of what has been said and written. It is not the return to the secret of the origin, it is the systematic description of a speech object. (Foucault, 1970:235).

On the other hand, without ignoring the importance of other approaches and their contributions, it is necessary to clarify that the study of architecture, from an archaeological standpoint, offers an interesting avenue of approaching the social world (Stedman, 1996). If we understand constructions as active elements in dynamic interaction with people, they become a useful tool for discussing historical processes related to the constitution of the modern world.

Foucault (1976) believes that the System uses different strategies, at times imperceptible to ordinary people, to produce disciplined individuals. One of these strategies is the manipulation of material culture. Loaded with social and personal meanings, this manipulation generates a symbolic violence (Bourdieu, 1989) which enables the system to impose and legitimate its own ideology (Bourdieu and Passeron, 1970). Therefore, within this context, the analysis of the ways in which the System builds essential categories and mental structures which contribute to naturalize the bases for its operation—for example inequality— becomes pivotal to this analysis. Again in this context, if we understand architecture as a technology of power, its manipulation can be seen as a strategy of power that seeks to reproduce itself.

Special importance must be given to the relationship between architectural structures and processes of socialization. Among these processes, Bourdieu (1977) highlights two: the family household and schools which are of special important they provide key environments where people incorporate most of the mental frameworks according to which the rest of their life will be structured.

A previous study focused on processes of change and transformation in middle class houses in Buenos Aires, from the 18th Century to the present. Its results have enabled us to establish a direct relationship between these changes and the development of the capitalist system in that part of the world (Zarankin, 1997, 1999a, b). It is necessary now to direct our attention to the material configuration of school buildings, to achieve a deeper understanding of one of the strategies central to the System's functioning and self-reproduction.

Architecture as Material Speech

In order to use space, people must transform it into a place. In other words, space is an empty plane which must be domesticated, or turned into a "place". Among the different ways of turning space into a place, we can distinguish:

1. An abstract dimension, including the of drawing maps and plans, which involves dividing space in specific fragments, according to diverse methods, and granting each fragment a name and specific characteristics.
2. A material dimension, whereby Space is transformed into place through modifications and transformations in its materiality, such as the pruning of a forest in order to turn it into working soil and the building of a road or a city.

The construction of social relationships by means of material speeches is an efficient power strategy for self-reproduction (Funari, 1999 and Funari's chapter in this volume). The capitalist system can be characterized by the special relationship between the production, circulation and consumption of objects (Johnson, 1996) it engenders, which occupy a central place and generate a "culture of consumption". However, material culture has no significance of its own and it is only within a certain cultural system that it acquires an active and ideological dimension. I agree with the idea that the objects used by humans are active, dynamic and generate meanings in their own right. Through this perspective exists an alternative way of studying both people and their social world. Several scholars have seen the relevance of this kind of approach to material culture (Andrade Lima, 1999; Austin and Thomas, 1986; Deetz, 1977; Funari, 1991; Hodder, 1982; Johnson, 1996; Leone, 1984; Miller, 1987; Shanks and Tilley, 1987; Tilley 1989; McGuire and Paynter, 1991; among others).

Three questions which have previously been asked (Zarankin, 1999b) help us structure our research on school buildings: First, how objects were socially built—understanding objects as systems of meanings; second, how they change through time; and third, which strategies are used to legitimate them. We are also interested in another issue: understanding the subjectivities contained in and generated by material culture. In order to answer these questions, one needs the references used by objects and understand how these developed through time. These "truths"—here, "legitimated objects"—are built through multiple practices, among which stands out those related to the manipulation of the material world (Leone, 1984; McGuire and Paynter, 1991; Miller and Tilley, 1984).

If architecture is also considered it a kind of language that can be read (Fletcher, 1989; Grahame, 1995, 1997, 2000; Monks, 1992; Markus, 1993; Parker Pearson and Richards, 1994), when we analyze its growth processes, we will be able to understand its significance throughout history. It also necessary to assume that the human landscape is built and resisted through a continuous struggle between dominance and resistance (De Certeau, 1980; McGuire, 1991; Miller et al., 1989; Parker Pearson and Richards, 1994; Shanks and Tilley, 1987). Within this context, architecture—as part of the cultural landscape—can be approached as a battlefield were powers and opposed ideologies face each other (i.e., Miller, 1984; Parker Pearson and Richards, 1994).

Archaeology of the School

In the film "The Matrix", Morpheus (Larry Fishbourne) says that people only tolerate reality in this world because they think that at any moment they will be able to wake up. This statement prompts the question: what are the devices created to constrain—a class, a group, a worker, a woman, a boy, etc.—and prevent the small resistances generated in our daily life from becoming an insurrection? The elementary public school, undoubtedly, has much to do with this situation (Althusser, 1968; Apple, 1979; Baudelot and Establet, 1971; Bourdieu and Passeron, 1970; Fernandez Enguita, 1985; Querrien, 1979; Varela and Alvarez Uria, 1991).

The history of the planning and construction of school buildings has been barely approached by scholars. The few works existing generally focus their analysis on formal questions such as pedagogy, hygiene, didactics and stylistic aspects, among others. A series of recent studies, however, have focused on studying the material dimensions of teaching (see especially Viñao Frago and Escolano, 1998). These authors understand the emergence, consolidation and current crisis of the public elementary school as part of a historical process.

Capitalism, by means of different strategies and mechanisms, has not ceased to expand its own limits (Deleuze, 1990). Among these strategies are found: the formation of an appropriate labor force for its changing necessities as well as the production of people who participate actively in the reproduction of the system without posing questions about their daily reality. Within this context, the history of modern school can be considered part of the history of the search for devices to achieve this aim.

Althusser (1968) points out that an ideology presupposes a series of practices and material representations, the material existence of which is a concrete apparatus. In the case of a school, an archaeological analysis, as proposed here, allows a better understanding of this new institution into the ideological apparatus of the State (Althusser, 1968). The ways in which this institution functions within the capitalist system as speeches contained in the walls and as a technology of power also figures heavily in the present analysis. The morphologic-space transformations in elementary public schools in Buenos Aires, from their appearance in the mid 19th to the late 20th Century, represents the case study with which the general propositions proposed above are evaluated.

The Buenos Aires Case

In Latin America, the development of education has been an essentially heterogeneous process. However, by the end of the 19th Century, the State in almost every country takes over the organization and monopoly of all educational devices which had resided previously under the control of different civil organizations, such as town councils, churches and private institutions. In Buenos Aires, access to education during the colonial period was not an exclusive privilege of the aristocratic class but an essential tool for the social promotion of the lower classes, especially for the acquisition of bureaucratic posts (Szuchman, 1990). Another factor which influenced the need to generate educational policies for children was related to the existence, in the hegemonic classes, of new ideas about childhood [1] (Aries, 1973). In response to these changes, educational methods were brought in from Europe including, among many, the Lancasterian system and the simultaneous method of Pestalozzi. However, and in spite of these new ideas, pedagogical methods were still predominantly in the hands of the teachers who continued to emphasize memorization and corporal punishment (Newland, 1991).

On the other hand, the certainty remained in Argentina that economic success was related to workers' competence. These ideas were mainly promoted by the President of the Nation, Domingo Faustino Sarmiento who, in the mid the 19th Century, devoted himself to building the foundation of the Argentine educational system.

> A model of identity that is linked to the imaginary of progress and civilization
> is proposed: the child has to be a pupil of the public school, and a scholastic
> generation is the main condition for a modern country to exist. (Carli, 1999:27)

This situation turned Argentina (and in particular its capital, Buenos Aires) into a pioneering country in South America for the construction of school buildings. The first school was built in the center of Buenos Aires in the year 1857: *the Escuela Catedral del Sur*. Since then, the long and complex process of planning and building schools has continued.

As a whole, we can say that the free elementary public schools of the mid 20th Century in Argentina had the following objectives:

1) Face a heterogeneous cultural immigrant population while attempting to establish a national identity.
2) Educate and discipline the future working classes while avoiding contact with socialist and anarchist ideas arriving with the immigration process.
3) Generate an educational common ground for the entire population which was based on an ideology imposed by hegemonic class.
4) Increase the political power of the State rather than that of the Church, thus construct elaborate, imposing and sacred church-like schools in competition.

The school architecture of the 19th Century, especially after the incentives of the 1882 Law # 1420 which establishes the foundation of the Argentine educational system, was characterized by the search for models which would represent both what a school was and what was expected of a school, in a functional as well as a symbolic sense. It was also believed that the importance of institutions was closely related to the solidity of their architecture. As a result, monument-schools were constructed, that is grand properties resembling palaces, temples or mansions, which represented the power of education and of the State (Figures 14.1 and 14.2). From that time, the kind of schools built in Argentina, particularly those in Buenos Aires, as well as the importance

Figure 14.1. General Roca School (1903).

Figure 14.2. Ministry of Education (1905) (previously Petronila Rodríguez School).

given to them, have changed according to different government policies and the power needs generated.[2]

The Schools of Buenos Aires

In relation to the typology of school building in Buenos Aires, there are two fundamental studies conducted by an interdisciplinary team belonging to the Head Office of Educational Research—MCBA (1991a, b).[3] Twelve different types of school buildings have been identified throughout time: Sarmientist, Waldorph, Gelly Cantilo, Closed Form, U Shape, Adapted Chorizo House, International Style, Republic, Park, Nineteen-Sixties, Plan 60 and Prenova schools (Tables 14.1 and 14.2).

Sarmientist Architecture was characterized by monumental structures and represented (in the late 19th and early 20th centuries) a desire to build a country according to the Illuminist principles of reason and education. These buildings were considered not only schools but "temples of knowledge"; they were created with an ahistorical conception of time and space, as shown in the "Roca" school example (Figure 14.1), which is still evident within its Neoclassical façade. Another characteristic of these structures was the European origin of most of their building materials.

Table 14.1. Frequency of Buildings
According to Architectural Tradition

School	Quantity	Percentage
Sarmientist	25	7.1
Closed Form	48	13.7
U Shape	69	19.7
Adapted *Chorizo* House	23	6.5
Waldorph	28	8
Gelly Cantillo	18	5.1
International Style	41	11.7
Republic	38	10.8
Nineteen-Sixties	15	4.2
Park	4	1.1
Plan 60	41	11.7
Total	350[14]	100%

Table 14.2. Date Ranges for Each Architectural Tradition

Typology	1850	1875	1900	1925	1950	1975	2000
Sarmientist		————————					
Closed Form		———					
U shape		————————					
Adapted *Chorizo* House		———					
Waldorph		————					
Gelly Cantillo		———					
International Style			———				
Republic			—				
Nineteen-Sixties			–				
Park			-				
Plan 60				————			

However, the technological and material effort of Sarmientist schools was not enough to meet the demands of a population that had grown exponentially in the late 19th and early 20th Century due to waves of European immigration. New options were employed, such as the adaptation of houses into schools or the building of new ones according to a domestic conception of space, i.e., the "Closed Form" and "U Shape". Another kind of buildings erected by the State in the early 20th Century were the "Waldorph Schools", planned from an academic point of view (DIE, 1991a) and the "Gelly Cantilo Schools", both named after the architects who designed them. Both Waldorph and Gelly Cantilo used elements of the Spanish American tradition (DIE, 1991a).

The technological and social changes during the thirties also had repercussions for school buildings. The influence of the "International Style", in which ornamental aspects were rejected and emphasis was placed on a holistic and technological style, using "modern" building materials such as concrete, metal and glass, created explicitly rational buildings labeled "International Style Schools".

Later, simultaneous with military coups and the growth of the Peronist party in Argentina, school architectural policies began constructing national norms for school architecture. Paradoxically, the outcome was a kind of building with expressive and formal elements from Italian architecture (DIE, 1991a) and named after—as well as supported by—Latin-American countries (i.e., The Republic of Mexico, The Republic of Peru, The Republic of Chile, and others). These are known as "Republic Schools".

In the late 1950s, and the 1960s, some of the international architecture principles were reestablished.[4] Two types of schools were built during this period, "Park Schools" and "Nineteen-Sixties schools". Both were built with standard materials, their façades were made of brick and concrete, and aluminum carpentry was used (DIE, 1991a). By the mid sixties, investments in educational facilities had begun to decrease, so the general answer to the problem of increasing numbers of pupils was to add new classrooms onto existing schools.

"Plan 60 schools" were the result of the dissolution of the old National Council of Education and the transfer of schools from national control to provincial, and in the case of the city of Buenos Aires, to municipal administration. The Federal Capital benefited from this shift, in contrast to the rest of the country. The military government (1976–1983) began a monumental plan for schools to be build by private architectural studios. These high budget buildings fit with the "international" style, following LeCorbusier, that is to say: macro-structures of concrete, covered with glass and aluminum carpentry, yards and cement terraces, few green spaces and visible facilities. They were usually located in high and middle-class neighborhoods within the city. This kind of school was defined by many intellectuals, precisely because of their layout and transparency, as "panoptical" (Nielsen, personal communication). During the military government, prefabricated elements called "PRENOVA"[5] were also used experimentally. When democratic governance was reinstated in 1983, most construction activities were related exclusively to finishing "Plan 60" schools, which continued through the nineteen-nineties. At the same time, educational policies were focused on pedagogical aspects, which led to an important reform—the Federal Educational Law—which does not include in its regulations issues related with school architecture.

How to Study a School Building?

Although there are different methods of making comparative studies among different architectural structures (Blanton, 1994; Hage, 1979; Hillier and Hanson, 1984; Samson, 1990; among other) the indices of "Scale", "Integration" and "Complexity" (4) developed by Blanton (1994) prove useful to our objectives and hypotheses. These require the application of the "Gamma" pattern, proposed by Hillier and Hanson (1984) which allows us to break down the plan of a building into different cells and establish connections among them to show its underlying structure. One of the interesting aspects of Hillier and Hanson's (1984) work has to do with the connection characteristics presented by a given architectonic tradition. Thus, they consider two types of spatial configurations: distributive and non-distributive.

Non-distributive spaces are those which you can reach or leave only through one opening (Figure 14.3). Distributive spaces are those which you can reach of leave through more than one opening (Figure 14.4). On studying this characteristic in one given structure, in general we observe that as many distributive and non-distributive spaces are likely to appear. Therefore, when analyzing a structure it is necessary to make a general evaluation in order to categorize its configuration as distributive or non-distributive. Non-distributive structures show high figures of low connections (that is, one connection every node). Distributive structures present high figures of high connections, that is two or more connections every node.

In those structures defined as distributive, power and control are distributed homogeneously, therefore they are more democratic in character (Hillier y Hanson, 1984; Markus, 1993a). On the other hand, non-distributive structures concentrate power and control heterogeneously, giving priority to some spaces over others so as to rank them hierarchically. A further central aspect in this Gamma analysis is related to the degree of access to spaces within a given structure. Accessibility is considered according to the remoteness of spaces to the outside. The result has to do with the isolation and difficulty of access of each space.

As Grahame points out (1995:62), the application of Hillier and Hanson's pattern does not consist of a mere translation of designs into schemes and graphics; on the contrary it is a very delicate job which involves both the decisions made by the researcher and the statement of the criteria he used in this process. In our case these decisions imply the generation of a model which will allow us to make a basic reading of the plans in order to establish a morphological comparison.

On the other hand, the indices set by Richard Blanton (1994), which require the application of the Hillier and Hanson pattern, help achieve a comparison of the different architectural structures to one another, and can be summed up as follows:

1) Scale index. This consists of counting the number of nodes[6] in the Gamma diagram. If possible, the surface area and number of

Figure 14.3. Schematic Representation of a Non-Distributive Space.

Figure 14.4. Schematic Representation of a Distributive Space.

inhabitants should be added, in order to get a measure of square meters per person.

> Scale Index = Number of Nodes

2) Integration index. This index is connected to circulation within the structure and expresses its degree of restraint. It is the result of dividing the number of nodes by the amount of doors or passages in the structure.[7] One (1) is the smallest figure possible, because a room must have at least one connection. The highest restraint, then, is 1 and it decreases while the integration index increases. Integration is achieved through creating alternate circuits so that many potential routes exist between places.

$$\text{Integration Index} = \frac{\text{Number of Connections}^{[8]}}{\text{Number of Nodes}}$$

3) Complexity index. In his model, Blanton refers to functional variation in the use of space. If the information on activities or specific functionality is scarce, the author proposes that calculations should be based on the degree of accessibility or intercommunication of each node. In this way not only do we know the amount of connections in the structure but also the degrees of accessibility and the circulation within each node

> Complexity Index A: Amount of Connections Among Nodes[9]
> Complexity Index B: Accessibility of Each Node to the Outside (number of spaces to be crossed)[10]

In light of these models, a Gamma diagram to which we apply the scale, integration and complexity indices can be attempted for different historic schools in Buenos Aires. The results allow us to make a qualitative and quantitative comparative analysis among the different architectural "types", and see more significant structural and accessibility changes in these buildings through time.

Schools in Buenos Aires

Having chosen the school building classification model proposed by the multidisciplinary team of the *Municipalidad de Buenos Aires* as a basis for our analysis, I selected a school from each type, and applied Hillier and Hanson's Gamma analysis and Blanton's indices (see Figures 14.5–14.15, and see legend Figure 14.16).

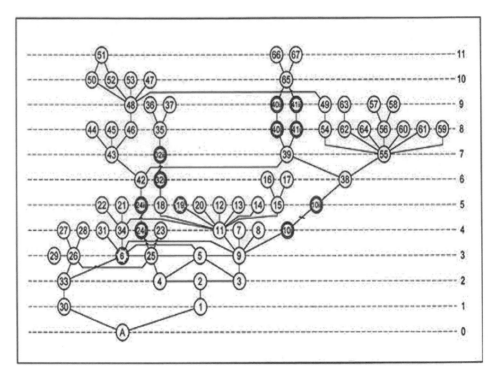

Figure 14.5. A Gamma Pattern of a Sarmientist School.

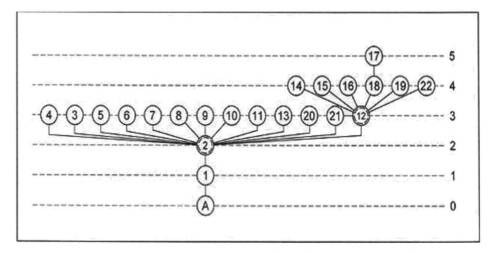

Figure 14.6. A Gamma Pattern of a Close Form School.

A first reading of the Gamma models allows the identification of a basic structural element common to all schools—a main central space surrounded by other secondary spaces linked to it—called a "panoptical shape" here. In the case of the "Sarmientist schools", however, there is another predominant shape of spatial structuring: a deep chain of spaces linked to each other, such that, in order to reach to one of them, it is necessary to go through others (Figure 14.17).

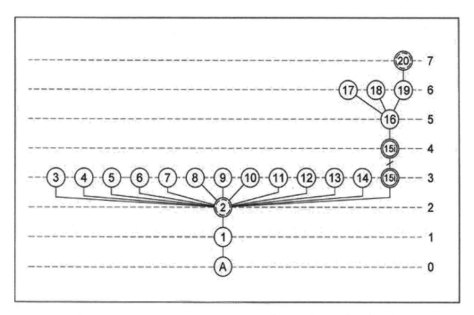

Figure 14.7. A Gamma Pattern of a U-Shaped School.

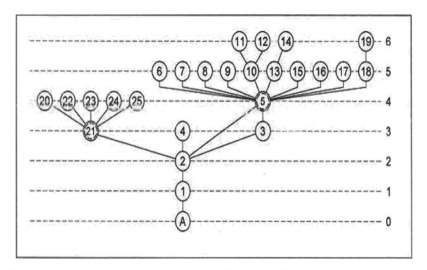

Figure 14.8. A Gamma Pattern of a Adapted *Chorizo* House School.

A "simple panoptical shape" is found in the "closed form" schools (Figure 14.18) as well as in the "U shape" schools. These buildings show this morphology, which will become the basic structure of all schools, for the first time. The in-depth chains of the "Sarmientist schools" also reoccur at a smaller scale.

In the later buildings, this panoptical shape was taken as a central axis from which a complex system of links radiated, resulting in

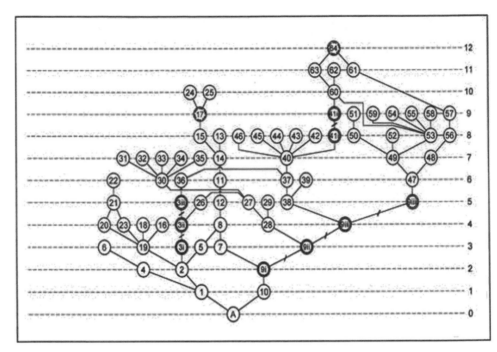

Figure 14.9. A Gamma Pattern of a Waldorph School.

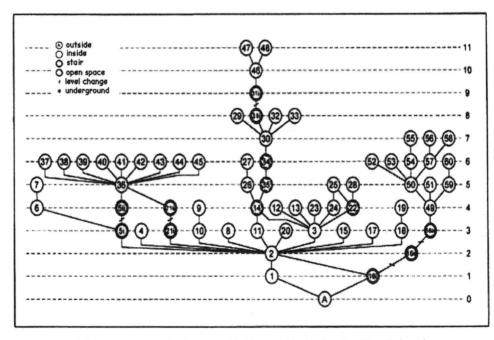

Figure 14.10. A Gamma Pattern of a Nelly Cantilo School.

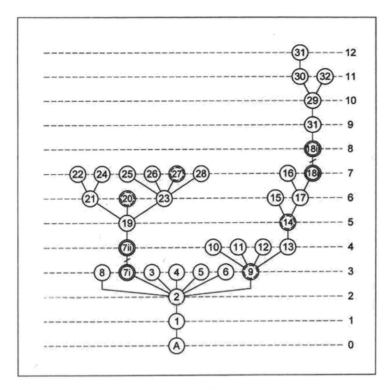

Figure 14.11. A Gamma Pattern of a Internacional Style School.

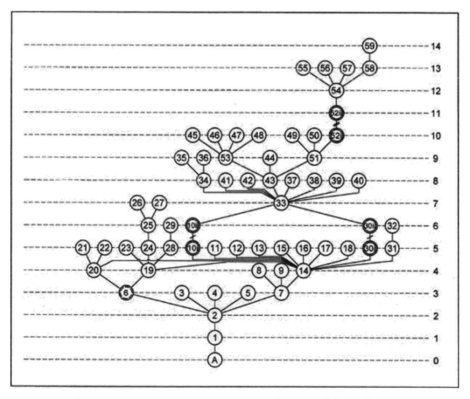

Figure 14.12. A Gamma Pattern of a Republic School.

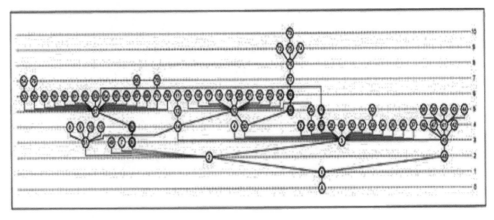

Figure 14.13. A Gamma Pattern of a Nineteen-Sixties School.

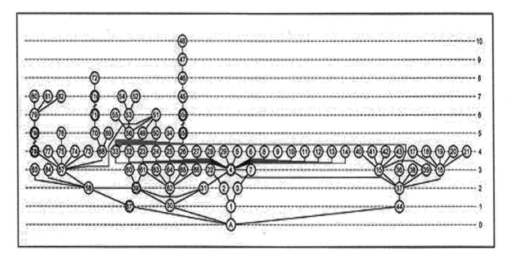

Figure 14.14. A Gamma Pattern of a Park School.

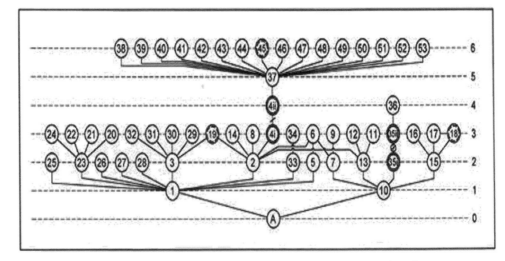

Figure 14.15. A Gamma Pattern of a Plan 60 School.

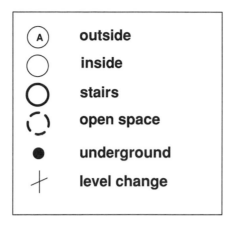

Figure 14.16. Legend for Gamma Patterns in Figures 5 to 15.

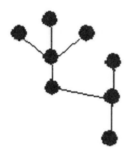

Figure 14.17. The Deep Structure of the Sarmientist School.

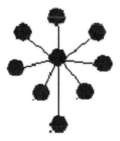

Figure 14.18. The Deep Structure of the Closed Plan School.

buildings made of 'sets' of panoptical shapes (Figure 14.19). All these models show how structures branch out as we move through the building. Thus there are one or two linked spaces from which access and exit are controlled and they usually constitute the essential structuring space of the school. They are strategically placed in the building to work as filters, from which one can control, regulate and watch people's movements. Classrooms, on the other hand, are placed at the end of these chains and are only reachable once the filters have been crossed, hence the tree-shape seen in the plans. Even more can be discerned by employing the various Blanton indices (Table 14.3).

Table 14.3. Blanton Indices by Architectural Tradition

School type	Scale index	Integration index	Complexity index A	Complexity index B
Sarmientist	72	1.13	166	6.2
Closed Form	22	1.04	45	3.2
U Shape	21	1	41	3.6
Adapted *Chorizo* House	25	1.04	50	4.4
Waldorph	70	1.14	158	6.3
Gelly Cantillo	65	1.06	136	5.1
International Style	35	1	69	5.74
Republic	62	1.04	141	7
Nineteen-Sixties	82	1.06	172	5.1
Park	87	1.13	194	4.2
Plan 60	55	1.09	118	3.6

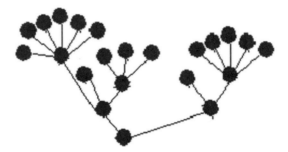

Figure 14.19. The Deep Structure of the 1960s School.

Scale Index

In general, we find a steadily increasing pattern in the amount of nodes in school buildings throughout time. Although the "Sarmientist school" is an exception, because of its high Scale index, the others schools built in the 19th Century and at the beginning of the 20th Century show an average of 21 to 25 nodes. In 1920, school buildings had at least two stories which helped to maximize covered space, even in small lots. Their scale indices range from 35 to 70 nodes. Finally, schools built after 1960 are the ones with the highest numbers of nodes, from 55 to 82 nodes. In Figure 14.20, the tendency toward larger school buildings is evident, while oscillations often represent schools belonging to the same period.

Integration Index

A common characteristic of all school buildings throughout history has been the non-distributive condition of spaces. This is shown in the very low levels of integration indices that range from 1 (the minimum possible figure) to 1.14. That is to say that In every case the average shows that most of the spaces have only one door.

On the other hand, the integration index also shows:

1. Proportionally, there is a concentration of spaces with low con-nection levels (1, in general),[11] demonstrating the non-distributive condition.
2. This panoptical organization leads to many spaces with few connections (1 access point per node) and a few spaces with many connections (10 or more access points per node) (Figure 14.21). Figure 14.22 shows a high number of nodes with low

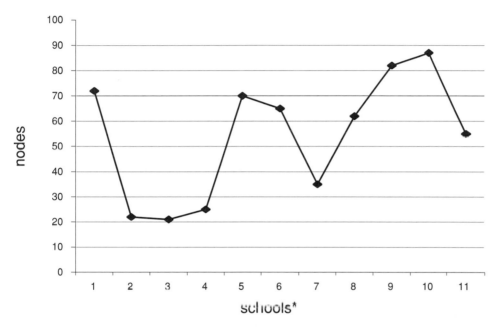

Figure 14.20. Comparison of Scale Index between School Types. 1. Sarmientist; 2. Closed Form; 3. U Shape; 4. Adapted Chorizo House; 5. Waldorph; 6. Gelly Cantilo; 7. International Style; 8. Republic; 9. Park; 10. Nineteen-Sixties; 11. Plan 60.

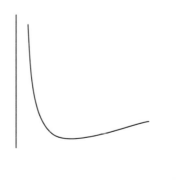

Figure 14.21. The Panopticon, Non-Distributive Model of School Building.

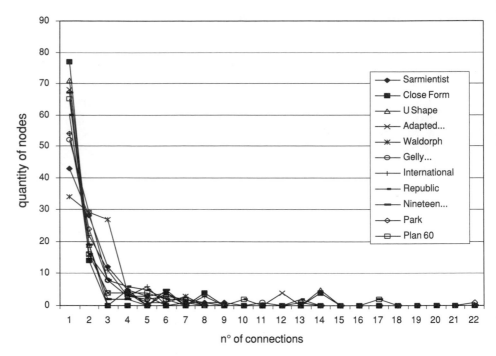

Figure 14.22. Connection Analysis: Comparison among all Schools.

connections, a dip in the number of nodes with average connections, and a slight increase in the numbers of nodes with high connections (10, 12 and even 22). In other words, these results show that there are many secondary spaces controlled by a few central ones. And when compared with Figure 14.21, Figure 14.22 also shows the two central aspects of the spatial organization of the school building: its panoptical and non-distributive structure.

Complexity Index A

At first sight, it might seem as of there are major differences in the complexity index A (that is, the proportion between nodes and connections) among different schools. Nevertheless, this index should be interpreted on a proportional basis in relation with the size of the school building, that is to say, taking into account the proportion of number of nodes and the number of connections (the average is 50 connections for every 25 nodes; or rather 100 connections every 50 nodes or 150 connections every 75 nodes). It is clear, then, that the results do not really vary in their indices of complexity A.

Index of Complexity B[12]

This index, that is the relationship between the internal spaces of a structure and the "outside", shows some temporal variation. In order to understand the data it is important to make this comparison while taking into consideration the size of the building as in Complex Index A. Figures that might seem relatively low, such as those for the "Closed Form", "U Shape" and "Adapted Chorizo House", are actually high. The result of the complexity indices of these buildings (from 3.2 to 4.4) and their reduced size (scale indices around 22), show the high degree of isolation and confinement of these spaces.

Thus we find a relatively homogeneous pattern of high index figures (i.e., low accessibility to spaces) for schools built before the 1960s (Figure 14.23). Then a sustained process of shortening distances between interior spaces and the outside takes place (i.e., the Plan 60 school is the one with the lowest index of complexity B: 3.6). This decrease in the distance between the "outside" and the "inside" can be understood in light of the fact that in the beginning, schools intended to isolate children from the rest of society, because that was where "dangerous" ideas and unacceptable knowledge lay. There was also an emphasis on making those transitional places separated the space inside the school building with the space outside more visible. In this way, the headmaster's office would generally be at the entrance of the building. In the sixties, "dangerous" ideologies seemed to be found "inside" the school space, probably brought by teachers and students. So then surveillance was reoriented

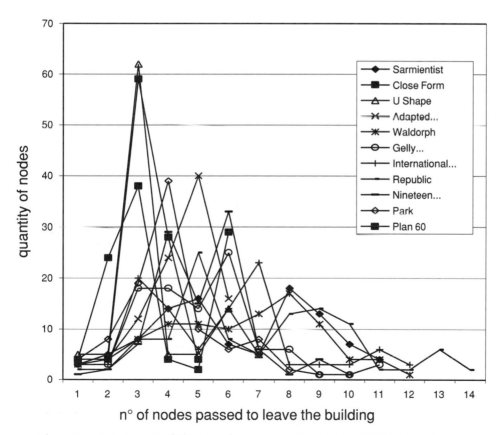

Figure 14.23. Accessibility Analysis: Comparison among all Schools.

toward each and every space within the school and its inhabitants. New "transparent" schools were built (i.e., the inside of the classrooms were visible through glass walls) and the headmaster's office was placed well inside the building, revealing new organizational criteria.

Conclusion

These results allow us to observe that, even though styles and shapes might seem different, the structures of the schools basically remain the same throughout time. Thus, while the indices of integration and complexity A do not vary, the indices of scale and complexity B show some minor changes through time. The scale index in particular shows an increase in the number of nodes (or discreet spaces) found in the buildings, while the index of complexity B shows a gradual decrease in the depth and isolation of nodes as related to the outside. As the Gamma plans show, the simple panoptical shapes become more complex. In the most recent models, the structure of the building becomes a panoptical chain, linked by corridors, halls, yards or staircases.

It could be said that, in general, there have been no structural changes in the public school buildings throughout time, therefore they still function as disciplinary institutions. Basically it is only their formal aspect that has changed in order to look more up to date in an aesthetic sense. Perhaps only "Plan 60" schools, with their possibilities to modify space, their projection of continuous visibility, and the reorientation of their focus of surveillance, that initiated a new trend more connected with the new requests of the system.

Some Ideas about the Public School in Argentina in a Post-Industrial Society

From the mid 20th Century there is a gradual process of emergence and growth of a new 'marginal' social figure, existing outside the system (Forrester, 1996, 2000). These are individuals that even in the "best situation" they cannot expect to be exploited by the system. From its ranks come the most radical and harmful resistance movements to capitalism—for example the landless movement (*Movimiento de los Sin Tierra*) in Brazil-. In opposition to other social groups within system, these groups have no future, nothing to lose, not even their putative freedom, thus they can confront power more effectively. In this way, resenting and in opposition to a system that excludes and ignores them, they create their own cultural values.

What is the way to disciplining those groups of people which grow far from the institution (such schools and families, or factories, hospitals and justice), designed by power to manage the mental tools that facilitate the later control of them? Otherwise, the only devices that the power structure has to face them are jails, physical repression and the hope that their own lack of organization will lead to self-destruction.

Education, once used as a mechanism social promotion, has now lost its power. To invest time, money and effort in training does not guarantee unemployment or success. In fact, education is now seen as generating anti-economic expenses.

> Education is no longer thought of as an automatic public good, to be funded without question from the public purse. (Beare 1998:18)

Nowadays in Argentina (as well as in many other countries) there exists a short-circuit between the needs of the system, the interests of the market, and the public educational training of individuals. This has led to a crisis in the educational system. The difficulty of achieving the goal of "training individuals who will be useful for society" —in fact, for the needs of the capitalist system—has led school into to a deep crisis. As Charlot (1976) points out, it is particularly in these times of crisis and social chaos that society worries about the kind of education given to the young.

It is necessary to consider that the productive unit of the post-industrial society, according to Deleuze, 1990)—the enterprise, does not require more people to repeat the same operations in a silent, mechanical, monotonous and standard way. The modern enterprise needs trained workers, who can be flexible, active and competitive. They have to be able to deal with different matters in specific ways. This is why many enterprises choose to train their own workers themselves. At present, working for an enterprise is not enough, it is necessary to believe in it and to feel that one, as an individual, has an important role in its development. To do so, new disciplinable devices that use emotions as the main method of persuasion are being created. For example, there are many places where employees are referred to as "associates", or they may even be called by their first names.

We can relate to the inability of public schools to adapt to this idea that, unlike the other establishments that constitute our society, it has been ruled by conservative ideas which help the same original principles prevail (Townsend, 1998). Thus, over a century after their consolidation, we can see that the same buildings, the same class organization (1 professor to 20 or 30 students), the same classrooms, the same curricula are still being used. In the Argentine case, the speed at which public schools changed was quick not enough to supply the new type of worker needed by the system (Figure 14.24). Private schools have therefore slowly begun to occupy this vacant space, creating a new kind of school (Zarankin, 2002).

If we consider what has happened in "developed" countries, we find public primary schools have changed radically in the last few years, both in their organization and material structure (Townsend 1998). However, in the case of Buenos Aires, unlike what could be expected of this new postindustrial reality, public schools only intensify the usage of the

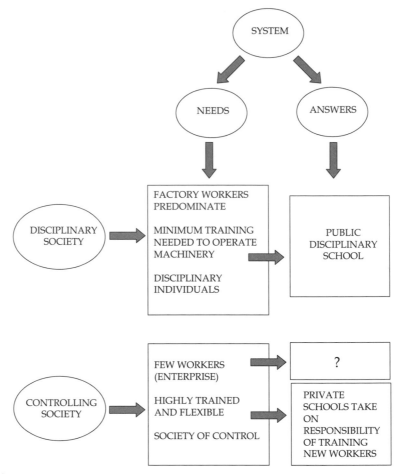

Figure 14.24. Relationship between Societal Orientation and Pedagogical System.

disciplinary model's criteria. The origin of the public school as an institution created within the frame of a disciplined and normalized organization of childhood reveals its inability to adapt to the new requirements of the system.

> I have visited many public schools, both in my country and in Latin America, and I have a feeling that, there, the 19th Century is not over yet. (Cangiano 2000)

It is possible to wonder, then, what kind of school will need a system in a society where only a few will have the chance to enter the productive sector and where most will became members of a new social group that exists outside the system (Forrester 1996). Perhaps they want a school with "eyes" and surveillance mechanisms that inculcates norms for living while watching and controlling it, or perhaps a school that transmits a false optimism about the future, or a school that, instead of training a working class, becomes a temporary storehouse, for lock up the children during the day.[13] Perhaps elementary public schools in Argentina only continue existing thanks to the legitimacy inherited from their functionality in the past and a belief in the positive effects of education.

Acknowledgements

First, I would like to thank Pedro Paulo Funari and Amalia Sanguinetti de Bórmida for their guidance and support. The suggestions and hints of the architects Miguel Cangiano, María Elena Longero, Rafael Iglesia, Gustavo Brandariz and Paula Moreno (who helped me in designing the plans and graphics) have been very useful, as were the comments of Carmen Soares and Margareth Rago. I must also thank Mathew Johnson (Durham University) and Charles Orser Jr. (Illinois State University) and Margarita Díaz Andreu (Durham University) with whom I had the chance to discuss my work to enrich it. I would also like to thank the FAPESP for making this research possible. For their unconditional support, I must thank my family (especially my sister Julieta, who helped me to translate this paper), and the Senatore family, particularly Lorena, who reviewed the translation.

Finally, I find it impossible to enumerate the reasons why I should thank María Ximena Senatore, a simple thank you is not enough.

Notes

[1] A synthesis of the speeches and policies of childhood in Argentina can be found in Carli (1999).

[2] For a history of school buildings in Argentina, please consult the work of Architect Gustavo Brandariz (1984, 1987, 1997, 1998).

[3] In 1991, an interdisciplinary team completed two reports (DIE, 1991a and 1991b) about school buildings in the Federal Capital. These studies are extremely important because they provided a level of detail and a quantity of information that had not been available previously. As such, these reports constitute the basis from which I organize the present cases under analysis.

[4] The construction of dining rooms in schools begins at this point too.

[5] Only 3 schools were built following this system. Morever, as they do not follow explicit models, but employ prefabricated materials, these buildings will not be analysed in this paper.

[6] The number of nodes implies the number of circumscribed physical spaces defined within an architectural structure. In contrast to Blanton (1994:52), outside spaces are not considered nodes here.

[7] In the present case, due to the examples used, it is useful for us to divide the number of connections by the number of nodes.

[8] In this case, it comes from the addition of each connection.

[9]The "number of connections between nodes" comes from the addition of the of "amount of connections".

[10]The work was done with the averages of the addition of the column "outside distance" and its division by the number of nodes.

[11]This means that a space has only one link (or door).

[12]This is the average number of spaces that have to be passed through in order to leave the building.

[13]How else could one explain that the last Argentine government made education obligatory yet reduced its budget?

[14]The typology mention 353 buildings. Our chart include only 350 because the PRENOVA buildings were not analized.

References

Althusser, L., 1968, Ideología y aparatos ideológicos del estado. In *La filosofía como arma de la revolución*, pp. 97–142. Siglo XIX, México.

Andrade Lima, T., 1999, El huevo de la serpiente: Una arqueología del capitalismo embrionario en el Rio de Janeiro del siglo XIX. In A. Zarankin and F. Acuto edited by, *Sed Non Satiata: teoría social en la arqueología latinoamericana contemporánea*, pp. 189–238. Ediciones Del Tridente, Buenos Aires.

Apple, M., 1979, *Ideología y Currículo*. Akal, Madrid.

Aries, P., 1973, *L'enfant et la famille sous l'ancien régim*. Seuil, Paris.

Austin, D., and Thomas, J., 1986, The 'Proper Study' of Medieval Archaeology: a Case Study. In *From the Baltic to the Black Sea: Studies in Medieval archaeology*, edited by D. Austin and L. Alcock, pp. 44–78. Unwin Hyman, London.

Baudelot, C., and Establet, R., 1975, *La Escuela Capitalista*. Siglo XXI, México.

Beare, H., 1998, 'Enterprise': The New Metaphor for Schooling in a Post Industrial Society. In *The Primary School in Changing Times: The Australian Experience*, edited by P. Townsend, pp. 3–20. Routledge, London.

Blanton, R., 1994, *Houses end Households*. Plenum Press, New York.

Bordieu, P., 1977, *Outline of a Theory of Practice*. Cambridge University Press, Cambridge. 1989, *O. poder simbólico*. Bertrand Brasil, Rio de Janeiro.

Bourdieu, P and J. Passeron., 1970 *A Reprodução. Elementos para uma teoria do sistema de ensino*. Alves Editora, Rio de Janeiro.

Brandariz, G., 1984, *El Edificio de la escuela Presidente Roca*. Manuscript. 1987, La Arquitectura de la Libertad. In *Libertad Responsable y Educación*, edited by C. Lazzari, pp. 41–51. Buenos Aires. 1997, Los lugares donde se enseña. *Todo es Historia* 356: 74–90. 1998, *La arquitectura escolar de inspiración sarmientina*. EUDEBA, Buenos Aires.

Cangiano, M. 2000, El espacio para la educación: en las puertas del siglo XXI? Paper presented at the Seminario sobre Espacios Educativos en Chile, América Latina y el Caribe, Buenos Aires.

Carli, S., 1999, *Niñez, pedagogía y política: transformaciones de los discursos acerca de la infancia en la historia de la educación argentina 1880–1955*. Ph.D. dissertation, University of Buenos Aires, Buenos Aires.

Charlot, B., 1976, *A mistificação pedagógica: realidades sociais e processos ideológicos na teoria da educação*. Zahar, Rio de Janeiro.

de Certeau, M., 1980, *La invención de lo cotidiano: 1 artes de hacer*. Universidad Iberoamericana, México.

Deleuze. G., 1990, Controle e devenir, *Conversações (1972–1990)*. Editora 34, São Paulo.

Deetz, J., 1977, *In Small Things Forgotten*. Anchor Books, New York.

Die, MCBA., 1991a, *Adaptabilidad del parque edilicio escolar instalado a los requerimientos de un plan de construcciones escolares y nuevos programas de necesidades: tipologías y funcionalidad.* Serie 8, Dirección de Planeamiento Educación, Dirección de Investigación Educativa, Municipalidad de la Ciudad de Buenos Aires, Buenos Aires.

   1991b, *Principales cifras del sistema educativo municipal: estado edilicio.* Serie 10, Dirección de Planeamiento Educación, Dirección de Investigación Educativa, Municipalidad de la Ciudad de Buenos Aires, Buenos Aires.

Fernández Enguita, M., 1985, *Trabajo, escuela e ideología.* Akal, Madrid.

Fletcher, R., 1989, The Messages of Material Behavior: a Preliminary Discussion of Non-verbal Meaning. In *The Meaning of the Things,* edited by I. Hodder, pp. 33–39. Harper Collins, New York.

Forrester, V., 1996, *El horror económico.* Fondo Económico de Cultura, México.

   2000, *Una extraña dictadura.* Fondo Económico de Cultura, México.

Foucault, M., 1970, *La arqueología del saber.* Siglo XXI, México.

   1976, *Vigilar y castigar: el nacimiento de la prisión.* Siglo XXI, México.

Funari, P., 1991, El Mito Bandeirante: elite brasileña, cultura material e identidad, *Boletín de Antropología Americana* 24: 112–121.

   1999, Historical Archaeology from a World Perspective. In *Historical Archaeology: Back from the Edge,* edited by P. P. A Funari, M. Hall and S. Jones, pp. 37–66. Routledge, London.

Grahame, M., 1995, *The House of Pompeii: Space and Social Interaction.* Ph.D. dissertation, Southampton University.

   1997, Public and Private in the Roman House: the Spatial Order of the Casa del Fauno. *Journal of Roman Archaeology* supplement 22: 137–164.

   2000, *Reading Space: Social Interaction and Identity in the Houses of Roman Pompeii.* Bar International Series 886, Oxford.

Hage, P., 1979, Graph Theory as Structural Model in Cultural Anthropology. *Annual Review of Anthropology* 8:115–136.

Hillier, B., and Hanson, J., 1984, *The Social Logic of Space.* Cambridge University Press, Cambridge.

Hodder, I., 1982, *Symbols in Action.* Cambridge University Press, London.

Johnson, M., 1996, *An Archaeology Of Capitalism.* Blackwell, Oxford.

Leone, M., 1984, Interpreting Ideology in Historical Archaeology: the William Paca Garden in Annapolis, Maryland. In *Ideology, Power and Prehistory,* edited by D. Miller and C. Tilley, pp. 25–35. Cambridge University Press, Cambridge.

Markus, T., 1993, *Buildings and Power: Freedom and Control in the Origin of Modern Buildings Types.* Blackwell, Oxford.

McGuire, R., 1991, Building Power in Cultural Landscape of Broome County, New York 1880 to 1940. In *The Archaeology of Inequality,* edited by R. McGuire and R. Paynter, pp. 102–124. Blackwell, Cambridge, MA.

McGuire, R., and Paynter, R., 1991, *The Archaeology of Inequality.* Blackwell, Cambridge, MA.

Miller, D., 1984, Modernism and Suburbia as Material Ideology. In *Ideology, Power and Prehistory,* edited by D. Miller and C. Tilley, pp. 37–49. Cambridge University Press, Cambridge.

   1987, *Material Culture and Mass Consumption.* Blackwell, Oxford.

Miller, D., and Tilley, C., editors, 1984, *Ideology, Power and Prehistory.* Cambridge University Press, Cambridge.

Miller, D., Rowlands, M., and Tilley, C., 1989, *Domination and Resistance.* Routledge, London.

Monks, G., 1992, Architectural Symbolism and Non-Verbal Communication at Upper Fort Garry. *Historical Archaeology* 26(2): 37–57.

Newland, C., 1991, La educación elemental en Hispanoamérica: desde la independencia hasta la centralización de los sistemas educativos nacionales. *Hispanic American Historical Review* 71(2): 334–364.

Orser Jr., Ch., 1996, *A Historical Archaeology of the Modern World.* Plenum Press, New York.

Parker Pearson, M. and Richards, C., editors, 1994, *Architecture and Order: Approaches to Social Space*. Routledge, London.

Querrien, A., 1979, *Trabajos Elementales sobre la Escuela Primaria*. Ediciones La Piqueta, Madrid.

Samson, R., editor, 1990, *The Social Archaeology of Houses*. Edinburgh University Press, Edinburgh.

Shanks, M., and Tilley, C., 1987, *Reconstructing Archaeology*. Routledge, London.

Stedman, S., 1996, Recent Research in the Archaeology of Architecture: Beyond the Foundations. *Journal of Archaeological Research* 4(1): 51–93.

Szuchman, M., 1990, Childhood Education and Policies in Nineteenth-Century Argentina: The Case of Buenos Aires. *Hispanic American Historical Review* 71(2): 334–364.

Tilley, C., 1989, Interpreting Material Culture. In *The Meaning of the Things*, edited by I. Hodder, pp. 185–194. Harper Collins, London.

    1993, *Interpretative Archaeology*. Berg, Oxford.

Townsend, T., editor, 1998, *The Primary School in Changing Times; the Australian Experience*. Routledge, London.

Varela, J., and Alvarez Uria, F., 1991, *Arqueología de la escuela*. La Piqueta, Madrid.

Viñao Frago and Escolano, A., 1998, *Currículo, Espaço e Subjetividade: a arquitetura como programa*. DP and A, Rio de Janeiro.

Zarankin, A., 1997, *Vivienda Familiar y Sistema Capitalista: una lectura arqueológico*. Master's thesis, Facultad de Arquitectura, Diseño y Urbanismo, Universidad de Buenos Aires, Buenos Aires.

    1999a, Casa Tomada: sistema, poder y vivienda domestica. In *Sed Non Satiata: Teoría social en la arqueología latinoamericana contemporánea*, edited by A. Zarankin and F. Acuto, pp. 239–272. Ediciones Del Tridente, Buenos Aires.

    1999b, Arqueología de la arquitectura: 'Another Brick in the Wall'. *Revista do Museu de Arqueologia e Etnologia da Universidade de São Paulo* (São Paulo) supplement 3: 119–129.

    2002, *Paredes que Domesticam: Arqueologia da Arquitetura Escolar Capitalista; O caso de Buenos Aires*. Centro de Historia da Arte e Arqueologia (IFCH-UNICAMP), Campinas.

15

Enlightened Discourses, Representations, and Social Practices in the Spanish Settlement of Floridablanca, Patagonia 18th Century

Maria Ximena Senatore

Enlightenment Discourses and the Spanish Project in Patagonia

The following question, posed by Roger Chartier, is an excellent starting point from which to begin a discussion of the motivations behind the Patagonian project, within the predominant ideological framework in force during its elaboration. It is in this context that we can detect the ideas of Enlightenment and the basis for modern society at work.

> Is it certain that Enlightenment must be characterized exclusively or principally as a corpus of self-contained transparent ideas, or a set of clear and distinct propositions? Should not the century's novelty be read elsewhere, in multiple practices guided by an interest in utility and a service that aimed at the management of spaces and populations and whose mechanism (intellectual or institutional) imposed a profound reorganization of the systems of perception an of the order of the social world? (Chartier, 1991: 17).

The Spanish Crown embarked on the incorporation of Southern Patagonian territories in the late 18th century. In order to achieve this, the Ministers of Charles the Third's court designed a plan of establishing settlements in different places along the southern Atlantic coast. In essence, this project may be considered an attempt to create Imperial reference points in spaces where there were none. One of our first questions concerns whether Patagonian settlements were organized according to social models already in use or whether they represented a trial for new models belonging to the particular body of ideas inherent to the Spanish Enlightenment, to which Charles the Third's Ministers adhered.

It is important to state that Spanish colonization projects were common in the 18th century (see Navarro, 1994). The one paradigmatic case within the Iberian Peninsula was the Sierra Morena colonization. According to historians, this project shows "that Spanish reformers, having looked at their society, knew what was wrong and what was needed" (Lynch, 1989: 213–214). The Sierra Morena case has many similarities to the Patagonian settlements in the late 18th century (Porro, 1995). In 1767, one of Charles the Third's Ministers outlined a plan meant to establish colonies in the empty regions of southern Spain, where German and Flemish catholic immigrants were taken in order to promote agriculture and industry (see Capel, 1970). It has been said that "Sierra Morena was more than a colony- that it worked as a model or social experiment, meant to demonstrate that agrarian problems could be solved by applying an enlightened program untrammeled of the Spanish past and free of latifundia, entail, and *mortmain*" (Lynch, 1989: 213–214).

Most historical research on the reformation projects found in Enlightenment Spain of the 18th century, has focused on the ideas of the learned men who were close to Charles the Third's court and on their discourse of Spanish Enlightenment (see Anes, 1969, 1982; Argemí, 1988; Elorza, 1970; Herr, 1964, Mestre, 1993; Palacio, 1964; Rodríguez, 1975; Sarrailh, 1954; among others). This paper seeks to explore how this theoretical discourse relates to the practical aspects that arise when such projects are put into practice through the lens of one particular case on the Patagonian coast.

The aim of this paper is to discuss the social order of the Patagonia Project and its implicit social tensions by using both material culture and documentary evidence. There is a variety of interesting approaches to the combined analysis of written and material evidence (see Funari et al., 1999). In Morris' (1997: 8–9) words, "both categories of evidence are generated by actors manipulating shared but contested cultural expectations in the process of living their lives. Words and things are responses to situations created by events beyond our control, but are also inventions aimed to shape the flow of events in ways which, we hope, will suit us". On the other hand we understand that "both archaeology and documentary evidence can be used as a form of discourse" (Johnson, 1996: 113). As Funari et al. (1999: 9) state, "verbal and artifactual discourses intersect with one another in diverse ways, and the development of techniques for addressing their interrelationships remains a fundamental methodological question binding together the field of historical archaeology". Following Hall (2000: 15), a better understanding of events in the past was sought by fitting propositions against documents, artifact assemblages, and other sources of evidence, by looking at what these sources reveal about eachother, and by modifying theoretical propositions during our research.

In colonial situations, it is common "to construct new spatial forms with the preconceived intention either of introducing or reinforcing a new set of behaviors to a colonized area" (Delle 1999b: 107); or at least "as a means of preserving colonists and their cultural values and to encourage economic growth" (Blades, 1986: 259). Patagonian settlements were built on a *tabula rasa*: that is to say there was no previous European settlement in these lands. Thus we start from the idea that built space worked as a starting frame of reference for the development of settlers' everyday practices and that such a space would be acting as the representation of the ideas underlying the Spanish project. It is our purpose to evaluate the context in which these practices were produced and the relation between these practices and the enlightened discourses.

Patagonia

The Southern Atlantic coast had been visited by vessels from different countries since the 15th century. Concerned by this situation, in 1580, the Spanish Crown developed a plan to settle two colonies in the coast of the Magellan Straits (Figure 15.1). This plan ultimately failed (Braun Menéndez, 1950; Saravia, 1988), thus until the 18th century, there were no permanent European settlements in Patagonia and the only inhabitants of those lands were indigenous groups with mobile hunter-gatherer economies.

In the 18th century, the design and careful planning of the Spanish project involved different levels of projection such as the integration of a geo-strategic mission and the economic use of settlements in the middle to long term. Overall, the plan consisted of establishing permanent settlements in specified places on the coast. From an economic point of view these settlements had three central goals: to support the exploitation of maritime resources that the Crown was planning to supply salt to the Rio de la Plata, and, according to some authors, to become ports that served the colonial trade system. The geo-strategic mission was to establish the physical presence of Spain in these southern territories, thus ensuring Spanish sovereignty in the region.

A close exploration and inspection of the Southern Atlantic coast occurred during the opening stage of the settlement project. These trips provided abundant information to facilitate the selection of the locations for the new settlements, such as sheltered natural ports which offered the best living conditions. The design for this plan considered the creation of two main settlements "Población de Nuestra Señora del Carmen

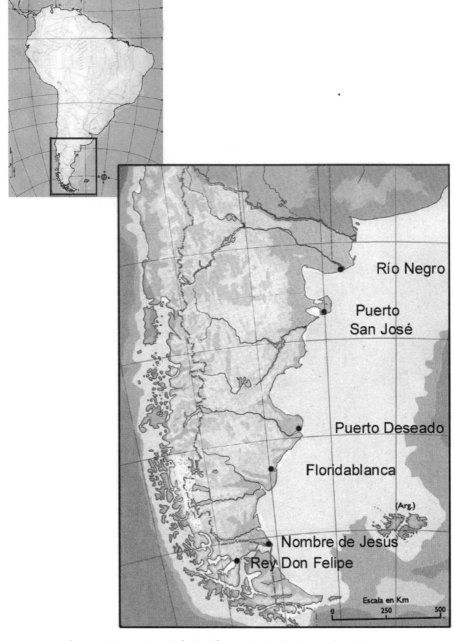

Figure 15.1. Spanish Settlements in Patagonian Coast.

del Río Negro" and "Nueva Población y Fuerte de Floridablanca", and two other subsidiary ones (Gorla, 1984) (Figure 15.1).

In the Floridablanca case, the concepts of agriculture and family were the centre of the discourse for each new colony. According to contemporary hierarchies of the possible economic activities for the Patagonian coast (such as fishing, maritime resources, or salt extraction), agriculture was selected as the main means of support for new populations. An attempt was made to guarantee agricultural development through building a society of principally farming families tied to the land. Households were seen as the essential unit of society and the basic elements needed for their maintenance was determined by the Spanish Crown (i.e., lodging, food, health, land, seeds, and production means). Nevertheless, when these key elements are examined closely, discord is evident between the theoretical discourse and resulting practices.

People

The recruitment of settlers was also organized and supervised by the Spanish Crown (Apolant, 1970; Porro, 1995). The Ministers who designed the project determined *a priori* the profile of the settlements to be established in the region. The *Real Orden* of 1778 expressed the intention of sending poor Spanish farming families who would develop permanent bonds with the land (Ramos 1984). A recruiting campaign was thus implemented in the northern Spanish provinces (Galicia, Asturias and Castilla-Leon). Posters promised lodging, tools, land ownership, seeds, and a daily food ration. Interested families signed an agreement such that they were sent to Rio de la Plata, where the Viceroyalty would determine which Patagonian settlement they would be sent to. Conditions stated in the agreement included 'subjection to destination', that is, settler families were not allowed to abandon the settlement by their own will, rather only by permission of the local authorities (Porro, 1995).

Even though Spanish families formed the main component of the settlement population, other social groups were present as well. Archaeologists can make use of written documents in more than one way, for instance by studying the structure of documents rather than by using them as a source of information (Johnson, 1996: 97). Documents clearly classify the people living in San Julian colony into six different groups, each with different rights and duties assigned to them by the Spanish Crown. These groups were: local representatives and officers of the Crown, troops, craftsmen, settlers, convicts, and crew members of the King's brigantines. The organization of each group is expressed in lists ordered hierarchically from the most important to the least important member. Settlers were listed as families. Each familial unit is registered under the name of the male settler or head of the family, followed by his wife and his children, including specifying whether the latter are under eight years of age ("*párvulos*"). These written lists may be understood as a representation of Floridablanca social structure. By means of expressing categories and subcategories, and the hierarchies between and within them, the lists both represent and reproduce the social order.

According to the information found in archives about the number of people in each group, farming settlers constituted largest group within

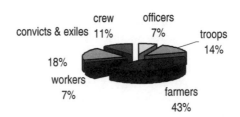

Figure 15.2. The Floridablanca Population, Composition of Social Groups, October 1781.

the settlement population. During the first year after the colony was established, there was a 20% mortality rate which affected all groups (Senatore and Insiarte, 2000), and as such, the composition of the population structure did not change, as demonstrated by Figure 15.2.

Analysis of documents and published data (Apolant, 1970; Porro, 1995) enables us to determine the composition and evolution of the Floridablanca population throughout its existence. In San Julian, for example, settler families came from thirteen villages in the Zamora, Leon, Valencia and Valladolid regions of central Spain (i.e., Castilla-León). Such homogeneity in settler origins enables us to homogeneity in terms of settler origins, which enables us to infer a certain regularity in everyday practices previous to their arrival in Patagonia. Moreover, when examining further the composition of families sent to Floridablanca, we find that many were related such that communities were in some sense extended families. These ties may have influenced the system of social relationships inside the settlement, reinforcing bonds of solidarity among families and even influencing the reorganization of the settlement after the significant mortality rate experienced during the first year.

A further group was formed by Crown officers- such as the Superintendent Don Antonio Viedma who headed the colony-, accountants, surgeons, priests, and other officers whose duties and pay were closely regulated. Troops from Infantry and Artillery Regiments of Buenos Aires were stationed in Floridablanca, and regulation of their duties, rights, activities, release conditions, and pay differed from those of the groups previously mentioned in relation to the regiments they belonged to.

Craftsmen constituted yet another group, appearing in the documents under the name of "*Maestranza*" (workers), and including masons, carpenters, blacksmiths, barrel makers, lantern makers, caulkers and laborers, among others. Living conditions established by the Spanish Crown for this particular group also differed from those established for the farmers. Interestingly, only men are found in this group. Most of them received monthly pay that varied according to their work, and some were given a daily food ration as well. Tools belonged to the craftsmen themselves and were not supplied by the Crown. Workers' mobility was higher than that of the farmers since their presence in Floridablanca was closely related to how much their work was needed. In addition, the crew of the Brigantine San Francisco de Paula, stationed in the San

Julián port, was also recorded as part of the population. Last of all, the documents mention a group of convicts and exiles send by the Rio de la Plata Viceroyalty to serve out their prison terms.

This document analysis demonstrates that Spanish farmer families were the principle and most homogeneous component of the Floridablanca population. They were also the most stable population in the settlement, whereas the members of other minority groups sent from the Viceroyalty (i.e., officers, troops, workers, convicts and exiles) lived there on a temporary basis only as their stay was tied to their job or positions.

Space

When analyzing built space in Floridablanca, the decisions made in the building and organization of domestic spaces were given particular weight because architecture is a technology of power (Foucault, 1976), while it helps fix the social order by establishing a certain spatial order (Grahame, 1995: 55). Our analysis of space involves the study of two lines of evidence: archaeological and documentary. Both are forms of discourse (Johnson 1996: 113). In the Patagonian case, built space in Floridablanca forms part of the Enlightenment discourse which served as the basis for the settlement endeavor.

In Patagonia, as far as the space-occupation model is concerned, the populating process emphasized concentrating populations devoted to agriculture into small villages, surrounded by cultivated land. If we consider that the only means of communication settlers had was by sea, the choice of the location for Floridablanca—10 km away from the coast—suggests that fresh water availability prevailed over a strategic location on the coastline in the decision-making process. There is still more evidence that the agricultural character of the settlement also entered in to this process, even though a location on the coastline would have meant more comfort and less isolation for the settlers.

The only existing historical design of the San Julian settlement is of a fortification and dates to the time of the establishment of the settlement in January 1781 (Figure 15.3). Because of the subject of this image, writers of historical narratives often mistake the character of this settlement to be defensive. According to the reports sent to the Rio de la Plata Viceroyalty, the fort sheltered the entire population during the first year until the village expansion was completed (Viedma, [1783] 1980). The fort was both 50m long and wide, made of wood, and surrounded by a moat. It was square, with a central open space surrounded by four barracks, two of which were meant to lodge settler families and another two to lodge the other members of the population (officers, troops, workers and convicts). The only kitchen was located in the middle of the central space. Bastions were devoted to specific functions common to all the population (hospitals and warehouses). Other productive spaces were located outside the fort (blacksmith's forge, bakery).

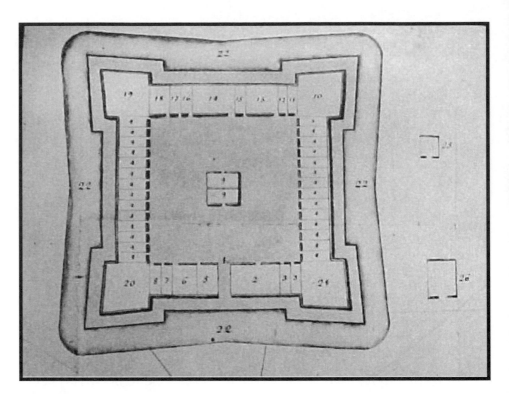

Figure 15.3. Historical Plan of the San Julián Settlement *'Nueva Población y Fuerte de Floridablanca'*, 28th January 1781: 1. Bastion and Tools Warehouse; 2. Accountant's Room; 3. Surgeon's Room; 4. Priest's Room; 5. Chapel; 6. Priest's Room; 7. Superintendent's House; 8. Superintendent Servants' Room; 9. Warehouse Warden's Room; 10. Bastion and Food Warehouse; 11. Bastion and Hospital; 12. Bleeders' Room; 13. Artillery-troop Room; 14. Worker's House; 15. Convicts' Barrack; 16. Troop Barrack; 17. and 18. Troop-officers' Rooms; 19. Bastion and Food Warehouse; 20. Kitchen; 21. Blacksmith's Forge; 22. Bakery; 23. Settler Family Rooms.

Interestingly, the lateral barracks devoted to Spanish farmers showed a marked homogeneity—all the rooms were similar in shape and size—whereas the barracks at the entrance and the back had a greater social and functional heterogeneity.

The village enlargement was financed by the Crown and supervised by Crown officers in San Julián and built by workers hired for that express purpose. During 1781, a hospital, a blacksmith's forge, a bakery, and nine houses for permanent settlers were built. From then on, living quarters for all Spanish settler families were located outside the fort. Two years later, and a few months before the abandonment of the colony, a new series of houses for the families was built opposite the previous one, thus closing the central square space. Archaeology shows that these houses remained unfinished.

As soon as the first stage of the village enlargement was finished, a report was sent from San Julián to the Rio de la Plata in which the state of the colony and the projects for new buildings are described.

In this report, spaces are described according to the use given to them, and in some cases, their size and construction materials. An interesting aspect of this report is that each group was attached to a specific living space. The typical cultural strategy of dominant actors and institutions is not so much to establish uniformity as it is to organize difference (Sewell, 1999:56). It is from this point on that we can start interpreting the social order at work in Floridablanca, as suggested by the documents.

In general terms, some characteristics of the initial organization and orientation were kept when the built area was enlarged, for instance the quadrangular disposition around a central space or plaza remained. On the other hand, changes were implemented in the number and location of entrances to this central area which had a subsequent influence on the entrance to and circulation within the settlement.

To begin, the shape and function of the lateral quarters of the fort were kept. Settler family houses were built along the two lateral wings of the plaza in parallel streets. The general homogeneity of living spaces for Spanish settlers was maintained, as well as the way into the central area. The description of houses enables us to deepen into some aspects related to settlers' living space.

By integrating documentary and archaeological information we can acquire some knowledge of daily life within living spaces and the different practices associated with them. Our archaeological approaches to the site resulted in the drawing of a plan of the San Julián settlement in which the location of the different buildings outside the fort is shown for the first time (Senatore, 2001, Senatore et al., 2001). Geophysical surveys are also provided (see Buscaglia, 2001, Buscaglia et al., 2001). In order to interpret the archaeological plan (Figure 15.4), spaces devoted to specific functions such as living, production and socialization were considered, as well as the location of public and private spaces and limitations to the access different groups or individuals had to specific spaces.

When focusing our analysis on living spaces, we can say that social space in Floridablanca was mainly structured on two components: Spanish settler families, and others (i.e., officers, troops, workers, and convicts). According to the information available, the fort -apart from its functional heterogeneity (church, warehouse, and lodging)—was a socially diversified space. It lodged officers, troops, workers and convicts that, however, shared two characteristics: they were all single men and they were in Floridablanca on a temporary basis. According to the historical plan, private space differed for each one of the social groups (i.e., individual private space in the case of officers or shared space in the case of troops or convicts). The kitchen was common to all, which possibly needed a certain level of organization to accommodate so many different groups.

The description of settler family houses enables us to deepen our understanding of their living space. As mentioned before, this group was formed by families residing in Floridablanca on a permanent basis. The living spaces provided by the Crown for them were identical in size

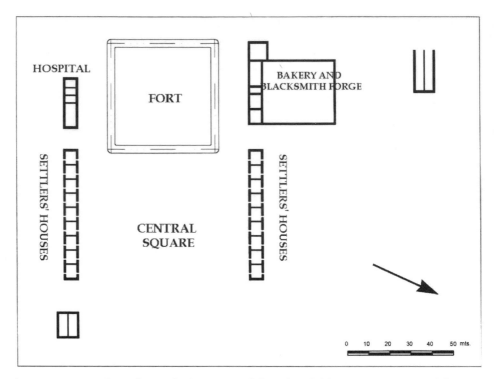

Figure 15.4. Archaeological Blueprint of the Floridablanca site, San Julián Bay, Santa Cruz Province.

and design for all settlers both inside and outside the fort. Every house was approximately 30m square and consisted of a room, a kitchen and a roofed yard. Archaeology shows that internal divisions were established at the time the houses were built. This is to say that an 'average' house was determined for each family with predetermined spaces for sleeping, eating, and storage. Private space was pre-established for a domestic unit since no differentiated spaces existed for individual members of the family.

Settler family houses were made of durable materials, such as clay-bricks for the walls and tiles for the roof, which may reflect part of their obligation to stay permanently in the settlement. In contrast, the material used for the fort was principally wood, less permanent, which may, in turn, be a product of the temporary commitment of the groups occupying this space (see Table 15.1).

The analysis presented suggests that social organization in Florid-ablanca was structured on the basis of two population groups: Spanish settler families and others. Differentiation was marked by the composition of each group (families *versus* single men), the length of time they were supposed to stay in the place (permanent *versus* temporary settlers), and differentiated living conditions. Those of the settler families, involving greater privacy and freedom for the organization of daily life. Moreover, absolute homogeneity in the design and

Table 15.1. Comparison of Farming and Non-Farming Structures

	Farmer families	Others
Condition	Permanent	Temporary
Function	Agriculture	Diverse
Composition	Families	Single men
Housing Space	Identical houses with differentiated space to cook, sleep and store	Individual or group shared inside the fort
Building Materials	Greater durability: clay bricks and tiles	Less lasting: wood

size of all houses suggests that the Crown determined an initial equality in the conditions of each settler family. They also shared the same legal and juridical rights and duties, as was shown in the contracts signed in Spain when formalizing the terms of the settlement agreement. Our analysis reinforces the idea that from the beginning, all the families in this group were hired under presumably egalitarian conditions.

Discourses and Social Practices: Family, House, and Land

A first interpretation of the organization of domestic living spaces may reflect a predetermined social order within which each settler family is concurrently a reproductive and productive unit isolated within discrete spatial units. But the meaning of any spatial order is not intrinsic, and must be invoked through practice (Moore, 1986: 6). Everyday practices demonstrate that there was no direct equivalence of family, domestic living space and productive unit.

To begin, each house was built to be occupied by one family, though at times, two families shared them. In spite of the fact that several official documents express the need of building one house for each family, during most of the settlement's existence, one house often lodged more than one family. Moreover, when a male settler (husband/father) died, his widow and children were forced to abandon the settlement since the family unit had become of no use to the development of the colony. Each unit was, therefore, considered productive only if headed by a man and as such there is no equivalence between the idea of the 'entire family' and that of a productive unit.

From the analysis of everyday practices in Floridablanca, we can see, quoting Moore (1986: 9), "that the danger of suggesting that the organization of space simply reflects social order or socioeconomic conditions is avoided by showing that what is reflected is a representation of the unity of the individual family rather than its real unity." Exploration of the meaning of these representations leads us to consider space as a kind of discourse. The discordance between practices and discourses leads us to return to the question posed by Chartier quoted at the beginning.

Society

In general terms, when we think of Enlightenment, we agree with Munck (2000: 26) that, although rural society is not the obvious place to start looking for signs of social and cultural innovation, despite intensive research in recent years, there is very little agreement about what early European popular culture really was. Therefore, the Floridablanca settlement enables us to propose some new questions about Spanish Enlightenment considering social order from the link between discourse and social practices.

In the Patagonian case, we stress certain ideas which are at the root of the discourse on settlement. One is the central importance given to agriculture, and that families were fundamental to achieving agricultural development. The family, however, "was not only the fundamental economic unit of society; it also provided the basis for political and social order. It is well-known that in this period the family served as a metaphor for the state; in conventional political thought the king was the father to his people, the father king is the household" (Amussen, 1988: 1, see also Johnson, 1996).

In the new colonies, households seemed to become the essential unit of society and basic conditions for its reproduction were ensured (i.e., lodging, food, health, land, seeds and production means). Nevertheless, when these key units are examined in detail, discordance between discourse and practices is evident. Discourse refers to a family as a reproductive and a productive unit, isolated in space as a domestic unit, but in practice this unit did not function as such.

In Floridablanca, domestic space was family space, based on the patriarchal idea that the man-husband-father is an essential component. When the *pater familias* died, his widow and children were sent to the Rio de la Plata since they were considered "useless for the colony", that is to say that the family worked as a productive unit only if the man was present. Thus, gender relationships were built on this patriarchal structure bearing a strong hierarchy.

From a material point of view, egalitarian conditions were established for all families from the start, though it remains to be seen whether these conditions ever became permanent. It is thus necessary to evaluate the development of differentiation later or—for instance in the regulation of production.

Moreover, gender relations in other settlements may differ from those found in San Julián where widows were considered useless for agricultural labor (Table 15.2). In Carmen de Río Negro, women appear in lists of volumes produced by each settler, such that here, the productive unit did not depend on the presence of a man and that in the Río Negro settlement, the productive unit and the family was considered more equivalent.

Land distribution and the regulation of production are key to understanding the projection of social development in Patagonian settlements in order to be able to link these practices in local contexts, belonging to

Table 15.2. Gender Roles at Floridablanca and Rio Negro

	Floridablanca	Rio Negro
Head of the family	Only the man	Man or widow
Head of the productive unit	Only the man	Man or widow
Man	Necessary	Not necessary
Woman	Cannot stay at the colony	
without a man	Useless or dangerous?	Useful

Table 15.3. Discourses vs. Practices at Floridablanca
and Rio Negro

	Floridablanca	Rio Negro
Discourses	Family = house = land	Family = house = land
Practices	Discord:	Concordance:
	Reproductive unit $\neq^a$ Productive unit $\neq$ Domestic space	Reproductive unit = Productive unit $\neq$ Domestic space

^{a} is not equal to

marginal sectors of Spanish expansion in America, to global socioeconomic trends present in the late 18th century. Differentiation between the structuring of gender relations within the domestic unit and that of the productive unit may very well be showing important social tensions at a smaller scale (Table 15.3).

In other words, in spite of the imposition of one Enlightenment understanding of social order on new colonies, each Patagonian settlement shows different ways of organizing social relationships involving gender and production. Some questions arise from this difference with regard to the social project according to which both settlements were established.

Conclusion

The interpretative potential offered by relating global and local scales (Orser, 1996) forces us to consider here larger social, economic, ideological and political changes characteristic of the late 18th century. The Patagonian project arises from the ideas of Spanish Enlightenment men and, as such, evaluating their discourse is central to our research. In general terms, when we think of Enlightenment, we follow Chartier (1991: 18) in that:

> To think of the Enlightenment as a web of practices without discourse (or at least without those varieties of discourse traditionally and spontaneously defined as 'enlightened') is to give oneself a way to postulate distances and even contradictions between ideological declarations and the 'formality of practice'.

The idea of family as a key unit in the social order was emphasized in the Patagonian case. In Enlightenment discourse, the family is conceived of as both a productive and reproductive unit, involving the organization of social relationships and agricultural production. The built space in Floridablanca is interpreted here representing this discourse insofar as domestic space represents the family as a single unit. Domestic space also captures the equalitarian premises under which the families were sent to the settlement. Even so, I argue here that there is no automatic equivalence of the concepts of family, domestic space, productive unit, and reproductive unit in the Floridablanca society. Space represents predefined social order, but not the real one. This real order is invoked as a result of everyday practices which—in the case under study—show internal tensions.

The relationship between Enlightenment discourse and everyday practices in other Patagonian settlements shows further tensions within that order. In the Rio Negro case, family is equivalent to the idea of both productive and reproductive units and is represented materially in the domestic space. So closely structured productive and gender relationships differ from those described for the Floridablanca case.

Within the frame of these discords and as a way to start discussion on their meaning, we understand the Patagonian project as one example of cultural conditions of the Spanish 18th century. As such, Enlightenment projects may have "resided not in any harmony that supposedly united acts and the ideology governing them, but in the discordances that existed between the (moreover competing) discourses that in representing the social world proposed its reorganization and the (moreover discontinuous) practices that, as they were put into effect, created new differentiation and new divisions" (Chartier, 1991:18).

We believe that fragmentation and integration may be an interesting avenue towards the understanding of modern society. The fragmentation of this society implies—particularly in this case—accepting that there are innumerable ways of structuring modernity in different times and spaces. Understanding modernity, then, involves learning the diversity of dynamics within these processes in their different versions, starting from the multiplicity of practices but bearing in mind that the meanings of those social practices are different if in different contexts.

Acknowledgements

I thank the following Institutions, all of whom provided different kinds of support which sustained my historical and archaeological doctoral research: Universidad de Buenos Aires, Academia Nacional de Ciencias de Buenos Aires, Fundación Antorchas-British Council, Fundación Rotaria. I am very grateful to Pedro P. Funari, Amalia C. Sanguinetti de Bórmida, José Luis Lanata, Angel Sánz Tapia, Matthew Johnson, for advice and comments. I thank Marcia Bianchi Villelli, Silvana Buscaglia, Marìa Marschoff and Paula Palombo, for their enthusiastic help in laboratory works at PREP-CONICET, and archaeological field-works in Floridablanca. I would also like to thank the Municipalidad Puerto San

Julián and Pablo Walker for logistic support in field-works. Particular thanks are due to Lorena Connolly for her help in the translation of this paper and to Andrés Zarankin for his criticism, comments and constant encouragement during this research.

References

Amussen, S., 1988, *An Ordered Society: Gender and Class in Early Modern England.* Columbia University Press, New York.

Anes, G., 1969, *Economía e Ilustración en la España del siglo XVIII.* Ediciones Ariel, Barcelona.

1982, Obstáculos para el crecimiento de la agricultura. In *España a finales del siglo XVIII*, pp. 33–40. Ediciones de la Hemeroteca de Tarragona, Tarragona.

Apolant, J., 1970, *Operativo Patagonia.* Letras, Montevideo.

Argemí d'Abadal, L., 1988, Estudio Preliminar. *Agricultura e Ilustración. Antología del pensamiento agrario ilustrado.* Ministerio de Agricultura, Pesca y Alimentación, Secretaría General Técnica, Madrid.

Barrett, J., 1988, Fields of Discourse: Reconstituting a Social Archaeology *Critique of Anthropology* 7(3): 5–16.

Blades, B., 1986, English Villages in Londonderry Plantation. *Post-Medieval Archaeology* 20: 257–269.

Bourdieu, P., 1977, *Outline of a Theory of Practice.* Cambridge University Press, Cambridge.

Braun Menéndez, A., 1950, Prólogo. *Pedro Sarmiento de Gamboa. Viajes al Estrecho de Magallanes (1579–1584)*, pp. 7–48, Buenos Aires: Emecé Editores.

Buscaglia, S., 2001, Métodos geofísicos y propiedades del registro arqueológico. Arqueología no intrusiva en el establecimiento de Floridablanca (San Julián) Prov. de Santa Cruz,, Honors Thesis, Universidad de Buenos Aires.

Buscaglia, S., Lanata, J. L., Lascano, M., Osella, A. and Senatore, M. X., 2001, Geofísica y Arqueología en Floridablanca. *Arqueología* (Buenos Aires). *In press.*

Capel, M., 1970, *La Carolina, capital de las Nuevas Poblaciones. Un ensayo de reforma socio-económica en España en el siglo XVIII.* CSIC, Instituto de Estudios, Giennenses.

Chartier, R., 1991, *The Cultural Origins of the French Revolution.* Duke University Press Durham and London.

Delle, J., 1999a, *An Archaeology of Social Space,* Plenum Press, New York.

1999b, Extending Europe's Grasp: An Archaeological Comparison of Colonial Spatial Process in Ireland and Jamaica. In *Old and New Worlds*, edited by G. Egan and L. Michael, pp. 106–116. Oxbow Books, Oxford.

Driscoll, S., 1991, Discourse on the Frontiers of History: Material Culture and Social Reproduction in Early Scotland. *Historical Archaeology* 26: 12–25.

Elorza, A., 1970, *La ideología liberal en la ilustración española.* Editorial Tecnos, Madrid.

Foucault, M., 1972, *The Archaeology of Knowledge.* Tavistock, London.

1976, *Vigilar y Castigar: El nacimiento de la prisión.* Siglo XXI, México.

Foucault, M., Donzelot, J., Grignon, C., Gaudemar, J.; Muel, F. and Castel, R., 1981, *Espacios de Poder.* La Piqueta, Madrid.

Funari, P., 1995, A cultura material de Palmares: O estudo das relacoes sociais de um Quilombo Pela arqueología. *Idéias* 27:37–42.

Funari, P. P. A., Hall, M., and Jones, S., editors, 1999, *Historical Archaeology: Back from the Edge.* Routledge, London.

1999. Introduction: Archaeology in History. In *Historical Archaeology: Back from the Edge*, edited by P. P. A. Funari, M. Hall and S. Jones, pp. 1–20. Routledge, London.

Gaudemar, J. P., 1981, Para una genealogía de las formas de la disciplina. *Espacios de Poder.* La Piqueta, Madrid.

Giddens, A., 1984, *The Constitution of Society.* Polity Press, Cambridge.

Gilchrist, R., 1994, *Gender and Material Culture: The Archaeology of Religious Women.* Routledge, London.

1999, *Gender and Archaeology.* Routledge, London.

Gorla, C., 1984, *Los establecimientos españoles en la Patagonia: estudio institucional.* Escuela de Estudios Hispanoamericanos de Sevilla, Consejo Superior de Investigaciones Científicas, Sevilla.

Grahame, M., 1995, The Houses of Pompeii: Space and Social Interaction. Ph. D. dissertation, University of Southampton.

Hall, M., 1992, Small Things and the Mobile, Conflictual Fusion of Power, Fear and Desire. In *The Art and Mystery of Historical Archaeology: Essays in Honor of James Deetz,* edited by A. Yentsch and M. Beaudry, pp. 373–399. CRC Press, Boca Raton.

1999, Subaltern Voices? Finding the Spaces between Things and Words. In *Historical Archaeology: Back from the Edge,* edited by P. Funari, S. Jones and M. Hall, pp. 193–202. Routledge, London.

2000, *Archaeology and the Modern World: Colonial Transcripts in South Africa and the Chesapeake.* Routledge, London.

Herr, R., 1964, *España y la revolución del siglo XVIII.* Aguilar, Madrid.

Hodder, I., Shanks, M., Alexandri, A., Buchli, V., Carman, J., Lastand, J. and Lucas, G., editors, 1995, *Interpreting Archaeology; Finding Meaning in the Past.* Routledge London.

Johnson, M., 1996, *An Archaeology of Capitalism.* Blackwell, Oxford.

Leone, M., and P. Potter., editors, 1988, *The Recovery of Meaning: Historical Archaeology in the Eastern United Stated.* Smithsonian Institution Press, Washington D.C.

Little, B., 1992, *Text-Aided Archaeology.* CRC Press, Boca Raton.

1994, People with History: An Update on Historical Archaeology in United States. *Journal of Archaeological Method and Theory* 1(1): 5–40.

Lynch, J., 1989, *Bourbon Spain 1700–1808.* Basil Blackwell, Cambridge, MA.

Mestre Sachís, A., 1993, *La Ilustración.* Editorial Síntesis, Madrid.

Moore, H., 1986, *Space, Text and Gender.* Cambridge University Press, Cambridge.

Morris, I., 1997, Archaeology as Cultural History. *Archaeological Review of Cambridge* 14(1):3–16.

Mukerji, C., 1983, Patterns of Modern Materialism. *From Graven Images,* pp. 1–29. Columbia University Press, New York.

Munck, T., 2000, *The Enlightenment: A Comparative Social History 1721–1794.* Arnold Publishers, London.

Palacio Atard, V., 1964, *Los españoles de la Ilustración.* Ediciones Guadarrama, Madrid.

Porro Gutiérrez, J., 1995, *La emigración asturiana y castellano-leonesa para el poblamiento de la Patagonia en là época de Carlos III.* Editorial Sever Cuesta, Valladolid.

Ramos Pérez, D., 1984, El sistema de creación de establecimientos en la época de Carlos III y su carácter antitradicional: el caso de la costa patagónica. *Estructuras, gobierno y agentes de la administración en la América española (siglos XVI, XVII y XVIII),* pp. 503–529. Editorial Sever Cuesta, Valladolid.

Rodríguez Díaz, L., 1975, *Reforma e ilustración en la España del siglo XVIII: Pedro Rodríguez de Campomanes.* Fundación Universitaria Española, Madrid.

Samsom, R., editor, 1990, The Rise and Fall of Tower-Houses in Post-Reformation Scotland. In *The Social Archaeology of Houses,* pp. 197–243. Edinburgh University Press, Edinburgh.

Saravia Viejo, J., 1988. Introducción. In *Pedro Sarmiento de Gamboa: Viajes al Estrecho de Magallanes,* pp. 9–32. Alianza Editorial, Madrid.

Sarraillh, J., 1954, *L'Espagne éclarée de la seconde moitié du XVIII siecle.* Klincksieck, Paris.

Schrire, C., 1991, The Historical Archaeology of the Impact of Colonialism in Seventeenth-Century South Africa. In *Historical Archaeology in Global Perspective,* edited by L. Falk, pp. 69–96. Smithsonian Institution, Washington D.C.

Senatore, M. X., 2001, Arqueología en Floridablanca: Plano arqueológico y espacio social. *Anales de la Academia Nacional de la Ciencias de Buenos Aires* 34(2): 743–753.

Senatore, M., and Insiarte, M., 2000, Dietas planificadas y expectativas de salud en los asentamientos españoles en Patagonia, siglo XVIII. Paper Presented at the Inauguration of the Ph.D Program, Facultad de Humanidades, Universidad del Salvador, Buenos Aires.

Senatore, M., Bianchi Villelli, M., Buscaglia, S. and Marschoff, M., 2001, Hacia la definición del Plano arqueológico de Floridablanca. *Relaciones de la Sociedad Argentina de Antropología* (Buenos Aires). *In press.*

Sewell, W. H., 1999, The Concepts of Culture. In *Beyond the Cultural Turn: New Directions in the Study of Society and Culture,* edited by V. Bonnell and L. Hunt, pp. 35–61. University of California Press, Berkeley.

Shammas, C., 1990, *The Pre-Industrial consumer in England and America.* Clarendon Press, Oxford.

Sofaer Derevenski, J., 1997, Engendering children, engendering archaeology. In *Invisible People and Processes: Writing Gender and Childhood into European Archaeology,* edited by J. Moore and E. Scott, pp. 192–202. Leicester University Press, London.

Steadman, S., 1996, Recent Research in the Archaeology of Architecture: Beyond the Foundations. *Journal of Archaeological Research* 4(1): 51–93.

Viedma, A., 1980 (1783), *Diario de Antonio Viedma.* Municipalidad Puerto San Julián, Santa Cruz.

Zarankin, A., 1999, Casa Tomada, sistema, poder y vivienda doméstica. In *Sed Non Satiata: teoría social en la arqueología latinoamericana contemporánea,* edited by A. Zarankin and F. Acuto, pp. 239–272. Ediciones Del Tridente, Buenos Aires.

16

Stylistic Units in Prehistoric Art Research

Archeofacts or Realities?

André Prous

Introduction

When modern Western thinking divided knowledge into several strictly separated areas by the 18th century, the idea then appeared that 'art' constituted its own category that Kant characterized as 'its own finality'. Actually, the concept of art does not exist in most cultures. Even in Latin, *ars, artis* means technological skill (of the craftsman—*artisan, artesão, artesano* in neo-Latin languages) as well the capacity to create a lovely thing (proper of our *artist*).

And while Plato wrote about Beauty, he did not create an aesthetic. The very word 'art', thus, when applied to a different cultural context, is an ethnocentric and problematic one. Can we truly study prehistoric productions like 'Rock Art' according to our own mental categories without speaking exclusively about ourselves?

There are two main groups among the many Western scholars that have studied artistic phenomena from the beginning of the 20th Century. In the first, we find mostly artists and aestheticians that study non-Western objects from an aesthetic point of view, as if there were *universal* categories; in the second, we find some archaeologists and ethnologists mainly from the second half the 19th Century who have tried to discover *ethnic* realities. But even the concept of ethnicity was created as a political instrument in Western culture, during the 19th Century.

Archaeologists that have studied prehistoric art have worked in three main directions:

1. Archaeometric studies that try to date objects, identify techniques of elaboration, and raw materials, etc.
2. Attempts to explore the significance of artifacts or iconography to their producers.
3. Studies that delve into *implicit information* (ethnic, sociological, aesthetic, economic, perceptions of reality) about the producers captured in their so-called 'artistic' production. Prehistoric people were, putatively, not always conscious of this type of information.

In this paper, only this last orientation will figure and the attempt to identify ethnic, social or gender groups. Concepts like 'style', 'tradition' (and, in Brazil, 'variety' or *'facies'*) are generally used to characterize the production of these alleged populations.

In this way it is important to know if these categories express objective realities, or if they are only a statement of our ethnocentrism. Are Rock Art descriptive units *archaeofacts*, or *realities*?

To discuss this point further, the objectives of each different archaeologist when they proposed stylistic units is pivotal. One must also test the validity of these categories within Western historical art. The utility and limitations of ethnographic examples to archaeologists will be demonstrated through concrete examples.

Research on Prehistoric Art: A Short History

The First Steps

Since the 16th Century, 'tourist' guides have mentioned the painting of Niaux cave in France. Obviously, these did not consider the prehistoric age (as this concept did not exist yet), but people imagined the paintings had been made by peasants that did not know how to paint (according to the naturalistic manner of Renaissance period, of course). The paintings were, thus, objects of curiosity but not of investigation or of aesthetic pleasure.

The first scientific interest arose in Europe during the late 19th Century, when engraved bones were found at Paleolithic levels. People was amazed by the fact that prehistoric Man should have time enough to waste on artistic productions; early Man, and even the so called 'primitive' living populations, were seen as poor people that had to cope with a world too difficult to allow high intellectual activities. In any case, the first scholars did not think that prehistoric art needed to be studied: they interpreted it as a purely aesthetic statement, in conformity with the Neoclassical or Parnassian ideas about art.

The Comparativist and Evolutionist Periods:
Magic and Hunting

285
STYLISTIC UNITS
IN PREHISTORIC
ART RESEARCH

In the beginning of the 20th Century, concurrent with a worldwide expansion of ethnological research, prehistorians remained evolutionists and thought that the behavior of modern 'primitives' should explain how past societies belonged to the same 'evolutionary stage'. The time of analogy had arrived. Some aboriginal populations were said to paint animals before they hunted them to catch their souls—and later, their body—in a 'sympathetic', magical way. Scholars like H. Breuil pointed to the frequency of animals in the recently-discovered rock art of Franco-Cantabrian Caves as evidence that they depicted hunting scenes. Linear geometric figures were considered representations of weapons while circular ones were seen as representations of wounds. Every animal with a round belly represented a pregnant female, portrayed to ensure propagation of game. These explanations were applied to the whole of European Paleolithic art.

Differences in the way animals were painted were seen as the result of the development primitive artists toward the laws of perspective from the Aurignacian to Magdalenian periods.

Rich rock art was soon discovered in non-European regions like Tassili, where H. Lhote identified successive chronological periods, each one characterized by different themes: hunter-gatherers depicting wild animals (Bubalin period); pastoralists illustrating livestock (Bovine period); and horse herders of the bronze period representing chariots. From such few regional sequences, evolutionists developed the idea (implicit or explicit) that each type of rock art should show the evolutionary stage of its authors.

This idea remains alive and well in Anati's work (1993: 47) that lists the characteristic themes of each evolutionary stage 1) archaic hunter (wild animals, masked human figures, psychograms; few actual scenes), 2) evolved hunters (anecdotal scenes, imaginary beings), 3) pastoral breeders (domestic animals, idealization of forms), and 4) complex societies (implements and weapons, mythological scenes, schematic and abstract graphics.

The Reaction against Ethnographic Comparativism:
The Structuralist Approach

A new era began in the 1960s, evident from independent studies carried out by of A. Laming-Emperaire and A. Leroi-Gourhan (embodying the perspective predicted by M. Raphael in the 1940s; Chesney, 1991). Neither accepted naive ethnographic analogy; they did not consider indigenous populations fossilized 'primitive' peoples capable of offering keys to interpret paintings made thousands of years ago and thousands of kilometers away. They asserted that scholars like Breuil always used the same figures in their publications to prove their ideas and that, in fact, most painted Paleolithic animals were not wounded or pregnant. As it was not possible to use living people in order to explain prehistoric art anymore, it was necessary to find information in the pre-historic *corpus* that could not be inspired by any ethnic discourse; nei-ther European, nor Indigenous. The new goal was to understand what themes were chosen by prehistoric people, which were excluded, and the way they reflect a structured, coherent body of organized symbols. Specific relationships between horse and bovine representations (Leroi-Gourhan later added deer/goats), or between linear/round shaped ge-ometric forms were recognized. Researchers sought relationships be-tween certain types of symbols and topographic features (i.e., horses and bovines in central places; dots at the entry of corridors, or 'danger-ous' animals at the end of corridors). These recurrent associations, gen-erally of a binary nature, were seen as structurally opposed, influenced by Boole's algebra and structuralist thinking. It is important to question whether this is really a universal or rather a historically determined vi-sion of the world.

Though Leroi-Gourhan (like Breuil before him) recognized the exis-tence of chronological modifications during the millennia (he proposed the existence of 4 successive styles), his approach let him to privilege statistics, using the whole corpus of Paleolithic figures, as if they were the product of only one mode of thinking. This served to underestimate abundant variability throughout millennia and many different loci.

After showing some underlying binary pairs in European Paleolithic rock art, Laming-Emperaire and Leroi-Gourhan tried to interpret their meaning (i.e., the bovine/equine pair was seen as reflecting a male/female duality). As such, the authors were no longer searching for 'objective' structures, but making subjective interpretations. All subse-quent semiotic work on rock art (like those of Sauvet and Wlodenczyck, 1977) continued in this structuralist way.

The Diversification of Approaches During the Late 20ᵗʰ Century

During the 1970s and 1980s, hundreds of new sites were discovered in all continents. It was no longer possible to study them in the same way and many new approaches arose. One of these is ethnographic interpre-tation which assumes modern indigenous traditions might offer some in-formation about the earlier meanings of regional rock art. This has been attempted on a regional level in Western Canada or northern Australia. But other interpretations are being proposed as tentative 'keys' for other places. Some authors, for example, have used the idea of J. Lewis-William and T. Dowson that many paintings or engravings should depict visions of shamans who had ingested hallucinogenic mushrooms or other psychoactive substances. Most geometric figures, found every-where, are thus considered phosphenes and thus universal. Much like Lewis William's proposal that South African animal representations were made to improve good results during hunting parties, the presence of geometric figures as phosphenes reinforced Breuil's old theories. This latter idea, however, reflects more our modern obsession with drugs. As a result, representations of hallucinogenic plants were sought throughout the world. San Pedro cactus was identified on Chavin sculptures in Peru; an old Salish woman explained North American engravings as visions and dreams of starving youths during initiation phases (York et al., 1993).

In any case, it appears that the Shamanistic theory could not explain all forms of rock art (Clottes and Lewis-William, 1996). The 'information' theory of the 1990s that tried to show (again principally from European rock art examples) that prehistoric figures were didactic representations used to improve hunting success (i.e., determining the type of tracks, for example) also proved not to be an all-embracing theory. From this approach, however, we know that some European Paleolithic paintings were far more naturalistic than had been thought before; i.e., seasonal differences and behavior can be shown by antlers, fur and gestures, (Bouvier and Dubourg, 1997). Medical problems and specific pathologies are evident in anthropomorphic figures (Duhard, 1993).

In the early 1970s, Marschack's and Ouy's work on European art and studies of Southern Brazilian cultures by Prous (Marshack, 1972; Ouy and Ouy-Parczszewska, 1972; Prous, 1977) tried to demonstrate the existence of mathematical or rhythmic records.

During the same period, archaeoastronomy became fashionable along with searching for celestial phenomena (i.e., comets, supernova explosions). Very recently observations have appeared on the acoustic properties of some sites (Dauvois, 1992). There is also ethnographic evidence that historic Californian tribes used places with special sound propagation for ritual purposes (K. Hedges, 1993).

Since then, a gendered perspective has been introduced too, such as in the study of the Paleolithic 'Venus' body (McCoid and McDermott, 1996). Systematic experiments to replicate and analyze the prehistoric preparations of pigments began with Couraud (Couraud and Laming-Emperaire, 1979) and have seen huge advancement in the last years, aided by growing cooperation between chemists and archaeologists. Chemists have found how to extract minute quantities of organic material to be dated by AMS (Russ et al., 1990) thus the direct dating of some rock paintings and engraving is now possible. At the same time, the gesture and chronology of engravings on walls and bones was studied through the micro-analysis of the grooves (d'Errico, 1989).

But the ostensible 'ethnicity research' has turned into an even more important approach. Frequent superimpositions were shown to be painted by successive populations, each in its different way, while scholars work to establish the chronology of styles or traditions, like Lhote has done in Sahara, Chaloupka in Australia, and Prous in central Brazil. In Australia, the identification of ancient tribal territories identification from the study of their mythological representations turned into a priority because aboriginal peoples were claiming their right to control the sites that symbolized their cultural identity. Notwithstanding, some ethnoarchaeological studies refute the presumed one-to one correspondence between styles and ethnic units (Franklin, 1989).

In Europe, regional styles are being valorized and the new dates allow the scholars to analyze modifications to technique and theme during the Late Paleolithic. Some speak of a 'post-stylistic era' (Lorblanchet) to clarify that the unilinear view of European rock art that characterized the Breuil and Leroi-Gourhan periods is finished. But this does not mean that the style concept will no longer be used, as it remains useful when applied in a more restricted context.

The Principal Approaches to Rock Art in Brazil

Both artists and naturalists have discussed the meaning of Brazilian rock art from the early 19th Century such as J. B. Debret (1972), who in 1839 reproduced the drawings of Spix and Martius, modifying the graphics in order to demonstrate their interpretation, but thereby partially falsifying their representation; or T. Sampaio (1918), who interpreted the paintings as descriptions of travels, battles or funerary inscriptions.

In the late 1960s, D. Aytai published a remarkable structuralist paper about Itapeva rock art (São Paulo state), where he tried to find an organization within the pictographs in a way that mirrored Leroi-Gourhan's work—although he did not know this author's publications on rock art. Aytai (1969) also suggested an interpretation using Gê mythology. This ethnographic analogy was renewed recently, when M. Beltrão (1994) explained some painting from the Bahia State, using the mythology of Tukano, a Western Amazonian tribe that live thousands of kilometers from the sites (moreover, the painting are claimed to be very ancient, some are even argued to date to the Pleistocene age). Even where there are modern indigenous traditions about rock art existing in their present territory (as occurs with the Krenak Indians, in Minas Gerais), it is quite clear that their interpretation is recent and that it helps them built a new ethnic identity and is not a fossilized 'original' interpretation (Baeta, 1998). For this reason, most Brazilian scholars, even if they sometime mention interesting local ethnographic similarities (Victor, 1997), generally avoid this approach.

In the 1970s, scholars preferred a stylistic treatment that could indicate social and cultural units (i.e., territories, ethnic groups). At that time, it was clear to V. Calderon (Bahia State), N. Guidon (Piaui state) and A. Prous (Minas Gerais state) that rock art differed from one region to another. In the last state, drastic chronological modifications were also evident in a number of places (Lagoa Santa region, Peruaçu valley, Montalvânia . . .), and regional chrono-stylistic sequences were attempted. *Many buried paintings or engraving were found and stratigraphic levels on the decorated walls were studied.* Buried pigments and their characterization became a new field of study used in combination with rock art (Prous, 1991). Chemical analysis also began in Piaui (Lajcs, 1990) and Minas Gerais (Costa et al., 1989).

In the 1980s, it seemed possible to know actually *who* had made *what*. Homogenous thematic complexes were credited to authors using a same code and were differentiated from other complexes presumably made by other tribes. *Traditions* were defined to express cultural continuity; for example, one characterized by the dominance of specific geometrical drawings; another by human beings organized into ritual scenes, a third by the association of certain kinds of animals.

Technical attributes (i.e., the method of drawing, the morphology of the figures) or minor variations in recurrent themes have been used to define stylistic sub-units (i.e., varieties, styles, *facies* typical of a small region or periods within one tradition.

The result should be seen, in a way, like a culture/historical approach (Wüst, 1991). This type of classification, that began with Prous and Guidon, became very popular, in the sense that almost 200 traditions, and styles, etc. were created in one decade. Consens and Seda (1989), though, have discussed how poorly characterized many of these stylistic units are. They highlight one case where the definition of one style was: "engravings on boulders near/on waterflows", without further information (Consens and Seda, 1989). In several papers, Prous and his collaborators also discussed what the meaning of differences and similarities identified in these stylistic units should be, for it was clear to them that they were not only ethnic markers (Prous, 1997; Solá, et al. 1981).

The Definition of Stylistic Units: What are 'Good' Criteria?

It is time to reflect on the classifications that archaeologists make and the significance of the attributes we choose to make them with.

Similarity and Difference

When creating classifications of bones, ceramics, stones or petroglyphs, archaeologists compare the artifacts, seeking similarities and differences. The first question that arises is: are we looking at what prehistoric man would have seen? Or rather, would that which is significant to us also be significant to prehistoric people? Second, if our classifications would have made no sense for prehistoric 'artists', are they worthwhile? Do they really increase our knowledge of the past?

In reference to the first question, I will recount a story about the anthropologist W. Chiara and what happened to her while she lived with a Brazilian tribe. An indigenous man showed two girls to the anthropologist, saying they looked very much alike. Looking at their faces, the Anthropologist saw no similarity and said so. The Indian answered 'look at the shape of the breast'. Obviously, we are used to seeing the similarities between people in their unclothed parts: their hands and face. Indigenous people, of course, see other parts because they do not hide their bodies. In a traditional Iranian village, it is probable that people compare the way the girls walked.

This case demonstrates that to perceive that which was significant for prehistoric cultures, one must be ready to look at a great number of attributes, with the hope that some of them are truly important (something like the *emblematic* category in Wiessner's sense) and that our study shall be able to demonstrate it. We must not use only one or a few dimensions, like iconography, to characterize a stylistic unit.

What Attributes Could Be Important?

In order to make comparisons among graphic complexes (i.e., within regions, between sites in one region, between panels at one site, or chronological levels within one panel), we must look not only at the drawings themselves, but also at the natural and cultural context in which they appear.

Prehistoric people could have chosen a site for many reasons: for its visibility in the landscape, its topographic location, its proximity to a water supply, its orientation and exposure to the sun. Moreover, one can judge this point only with caution. In 1976, 20 rock art sites were found during a survey in Montalvânia (Brazil), all with the same orientation. The next year, 30 more were discovered along other cardinal orientations and it therefore appeared that their orientation was not important.

Inside a site, the selection of the wall to be worked is not neutral. In Lapa Vermelha dolina, near Lagoa Santa, the many wide, flat, smooth and well illuminated walls that Western people might have used were not decorated (Baeta et al., 1992). Prehistoric artists preferred less regular surfaces. In Peruaçu valley, each tradition had its own preferences: S. Francisco people chose the higher part of large and flat surfaces while at the same sites, Piolho do Urubu people painted the lower part of the same panels. Desenhos artists also used lower places, but mostly fallen blocks while Nordeste people used discrete and generally marginal places. In fact, it is equally important to know why a site or a panel has been used and why another one has not been used.

In the same way, when we study iconography, it is not sufficient to point out the primary and secondary themes. It is also worthwhile to identify what has not been depicted. In central Brazil, the animals most coveted by recent indigenous hunters are deer, peccari (wild American pigs) and tapirs. But in the rock art of Minas Gerais state, deer are the most popular animals painted in the Planalto tradition, while peccaris and tapirs are almost completely absent; the same occurs in the domestic refuse in archaeological layers. In other words, we find many bones of deer, but few or none of peccari: why, thus, are some worthy of representation and consumption and others not?

Obviously, a dominant iconographic theme cannot create a tradition alone. In such a system the Planalto tradition would thus exist over several continents, where numerous deer are also depicted.

In fact, the way that figures are made is full of information, even if they might be of a more assertive nature than emblematic. In Brazil, for instance, anthropomorphic figures of the Planalto Tradition are generally very small (i.e., smaller than the associated animals) and schematic in their representation, but in the Agreste tradition they are large and more naturalistic.

The very disposition of figures may also be typical of a stylistic unit. Spear throwers, for example, always appear in the hands of a hunting human being in the *Nordeste* tradition. In the *São Francisco* tradition, however, the same implements are depicted far away from anthropomorphic figures, either isolated (*Januaria* style) or in alignment (*Montalvania complex*).

Some aspects of the aesthetic sense of prehistoric people can also be approximated. In central Brazil, *São Francisco* people liked splendid drawings and bright colors that can be seen from a distance. *Nordeste* people liked to express movement in their little figures that must be examined closely. A clear spatial logic and iconographic organization is characteristic of the *Montalvânia* phase, while *Planalto* paintings are distributed on walls in a confused, more random fashion.

We can even go further than the main stylistic units (i.e., tradition, style, *facie*, variety) that are used to characterize wide social groups. It is not unrealistic to attempt to identify individuality through the observation of idiosyncratic patterns. Brazilian archaeology may not at present view this as a worthy enough endeavor to justify high investment, but the discrete styles of specific artists have been recognized in the deer representations of Serra do Cipó (Prous and Baeta, 1992/3).

The Significance of Archaeological Categories

What Reality, if Any, Do Our Classifications Reflect?

We saw that the stylistic units that have been proposed in Brazil have, consciously or not, reflected an attempt to identify prehistoric people through what A. Leroi-Gourhan named an 'ethnic style'. Is it possible to do this? During the last years, it has become clear that archaeology cannot help us find 'cultures' or ethnic groups in the modern sense, but only the remains of some behaviors.

Let us consider some historical examples. If we look at European and Vietnamese Catholic churches, we hope that iconography will be the same (i.e., a Cross, the Virgin Mary, and some Saints) because they belong to the same tradition (in the way we use this term in Brazil); but some stylistic patterns might be different, introducing oriental conventions (or at least a Southeastern Asiatic inspiration). We used to associate eastern cultures not with Catholic religion (or iconography), but with the way they depict reality. But although Vietnam Catholics have the same rituals and ideas of God as their European brothers, there are many different of representing them. In the same manner, we cannot be sure that *Nordeste* rock art tradition was produced by one tribe, nor one linguistic, racial or one technological group; nor can we suppose they had the same lithic technology. Even so, the stylistic units created by the archaeologist do have analytical importance: it expresses a kind of sensitivity, of knowledge and of thinking that is the same for every *Nordeste* artistic person.

At the same time, we cannot be sure that every type of social unit has only one stylistic form of expression. For example, there is, among Brazilian tribes, a significant difference between women's art and men's, even in the drawings made with a pencil on paper. The former produce angular geometric figures that use one element to represent a whole reality. Men generally draw curvilinear figures that fit better into our concept of 'realism'. Scholars explain this difference as the product of coiling and basketry activities, that allow only geometric figures, which are strictly women's domain and thus would have influenced their perception of reality (Prous, 1977).

Such gender differentiation also exists in our culture: in France, baby girls traditionally use pink and baby boys, mostly blue clothes. Classic Ballet has been considered a feminine—or rather, not male—activity since the 19th Century. In our society, there are also many styles that co-exist. Classic music is listened to by old people and rock, by youngsters in the 1960s. Rock and classic belong to the same modern Western tradition (heptatonic temperate tonal music from the 18th Century) but they are different styles, one of them showing non-European influences. Could some Brazilian rock art styles be expressing the same thing?

To be sure, as the styles we create are actually chronological, we have to be sure that their figures are separated by a long period of time. In Lapa Vermelha dolina (Baeta et al.,1992), we tried to see if different styles could have coexisted in time. I shall once again use an historic analogy. The iconography of Christian churches is not homogenous, even in the Western World: both Catholics and Orthodox believers pray to the Virgin, but the Greek Church prays to Saints (such as St John Chrysostome) that don't appear in Western Europe (St. Francisco or St. Anton are more typical Latin Saints). We can thus say that there are geographical *facies* to Christian Mediterranean art. Other differences are less geographic, like those between catholic and protestants churches: one does not see the Virgin or Saints in the latter, though both churches can be found in the same territory. There are also more subtle differences, like those between churches of the same period, same region and belong to the same faith: i.e., the brightly decorated Clunisian monuments *versus* the ascetic and plain Cistercian ones. Both constitute varieties within the same medieval Christian community.

Diversity can also be functional. In Ouro Preto, a baroque Brazilian town, two churches, both consecrated to St. Mary, exhibit the images of distinct Saints because one (Sta. Maria do Rosário) was the temple of the African congregation and the other, belonged to the local aristocrat's godmother (Sta. Maria do Carmo). The same thing may have occurred in prehistoric times and it is quite possible that *moieties*, clans, genders, and age classes have left distinctive marks on these shelters. Obviously, there is also the progressive modifications of fashion throughout the millennia (i.e., a roman sculpture is different from a gothic one, even though they are both found in the same church). The products of all these kinds of variation can be used by archaeologists to create stylistic sub-units (styles, varieties) within a tradition.

It is also sometimes possible to study the relationship between different traditions (Prous and Seda, 1987). In Peruaçu valley, we found evidence of *respect* when figures of *Caboclo* style are painted on the periphery of elder *Januaria* pictograms. We see *neutrality* among Januaria paintings, that do not avoid superimposition. But the authors of *Desenhos* petroglyphs express a negative appreciation of older traditions by hiding them under a red layer of dye before they re-pecked zoomorphic figures. In Lagoa Santa and Serra do Cipo regions, the 'artists' of a new tradition sometimes 'peeled' the rock to destroy previous works.

Events such as the *recovering* or *renewal* of ancient paintings are also frequent. The first occurs when an ancient painting is put in a new context. Example of recovering is an ancient isolated zoomorphic fig-ure that receives a new interpretation when surrounded by anthropo-morphic ones, as if it were hunted; or, in Peruaçu valley, a geometric figure that has been transformed into a vegetal. Renewal occurs when some part of a figure is reinforced, like many old and patinated images that received a new layer of dye (frequently of another color) in Lagoa Santa; or the eyes of animals that were painted over and over again in the Australian desert.

These attitudes are the same we know from art history in Europe: there is a social continuity between 'classic' masterpieces that glorify the elites and that are preserved by their successors. But when there is an ideological gap, as when Protestants broke statues of Saints, French revolutionaries broke images of the King, and Catholics and Jews de-stroyed idols. But we also see missionaries recovering pagan sacred places through cross engravings.

The Many Possible Classifications for One Social Group

A question we have heard many times is 'how can we justify the creation of rock art traditions, the work of people that have also been classified according to their stone or ceramic production?' Would it not be prob-lematic, however, to have two labels for the same people that made *Serranopolis* phase lithic instruments and that may have painted *São Francisco* pictograms? First, it is very hard to make chronological cor-relations between art and technology. Classifications are needed for all these kinds of reality. Last, but not least, we use parallel classifications for our own historic framework; the same people or 'culture' are said to be Catholic (a religious concept) and mercantilist (an economic one). We also know that not every Catholic is a mercantilist, nor that every mercantilist is a Catholic. Today, the same person belongs to a number of different groups: family, social class, religious congregation, political party, etc., and can be considered within the different categories that are used to study each group. It would be tragic if archaeology were more totalitarian than others fields of knowledge and wanted to lock up a mul-tifaceted reality within only one strictly controlled and labeled drawer.

Conclusion

Consens and Seda (1990) have written about the hundreds of stylistic units created by archaeologists, commenting that if Brazilian scholars have seen differences, these should be considered real. These archaeological categories probably express some kind of reality, *if they are well defined*. To give a name to the phenomena, we can see it is correct and useful to discover cultural or social identities, but this is not sufficient.

The problem is how to interpret these units. We have seen that the differences in the rock art corpus are significant to several kinds of reality. Some of them may be similar to ethnic groups labeled in the modern period. In fact, people that lived in 14th Century in the southwestern part of France were not 'ethnically' nor politically 'French', nor 'English', nor even, maybe, 'Gascon' in the modern sense of these concepts. They knew they were subjects of the king of France and may be subjects of the king of England tomorrow, but that they really depended on the Earl of Pau. They shared a universal religion, were members of a little peasant community, and spoke a regional dialect. On the same way, most people that lived in Gallia in the 5th Century AD did not know they were on the doorstep of the Medieval period (Prous, 1967). These realties do not invalidate our concepts which remain useful *from our point of view*. What matters is we know that similarities and differences may expresses realities that are not those of our own society.

Even if we diversify our observations, we can never be sure we will be able to perceive what was essential for prehistoric peoples. But our typologies are valid if they are useful to the approach we have chosen. We are no longer searching for the old *adaequatio rei et intellectu*, but for an *adequatio instrumentis et quaestionis*. Our work is not an illusion, as it helps us to contrast our values with those of others cultures. We know that our point of view is not the only possible, but it can produce significant observations about the phenomena of which prehistoric men were not aware. Surely, our view of rock art manifestations is more sensitive to their 'artistic' aspect than prehistoric peoples' were. This is because we express our linkage with a consumerist society in which art is a *per se* product. In its 'art', Karajá Indians should express their gender complementarity; other tribes should project their clanic o class values.

The archaeologist must therefore avoid three dangers. The first is creating a great number of small, irrelevant stylistic units (a real danger at this moment in Brazilian archaeology). The second is to trust that these units are objectives realities. They should be used as simple instruments, as long they are worthy, but cast out when they are no longer useful. A fossilization of the classification system would break the energy of the research. The third danger, maybe the worst in this post-modern era, should be to prevent investigation because of the impossibility to fully understand the cultures of the past. This attitude will conduce to a sterile skepticism of the archaeological discourse, or to the idea that we are free to make a subjective discourse without serious implications for a real—though partial—understanding of the past.

As we intend to participate in the expansion of some kind of knowledge, we are not afraid if we have to use stylistic units that are *archaeofacts* (i.e., created by the archaeologist rather than the prehistoric subject) for research purposes that express the kind of interest we have about the past. The descriptive units may change, but the reality that they express is not an illusion. In this way, we reconcile the consciousness we have of our subjectivity with our scholarly exigency. We are not engaging an empty discourse upon ourselves only to excuse the pretext of an invented Other.

References

Anati, E., 1993, *World Rock Art, the Primordial Language*. Centro Camuno di Studi Preistorici.

Araújo, Victor P., 1997, Vestígios na arte rupestre de ancestralidade autóctone. *SIARB Documentos* (Cochabamba): 74–75.

Aytai, D., 1970, As gravações rupestres de Itapeva. *Revista da Univ. Católica de Campinas* 14(33): 69–61.

Baeta, A., 1998, *A Memória Indígena no Médio Vale do Rio Doce—Arte Rupestre e Identidade Krenak*. Master's thesis, Belo Horizonte.

Baeta, A., Silva, M., and Prous, A., 1992, Organização do espaço pictural nos sítios rupestres da região de Lagoa Santa-MG. In 3° Congresso Associação Brasileira de Estudos Quaternários, Belo Horizonte, *Anais*: 417–430.

Bahn, P., 1991, Where is the beef? The myth of hunting magic in Paleolithic Art. In P. Bahn and A. Rosenfeld edited by, *Rock Art and Prehistory*, pp. 1–13. Oxbow Monographs, Oxford.

Bahn, P., and Fossatti, A., 1996, *Rock Art Studies, News of the World*. Oxbow Monograph, Oxford.

Beltrão, M. da C., 1994, *Arte Rupestre: As pinturas da Chapada Diamantina e o mundo mágico-religiosos do homem pré-histórico brasileiro*. Catalogue of Exposition, Rio de Janeiro.

Bouvier, J-M., and Dubourg, C., 1997, Karst et saisonnalités paléolithiques. In *Karst et Archéologie*, Colloque du CNRS et de l'AFEQ. *Quaternaire*, 8 (2–3): 233–244.

Breuil, H., 1952, *Quatre-cents siècles d'art pariétal*. Montignac.

Chesney, S., 1991, Max Raphael's contributions to the Study of Prehistoric Symbol System. In *Rock Art and Prehistory*, edited by P. Bahn and A. Rosenfeld, pp. 14–22. Oxbow Monographs, Oxford.

Clottes, J., 1990, La préparation des peintures magdaléniennes des cavernes ariégeoises. *Bulletin de la Société Préhistorique Française* 87: 170–192.

Consens, M., and Seda, P., 1990, Facies, estilos e tradições na arte rupestre do Brasil: a incomunicabilidade científica. *Revista do CEPA* (Sta. Cruz do Sul) 17(20): 33–58.

Costa, G. M.; Jesus Filho, M. F.; Moura, M. T, and Prous, A., 1989, Pigmentos minerais e corantes pré-históricos, *Dédalo* 1: 362–373.

Couraud, C. and Laming-Emperaire, A., 1979, Les colorants. In *Lascaux inconnu*, edited by A. Laming-Emperaire, pp. 153–171. CNRS, Paris.

Dauvois, M., 1992, Les témoins sonores paléolithiques extérieurs et souterrains. In *Sons originels—préhistoire de la Musique. Etudes et recherches archéologiques* (Univ. Liége) 61: 11–35.

Debret, J-B., 1972 [1839], *Viagem Pitoresca e Histórica ao Brasil*. Martins/USP, São Paulo.

Duhard, J-P., 1993, Réalisme de l'image féminine paléolithique. *Cahiers du Quaternaire* 19. CNRS, Paris.

D'Errico, F., 1989, Mémoires et Rythmes au Paléolithique: le mythe des calendriers lunaires. 2° Congresso Internacional de Paleontologia, Torino. *Hominidae*: 507–510.

Franklin, N., 1989, Research with Style: a Case Study from Australian Rock Art. In *Archaeological Approaches to Cultural Identity*, edited by S. Shennan, pp. 278–289. Routledge, London.

Hedges, K., 1993, Places to See and Places to Hear: Rock Art and Features of the Sacred Landscape. In *Time and Space*, edited by J. Steinbring, A. Watchman, P. Faulstich, and P. Taçon. Occasional papers of AURA (Melbourne) 8: 121–127.

Hobsbawn, E, and Ranger, T., 1984, *A invenção das Tradições*. Paz e Terra, Rio de Janeiro.

Kant, I., 1788, *Critique de la Raison Pratique*. PUF, Paris.

Laje, M., and Menezes, C., 1990, *Etude archéométrique de l'Art rupestre du sud-ouest du Piaué, Brasil*. Ph. D. dissertation, Paris.

Laming-Emperaire, A., 1962, *La signification de l'art rupestre paléolithique*. Picard, Paris.

Leroi-Gourhan, A., 1965, *Préhistoire de l'art occidental*. Mazenod, Paris.

1973, *L'Homme, Hier et Aujourd'hui: recueil d'études en hommage à A. Leroi-Gourhan*. Cujas, Paris.

Marshack, A., 1972, *The Roots of Civilization*. McGraw-Hill, New York.

McCoid, C., and McDermott, Le Roy D., 1996, Towards Decolonizing Gender: Female Vision in the Upper Paleolithic. *American Anthropologist* 98(2): 319–326.

Ouy, G., and Ouy-Parczsewska, K., 1972, Les origines des règles de l'art. *Annales Economie Sociétés, Civilisations* 6: 1264–1316.

Prous, A., 1967, *Sidonius Apollinaris, un évêque des Gaules au VI° siècle*. Master's thesis, Université de Poitiers.

1977, Les sculptures zoomorphes du sud brésilien et de l'Uruguay. *Cahiers d'Archéologie d'Amérique du Sud 5*.

1985, Direções de pesquisa na análise da arte rupestre em Minas Gerais. *Arquivos do Museu de História Natural* (Belo Horizonte) 10: 196–224.

1994, "L'art rupestre du Brésil", Bulletin de la Société Préhistorique de l'Ariége, Foix, 49: 77–144.

1996, Recent Studies on Rock Art in Brazil. In *Rock Art Studies: News of the World*, edited by P. Bahn and A. Fossati, pp. 215–220. Oxbow Books, Oxford.

1997, Rock Art Traditions: Archaeofacts or Realities? Paper presented at Congreso Internacional de Arte Rupestre, Cochabamba.

Prous, A., and Batea, A., 1992/3, Elementos de cronologia, descrição de atributos e tipologia. In *Arquivos do Museu de História Natural UFMG* 13/14: 241–332.

Prous, A., Lanna. A. L., and Paula, F., 1980, Estilística e cronologia na arte rupestre de Minas Gerais. *Pesquisas* (série Antropologia, São Leopoldo) 31: 121–146.

Prous, A., and Seda, P., 1987, Cronologia, tradições e metodologias na arte rupestre do Sudeste. *Boletim do Insituto Arqueologico do Brasil série Catálogos* 3: 177–181.

Russ, J., Hyman, M., Schaffer, H., and Rowe, M., 1990, Radiocarbon Dating of Prehistoric Rock Paintings by Selection Oxidation of Organic Carbon. *Nature* 348: 710–711.

Sampaio, T., 1918. Inscrições lapidares indígenas no vale do Paraguassú. *5° Congresso Brasileiro de Geografia*, pp. 6–32. Salvador, Bahia.

Sauvet, G and S., and Wlodarczyk, A., 1977, Essai de sémiologie préhistorique. *Bulletin de la Société de la Préhistoire Française* 74: 545–558.

Shennan, S., editor, 1989, *Archaeological Approaches to Cultural Identity*. Routledgc, London.

Wüst. I., 1991, A arte rupestre: seus mitos e seu potencial interpretativo, *Ciências Humanas em Revista* (UFGO, Goiânia) 2(1–2): 47–74.

York, A., Daly, R. and Arnett, C., 1993, *They Write their Dreams on the Rock Forever—Rock Writings in the Stein Valley of British Columbia*. Talonbooks, Vancouver.

Water and Olive Oil

17

An Analysis of Rural Scenes in Black and Red Figure Attic Vases and the Construction of the Athenian Empire

André Leonardo Chevitarese

This chapter proposes to establish a discussion on the following hypothesis. The images on the Attic pottery show a drastic reduction of the rural scenes by the end of the sixth and beginning of the fifth centuries. This decrease was the direct result of a flagrant shift made by the Athenians towards urban space (*asty*) to the detriment of rural space (*khora*) after the victory in the Greek-Persian war.

This should not be understood, however, as a policy of abandonment undertaken by the Athenians in relation to landed properties, agriculture and pastoral rights in the fifth century B.C. On the contrary, not only did landed properties remain in force, but also several rural activities continued throughout the Attic period (for a detailed historiographic and documentary discussion of the Athenian shift, see Chevitarese, 2001a: 181–195)

The last three decades of the 20th century witnessed the development of uncountable archaeological studies related to ancient Greek rural space. We can even speak of a "true discovery" of the Greek *khora* when comparing the great volume of publications in the last thirty years with the historiographic production previous to 1970. One can see, however, that the results obtained by these studies remain unrecognized by the larger public and by a significant number of researchers of Ancient Greek history. Five points can be highlighted that help us understand the reason for this lack of connection between recent work on Ancient

Greek rural space and the majority of individuals interested in the history and archaeology of the Ancient World:

First, there is a generally accepted perception disseminated by many researchers (historians, archaeologists, classicists), who seem unaware of its implications, that *polis* is a synonym for city-state or city. This conception is based on three principles:

1. The majority of the *poliad* population lived in urban spaces;
2. The calendar that ruled life in the *poliad* community was established by urban activities;
3. A greater part of *poleis* production came from the urban sector.

These three points constitute situations that actually appear anomalous to the dynamics of the *polis*. As I have observed elsewhere (Chevitarese, 2001a: 23, footnote 2), the majority of citizens lived in rural areas, the calendar that regulated the community's life was related to agriculture, and that in fact agricultural production was predominant in the Greek *polis*. Even so, the recurrent use of *polis* as a synonym for city ends up suggesting (to any unaware reader) that ancient Greek culture was predominantly urban, with a strong emphasis in urban life and habits. This analysis perspective contributes to the overlooking of rural space in many history books.

Second, and strongly related to the first point though it demands separate attention, Snodgrass (1987: 67–68) has observed that ancient Greek texts emphasize urban life themselves, with exception of military campaigns and battles, such as assemblies, tribunals, sanctuaries, and marketplaces. This inclination in the written sources to reinforce city data instead of rural, has also helped consolidate the argument that archaeological fieldwork in Greece must be, basically, if not entirely, directed towards urban sites.

Another piece of information that helps us explain the absence of the *khora* from recent studies is related to a long literary tradition (with strong implications for Western political thought), starting with ancient Greek literature, which has sought to disqualify the peasant. This element is very meaningful since the readings made by the *kaloi kagathoi*, who were responsible for literary production, sought to confine the *agroikos* into a certain pattern: a rude person (Teophrastus, *Characters* 4.7, 4.11–12, 4.16), ignorant (Aristophanes, *Clouds* 627–631), devoid of any kind of social refinement (Aristophanes, *Wasps* 1120–1537), against politics (Aristophanes, *Acharnians* and *Peace*), who tries to maintain distance from the habits and novelties of the *asty*, who is seen as rejecting rurality (Teophrastus, *Characters* 4.8; Aristophanes, *Acharnians* 33–39; *Clouds* 43–52). These texts reinforce the assumption that the peasant was worried exclusively about his day-to-day life or, in the best of cases, with his survival.

We can also verify the prejudice of elites toward manual crafts (this too is greatly disseminated in Western political thought); not only towards the work realized by the *agroikos* but also towards craftsmen (*banausos*). This points to a very interesting question in ancient

Greek texts: why write about individuals that should not be counted among the citizens but among the *douloi* (Aristotle, *Politics* 1328b 40–1329a 2, 1329a 25–27)? Why waste time with men that live on the brink of death, that need to work hard, using their own hands, just to keep themselves alive? The answers to such questions are found in the elite Greek understanding of citizenship: a true citizen should hold a *skole* which signified knowledge of music, philosophy, rhetoric, oratory and other activities that ennoble him, and should never have to work with his own hands or be submitted to another's will.

The last point, but no less important, is the close relationship between archaeology and public investment policies. We find a flagrant preference in Grecian governmental archaeological funding for urban areas or areas close to urban centers. This choice reflects the fact that tourism is one of the most important sources of income for the Greek government. This results in the concentration of archaeological research in sites well served by streets, avenues and paved roads and not far from hotels, so as to avoid tourists getting tired or wasting time inside buses, cabs or other means of transportation. This concern for channeling public resources to archaeological activities in sites close to urban centers reinforces the idea, for the general public, that ancient Greek culture was basically (if not exclusively) urban.

Recent studies related to the ancient rural world have given little attention to the valuable information contained in the paintings of black and red figure Attic vases. We shall emphasize them in this study, so as to contribute new data from this area of material culture, consisting of Athenian figured pottery from the Archaic and Classical periods. This material is extremely important as a means of verifying the validity of the hypothesis mentioned above. The procedure employed here to recover rural images consisted of a systematic examination of the *Corpus Vasorum Antiquorum (CVA)* in reference publications and in the large bibliography that uses scenes related to the rural world from black and red figure Attic vases. This task resulted in two systematic catalogs— one of rural scenes from black figure Attic pottery and the other of rural scenes from the red figure Attic ceramic.

For the first catalogue we followed the model supplied by the pioneer work of Nassi Malagardis (1988: 95–134) closely. In her analysis of the Archaic period, she drew extensively, but not exclusively, on black figure Attic pottery. She established the major themes in the rural spaces represented in Attic pottery, including (with modifications made by the author of this chapter) hunting scenes, fruit harvest, vintages and treading of grapes, shepherds and flocks, agricultural labor, olive harvest, apiculture, bird hunting, oil making and selling, flour and bread making, grape harvest, fishing, rustic fountains, and sea or river bathing.

From the themes identified by Malagardis on the black figure Attic vases, only six appear on the red figure Attic pottery: hunting scenes, fruit harvest, shepherds, treading of grapes, bird hunting, and fishing. During research conducted for the present paper, four new themes were identified: *hoplites* and *peltastes* in rural space, breeding and characterization of animal husbandry, Attic peasants and women retrieving water from rural wells.

The data are organized into two Tables (17.1 and 17.2). Both seek to establish the relationship between vase shape and scenic theme found on black and red variants. Table 17.1 offers a total of two hundred and fifty-one images, distributed between fourteen types of scenes and nineteen ceramic forms. A wide range of themes developed by the painters encompassing a big number of situations present in the Attic *khora* are included, in addition to some that have passed relatively unnoticed: the making of flour and bread, rustic fountains (of water) and sea or river bathing. These themes are, without a doubt, a rare repertoire among the rural scenes in all the Attic pottery.

Table 17.2 offers a total of one hundred and nine images, distributed between ten types of scenes and fourteen ceramic forms. Two themes may be classified as rare, concerning the kind of information they offer to the researcher: *hoplites* in the *khora* and women next to wells. Two topics arise when analyzing Table 17.2:

1. Only six of the fourteen themes present on Table 17.1 date to the Classical period.
2. There is a drastic reduction of the scenes involving the rural world in the red figure Attic vases from the second half of the fifth century, disappearing in the next century.

From a total of one hundred and nine vases only thirteen of them, or 11.92%, occur in this period. It must be observed, however, that from this total only one vase, or 0.92% of the total, is securely dated to the fourth century. These data reveal that rural themes were appreciated by a very restricted number of people during the Classical period (Burford, 1993: 10).

The two topics identified above constitute very interesting problems that are common to other types of documents, such as ancient texts. Both present a partial and fragmentary description of the Attic rural space while representing (in iconography) and describing (in texts) a *khora* that is practically deprived of inhabitants. When referring to texts, we can also add a certain inclination in presenting the Athenian peasants as politically ignorant and incapable of sociability (Chevitarese, 2001a: 237–239). These two topics, however, allow for further exploration of the issue in the form of relative percentages of themes found on the black and red variants (Table 17.3). This Table provides the following observations and opportunities.

A close analysis of the six themes that remained unaltered during the transition from the black to the red figure vases—hunting, fruit harvest, vintages and treading of grapes, shepherds and flocks, bird hunting, fishing—confirmed continuities and variation between the two styles. Of these six, two suffered a proportional reduction, such that hunting decreased from 70.92% of the total images in black to 55.96% in red; fruit harvest changed from 11.95% of the total images in black

Table 17.1. Relationship between Vase Shape and Rural Themes on Black Figure Attic Vases

Rural scene	KYLIX	AMPHORA	LEKYTHOS	HYDRIA	OINOCHOE	SKYPHOS	DINOS	BOL	KYATHOS	KRATER	COVER	PINAX	KOTHON	PHIALE	KANTHAROS	LEKANIS	PELIKE	KLEPSYDRA	EXALEIPTRO	TOTAL
Hunt	61	29	23	32	5	3	5	4	2	3	4	3	1	1	1	—	—	—	1	178
Fruit Harvest	3	4	15	—	4	2	—	—	—	—	—	1	—	—	—	—	—	1	—	30
Vintages and Treading of Grapes	2	10	1	—	1	—	—	—	—	—	—	—	—	—	—	1	—	—	—	15
Shepherds and Flocks	2	1	—	1	2	—	—	—	1	—	—	—	—	—	—	—	—	—	—	7
Agricultural Labor	3	1	—	—	—	1	—	—	—	—	—	—	—	—	—	—	—	—	—	5
Olive Harvest	—	2	—	1	—	—	—	—	—	—	—	—	—	—	—	—	—	—	—	3
Apiculture	—	2	—	—	—	—	—	—	—	—	—	—	—	—	—	—	—	—	—	2
Bird Hunting	—	2	—	—	—	—	—	—	—	—	—	—	—	—	—	—	—	—	—	2
Oil Making and Selling	—	—	—	—	—	1	—	—	—	—	—	—	—	—	—	—	1	—	—	2
Flour and Bread Making	—	2	—	—	—	—	—	—	—	—	—	—	—	—	—	—	—	—	—	2
Grape Harvest	—	1	1	—	—	—	—	—	—	—	—	—	—	—	—	—	—	—	—	2
Fishing	—	1	—	—	—	—	—	—	—	—	—	—	—	—	—	—	—	—	—	1
Rustic Fountain	—	—	1	—	—	—	—	—	—	—	—	—	—	—	—	—	—	—	—	1
Sea and River Bathing	—	1	—	—	—	—	—	—	—	—	—	—	—	—	—	—	—	—	—	1
Total	71	56	41	34	12	7	5	4	3	3	4	4	1	1	1	1	1	1	1	251

Table 17.2. Relationship between Vase Shape and Rural Themes on Red Figure Attic Vases

Rural scene	KYLIX	AMPHORA	LEKYTHOS	HYDRIA	SKYPHOS	DINOS	KYATHOS	KRATER	PELIKE	CHOUS	PSYKTER	PIXIS	ASKOS	RYTHON	TOTAL
Hunt	30	4	12	1	1	1	1	6	2	—	—	1	1	1	61
Treading of Grapes	5	—	—	—	—	—	—	10	—	—	1	—	—	—	16
Fruit Harvest	3	—	1	2	—	—	—	1	1	—	—	1	—	—	9
Fishing	5	—	—	—	—	—	—	1	1	—	—	—	—	—	7
Shepherds and Flocks	1	1	—	—	2	—	—	—	—	—	—	—	—	1	5
Breeding of Animals	3	—	—	—	—	—	—	—	—	1	—	—	—	—	4
Bird Hunting	1	—	—	—	2	—	—	—	—	—	—	—	—	—	3
Women at Wells	2	—	—	—	—	—	—	—	—	—	—	—	—	—	2
Attic Peasants	—	—	—	—	—	—	—	—	1	—	—	—	—	—	1
Hoplites in the Khora	1	—	—	—	—	—	—	—	—	—	—	—	—	—	1
Total	51	5	13	3	5	1	1	18	5	1	1	2	1	2	109

Table 17.3. Relative Percentage of Rural Themes on Black and Red Figure Attic Pottery

Rural scene	Black Figure Total	%	Red Figure Total	%	Total (Black and Red Figures)	%
Hunt	178/251	70.92	⇓61/109	55.96	239/360	66.40
Fruit Harvest	30/251	11.95	⇓ 9/109	8.26	39/360	10.83
Vintages and Treading Grapes	15/251	5.98	⇑16/109	14.68	31/360	8.61
Shepherds and Flocks	7/251	2.79	⇓ 5/109	4.60	12/360	3.33
Agricultural Labor	5/251	1.99	—	—	5/360	1.40
Olive Harvest	3/251	1.19	—	—	3/360	0.83
Apiculture	2/251	0.80	—	—	2/360	0.55
Bird Hunting	2/251	0.80	⇑ 3/109	2.75	5/360	1.40
Oil Making and Selling	2/251	0.80	—	—	2/360	0.55
Flour and Bread Making	2/251	0.80	—	—	2/360	0.55
Grape Harvest	2/251	0.80	—	—	2/360	0.55
Fishing	1/251	0.40	⇑ 7/109	6.42	8/360	2.22
Rustic Fountains	1/251	0.40	—	—	1/360	0.30
Sea or River Bathing	1/251	0.40	—	—	1/360	0.30
Breeding of Animals	—	—	4/109	3.67	4/360	1.11
Attic Peasants	—	—	1/109	0.92	1/360	0.30
Hoplites in the Khora	—	—	1/109	0.92	1/360	0.30
Women at Wells	—	—	2/109	1.83	2/360	0.55

to 8.26% in red. On the other hand, two other themes presented an increase in the number of scenes developed by the painters, which are: vintages and treading of grapes changed from 5.98% of the rural scenes developed by the black figure painters to 14.68% of the total in red figure pottery; and fishing changed from 0.40% of scenes in black to 6.42% of the total in red. Of the themes that ceased to be developed by the Attic red figure painters, all, without exception, are directly associated with production activities performed by agricultural workers: plowing and sowing of the fields, olive harvest, apiculture, oil making, flour and bread making and grape harvest. Of the four new themes identified on the red figure Attic pottery, only one is directly related to a rural productive activity—breeding of animal husbandry—while the other three show, in general, individuals in the *khora*—peasants, hoplites and women.

Table 17.3 shows us that there are only three rural themes that stand out in both the black and red figure Attic pottery: the hunting scene—without a doubt the scene developed the most by painters—the fruit harvest and vintage and treading of grapes. It is not an easy task to explain this preference. We can concede, at least for the hunting scenes, the existence of three arguments that would explain the fascination for this theme among Attic painters engaged in representing rural scenes. The following arguments are not presented in hierarchical order nor should be seen as mutually exclusive, but rather as complementary.

1. This emphasis may be related to an interest in the urban rather than the rural universe, encompassing the connections between

hunting (hunter/hunting pursuit/capture) and homoerotic relationship (*erastes/eromenos*, pursuit/capture) (for a more detailed
discussion, see Chevitarese, 2002: 32–33);

2. Athenians, especially the elite, found pleasure in hunting, not
   only as a sport but as a training for war (for a more detailed discussion, see Chevitarese, 2002: 32);

3. Hunting had an alimentary function to the Athenians (Chevitarese,
   2001a: 203, footnote 107), and for this reason too it was
   considered one of the most important activities conducted in rural environments.

Scenes of fruit harvest and treading of grapes also reached considerable percentages in the both black and red figure pottery, and some
observations, more than explanations of their choice, will be presented
separately here. Interestingly, most of the characters involved in fruit harvesting are women (Chevitarese, 2000: 175–187; Chevitarese, 2001b:
7–15), the only exception being one scene which shows a beardless
youth carrying a bunch of grapes (Chevitarese, 2001a: 287–288). It is interesting to observe that this direct association—woman/fruit harvest—
may be the result, as suggested by Webster (1972: 247), of these scenes
having been painted by women or, even more probable, that it was a
rural activity conducted predominantly by women. The latter calls into
question a significant part of the historiography that insists on placing
women (as well as the activities practiced by them) inside the house
(for critics on this historiographic model see de Andrade, 2001; Lessa,
2001). In the treading of grapes, we see only a very small number of representations directly associated with human beings. There is only one
scene dated to the first quarter of the fifth century (# 73, Chevitarese,
2001a: 292–293) that shows men, never women, involved in the process of treading grapes. This almost complete absence of human representations would be the result of the ritual character of the images
with their great numbers of satyrs, maenads, and even of Dionysios
(Chevitarese, 2001a: 220).

From Tables 17.1 and 17.2, a discussion of the percentages of different rural scenes found on black and red figure Attic pottery allowed
the organization of Table 17.4. To begin, rural scenes appear better distributed throughout the black figure Attic vases. Of the twenty-four types
of forms used (we include in this total the four lids: of the *amphora*, the
lekanis, the *pixis* and that of a non–specified vase), nineteen were used
by painters of black figure against only fourteen used in red figure painting. Among the forms chosen for the development of black figure rural images, four employ almost 81% of all identified scenes—*kylix* with
seventy-one, *amphora* with fifty-six, *lekythos* with forty-one and hydria
with thirty-four. The same pattern is also observed in the case of red
figure vases. There we find three forms display 75.34% of all identified
images—*kylix* with fifty-one, *krater* with eighteen and *lekythos* with thirteen. There is an obvious preference shown by Attic painters for the
kylix form for images involving the rural world. This evidence is shown
on two levels:

Table 17.4. Relative Percentage of Vase Shape among Rural Themes in Black and Red Figure Attic Pottery

Vase Shape	Black Figures	%	Red Figures	%	Black and Red Figures	%
Kylix	71/251	28.30	⇓51/109	46.90	122/360	33.90
Amphora	56/251	22.31	⇓ 5/109	4.60	61/360	16.94
Lekythos	41/251	16.33	⇓13/109	11.93	54/360	15.00
Hydria	34/251	13.54	⇓ 3/109	2.75	37/360	10.30
Oinochoe	12/251	4.78	—	—	12/360	3.33
Skyphos	7/251	2.90	⇓ 1/109	0.92	8/360	2.22
Dinos	5/251	2.00	⇓ 1/109	0.92	6/360	1.70
Bol	4/251	1.59	—	—	4/360	1.11
Kyathos	3/251	1.19	⇓ 1/109	0.92	4/360	1.11
Krater	3/251	1.19	⇑18/109	16.51	21/360	5.83
Cover	4/251	1.59	—	—	4/360	1.11
Pinax	4/251	1.59	—	—	3/360	0.83
Kothon	1/251	0.40	—	—	1/360	0.30
Phiale	1/251	0.40	—	—	1/360	0.30
Kantharos	1/251	0.40	—	—	1/360	0.30
Lekanis	1/251	0.40	—	—	1/360	0.30
Pelike	1/251	0.40	⇑ 5/109	4.60	6/360	1.70
Klepsydra	1/251	0.40	—	—	1/360	0.30
Exaleiptron	1/251	0.40	—	—	1/360	0.30
Chous	—	—	1/109	0.92	1/360	0.30
Psykter	—	—	1/109	0.92	1/360	0.30
Pixis	—	—	2/109	1.83	2/360	0.55
Askos	—	—	1/109	0.92	1/360	0.30
Rython	—	—	2/109	1.83	2/360	0.55

1. of the three hundred and sixty vases containing these scenes, one hundred and twenty-two are *kylix* bringing up to a total of 33.90% of all the Attic rural images;
2. of the eighteen identified themes in Tables 17.1 and 17.2, the *kylix* appears in thirteen of them, in the following proportion: five of the fourteen themes among black figure vases and eight of the nine themes among red figure vases.

We can also see a direct relationship between the *kylix* and hunting: of the total one hundred and twenty-two *kylix* forms used for the different rural scenes, 74.59% of them were devoted exclusively to hunting scenes. This association, observed previously elsewhere (Chevitarese, 2001a: 201), is related to wine consumption at banquets, suggesting the values of masculinity, youth, aristocratic ideals, leisure among friends (and lovers—*erastai*), and eating and drinking together.

In the shift from black to red figural representations some vase shapes diminish in popularity. *Amphora*, for example, drop from fifty-six to five, *lekythos* from forty-one to thirteen, *hydria* from thirty-four to three, *skyphos* from seven to one, and *dinos* from five to one. Other vase shapes cease to be used by red figure Attic painters: the *oinochoe*, the *bol*, any lid (of different vases), the *pinax*, the *kothon*, the *phiale*, the *kantharos*, the *lekanis*, the *klepsydra*, and the *exaleiptron*. The *amphora*, which appears in twelve of the fourteen rural themes developed in the Archaic period, also suffers a retraction of its use during the Classical period: it is present in only two of the nine rural themes. On the other hand, two other forms grew in their use by painters:

1. The *krater*, that had been used only three times previously (Table 17.1)—always with hunt scenes—leaps to eighteen (Table 17.2)—with four different themes: hunting, fruit harvesting, treading of grapes, and shepherds and flocks—in the red figure Attic pottery. The growth in use of this form with the treading of grapes theme is particularly marked;
2. The *pelike*, used only once previously (Table 17.1) with representations of oil making and selling was used five times (Table 17.2) with four different themes—hunting, shepherds and flocks, Attic peasants, and fishing—in the red figure Attic pottery.

In addition, some vase shapes that had never been used as forms for rural scenes in the Archaic period came to be used by the red figure Attic painters: *chous, psykter, pixis, askos, and rhyton*.

It seem clear, then, in consideration of the data provided in Tables 17.1 to 17.4, that a direct relationship existed between the function of each vase (as suggested by its form) and the type of rural scene used in its decoration. This relationship could explain why 74.59% of the plates containing hunt scenes were associated with *kylix*. The wine consumed by the citizens in this vessel form present at banquets can suggest masculinity, youth, aristocratic ideals, the leisure among friends, and eating and drinking together. The massive presence of *amphoras, hydrias*, and *kraters* in hunting scenes, vintages and the treading of grapes could be explained by the use of these vases in the preparation and storing of wine. It is not surprising that most of these scenes include elements related to Dionysism. The frequent use of *lekythos* for hunting scenes can be explained especially for the Classical period due to the fact that the white background of the *lekythos* made it particularly useful for funerary ritual. In this way the scenes could possibly symbolize someone killed during a hunt or even represent an homage to the deceased by their family recalling a favorite activity.

The hypothesis proposed here suggests a program developed by the Athenian democratic leadership. This program would have had its foundations in the following:

1. The development of a new military-political power—the trireme rowers—that arose after the Greek-Persian confrontation. At this moment, this group constituted the main military defense and attack force of Athens (Meiggs, 1987: 205ss) It was the rowers, mainly native to popular urban strata, who guaranteed much more than the *hoplites* and the knights, including the control of the sea routes, the submission of allies and a vast part of the safety of the Athenian territory (for a discussion involving

the number of men aboard these warships see Morrison and
Coates, 1986: 107–127).

307

RURAL SCENES

2. The significant increase in income that Athens witnesses not
   only with the creation of the Delos League, but also with the
   transposition of the League's treasure to Athens.

These two pillars provided tangible benefits to the entire Athenian
civic community after the third quarter of the fifth century. Moses Finley
(1989: 43–64; see also De Ste Croix, 1972: 43–48; Meiggs, 1987: 255–
272) considers them in more detail, developing six main topics: 1) the
payment of tribute by allies; 2) the massive use of citizens in the navy; 3)
the confiscation of allied *poleis* land thus integrating the empire for the
use of its citizens; 4) the control of commercial routes on the Aegean and
oriental Mediterranean seas; 5) the institution of the *misthophoria*; and
6) the access of Athens to the internal affairs of allied *poleis*. One must
consider that the advent of democracy precedes the Athenian empire.
The stabilization of this kind of government, however, involves the at-
tainment of lands for citizens and the importation of cereals, especially
of wheat (for an association of the imperialism with nourishment see
Austin and Vidal-Naquet, 1986: 117–118; Finley, 1984: 54; Hornblower,
1988: xxii; for a critical position about this postulate in historiography
see Bloedow, 1975: 20–29), which defines the six benefits the empire
provided Athens with. In other words, we can confirm that the stability
of the *polis* was connected to its capacity to mitigate internal problems
(Finley, 1985: 129ss).

Therefore, the two bases shown here form part of the same objective: since the conclusion of the Persian wars and the construction of a maritime empire, Athens assumed a new role in the Greek
social-political, economic and ideological spheres. It begins to exert
an almost incontestable hegemony through the Aegean and oriental
Mediterranean seas. This prominence in an international setting is complemented by a decided preference in representation on the part of the
Athenians for urban space. This shift is strongly evident in numerous
kinds of documents, including ceramic iconography. The city was associated with complexity, as if it were a privileged space for the execu-
tion of political activities, the location par excellence for the citizen to
live. The city acquires before the eyes of the ancient Greek writers and
artists a political, economic, social and ideological supremacy over the
rural world. The latter continued to be present—it is a common element
in the black and red figure Attic pottery—but is represented as uniform
and simple. It seems as if all the different types of rural themes developed by the painters could be found anywhere and everywhere in the
Attic *khora*.

We can confirm an almost direct relationship between the development of Athenian imperialism and the meaningful reduction of rural
scenes on Attic vases after the second quarter of the fifth century, and
its virtual disappearance during the following century. This association
may be related to the control of commercial routes, especially those
that guaranteed Athens' wheat supply.

The construction and development of imperialism since the second quarter of the fifth century reinforced characteristic urban ideas, visions and values. The Empire can be seen as a chronological mark of the choice made by the Athenians—at least by the democratic leadership, of the elites who produced texts and of the artisans involved in the elaboration of the themes developed on the red figure Attic vases—to emphasize a group of elements related to urban life to the detriment of those associated with rural space. The title of this chapter was elaborated through reflecting on this chronological mark: in the same way olive oil and water do not blend with each other, so the decision made by Athenians to throw themselves to the sea—in the throes of constructing an empire—led Athens to accept urban values and reject the rural oil.

References

Austin, M., and Vidal-Naquet, P., 1986, *Economia e Sociedade na Grécia Antiga*. Edições 70, Lisboa.

Bloedow, E. F., 1975, Corn Supply and Athenian Imperialism. *Antiquité Classique* 44: 20–29.

Burford, A., 1993, *Land and Labor in the Greek World*. John Hopkins University Press, Baltimore.

Chevitarese, A. L., 2002, A Caça na Polis Ateniense nos Períodos Arcaico e Clássico. *Phoînix* (Federal University of Rio de Janeiro) 8: 24–48.

2001a, *O Espaço Rural da Pólis Grega. O Caso Ateniense no Período Clássico*, Fábrica de Livros (SENAI), Rio de Janeiro.

2001b, Uma Nova Proposta de Interpretação do Prato Ático de Figuras Negras do Santuário de Hera. *História: Revista do Departamento de História da Universidade Federal do Espírito Santo* 9: 7–15.

2000, Mulher e Colheita de Frutas na Pólis Ateniense. Análise Iconográfica dos Vasos Áticos de Figuras Negras e Vermelhas, *Revista do Museu de Arqueologia e Etnografia da Universidade de São Paulo* 10: 175–187.

De Andrade, M. M., 2001, *A Cidade das Mulheres: Cidadania e Alteridade Feminina na Atenas Clássica*. Editora Laboratório de História Antiga, Rio de Janeiro.

de Ste. Croix, G. E. M., 1972, *The Origins of the Peloponnesian War*. Duckworth, London.

Finley, M. I., 1989, *Economia e Sociedade na Grécia Antiga*. Martins Fontes, São Paulo.

1985, *A Política no Mundo Antigo*. Zahar, Rio de Janeiro.

1984, *Os Gregos Antigos*. Edições 70, Lisboa.

Hornblower, S., 1988, Introduction: the Archaic Background to the Fifth-Century Empire. In *The Athenian Empire*, S. Hornblower and M. C. Greenstock. London Association of Classical Teachers, Cambridge.

Lessa, F. S., 2001, *Mulheres de Atenas: Mélissa do Gineceu à Ágora*. Editora do Laboratório de História Antiga, Rio de Janeiro.

Malagardis, N., 1988, Images du monde rural attique á L'Èpoque Archaïque. *ARKHAIOLOGIKE EPHEMEPIS* 127: 95–134.

Meiggs, R., 1987, *The Athenian Empire*, 7th edition. Clarendon Press, Oxford.

Morrison, J. S., and Coates, J. F., 1986, *The Athenian Trireme: The History and Reconstruction of an Ancient Greek Warship*. Cambridge University Press, London.

Schnapp, A., 1997, *Le Chasseur et la Cité: Chasse et Érotique dans la Gréce Ancienne*. Albin Michel, Paris.

Snodgrass, A., 1987, *An Archaeology of Greece. The Present State and Future Scope of a Discipline*. University of California Press, California.

Webster, T. B. L., 1972, *Potter and Patron in Classical Athens*, Metheun, London.

Between Motorcycles and Rifles

Anglo-American and Latin American Radical Archaeologies

18

Randall H. McGuire and Rodrigo Navarrete

The recent English publication of Che Guevara's (1995) journal of his youthful motorcycle trip through South America, *The Motorcycle Diaries*, has generated a resurgence of public interest in the iconic figure of Che. The publicity blurb on the back of the book represents Che as a South American James Dean who embarked on a journey of discovery and adventure. In our opinion this comparison is extremely misleading because it confuses individual rebellion with true social revolution. This confusion makes the formulation of a radical praxis difficult because it mistakes the angst of youth for transformative social struggle. Just as Che and James Dean may be muddled so too may the attempts to build a radical praxis in Anglo-American and Latin American archaeologies be confused.

The differences between James Dean, the archetypal American rebel without a cause, and Che Guevara, the most renowned Latin American revolutionary with a cause, are clearly more notable than the similarities between these two men. The rebellion of James Dean can be characterized as an intimate, individualistic, self-serving, safe, and introspective transgression that lacked efficacy as a means to change the world. In contrast, the revolution of Che Guevara formed part of an effective and significant sociopolitical program that involved a high degree of personal sacrifice, and real danger. Both men died in a violent manner.

James Dean crashed his car while traveling at a high speed on a country road. Che Guevara left the security of a post-revolutionary Cuba to help advance the revolution in Bolivia and died at the hands of the Bolivian army. Victims and symbols of the same convulsive decade, these men represent the extremes of approaches to confront established authority.

We would argue that those scholars who seek to develop a radical theory of archaeology also can be identified within these same extremes, the contrast between rebellion and revolution, the difference between James Dean and Che Guevara. For us these two cultural icons are metaphors for the disparity between Anglo-American and Latin American attempts to create a radical archaeology. The radical archaeology of Great Britain and the United States often looks very much like the teenage rebellion of James Dean. The radical archaeology of Latin American, on the other hand, has struggled to build a revolutionary practice like that of Che Guevara.

The Praxis of Archeology

A radical praxis of archaeology that seeks to effect the social world in a meaningful and beneficial way necessarily involves three goals: 1) to know the world, 2) to critique the world, and 3) to take action in the world. Knowledge, critique, and action lie at the core of a radical praxis. Without a praxis that integrates these three goals, intellectuals cannot fully realize their place in society nor their capacity to transform society.

In order to change the world we must have accurate knowledge of the world. Action based upon false or flawed knowledge can only lead to failure and error. Accurate knowledge does not, however, exist independently of the social consciousness of the researcher simply waiting to be discovered in the world. It is instead a complex product of the dialectic between the reality that we observe as archaeologists and the consciousness that we bring to our research. Knowledge for knowledge's sake is often self-serving or trivial. Knowledge becomes meaningful and important when the process of gaining knowledge is intimately interconnected both with social concerns and with the social position and interests of archaeologists as social agents. Accurate knowledge, therefore, is only possible with a critical stance. If we do not question the ethics, politics, epistemology, and reality behind our knowledge, then our actions in the world will be unsound and may result in unanticipated, pernicious, and/or counterproductive consequences.

By critique, we mean a challenge to how archaeologists use the reality of the world, the social context they exist in, and their own interests in creating knowledge. This critique involves both a questioning of different archaeological visions or interpretations of knowledge, and an auto-critique of our own perspectives. It must ultimately rest in the reality of the observable world, however, because if it does not, then it will only lead to self-delusion and fantasy. By the same token, critique should be coupled with social action. Just as critique without reality equals self-delusion, critique without social action produces only nihilism and despair. Critique without social action spawns James Dean, the rebel without a cause.

Along these lines, we argue that to take effective social action in the world archaeologists need to step outside of often-sterile debates and reflect on our larger social context. The political, ideological, and ethnic confrontations of the last three decades have led many social scientists to conclude that taking action in the world without concrete knowledge of that world inevitably leads to erroneous and pernicious results. In the same way social action that springs from knowledge and converts it into a rich platform for debate and critique avoids the tendency towards self-delusion and totalitarianism that lurks in isolated and unexamined knowledge or in absolute truths.

It is in the articulation of knowledge, critique, and social action, all based in the concrete world, that praxis is realized. Praxis enriched by knowledge, critique, and action can only exist within real contexts of social relations, social struggles, social interests, and social agents. Praxis cannot exist in the abstract. To understand then why Anglo-American and Latin American archaeologies developed different forms of praxis and why one is more like James Dean and the other like Che Guevara, we must critically compare and contrast their social contexts.

Two Worlds

In order to compare the development of Anglo-American and Latin American radical archaeologies we will consider both the general trends of each and the internal differentiation found within them. These similarities and differences are only understandable in their historically specific social contexts.

In the Anglo-American context, the appearance of a radical archaeology was the result of a tacit alliance between diverse theoretical approaches unified against a common enemy, processual archaeology. These different approaches never formed a unified theoretical perspective (McGuire 1992; Trigger 1989a). They included the primarily British development of post-modernist and post-structuralist theory (Bapty and Yates, 1990; Hodder, 1982, 1986; Hodder et al., 1995; Preucel 1991; Shanks and Tilley, 1987a, b; Tilley, 1990, 1993), and the evolution of a feminist archaeology firmly rooted in the social movements of both the United States and Great Britain (Claasen and Joyce, 1997; Conkey and Spector, 1984; Gilchrist, 1994; Moore, 1994; Sweely, 1999; Wall, 1994; Wright, 1996; Wylie, 1992). Perhaps the weakest of these Anglo-American approaches has been a heterogeneous set of Marxist based theories (Bender, 1989, 1990, 1998; Handsman, 1983; Kohl, 1985, 1989; Leone, 1982, 1988, 1995; McGuire, 1992; Patterson, 1986; Paynter, 1989; Rowlands, 1989; Saitta, 1988, 1989, 1997; Trigger, 1984; Wurst, 1991).

In contrast, the development of a radical archaeology in Latin America has been much more homogeneous because of the centrality of Marxism to the development of a Latin American Social Archaeology (Bate, 1998; Lorenzo, 1976; Oyuela-Caycedo, 1997; Patterson, 1994; Vargas and Sanoja, 1999). Feminist and post-modernist theories have had much less impact in Latin American than in Anglo-American archaeology and there are few examples of these approaches in the Latin American literature (although a well established and growing feminist archaeology exists in Spain. i.e., Sanahuja, 2002) (Navarrete, 1995; Politis, 1995; Politis and Alberti, 1999).

There exist many significant differences between post-modernist or post-structuralist thought and both Marxism and feminism (Kohl, 1985; McGuire, 1992; Navarrete, 1995; Trigger, 1989b). At their extreme, post-processual theories embrace a severe relativism, advocating an excessive degree of contextualization that negates the possibility of making any generalizations about social change, and accepting a notion of multi-vocality that inhibits the development of general theories of society. In the most extreme interpretation of this theory, any archaeological proposition is only valid in its specific context of theoretical production and each individual or group can construct a past consistent with its own vision of the world (Kohl, 1985; McGuire, 1992; Navarrete, 1995; Trigger, 1989b). Post-modernism tends to offer a nihilistic and pessimistic vision for the future of archaeology that does not provide an effective base for political action in the world. The perspective of Post-modernism emphasizes how knowledge is constructed in consciousness without giving sufficient attention to the dialectical relationship between consciousness and the concrete world. From this perspective, knowledge is captive to the specific logic of representation, ideas, and cultural perceptions of the individuals that create it. It is difficult or impossible to effect change in the world when our knowledge of it dissolves into a constellation of infinite, unstable, and irreconcilable perspectives.

We do not think that it is an accident that post-modernist theory has developed, thrived, and been rewarded in the world's most prestigious universities, such as Cambridge, Berkeley, and Stanford. Such universities are not just sanctuaries for the production of knowledge; they are also factories for the production of the dominant ideologies of our time (Chippendale, 1993). Thus we find the political program of postprocessualism provocative and challenging, but never revolutionary. Rather we would see it as more reformative than transformative of modern social relations. Once again, like James Dean, the rebellion begins and ends with the individual, in this case with archaeologists and our own internal discourse.

Feminist theory for its part has generated a vibrant and useful debate concerning the praxis of archaeology by social agents. In fact, as has happened with Latin American Social Archaeology, feminist archaeology has produced an interesting encounter between social movements and theory in the Anglo-American context. When feminists integrated the study of symbols and representations into the study of power relations and the analysis of class, they produced the necessary tools to understand gender discrimination as a historical process intimately linked to inequalities of class, race, and ethnicity (Conkey and Gero, 1991; Sanahuja, 2002; Wylie, 1992).

Our own perspective is a Marxist one. Marxist thought assumes the existence of social actors in specific historical contexts that act within a political and economic dialectic. Marxism places knowing subjects within a social context comprised of the relations of production, and considers the dynamic of the actions of social actors and reactions within both the social context and the natural environment. The dialectical nature of social action means that knowledge does not exist for its own sake, but instead that knowledge is necessary to take action in the world. Equally, our position assumes that archaeologists as social agents produce knowledge conditioned by their historical social context but that this knowledge can also be used to transform that context. Such transformation is only possible when archaeologists maintain a critical perspective on how well this knowledge reflects the concrete world and on the social relations of its production.

Aspects of Marxist theory have frequently appeared in Western archaeological thought since the middle of the 20th century (McGuire, 1992). In some cases Marxism has arrived indirectly, for example via Leslie White's theory of cultural materialism, and in other cases more directly, usually via the work of V. Gordon Childe (Trigger, 1989a). It is, however, undeniable that the development of Marxist archaeology owes a great debt to Latin American archaeologists and their theory of Social Archaeology (Patterson, 1994). The existence of Che as a global symbol of revolution gives testimony to the broad contribution of Latin American thought to the construction of an international revolutionary praxis.

Making History

Cultural Historical archaeology preceded both the Marxist archaeologies of Latin America and the United States and was dominant in both areas throughout the 1950s (Politis, 1995; Trigger, 1989a). In Latin America, Social Archaeology developed as a scientific alternative to a hegemonic culture history. By contrast, in North America Marxist archaeology developed later in reaction to the positivist currents of a processual archaeology that had replaced the Cultural History of the first half of the century.

At the beginning of the 20th century, theories of Cultural Evolution dominated archaeology. Cultural History displaced this approach, however, in the second and third decades of the century. Culture History throughout the Americas was a product of German Natural History with an emphasis on the importance and uniqueness of cultures (Politis, 1995; Trigger, 1989a). Cultural Historians used the existence of variation between cultures as the starting point of their approach. They rejected both the idea that this variation had any evolutionary significance and that value judgments could be made with respect to it. This Normative

Archaeology resisted theoretical and methodological elaboration but did develop an extensive body of techniques to observe and classify the archaeological record. It also resisted any ethical or political contamination of its practice. Despite this abhorrence of politics, Cultural Historical archaeology remained at the center of nationalist discourses in both North and South America (McGuire, 1992; Politis, 1995; Trigger, 1989a).

By the second half of the century, over 50 years of Culture History research had resulted in an extensive, and some time intensive, classification of the archaeological record of North and South America. Also at this time, the rise of U.S. hegemony in the world altered the larger political context of archaeology in both continents. In the 1960s, in both Latin America and in the United States, archaeologists responded to these changes in the social context of their production of knowledge by formulating new approaches to the study of archaeology. Not surprisingly, given the dissimilar position of the two archaeological communities in this social context, these new approaches differed considerably.

In Latin America, Culture History dominated archaeology through the 1960s and into the 1970s. The continued emphasis on chronological and stylistic studies of artifacts did not produce a past for Latin America that was relevant to the then contemporary conditions or needs of the region (Lumbreras, 1974; Sanoja, 1983). At the same time Capitalism was in crisis in Latin America with Marxist revolutions and/or revolutionary movements afoot in practically every nation of the continent. Indeed, U.S. imperialism was under attack in many parts of the world during this epoch. In this context a Marxist archaeology developed earlier in Latin America than in the United States (Patterson, 1994; Politis, 1995; Vargas, 1995). Latin American Social Archaeology had its origin as part of political and intellectual movements within Latin America in opposition to the hegemonic power of U.S. ideologies. It represented an anti-imperialist rejection of dominant ideas from Europe and the United States that had lost their relevance in Latin America as a product of the convulsive struggles during this period (Lorenzo, 1976).

One of the crucial elements necessary to understand the development of Latin American theory is the relationship of scholars with political and ideological institutions both within and between the varied nations of the region. Latin American intellectuals have produced many important theoretical currents, such as *indigenismo*, nationalism, and dependency theory (Sturm, 1998). These currents can only be understood in terms of the tensions between the popular sectors of society and the elites of the various nation states and the relationship of these tensions to global relations of power (Badillo, 1995; Vargas, 1995). Also, at least since the 19th century, Latin American intellectuals have taken an active and leading role in the political movements and political parties of the region. This trend was accentuated during the convulsions of the 1960s. Radical theoretical developments such as Paulo Freyre's Pedagogy of the Oppressed, Dependency Theory, and Fals Borda's Revolutionary Science sprang up in this decade (Navarrete, 1995, 1999).

Within this larger Latin American context Latin American Social Archaeology has always maintained a contradictory relationship with

European and especially U.S. archaeological theories. This relationship rests in the irresolvable contradiction between imperial domination and cultural dependency (Navarrete, 1995). On the one hand Social Archaeology represented a definitive political and epistemological break with the Cultural Historical approach and its emphasis on chronology and description. On the other hand it cannot escape the dead weight of the tradition of Cultural History in its work. Towards the end of the 1960s, Social Archaeology began to develop a common theoretical program and this effort culminated in the Teotihuacán Group (Lorenzo, 1976). The work of this group resulted in a shared body of theory and scientific program, but this larger corpus of theory bore the mark of the various national traditions of archaeology that it drew on.

The articulation of Latin American archaeology with political movements is clear in the case of Cuba. The Cuban Revolution of 1959 represented a significant political and ideological event that challenged the balance of power in global politics. In Latin America, the Cuban Revolution opened the door for political and revolutionary endeavors that included intellectuals. Within Cuba itself the implementation of a socialist society included the immersion of cultural and scientific production in a Marxist discourse. This was especially true for the social sciences, including archaeology (Tabío and Ray, 1985). This transformation in Cuba reinvigorated revolutionary movements in other Latin American countries and in many of these nations, including Venezuela, Colombia, and Perú, armed revolutionary guerrilla forces appeared. These movements had extensive membership and support among the intellectual sectors of their nations. This process was one of the principle motivations for the development of Marxist archaeology in Perú and Venezuela (Oyuela-Caycedo et al., 1997; Patterson, 1994).

Developments in Chile and Argentina followed a somewhat different course. Traditionally Argentina had been one of the principal centers for progressive intellectual thought in South America. Chile became the first nation of Latin America to elect a socialist government in 1971. In the 1970s, reactionary forces in both nations moved violently to establish military dictatorships that sought to crush these leftist ideas and actions. This repression drove many intellectuals, including archaeologists, to more democratic countries including México, Venezuela, Canada, and Switzerland. In México these archaeologists came into contact with an already established progressive tradition of nationalism and *indigenismo* (Bernal, 1979; Caso, 1958). As a result of this process México became the center for the intellectual development of Social Archaeology in the 1970s and 1980s (McGuire, 1992; Navarrete, 1999).

In the Anglo-American context, especially in the United States, Marxist archaeologies developed at a later point. By the 1970s processual archaeology had replaced Cultural History as the dominant theoretical approach to archaeology in the United States. The early 1970s were also a time of turmoil as the United States lost the Vietnam War and the Watergate scandal unfolded. Economic recession added to this malaise. Within archaeology, the optimistic beginnings of

New Archaeology ended because of growing questions about its basic premises and assumptions. Several U.S. archaeologists including Bruce Trigger (1978), Thomas Patterson (1986), Philip Kohl (1981) and Antonio Gilman (1984) had never adopted processual archaeology and began to investigate Marxist approaches during the 1970s. These authors and those who followed them in the 1980s tended to be self-taught in their Marxism and as such they adopted a wide range of Marxist theoretical perspectives. In Great Britain, by the end of the 1970s, a postprocessual critique was developing that challenged the positivist method, technological determinism, and systems perspective of processual archaeology (McGuire, 1992; Trigger, 1989a). Anglo-American Marxist archaeology developed in this context primarily as a critique of processual archaeology and positivism, rather than as a critique of Culture History.

This difference, in relation to previous theories and especially to positivism, lies at the heart of the differences in emphasis between Latin American Social Archaeology and Anglo-American Marxist archaeologies. The Latin American reaction to the empiricism of Culture History was to develop a structured, scientific, objective and substantive approach that stressed Marxism as a way of knowing the world. The archaeological perspectives that developed in the U.S. and Great Britain during the 1980s occurred in reaction to the positivism of the processual archaeology, emphasizing Marxism as a means of critiquing the world. Their critique tended to be anti-programmatic and to focus on the social construction of knowledge, the political nature of science, and on ideology (McGuire, 1992).

Two Visions of The World

It is clear that differences in the development of radical archaeologies in Latin America and in the United States reflect the different positions of these two regions in a global context. The tensions, institutions, politics, and social relations that archaeologists enter into and help shape, differ greatly between nations in the core and the periphery of that world.

Nowhere is this clearer than in how archaeology is financed. The most obvious contrast is the fact that there is far more money spent on archaeology in the core states than in the periphery, but the sources of this money also differ. In the United States and Great Britain archaeologists draw their financial support from a multitude of sources, including government grants, state and local governments, private foundations, public and private colleges and universities, museums, and private companies. In Latin America, with few exceptions, federal governments alone fund archaeology, providing both the money for research and the jobs that archaeologists hold on a day-to-day basis (Gándara, 1992b; Oyuela-Caycedo et al., 1997; Patterson, 1994).

These differences in funding sources and amounts result in different behaviors and contradictions within the two contexts. Anglo-American archaeologists with more money and more varied sources for that money have more independence in their research. It would seem that this should permit a greater liberty in the range of ideas they can consider. But, as private firms and the state most often direct research objectives, and access to this abundance of funding, they require the archaeologist to take an uncritical stance to fulfill these objectives. In Latin America, state control of funding should mean less freedom of ideas, but the cracks and imperfections that exist in the state systems frequently permits the appearance of critique within the state-supported institutions and universities (Vargas, 1990; Vargas and Sanoja, 1993). The state often, however, does not permit such a critique outside of those institutions and universities (Gándara, 1992b).

At an even more general level the development of Anglo-American critical thought occurred in an imperialistic milieu while critical thought in Latin American archaeology exists within an anti-imperialist, usually nationalistic, archaeology. The goals of critique in these two contexts differ. Following Trigger (1984), a nationalist archaeology serves to define a distinct heritage for a nation state and as such is particular and local in its focus. In contrast, an imperialist archaeology focuses on the application of general methods to answering universal and broad ranging theoretical questions with little consideration of the national context.

The political and economic domination of the periphery by the core also entails ideological hegemony. This ability to define or impose hegemonic discourses also characterizes an imperialistic archaeology (Trigger, 1984). The major Anglo-American theoretical approaches to archaeology, including Culture History and processual archaeology, entered Latin America as part of such a hegemonic discourse. It is for this reason that the development of Latin American Social Archaeology as a rejection of first Culture History and then of the processual archaeology is both a scientific critique of these perspectives, a way of knowing the world, and a political critique of hegemonic ideologies. Archaeologists in the United States and Great Britain have to transcend their position in the social relations of the world and recognize these hegemonic discourses in order to take radical political action. The position of Latin American archaeologists is in some ways more contradictory. From their position in the periphery the hegemonic nature of the discourse should be clear, yet they are formed within this discourse and are often educated in the universities and colleges of the center where these ideologies are manufactured.

To paraphrase Carlos Fuentes, Anglo-American archaeologists live in the belly of the beast. They produce and reproduce their critique within the center of power and they participate in the very processes and institutional contexts of dominant ideology production that they wish to criticize. In the case of Latin American archaeology, the relationship with the beast is more complicated. From the periphery they can clearly see the form of the animal yet many have nourished themselves from the beast and many have also spent time within its entrails. As a consequence, many of the critiques originating from Latin

America reflect genuine expressions based on local relations antagonistic to hegemony, even as other critiques simply reproduce the debates going on in the center. In this way the peripheral position represents the strongest and easiest space from which to formulate a critique but those intellectuals in this position are also inescapably immersed in the hegemonic discourse of the center. To put it another way, it is possible to better perceive the beast from outside but all of us are ensnared within its lair.

Another factor in understanding the differences between both radical archaeologies is the differing role of intellectuals in these societies. One of the elements that define the intellectual culture of Latin America is its engagement with political praxis in society. At the beginning of the 20th century this started with propositions such as the state ideologies of *indigenismo* in México (Bernal, 1979; Caso, 1958; Gándara, 1992b; Ochoa, 1989) and Perú (Mariategui, 1973; Valcarcel, 1978, 1981). More recently this engagement was manifested in notions such as Paulo Freyre's Pedagogy of the Oppressed, Dependency Theory, and Fals Borda's Revolutionary Science. Latin American intellectuals have commonly integrated their scholarship with political struggles in their societies. In general in Latin America, political and intellectual elites greatly overlap or are the same people. Latin American scholars who practice science and produce knowledge can also become political leaders of their countries, or rather people who effect change in their nations, or conserve the status quo. This situation contrasts convincingly with the strong separation of political and intellectual elites in the English-speaking world.

In general, intellectuals in the United States and Great Britain represent a sector of the national elites restricted to the production of knowledge. Within society, the justification for such knowledge most often lies in its practical technological application. Such practical application is seen as existing outside politics. For this reason the intellectual lives an ivory tower and his or her participation in the public realm of politics is limited. Within this context there also exists an ideology that active participation in politics by intellectuals corrupts and compromises objective science and knowledge.

These differences not only pertain to the actions and politics of scientists and intellectuals but also to the institutions, universities, research centers, and museums that house them (Vargas and Sanoja, 1993). A guiding principle for universities in Latin America is the model of the autonomous university. Students in Córdoba, Argentina won the first rights of autonomy for a Latin American university in 1917 and these rights have been defended, often with blood, at many Latin American universities since then. The state funds autonomous universities but the university community controls the fiscal, intellectual, moral, and political integrity of the university through internal governance. The intellectual community controls not only the curriculum but also the leadership and priorities of the university. Agents of the state, such as the police and army, cannot enter the campus of a Latin American autonomous university. Within Latin America an affront to the autonomy of the universities is considered a violation of academic freedom and of liberty in the nation. The only regimes in recent history to violate the autonomy of their national universities have been the most repressive military dictatorships of Argentina and Chile. For these reasons Latin American universities are not only symbols of liberty and free speech but also havens for political and intellectual currents and personalities that are opposed to the state.

In contrast North American universities are not autonomous. The state or an external board of governors directs the administration of such universities and increasingly corporations and the marketplace hold sway in their corridors. The U.S. author of this paper has often heard Latin American colleagues question how free inquiry can in fact occur when external bodies control the university and when agents of the state can enter a campus, or even a professor's office, at will. With this comparison we do not wish to suggest that the autonomy of Latin American universities is absolutely inviolable. On the contrary there exist many examples of how national and global political and economic forces shape Latin American universities. The difference is that in the U.S. the university functions within the regulation of the state and the market place and not through internal, democratic, decision making processes. What we see here are two distinct types of institutions. In Latin America the intellectual community has an autonomy that allows it to dissent from the state, while in North America the university is part of the apparatus that legitimates the state and capitalism.

Another basic difference rests in the nature of political organizations in the two regions and the role of political parties in public opinion and action. In Latin America political parties are much more structured, autonomous, and socially far reaching than the political parties of the United States that serve primarily to get individuals elected.

In Latin America political parties are involved not only in the politics of government but also in programs of social transformation. Public action in Latin America has in large measure been a product of the level of participation in national life by political parties, and of the extent of connections between these parties and both the state and foreign interests (Coronil, 1997). In this manner the populist parties of the right have formed a symbiotic existence with the state, feeding it and being fed by it. In contrast, leftist parties have traditionally been in opposition to state programs and to imperialism and these efforts have included armed struggle.

During the 1960s and the 1970s this struggle included guerrilla movements that functioned as the strong arm of leftist parties. They coordinated with intellectuals in solidarity with their struggle. These intellectuals participated actively in all aspects of these struggles including the formulation of theory, clandestine activities, mobilization of public opinion, legitimate political action, and guerrilla war. Labor unions were also essential in these struggles and they formed a base for revolutionary action with the political parties, the guerrillas, and the intellectuals. In a situation such as this it is virtually impossible to escape the need for an explicit consideration of the class relations and of the class-consciousness of the social actors involved. Thus, Latin American intellectuals based their radical theory and praxis in class struggle. It is only recently with the rise of Neoliberalism in Latin America that we find societies atomized and stripped of such consciousness (McGuire, 1992; Navarrete, 1999).

In the English-speaking world, especially in the United States, the role of political parties is more tenuous. Attempts to manipulate public opinion to serve the interests of global sources of power tend to dominate in this role. The Cold War, particularly McCarthyism, destroyed leftist parties and weakened the left wing of the Democratic Party. Labor unions expelled radical members and turned away from social action to focus on economic benefits for their members. This led to an estrangement between the unions and the left that was amplified by the war in Vietnam. The ultimate consequence of these changes was that the second half of the 20th century witnessed a depoliticization of public opinion, a rejection of radical movements, and an estrangement of workers from working class interests. This was the triumph of an existing ideology that the United States is a classless society. It also saw a rise in debate and discussions based in issues of race, gender, and culture rather than in issues related to economic exploitation. It is for these reasons that radical scholarship in the English-speaking world has tended to focus more on ideology, and how ideology masks inequalities, especially in class (McGuire 1992; Trigger 1989b). It is also for these reasons that issues of culture and representation became so important near the end of the century.

The Italian Marxist Gramsci (1971) identified two strategies to confront the existing social order and transform it. First, the war of movement involves an open confrontation that often includes armed struggle to make revolutionary change. Second, the war of position involves a more subtle confrontation with the ideology and the ideological apparatus that legitimates the state and the social order. For Gramsci, the appropriateness of each strategy depends on the form of exploitation that exists in each specific context. When exploitation takes the form of the iron fist of violence and repression, the war of movement is appropriate; but when exploitation takes the form of the velvet glove of ideological manipulation, a war of position is necessary.

Gramsci's contrast is useful for understanding the differences between Latin American and Anglo-American radical archaeologies. Archaeologists created the Social Archaeology of Latin America in a context of a revolutionary war of movement during the 1960s and 1970s. Archaeologists formulated the radical archaeologies of the English-speaking world in the context of a war of position that has been called the "culture wars" in the U.S. (Nash et al., 2000). These "culture wars" began with the political victory of conservative forces in Great Britain and the United States in the late 1970s and continue today. Marxist Latin American archaeology laid out in the Manifesto de Teotihuacán (Lorenzo, 1976) a plan to use historical materialism as a tool to know the past and to act in the present. In the English-speaking world the focus has been on theoretical problems and the application of this theory to the past in order to challenge ideologies in the present.

A Comparison of Radical Archaeologies

Differences in the political and ideological contexts of archaeology have consequences for the traditions of thought and for the organization of the radical approaches that we are considering here. Latin American social archaeology has fought to produce a consistent, structured, programmatic praxis to address substantive and practical issues in prehistory. In contrast, the praxis of Anglo-American radical archaeology has been more diverse, more introspective, and more focused on critique than that of Latin America.

Latin American Social Archaeology, from its inception, strove for a coherent, integrated theory based in a vision of unified action by organized political groups. Archaeologists such as those that met at Teotihuacán and Oxctepec did not convene just for theoretical and academic discussions. They met primarily to formulate programs of political praxis. These intellectuals sought to elaborate, discuss, and critique these programs for further political action. Again, these goals are clear in the Manifesto de Teotihuacán (Lorenzo, 1976). In this document the relevance of archaeology is framed almost exclusively in terms of its significance for action in the present. Knowledge of the past was valued as the basis for a critically informed effort to transform the present (Navarrete, 1999; Patterson, 1994).

Latin Americans proposed a comprehensive program of work to implement this political praxis. In books such as *La Arqueología Como Ciencia Social* (Lumbreras, 1974), *Arqueología y Materialismo Histórico* (Bate, 1977) and *Arqueología y Sociedad* (Montané, 1980) they refined a methodology to generate a scientific, "objective" understanding of real pasts and the connections of those pasts with the present. A consequence of these efforts has been a tendency for these archaeologists to unify around a common project of research with a shared overall vision. Within this commonality, however, it is possible to identify variations in the implementation of this program based on differences in the national contexts where it is applied (Navarrete, 1999).

Marxist thought in Anglo-American archaeology is much more diffuse and varied than is the case in Latin America. Few if any of the archaeologists who initially formulated this theory had any formal education in Marxism and as a result they were largely self-taught. They therefore came to their theoretical positions independently and replicated the full range of Marxist theoretical positions that existed in English in the early 1980s (McGuire, 1992; Trigger, 1989b). Their theories are more a product of individual struggle than of organized political movements. Also, the relative isolation of the academy from political parties, unions, and other political organizations contributed to the isolation of these intellectual efforts from concrete political action. The Marxist perspectives that exist within Anglo-American archaeology include a traditional or Second International Marxism (Kohl, 1985; 1989; Patterson, 1986; Trigger, 1984; 1995), theories derived from French Structural Marxism (Bender, 1989, 1990, 1998; Rowlands, 1989; Saitta, 1988, 1989, 1997), a critical archaeology based in the Critical Theory of the Frankfurt School (Handsman, 1983; Leone, 1982, 1988, 1995), and Hegelian Marxism (McGuire, 1992; Paynter, 1989; Wurst, 1991).

Latin American Social Archaeology stressed the development of methods, categories, and concepts to gain a scientific understanding of the past from the archaeological record. Key works such as *Antiguas Formaciones y Modos de Producción Venezolanos* (Sanoja and Vargas, 1992), *La Arqueología Como Ciencia Social* (Lumbreras, 1974), *Arqueología Ciencia y Sociedad* (Vargas, 1990) and *El Proceso de Investigación en Arqueología* (Bate, 1998) begin with the scientific conviction that the transformation of social relations in the present depends upon a true knowledge of both the past and of general historical processes. We would argue that this emphasis on knowing the world springs from a Gramscian war of movement. In order to take effective action in the world it is first necessary to establish a plan based on a concrete and objective understanding of the world.

For its part, Anglo-American radical theory has emphasized the self-reflexive aspects of Marxist theory. These archaeologists have focused on a critique of the production of knowledge and of the contexts in which knowledge is produced. They do not seek to generate scientific and objective knowledge of the past but rather try to reveal how knowledge of the past is manipulated and produced within contemporary historical discussions. We would characterize this as a war of position in which scholars develop a critical consciousness to critique a hegemonic culture and ideology (Leone et al., 1987).

A pragmatic and programmatic emphasis on praxis springs from the substantive theory of Latin American Social Archaeology. It is built from a classic vision of historical materialism. This view gives primacy to the material conditions of life over social consciousness and emphasizes social and technical relations of production as determining the form of society and how it changes (Lumbreras, 1974; Vargas, 1990). From this perspective the actions of humans to transform nature are the basis for change in all social processes and in all historical moments. It also ensues from the tradition of progressive nationalism and *indigenismo* in Latin America. Linking the theory of the past with a critique of the present these archaeologists understand that contemporary class inequality and imperialism are connected to this past. More importantly they argue that just as people changed their social conditions in the past, so too can people change these conditions in the present (Vargas, 1990). In this way Latin American Social Archaeology connects with the notion of a war of movement as a historical development from revolutionary theory and linked to the struggles of political parties and movements. The period of development of this archaeological theory corresponds exactly with the epoch of the highest politicization of intellectuals and academic institutions in Latin America.

In contrast, Anglo-American radical archaeology has historically adhered to a more reflective position. Its emphasis on the Marxist notion of ideology is a product of both the role of intellectuals in English-speaking societies and of the specific evolution of Marxist theory in both Great Britain and the United States. The isolation of intellectuals, the suppression of Marxist theory during the Cold War, the ideological denial of class in the U.S., the weakness of true leftist political parties, and the position of these intellectuals within the imperialist center all pushed archaeologists to use Marxism as a critical tool. This activist position confronted the hegemonic ideological apparatus in the spirit of a war of position. As a consequence, English-speaking Marxists mounted a self-reflexive archaeology based in the development of profound critiques of the archaeological perspective. They also launched a critique of archaeological discourse and how it is profoundly interwoven with the ideological and cultural process of the context of its production (Yoffee and Sherratt, 1993).

This critique has resulted in a reevaluation of the theories and methods that archaeologists use to view the past. The Anglo-American position has set in motion a productive internal dialogue and self-critique of archaeological discourse, the social function of archaeology, and the role of archaeologists as social agents. This internal discourse, however, risks the danger of the ivory tower, whereby a nihilistic academic dialogue increases the isolation of the intellectual from political action in the world. As part of this same contrast we note that Latin American Social archaeology is actively involved in intellectual and political debates at the national, continental, and global level, whereas in the United States these debates largely exist within archaeology.

By pointing out the politically active nature of Latin American archaeologists in contrast to the self-reflection of Anglo-American archaeology we do not wish to present an idealized or romanticized picture of the role of intellectuals in Latin America. Indeed Oyuela Caycedo et al. (1997) have highlighted the bourgeois weaknesses and internal contradictions of Latin American Social Archaeology. With both of these schools of thought we recognize the political and practical contradictions that characterize each (McGuire, 1992; Navarrete, 1999). We, however, find the key to understanding how they differ in the comparison of their explicit political goals and plans for social action.

Shared Struggles

Aside from the notable differences that separate them, both of these Radical Archaeologies share achievements and challenges. Both have constructed useful critiques of the world and they have pushed the bounds of Marxist theory by extending it to non-capitalist societies. In both Latin America and in the English-speaking world, archaeologists struggle to build a radical praxis that transcends their own social position in history and society. In considering this social position we must reflect on both the reality of archaeology as both an elite and a colonial practice throughout the Americas. For these reasons radical archaeologists are often alienated from the interests of the working class and indigenous peoples whose interests they wish to advance.

Both approaches have had some success in building critical alternative visions of the past and of the present. The reach and scope of each of these visions reflect the social, political, and cultural factors we have already discussed. In Latin America the intention has always been to transcend the academic debate. For this reason Latin American Social Archaeology has always framed its internal critique of archaeological discourse within an endeavor to engage in a larger social and political analysis. In this effort they have always maintained connections with groups active in the political life of their nations (Vargas and Sanoja, 1993). Without exception an evaluation of their success at taking action in the world would find that it is difficult for them to unburden themselves of the world of intellectual discussion and to take action in the real world. In the English-speaking community radical archaeologists have intentionally positioned themselves within this intellectual discussion and they have fruitfully advanced it. It has been rare, however, for these archaeologists to transcend their internal critique and to take action in the world. In this way, in both contexts, archaeologists have developed useful but limited critical perspectives.

Both of these approaches engaged in critical discussions of Marxist theory and from these discussions they have generated novel and original theoretical proposals. They have worked to expand Marxist analysis to a far greater range of history than it has traditionally been applied to. Marxist theory has traditionally been directed to the study of Capitalism and to other modes of production that articulates with it. These archaeologists have sought in the writings of Marx a broader theory of history that is relevant to all times and to all places. They have applied it to societies that predate Capitalism and to social structures and social processes very different from Capitalism. These efforts require the constant critical elaboration and reevaluation of Marxist theory because this theory does not directly address such time periods and social forms.

Latin American archaeologists have sought to accomplish this goal through highly rigorous, programmatic, and structured systems of classification. These systems attempt to capture in a Marxist theory social forms and social relationships that are not Capitalist. The most elaborate of these systems is the Three Category System developed by the Grupo Oxtepec (Vargas, 1995). These discussions have been productive but an over-emphasis on definitions and the search for a general system of classification has limited attention to the critique and application of the system to the study of specific historical contexts. Specific studies would include those by Sanoja and Vargas of sites in the Orinoco River Valley and along the eastern coast of Venezuela (Sanoja, 1979; Vargas, 1979; 1981) and by Lumbreras at the site of Chavín de Huantar (Lumbreras, 1989). In contrast there exist a plethora of general studies on the evolution of social formations at a national or continental level

(Bate, 1983; Gándara, 1992a; Lumbreras, 1974, 1983, 1986, 1988a, b; Sanoja, 1983, 1994; Sanoja and Vargas, 1992; Vargas, 1990).

English-speaking radical archaeologists, however, have emphasized the critical aspects of Marx and consequentially not attempted to revise or develop a method of historical materialism. Instead they have applied cognitive models derived from other theories or developed particular concepts and categories to fit particular cases.

Both of these approaches confront the challenge of how to move beyond the bounds of intellectual and academic debate to take action in the world. Each has to struggle with the problem of how to span the gap that separates their academic discourse from social action. The key problem here is how to relate the findings of archaeological research on local histories with more general debates that have relevance to the problems of modern society.

From Latin America we would cite the experience of the Museo del Hombre Venezolano between 1984 and 1987 as an example of this struggle (Vargas and Sanoja, 1990). Mario Sanoja and Iraida Vargas developed this project within the Universidad Central de Venezuela in Caracas. This university has been one of the intellectual centers in South America for the development of alternative radical theories and for political activity. The purpose of the museum was to offer an alternative history of the Venezuelan nation to an audience of children and young people. This alternative history stressed social processes more than events, social groups more than heroes, struggles and contradictions more than accomplishments and progress, and the construction of a national identity more than legendary anecdotes.

With this goal the first and only exhibition—"Three Cultures, One Nation"—sought to challenge the official state vision of history from various angles. The exhibit covered an immense span of time from the first population of the continent until the 1980s. It broke down the traditional periodization of official history and instead emphasized the continuity of processes within this great span. The exhibit's consideration of the prehispanic indigenous history stressed both the importance of this history and its long-term effects on the development of the nation. The incorporation in the exhibit of themes related to Africans, Indians, and the working class represented a clear break with official, elitist, Eurocentric, hegemonic history. In terms of museology, the exhibit emphasized the substantive content of the history rather than the display of objects. Museum guides were also on hand to conduct the visitor through the exhibit. These guides sought to enhance the critical appreciation of the visitor and also present the exhibit as part of programmed cultural action.

In the end the museum was not a success. The reasons for this failure are multiple and complex and they spring from both national developments and from the social practice of individuals.

One of the major reasons for failure was the lack of interest on the part of the public in the activities of the museum. This lack of interest reflects a broader disinterest in history in a country that does not have a national history museum. The museum was also located within the university which is a place not frequented by the general public. Mainly the people who normally inhabit a university—intellectuals and professionals—saw the exhibit. The only exception to this was the school groups who were brought in to the university to see the museum.

Even though the exhibit explicitly confronted the hegemonic national history of Venezuela some of the concepts embedded in the exhibit and in its title "Three Cultures, One Nation" ran the danger of reinforcing basic beliefs of national ideology. The state of Venezuela celebrates the idea of miscegenation in a national holiday, *el Día de la Raza*, on the 12th of October. This idea has been one of the principle instruments that the European elites of Latin American have used to absorb and dilute the political potential of racial groups in their countries (Badillo, 1995; Sorensen, 1997). Although the exhibit presented a critique of this idea, in another manner it continued to advance the same ideology of cultural and racial equality by asserting that the three cultures (Indian, European, and African) did indeed form a single nation.

In the United States radical archaeologists undertook a similar experiment and perhaps surprisingly it encountered very similar challenges and disappointments. Annapolis, Maryland is a small city near Washington, D.C. It was founded in AD 1650 and throughout the 18th century it was an important sociopolitical and cultural center of the North American colonies. It has been the capital of the state of Maryland from 1695 until today and numerous important figures of the U.S. revolution lived or visited the city. Today this history is used to attract tourists and heritage tourism is the major contemporary industry of the city. In 1981, the Annapolis project began an archaeological program aimed at questioning the ideological construction of Annapolis' past, on paper, in reconstructed and restored buildings, and in the ground. The project sought to reveal the contradictions and social inequalities that the hegemonic history of Annapolis obscured (Leone, 1995; Leone et al., 1987). The organizers of the project sought to set up a participatory experience that would engage the tourists in a critical reflection on the colonial history of the United States.

As a result of their initial investigations the project organizers concluded that the history of Annapolis presented to the public was fragmented and that it reflected a nationalist ideology. This history pulled apart the temporal and cultural continuums of the city such as the 18th and 19th century, and the relationship between Euro-Americans and African-Americans. This dismembering reinforced a static and harmonic vision of the national past and it justified the inequalities of the present. These archaeologists embraced Althusser's (1969) notion of a dominant ideology that creates a false consciousness for all members of society. They sought to challenge this ideology by demonstrating to the tourists that the history and the historic Annapolis that they were presented with had been 'falsely' constructed. The project used guided tours of the historic center of the city and of their excavations to demonstrate that the hegemonic history was constructed and to reveal the inequalities and exploitation of the past. These archaeologists stressed how industrialization led to the increased consumption of goods and created the division between those who could acquire such goods and others who were marginalized in this consumption. They also emphasized how common goods used in daily life were used to establish and enforce social divisions in the formation of the United States. The concern here was not only with how day-to-day life defined the new class structure but also with how common things served to ideologically legitimate this structure.

In the end this challenge to the standard ideological history of Annapolis failed to overcome the official history and the cultural and social relations that produce it (Leone, 1995). The public generally responded to the alternative vision that the project offered by reinterpreting this vision in terms of their preconceptions derived directly from the ideology being critiqued. The archaeologists wanted to demonstrate the relationship between the inequalities of the past with relations of discrimination in the present. The visitors, however, were more interested in the exotic and odd features of the past. Their responses focused on the exotic, the monumental, and the extraordinary, and expressed assumptions directly derived from a Capitalist ideology such as a preoccupation with the value of objects, the time necessary to produce goods, and their availability in the market.

This range of responses should not have been surprising given the background of the tourists who visit Annapolis and the types of historical interpretations that they were already exposed to. In general, those people who have the most interest in heritage tourism are themselves members of the professional middle class in U.S. society (McGuire, 1992). The fact that Annapolis is a high-end tourist destination only amplifies this trend. It is clear here that relationships of power affect the distribution of knowledge within society. Leone, following Luckás (1971), noted that a hegemonic ideology reifies and distorts the history produced for the mass of people. This history naturalizes and makes universal the inequalities and forms of exploitation that exist in the past and the present. Clearly, in Annapolis, the privileged classes of U.S. society did not question this history even when presented with alternatives.

As a result of this experience Leone (1995) adopted Habermas' (1984) notion of communicative action. He recognized that those people who would be the most open to alternative histories were those who had been most directly affected in a negative ways by the contradictions, inequalities, and exploitation in society. He also shifted the focus of the research in Annapolis to an African American community in the city and to a project that actively incorporates members of that community. With this integration it becomes difficult for the archaeologist as part of the intellectual vanguard to assume they know the interest of the masses. Instead they must actively work with the community to develop an alternative historical discourse that meets the interests of both parties. This process of cooperation also revealed to the archaeologists how African-Americans incorporated the symbols and beliefs of the hegemonic ideology but in their own terms and giving them their own meaning (Mullins, 1999).

In these two examples we see that the efforts that a committed archaeology must make to implement a theory of praxis is rife with conflict and contradictions. Archaeology has traditionally been a middle class or bourgeois practice and this social position creates contradictions when it seeks to articulate and address problems and issues of the popular classes (McGuire and Walker, 1999). When archaeologists attempt to enter into a dialogue with social actors they enter into the complex sets of social relationships that structure the production of knowledge (Kohl and Fawcett, 1995; Yoffee and Sharrett, 1993). We would argue that, in order to enter into a dialectical praxis that allows action in the world, archaeology should be seen as a craft (Shanks and McGuire, 1996). Archaeology-as-craft rejects the idea that archaeology exists as an abstract search for absolute truths or objective scientific conclusions. It argues instead that archaeology should serve the interests of a variety of communities. These communities include the traditional ones of the academy and the middle class but also Native American, working class and other communities that archaeologists have not addressed. Craft implies a constant process of engagement with the archaeological record and the application of the knowledge derived from that engagement to a variety of different interests. Craft also requires a constant reevaluation of the interests of communities and how archaeology as a craft can serve those interests. Craft dissolves the dichotomies that have dominated archaeological discourse, including science versus humanism, objectivity versus subjectivity, arts versus crafts, and style versus function. It proposes a unification of reason and sensibility, politics and science, and most importantly of hand, heart, and mind, that is, of action, emotion, and consciousness. It is only here, in constant interaction between knowledge, critique and action, that we can, like Che Guevara, develop a truly revolutionary praxis of archaeology.

The realization that knowledge is produced in a complex interaction with social context necessitates a critical confrontation with history both as a process and as knowledge. The first step of this confrontation is to ask, "Who is our audience?" At one level this is a question of at what level, in what words and through what outlets we should reach this audience. It should be obvious that we need to speak to our audience in a language that they can understand and using outlets that are both available to them and of interest to them. Archaeologists have developed the language and the means to reach an academic audience and, to a somewhat lesser extent, a popular middle class or bourgeois audience. Once we step outside of these traditional communities, however, we are not so adept. At a more complex level we need to ask what the needs and interests of our audience are and how best we serve them. This requires that we ask the communities that we study what their interest in the past is rather than simply telling them what the realities of their past were. As the experience of the Annapolis project shows, if our goal is to formulate an archaeology that challenges a hegemonic ideology we need to do this in cooperation with communities that are victims of that ideology rather than communities that both create and benefit from it.

The standard means that archaeologists have used to communicate with public audiences are themselves products of social relations and thus are more effective with some communities than with others. Museums, national monuments, universities, and the whole of the educational apparatus are products of, and controlled by, the middle or bourgeois classes. We should not be surprised to learn that these institutions are most effective at educating and communicating with these classes (McGuire and Walker, 1999). Recently many scholars have argued that the Internet and cyberspace are the new democratic tools to tear down the hegemonic control of knowledge (Leotard, 1984; Poster, 1990) and some archaeologists have jumped on this bandwagon (Hodder, 1999). We are more cautious about these new media because access to them is class based, especially outside of core industrial states. The vast majority of the world's population does not have access to telephones let alone computers. It is clear that archaeologists who wish to advance a radical program need to seek media of communication that allows them to speak effectively with the popular classes. In both Latin America and the English-speaking world archaeologists have not been particularly successful at finding these media.

This lack of success springs in part from the position of archaeologists in society. It is clear that archaeologists in both Latin America and in the United States represent a privileged sector of society that has often been in opposition or simply irrelevant to the popular classes. We would propose five reasons why this is so. First, in both contexts archaeologists are associated with anthropology, a scientific and academic discipline that is a historical product of both colonialism and imperialism and that has in its history frequently served as an instrument of domination over indigenous peoples. Second, archaeology has generally held a Eurocentric, global view of history and the past that does not consider the visions of other traditions, cultures, and societies. Third, archaeology as a social product is directly associated with the professional middle and bourgeois classes, making it difficult to escape the assumptions, ideologies, and preconceptions of those classes. It is precisely these ideologies that justify the inequalities and exploitation that a radical archaeology wishes to challenge. Fourth, archaeology is frequently established and maintained as part of the ideological apparatus of states. Archaeology is a means to construct, depict, or rescue national heritages that justify national identities. In this capacity it is part of the ideological apparatus of the state (Gándara, 1992b). Fifth, the political position of archaeology is usually ambiguous and when archaeologists propose a critical view of the world they are doing so from an elitist social position, using elite language, and elite institutions and mediums of communication. Unless a considerable effort is made, such views are not linked to the interests and needs of popular classes.

When archaeologists lack a critical vision of our praxis it is easy for us to be part of the oppression. Nowhere is this clearer than in the relationship between archaeologists and Indian peoples in the Americas. In both North and South America archaeology has traditionally been a colonial practice, the study of the conquered by the conquerors. This practice flows directly out of the conquest of the continents. First the Europeans took the lands and wealth of the Indians, and then the archaeologists took their pasts. In the United States, as the U.S. army pushed the Native Americans to the far corners of the west and onto reservations, anthropologists and archaeologists claimed the Native past as their object of study (McGuire, 1992).

In the United States the colonial nature of archaeology was made forcibly apparent in the debates over repatriation during the last decades of the 20th century. At the end of the 19th century, Euro-American scientists dug up fresh Native American graves and collected bodies and artifacts from the battlefields to fill the museums of the eastern United States. The seizure of the Native American past was therefore both a physical seizure of bodies and things and a symbolic capture of authority over that past. Many modern Native Americans regard modern archaeology in the United States as simply a continuation of these macabre practices. Many have argued that archaeologists should be arrested for grave robbing rather than rewarded with positions in museums and universities.

For this reason, when Native Americans say that archeology is a locus of struggle they are pointing out that archaeology has been a source of their oppression in the United States (Antoine, 1986; Deloris, 1973, 1995). Within the archaeological community of the United Sates the fight over repatriation required a commitment to real social action and a far greater risk than abstract debates about the content of university lectures. Many in the field saw U.S. archaeologists who supported the rights of Native American communities to have a say in their own pasts and who pressed for the reform of archaeology as traitors. Many archaeologists who supported a Native American position had chapters rejected by journals, were passed over for jobs, and were denied the opportunity to present papers in national meetings because they were considered "too political" (Zimmerman, 1997). This history demonstrates the those archaeologists who choose to employ their craft in the service of other than the traditional communities of the discipline may do so at their own peril.

Similar contradictions and relations of exploitation exist between archaeologists and Indian people in Latin America to those that exist in the United States. The context is somewhat different in Latin America because of the *indigenismo* movement of the 1930s and 1940s. This movement appropriated Indigenous identity to further nationalist social, political, and cultural programs. Since the 1970s a new ethnic nationalism or *Indianismo* has arisen among the Native Peoples of Latin America and this movement tends to dismiss *Indigenismo* as paternalistic assimilation (Wearne, 1996). In Latin America there have been some faint stirrings on issues of repatriation and the control of Native histories (Condori, 1989), however the debate and conflict has not reached the level or importance that it has in the United States. We see no reason to think that this difference in conflict is the result of differences in the relations between archaeologists and Indians in the two regions. Rather, we think that it reflects differences between the economic, political, and cultural struggles that Indian people face in the two regions.

Defiance or rebellion, reform or revolution, James Dean or Che: at the beginning of the 21st century these icons appear feeble but they still have meaning in the alternative politics of many sectors of society including intellectuals, and among them archaeologists. We see these oppositions manifest in the differences between an Anglo-American and a Latin American radical archaeology. Much of the program for a radical archaeology in the English-speaking world resemble the rebellion of James Dean. This rebellion was individualistic, self-reflective, and reformist. We have argued in contrast that collective, political, and socially committed programs characterize Latin American social archaeology. We do not wish to conclude, however, that each of these traditions is trapped within the patterns of their development. In reality we think that contemporary processes may invert the oppositions that we have drawn between the two perspectives. In Latin America, on-going economic and political crises are eroding the integration and cohesion of social archaeology. In the English-speaking world we see evidence for more convergence between Anglo-American radical archaeology and the Latin American Social Archaeology. Is it by chance that we do not have a revolutionary vision in the English-speaking world? Is it by chance that we have proposals for reform in the Latin American contexts? What we have argued here is that it is only through a critical vision of the social context of science and of the relationship between theory and practice that it is possible to build a radical praxis of archaeology.

References

Althusser, L., 1969, *For Marx*. Vintage, New York.

Anton, C. F., 1986, Reburial: A Native American Point of View. *World Archaeological Congress*, Southampton.

Badillo, J. S., 1995, The Theme of the Indigenous in the National Projects of the Hispanic Caribbean. In *Making Alternative Histories: The Practice of Archaeology and History in Non-Western Society*, edited by P.T. Schmidt and T. Patterson. School of American Research, Santa Fe.

Bapty, I., and Yates, T., editors, 1990, *Archaeology after Structuralism*. Routledge, London.

Bate, L. F., 1977, *Arqueología y materialismo histórico*. Ediciones de Cultura Popular, México.

   1981, Relación general entre teoría y método en arqueología. *Boletín de Antropología Americana* (México) 4: 7–54.

   1982, Hacia la cuantificación de las fuerzas productivas en arqueología. *Boletín de Antropología Americana* (México) 6: 17–24.

   1983, *Comunidades primitivas de cazadores y recolectores en Suramérica*. Historia General de América, N. 1. Ediciones de la Presidencia de la República, Caracas.

   1984, Hipótesis sobre la Sociedad Clasista Inicial, *Boletín de Antropología Americana* (México) 9: 47–86.

   1986, El modo de producción cazador recolector o la economía del salvajismo. *Boletín de Antropología Americana* (México) 13: 5–31.

   1989, Notas sobre el materialismo histórico en el proceso de investigación arqueológica. *Boletín de Antropología Americana* (México) 19: 5–29.

1992a, Las sociedades cazadoras recolectoras pre-tribales o el 'Paleolítico Superior' visto desde Suramérica. *Boletín de Antropología Americana* (México) 25: 105–155.

1992b, Del registro estático al pasado dinámico: entre un salto mortal y un milagro dialéctico. *Boletín de Antropología Americana* (México) 26: 49–67.

1993, Teoría de la cultura y arqueología. *Boletín de Antropología Americana* (México) 27: 75–93.

1998, *El Proceso de investigación en arqueología.* Crítica, Barcelona.

Bender, B., 1989, The Roots of Inequality. In *Domination and Resistance*, edited by D. Miller, M. Rowlands, and C. Tilley, pp. 83–95. Unwin and Hyman, London.

1990, The Dynamics of Nonhierarchical Societies. In *The Evolution of Political Systems: Socio-Politics in Small Scale Sedentary Societies*, edited by S. Upham, pp. 247–263. Cambridge University Press, Cambridge.

1998, *Stonehenge: Making Space.* Berg, Oxford.

Bernal, I., 1979, *Historia de la arqueología en México.* Editorial Porrúa, México, D.F.

Caso, A., 1958. *Indigenismo.* Instituto Nacional de Indigenismo, México D. F.

Chippendale, C., 1993, Ambition, Deference, Discrepancy, Consumption: The Intellectual Background to a Post-Processual Archaeology. In *Archaeological Theory: Who Sets the Agenda?*, edited by N. Yofee and A. Sherrat, pp. 27–36. Cambridge University Press, Cambridge.

Claassen, C., and Joyce, R., editors, 1997, *Women in Prehistory: North America and Mesoamerica.* Pennsylvania University Press, Philadelphia.

Condori, C. M., 1989, History and Prehistory in Bolivia: What About the Indians? In *Conflict in the Archaeology of Living Traditions*, edited by R. Layton, pp. 46–59. Routledge, London.

Conkey, M., and Gero, J., 1991, *Engendering Archaeology.* Basil Blackwell, Oxford.

Conkey, M., and Spector, J., 1984, Archaeology and the Study of Gender. *Advances in Archaeological Method and Theory* 7:1–29.

Coronil, F., 1997, *The Magical State: Nature, Money, and Modernity in Venezuela.* The University of Chicago Press, Chicago.

Davies, D. D., 1996, Revolutionary Archaeology in Cuba. *Journal of Archaeological Method and Theory* 3(3): 159–188.

Deloria, V., Jr., 1973, *God is Red.* Grosset and Dunlap, New York.

1995, *Red Earth, White Lies: Native Americans and the Myth of Scientific Facts.* Simon and Schuster, New York.

Fernández Leiva, O., 1992, Desarrollo del pensamiento arqueológico en Cuba. In *Arqueología en América Latina Hoy*, edited by G. Politis, pp. 32–44. Fondo de Promoción de la Cultura del Banco Popular, Bogotá.

Gándara, M., 1980, La vieja nueva arqueología. Primera parte. *Boletín de Antropología Americana* (México) 2: 7–45.

1981, La vieja nueva arqueología. Segunda parte. *Boletín de Antropología Americana* (México) 3: 7–70.

1985, Arqueología y Marxismo en México. *Boletén de Antropología Americana* (México) 11: 5–17.

1987, Hacia una teoría de la observación en arqueología. *Boletín de Antropología Americana* (México) 15: 5–13.

1988, Observaciones sobre el término teórico 'Estado Arcaico'. In *Coloquio V. Gordon Childe. Estudios sobre las revoluciones neolítica y urbana*, edited by L. Manzanilla, pp. 221–234. Universidad Nacional Autónoma de México, México D. F.

1990, Algunas notas sobre el análisis del conocimiento. *Boletín de Antropología Americana* (México) 22: 5–19.

1992a, El análisis teórico: aplicaciones al estudio del origen de la complejidad social. *Boletín de Antropología Americana* (México) 25: 93–104.

1992b, *La arqueología oficial mexicana: causas y efectos.* Instituto Nacional de Antropología e Historia, Mexico D.F.

1993, El análisis de posiciones teóricas: aplicaciones a la arqueología social. *Boletín de Antropología Americana* (México) 27: 5–20.

Gasson, R., and Wagner, E., 1994, Venezuela: Doctors, Dictators and Dependency (1932 to 1948). In *History of Latin American Archaeology*, edited by A. Oyuela-Caycedo, pp. 124–136. Avebury, Glasgow.

Gero, J. M. and Conkey, M. W., editors, 1991, *Engendering Archaeology: Women and Prehistory*. Basil Blackwell, Oxford.

Gilchrist, R., 1994, *Gender and Material Culture: The Archaeology of Religious Women*, Routledge, London.

Gilman, A., 1984, Explaining the Upper Paleolithic Revolution. In *Marxist Perspectives in Archaeology*, edited by M. Spriggs, pp. 115–126. Cambridge University Press, Cambridge.

Gramsci, A., 1971, *Selections from the Prison Notebooks*. International Publishers, New York.

Guarch, J. M., 1987, *Arqueología de Cuba. métodos y sistemas*. Editorial de Ciencias Sociales, La Habana.

Guevara, E., 1994, *Mi Primer Gran Viaje: de la Argentina a Venezuela en motocicleta*. Seix Barral, Buenos Aires.

1995, *The Motorcycle Diaries: A Journey Around South America*. Verso, London and New York.

Habermas, J., 1984, *The Theory of Communicative Action*. Beacon Press, Boston.

Handsman, R. G., 1983, Historical Archaeology and Capitalism, Subscriptions and Separations: The Production of Individualism. *North American Archaeologist* 4 (1): 63–79.

Harnecker, M., 1969, *Los conceptos elementales del materialismo histórico*. Siglo XXI, México.

Hodder, I., editor, 1982, *Symbolic and Structural Archaeology*. Cambridge University Press, Cambridge.

1986, *Reading the Past: Current Approaches to Interpretation in Archaeology*. Cambridge University Press, Cambridge.

1999, *The Archaeological Process: An Introduction*. Routledge, London.

Hodder, I., Shanks, M., Alexandri, A., Buchli, V., Carman, J., Last, J., and Lucas, G., editors, 1995, *Interpreting Archaeology: Finding Meaning in the Past*. Routledge, London.

Kohl, P. L., 1981, Materialist Approaches to Prehistory. *Annual Review of Anthropology* 10: 89–118.

1985, Symbolic, Cognitive Archaeology: A New Loss of Innocence. *Dialectical Anthropology* 9.105–117.

1989, The Use and Abuse of World Systems Theory: the Case of the 'Pristine' West Asian State. In *Archaeological Thought in America*, edited by C. C. Lamberg-Karlovsky, pp. 218–240. Cambridge University Press, Cambridge.

Kohl, P. L. and Fawcett, C., editors, 1995, *Nationalism, Politics, and the Practice of Archaeology*. Cambridge University Press, Cambridge.

Leone, M. P., 1981, The Relationship Between Artifacts and the Public in Outdoor History Museums. In *The Research Potential of Anthropological Museum Collections*, edited by A. Cantwell, N. Rothschild and J. Griffen, pp. 301–314. New York Academy of Sciences, New York.

1982, Some Opinions About Recovering Mind. *American Antiquity* 47: 742–760.

1988, The Georgian Order as the Order of Merchant Capitalism in Annapolis, Maryland. In *The Recovery of Meaning: Historical Archaeology in the Eastern United States*, edited by M. P. Leone and P. B. Potter Jr., pp. 263–292. Smithsonian Institution Press, Washington D.C.

1995, A Historical Archaeology of Capitalism. *American Anthropologist* 97 (2): 251–268.

Leone, M. P., Potter, P. B., and Shackel, P. A., 1987, Toward a Critical Archaeology, *Current Anthropology* 28 (3): 283–302.

Lukacs, G., 1971, *History and Class Consciousness*. MIT Press, Cambridge MA.

Lorenzo, J. L., editor, 1976, *Hacia una arqueología social: reunión de Teotihuacan*. INAH, México.

Lorenzo, J. L., 1991, *Prehistoria y arqueología*. Instituto Nacional de Antropología e Historia, México D.F.

Lumbreras, L. G., 1974, *La arqueología como ciencia social*. Ediciones Histar, Lima.

1981, Organización y economía Inka. In *Los modos de producción en el imperio de los Incas*, edited by W. Espinoza Soriano, pp. 89–93. Amaru Editores, Lima.

1983, *Las sociedades nucleares de América*. Historia General de América, N. 4. Ediciones de la Presidencia de la República, Caracas.

1986, *Una nueva visión del antiguo Perú*. Municipalidad de Lima Metropolitana, Lima.

1988a, *De los orígenes de la civilización en el Perú*. Peisa, Lima.

1988b, Childe y la tesis de la revolución urbana: la experiencia central andina. In *Coloquio V. Gordon Childe. estudios sobre las revoluciones neollítica y urbana*, edited by L. Manzanilla, pp. 349–366. Universidad Nacional Autónoma de México, México D. F.

1989, *Chavín de Huantar*. Indea, Lima.

1990, *Visión arqueológica del perú milenario*. Editorial Milla Batres, Lima.

Lyotard, J. F., 1984, *The Postmodern Condition: A Report on Knowledge*. University of Minnesota Press, Minneapolis.

Mariategui, J.C., 1973, *Siete ensayos de interpretación de la realidad peruana*. Editorial Crítica, Barcelona.

Matos Mendieta, R., 1994, Peru: Some Comments. In *History of Latin American Archaeology*, edited by A. Oyuela-Caycedo, pp. 104–123. Avebury, Glasgow.

McGuire, R. H., 1992, *A Marxist Archaeology*. Academic Press, San Diego.

McGuire, R. H., and Walker, M., 1999, Class Confrontations in Archaeology. *Historical Archaeology* 33(1):159–183.

Montane, J., 1980, *Marxismo y arqueología*. Ediciones de Cultura Popular, México.

Moore, H., 1994, *A Passion for Difference*. Indiana University Press, Bloomington.

Mullins, P., 1999, *Race and Affluence: An Archaeology of African America and Consumer Culture*. Plenum Press, New York.

Nash, G. B., Dunn, R.E., and Crabtree, C. A., 2000, *History on Trial: Culture Wars and the Teaching of the Past*. Vintage Books, New York.

Navarrete, R., 1995, Antiguos caminos y nuevos senderos: existe una arqueología postmoderna en Venezuela? *Cuadernos de Postgrado* (Caracas, Venezuela, Fondo Editorial Tropykos-Universidad Central de Venezuela) 10: 101–139.

1999, *Latin American Social Archaeology: One Goal, Multiple Views*. Master's thesis, SUNY Binghamton.

Ochoa, L., Sugiura, Y., and Serra, M. C., 1989, Reflexiones en torno a la arqueología mexicana. In *Homenaje a José Luis Lorenzo*, edited by L. Mirambell, pp. 297–310. Instituto Nacional de Antropología e Historia, México.

Oyuela-Caycedo, A., 1994, Nationalism and Archaeology: A Theoretical Perspective. In *History of Latin American Archaeology*, edited by A. Oyuela-Caycedo, pp. 3–21. Avebury, Glasgow.

Oyuela-Caycedo, A., Anaya, A., Elera, C.and Valdez, L., 1997, Social Archaeology in Latin America?: Comments to T. C. Patterson, *American Antiquity*, 62 (2): 365–374.

Patterson, T., 1986, The Last Sixty Years: Towards a Social History of Americanist Archaeology in the United States. *American Anthropologist* 88 (1): 7–26.

1994, Social Archaeology in Latin America: An Appreciation. *American Antiquity*. 59 (3): 531–537.

1995, Archaeology, History, *Indigenismo* and the State in Peru and Mexico. In *Making Alternatives Histories: The Practices of Archaeology and History in Non-Western Societies*, edited by P. T. Schmidt and T. Patterson, pp. 69–85. School of American Research Press, Santa Fe.

1997, A Reply to A. Oyuela-Caycedo, A. Anaya, C.G. Elera, and L.M. Valdez, *American Antiquity* 62 (2): 375–376.

Paynter, R., 1989, The Archaeology of Inequality. *Annual Review of Anthropology* 18: 369–99.

Politis, G., 1995, The Socio-Politics of the Development of Archaeology in Hispanic South America. In *Theory in Archaeology: A World Perspective*, edited by P. Ucko, pp. 197–235. Routledge, London..

Politis, G., and Alberti, B., editors, 1999, *Archaeology in Latin America*. Routledge, London.

Poster, M., 1990, *The Mode of Information*. University of Chicago Press, Chicago.

Preucel, R., editor, 1991, *Processual and Post-Processual Archaeologies: Multiple Ways of Knowing the Past*. University of Southern Illinois, Carbondale.

Rowlands, M., 1989, A Question of Complexity. In *Domination and Resistance*, D. Miller, M. Rowlands and C. Tilley edited by, pp. 29–40. Hyman Unwin, London.

Saitta, D., 1988, Marxism, Prehistory, and Primitive Communism. *Rethinking Marxism* 1(4):146–168.

1989, Dialectics, Critical Inquiry, and Archaeology. In *Critical Traditions in Contemporary Archaeology*, edited by A. Wylie and V. Pinsky, pp. 38–43. Cambridge University Press, Cambridge.

1997, Power, Labor, and the Dynamics of Change in the Chacoan Political Economy. *American Antiquity* 62(1): 7–26.

Sanahuja, M., 2002, *Cuerpos sexuados, objetos y prehistoria*. Ediciones Cátedera, Universitat de Valéncia, Valencia.

Sanoja, M., 1979, *Las culturas formativas del oriente de Venezuela: La Tradición barrancas del bajo Orinoco*. Biblioteca de la Academia Nacional de la Historia, Caracas.

1981, *Los Hombres de la Yuca y el Maíz: un ensayo sobre el origen y desarrollo de los sistemas agrarios en el nuevo mundo*. Monte Avila Editores, Caracas.

1983, *7 Temas de Debate en la Arqueología Social*. Cuadernos de Antropología No. 2. Universidad de Costa Rica, San José.

1983, *De la recolección a la agricultura*. Historia General de América, N. 3. Ediciones de la Presidencia de la República, Caracas.

1984, La Inferencia en arqueología social. In *Actas del Primer Simposio de la Fundación de Arqueología del Caribe. Hacia una arqueología social*, edited by O.Fonseca. Latin American Foundation, Washington D.C.

1987, *Historia ilustrada de Venezuela: período indígena*. Tomo I. Ediciones Mediciencia, Caracas.

1989, Los orígenes del cultivo en el noroeste de Venezuela. In *Homenaje a José Luis Lorenzo*, edited by L. Mirambell, pp. 365–379. Instituto Nacional de Antropología e Historia, México.

1990, The Venezuelan Colonial Way of Life. *Revista de Arqueología Americana* (México. Instituto Panamericano de Geografía e Historia) 2: 157–167.

1991, *La Huella asiática en el poblamiento de Venezuela*. Cuadernos Lagoven, Caracas.

1994, *Gente de la Canoa: Ensayo sobre los antiguos modos de vida recolectores del noreste de Venezuela*. Fondo Editorial Trópikos, Caracas.

Sanoja, M., and Vargas, I., 1992, *Antiguas formaciones y modos de producción venezolanos*. Monte Avila Editores, Caracas.

Schmidt, P. T. and Patterson, T., editors, 1995, *Making Alternatives Histories: The Practices of Archaeology and History in Non-Western Societies*. School of American Research Press, Santa Fe.

Shanks, M., and Tilley, C., 1987a, *Re-Constructing Archaeology*. Cambridge University Press, Cambridge.

1987b, *Social Theory and Archaeology*. Cambridge University Press, Cambridge.

Shanks, M., and McGuire, R., 1996, The Craft of Archaeology. *American Antiquity* 61 (1):75–88.

Sorensen, N. N., 1997, There Are No Indians in the Dominican Republic: The Cultural Construction of Dominican Identities. In *Siting Culture*, edited by K.F. Olwig and K. Harstrup, pp. 292–310. Routledge, London.

Sweely, T. L., 1999, *Manifesting Power: Gender and the Interpretation of Power in Archaeology*. Routledge, London.

Sturm, F. G., 1998, Philosophy and the Intellectual Tradition. In *Latin America: Its Problems and Its Promise*, edited by J. Knippers Black, pp. 91–103. Westview Press, Boulder.

Tabio, E., and Rey, E., 1985, *Prehistoria de Cuba*. Editorial de Ciencias Sociales, La Habana.

Tilley, C., editor, 1990, *Reading Material Culture: Structuralism, Hermeneutics and Post-Structuralism*. Basil Blackwell, Oxford.

1993, *Interpretative Archaeology*. Berg, London.

Trigger, B. G., 1978, *Time and Traditions: Essays in Archaeological Interpretation*. Columbia University Press, New York.

1984, Alternative Archaeologies: Nationalist, Colonialist, Imperialist. *Man* 19: 355–370.

1989a, *A History of Archaeological Thought*. Cambridge University Press, Cambridge.

1989b, Hyperrelativism, Responsibility and the Social Sciences. *Canadian Review of Sociology and Anthropology* 26: 776–97.

1995, Archaeology and the Integrated Circus. *Critique of Anthropology* 15(4):319–335.

Valcarcel, L. E., 1978, *Historia del Perú Antiguo*, Vols. I and II. Editorial Juan Mejía Baca, Lima.

1981, El Estado Inca. In *Los modos de producción en el imperio de los Incas*, edited by W. Espinoza Soriano, pp. 141–170. Amaru Editores, Lima.

Vargas, I., 1976. Introducción al estudio de las ideas antropológicas en Venezuela: 1880–1936. *Semestre Histórico* (Caracas) 3: 151–175.

1979, *La tradición Saladoide del Oriente de Venezuela. La fase cuartel*. Biblioteca de la Academia Nacional de la Historia, Caracas.

1981. *Investigaciones arqueológicas en Parmana. Los sitios de la gruta y ronquen*. Biblioteca de la Academia Nacional de la Historia, Caracas.

1986, Evolución histórica de la arqueología en Venezuela, *Quiboreña* (Quíbor, Venezuela, Museo Arqueológico de Quibor) 1: 68–104.

1990, *Arqueología, ciencia y sociedad. Ensayo sobre teoría arqueológica y la formación económico social tribal en Venezuela*. Editorial Abrebrecha, Caracas.

1995, The Perception of History and Archaeology in Latin America: A Theoretical Approach. In *Making Alternatives Histories: The Practices of Archaeology and History in Non-Western Societies*, edited by P. T. Schmidt and T. Patterson, pp. 47–67. School of American Research Press, Santa Fe.

Vargas, I., Toledo, M. I., Molina, L., and Mountcourt, C., 1984, *Los Artífices de la Concha*. Biblioteca de la Academia Nacional de la Historia, Caracas.

Vargas, I. and Sanoja, M., 1990, Education and Political Manipulation of History in Venezuela. In *The Excluded Past*, edited by P. Stone and R. Mackenzie, pp. 50–60. Routledge, London.

1993, *Historia, Identidad y Poder*. Fondo Editorial Tropykos, Caracas.

1999, Archaeology as a Social Science: Its Statement in Latin America. In *Archaeology in Latin America*, edited by G. Politis, and B. Alberti, pp. 59–75. Routledge, London.

Vasquez Leon, L., 1994, Mexico: The Institutionalization of Archaeology, 1885–1942. In *History of Latin American Archaeology*, edited by A. Oyuela-Caycedo, pp. 69–89. Avebury, Glasgow.

Wall, D., 1994, *The Archaeology of Gender: Separating the Spheres in Urban America*. Plenum Press, New York.

Wearne, P., 1996, *Return of the Indian: Conquest and Revival in the Americas*. Temple University Press, Philadelphia.

Wright, R., 1996, *Gender and Archaeology*. University of Pennsylvania Press, Philadelphia.

Wurst, L. A., 1991, Employees Must Be of Moral and Temperate Habits: Rural and Urban Elite Ideologies. In *The Archaeology of Inequality*, edited by R. H. McGuire and R. Paynter, pp. 125–150. Basil Blackwell, Oxford.

Wylie, A., 1992, The Interplay of Evidential Constraints and Political Interests: Recent Archaeological Research on Gender. *American Antiquity*. 57: 15–35.

Yofee, N., and Sherrat, S., 1993, *Archaeological Theory: Who Sets the Agenda?* Cambridge University Press, Cambridge.

Zimmerman, L. J., 1997, Anthropology and Responses to the Reburial Issue. In *Indians and Anthropologists: Vine Deloria, Jr. and the Critique of Anthropology*, edited by T. Biolsi and L. J. Zimmerman, pp. 92–112. University of Arizona Press, Tucson.

19

Footsteps of
the American Race

Archaeology, Ethnography, and Romantism
in Imperial Brazil (1838–1867)

Lúcio Menezes Ferreira

> ...Azarias kisses her hand. Barral (Countess Barral) looks at Carlos (Carlos Gomes) with some curiosity. She couldn't expect that the young lad recommended by Azarias was half an Indian, or half black; she thinks about the blacks and the Indians in an ambiguous way: she feels affection for them, in a romantic way, but considers them as inferior...(Fonseca, 1994: 17)

In 1839, when the first issue of the Brazilian Journal of Historical and Geographical Institute (IHGB) was published, Januário da Cunha Barbosa (1839) wrote the new members of the Institute a list of documents and information which they should look for in the Imperial Provinces. Among the listed items, Father Januário da Cunha asked records of indigenous populations and their customs which could be used in the future to help bring these populations to civilization. He also requested a statistic list enumerating the number of indigenous groups, their principle activities and comments related to any economic advantage to be made of them. He also asked for a meticulous geographical examination of the provinces, a map showing natural resources, native products, and a careful topography of their rivers and mountains. A study of the quality and size of their lands was required as well. In sum, the first secretary of the IHGB, Januário da Cunha Barbosa, already in the first issue of the journal, set up a kind of overture, including two themes which would become the basis of IHGB's archaeological and

Ethnographic thinking: spreading civilization over the entire interior of the country and civilize indigenous populations. Agreement with these themes, important to centralizing political projects of the Monarchy, gave a certain rhythm to the Archaeology and Ethnography practiced by the Institute. It provided ideas to help set up the romantic picture used in the formation of a national identity and Indian policy.[1]

In this paper, using the texts of Francisco Adolfo Varnhagen (1816–78), Domingos José Gonçalves Magalhães (1811–82) and Gonçalves Dias (1823–64), I shall analyze how Archaeology, Ethnography and the Romanticism were articulated inside the IHGB and discuss the reason for such a picture, characterized, as we shall see, by racial overtones.[2] In considering of this, two analytical possibilities arise. First, Robert Miles (1989) has an advocated studying the "processes of signification and representation of the Other" or, as I would rather name it, a short History of the process of qualifying social groups. Another analytical possibility follows Foucault (1988, 1994a, b, c, and d, 1999), including the discovery of the population phenomena and its correlated fields of knowledge, the development of the biopower and State-sponsored racism.

Allegro con Brio: Varnhagen and the Use of Force

> ... for such people, that still live in childhood, there is no History, only Ethnography. Childhood is always accompanied by insignificance and miseries ... (Varnhagen, 1975[1854]: 30)

> ... Cheer up! Human enterprise domesticates everything! It's up to civilization to size and improve what is already good, and prevent or destroy evil... (Varnhagen, 1975[1854]: 19)

Varnhagen, a military engineer graduated from the cadet's school of Portugal, was able to use his historiographic knowledge of questions of politics and strategy. He argued with other Latin American Republics about Brazil's geopolitical boundaries and also wrote the *História das Lutas Holandesas no Brasil* (1943[1871]) which sought to encourage the spirit of the Brazilian nation to fight against Paraguay. In a moment during which physical and administrative integration of the territory was imperative to the Monarchy's political scheme, it is easy to understand why the diplomat Varnhagen, with all his historiographic knowledge, spent so much time thinking about ways to unify the Empire. For instance, in the *História Geral do Brasil* (1975 [1854]: 13–14), he suggests the Prata region was privileged for the future union of the State. It was the ideal *locus* to build the capital, on account of the pleasant weather it offered and its proximity to a hydrographical basin that could link the whole Empire. History, *Magistra Vitae*.

Lieutenant Varnhagen also exercised his potential as a strategist with respect to the indigenous populations. As a member of the IHGB, he thought about the possibilities of integrating indigenous groups into a territory defined geopolitically as the nation. He wished to submit the indigenous population to a new social order and to the social principles that emerge from this new ordering. It is also important to postulate a place for Indians within the hierarchy of national identity that was being defined and whose contours were particularly stressed by the concept of civilization. In other words, the main problem was the possibility of civilizing the indigenous populations through a policy of integration.

In 1841, Varnhagen wrote *Sobre a Necessidade do Estudo e Ensino das Línguas Indígenas do Brasil* (1841: 53–63). In this text, he proposed the creation of a section of Archaeology and Ethnography at the IHGB's Journal, to be added the section that included History and Geography. According to Varnhagen, this new section would have as its main purpose the investigation of Indian languages. These studies should also determine as accurately as possible indigenous movements and immigration. The same section should also examine different ways of civilizing indigenous people and use, if necessary, statistical methods to help the IHGB measure the indigenous population and locate each group. In essence, the IHGB sought to elaborate an "ethnography chart" (Varnhagen 1841: 63).

For Varnhagen, this section was to be created immediately, because the Indians belonged to a decadent and degenerating race. He also thought that in a very short time, the different languages will have lost their original purity, and in the near future, one would not be able to recognize the color of the Indian skin. Varnhagen believed in the ideas and principles of Buffon (1707–88), Gobineau (1818–82) and Von Martius (1794–1868), and presumed that Indians, due to their biological qualities, were condemned to imminent extinction. It would therefore be necessary to study indigenous languages as soon as possible. These languages studies were also fundamental to National Literature, because according to Varnhagen, they were the base upon which the independence and integrity of nations was built. Varnhagen's romanticism was based on general consensus—the Indians and their languages' myths were certainly useful in the inspiration of the National Poetry.

This Romantic argument, however, was abandoned in his subsequent work. Although in a letter sent to IHGB, in 1849, entitled *Línguas, Imigração e Arqueologia*, (1849: 366–376), Varnhagen still shows some romantic indigenist sentiments, this is no longer evident in *História geral do Brasil* (1854) In this work, only the author's discursive attitude and his archaeological and ethnological interpretation remains. Only Ethnography could study races that lived in intellectual childhood, or brutish peoples without a written system or History. As Ethnography, he understood not only fieldwork—and Varnhagen, in his travels around Brazil, made many observations on Indians and collected vocabularies—but also the descriptions of colonial chroniclers and the reports of naturalist travelers. One could understand this as incipient Ethnohistory. The fundamental discipline, however—and here Varnhagen reaffirms his texts of 1841 and 1849—was Philology. The study of the indigenous races could not be made by a historian without philological knowledge. It would be impossible otherwise to discern the variety and contrasting nominations given by the indigenous groups. Above all, he asserted, the customs of the American races were almost the same from the Andes to Patagonia, and only Philology could contribute to a sharp classification of these infant people (Varnhagen, 1849: 366). Only Philology could tell whether that names designated to Indians correspond, in reality, to one or to many races.

Finally, if Ethnography and Philology revealed the customs, myths, rituals, records and legendary memories of ancient and nebulous immigrations, they would be also studying Archaeology.[3] Thus, he believed in the deductive determination of American racial origins through the small footsteps or far-off monuments of a degenerated people, fated by their organic constitution and their decadent practices, to an inescapable disappearance.

Considering these procedures, Varnhagen (1975: 24) concluded:

> ... These vagabond people that always fought, populated the land that nowadays belongs to Brazil, were emanations of only one race or great nation; that means, they had a common origin, spoke dialects of the same language ...

In fact, the different "nations" spoke the variations of the same language, *Tupi*. Although they were degenerated by miscegenation with people wrongly called by different names, a detailed examination of the various languages and customs reveals that the *Tupi* were an invading race, "outer aliens" (Varnhagen, 1975[1854]: 52). They had a Caribbean origin and, when they left the Northeast, came in successive waves to the South, occupying the interior of the country and, above all, the Brazilian coast. New hordes from the same race then migrated from the North, especially from the Amazon region, fighting, exterminating, submitting the defeated to slavery, until they had occupied, once again, the same coastal area. Thus, those who lived on the coast, before the influx of the new warrior *Tupi* groups, dispersed to the South or to the interior. The *Tupi*, a conquering race, came from North, from the Caribbean and the Amazon Basin, and not from the South, from Prata and Paraguay, are as like those Martius (1844, 1907) wished they came from.

Because of their continued wars to occupy the territory that "today belongs to Brazil", the *Tupi* eventually fragmented themselves into smaller tribes. The decadent *Tupi* had become nothing less than one million nomadic souls engaged in incipient or inexistent agriculture when the Portuguese first arrived. Such an analysis is followed by the assertion of a statistical axiom established by Malthus (1766–1834): in any country, the population only develops when their inhabitants abandon their wandering lives, start working the land and set up permanent dwellings.[4] Before the Portuguese conquered, therefore, "the country was very little populated" (cf. Varnhagen, 1975[1854]: 23), and the chances of reaching development were small. Confirmation of this is found in, first, their lack of population, explained by the great importance of war to *Tupi* daily life: wars were their main reward, their hordes were moved by the instinct of revenge, they harassed each other, fought for the best spots for hunting and fishing, waited anxiously for the loot from conflicts—slaves and human flesh for anthropophagic celebrations. Second, *Tupi* cannibals, in their present decadent condition, did not have a metaphysical vision of the world. No religion ruled them. Thus, among the myriad of vices they had, they were also corrupted by the *peccatum nefandum*, the sin execrated by Saint Paul. In other words, the *Tupi* practiced homosexuality, and this helped to slow population growth. Finally, the social bonds of degenerated Indians were weak. Etymology reveals that the word *Tupi* was not related to any specific country, nor was the name of a great leader. Thus they lived in a wild anarchy, for nor did they have a centralized State like the Incas that could save them from their precarious situation. Nor did they have an aristocracy that could guide them into a civilized condition and a population increase (cf. Varnhagen, 1975[1854]: 26).

However, for Varnhagen, the viscount of Porto Seguro, there is no reason to be ashamed of this problematic image. After all, to him it was entirely probable that the *Tupi*, descending from the Northeast, specifically from the Caribbean islands, or coming from the Bering Straits, descend from the civilized navigators of the Ancient World. The viscount of Porto Seguro and others IHGB's intellectuals, searched for a "noble" genealogy for the young nation and Archaeology was fundamental to this process of definition (Ferreira, 1999; Piñón 2000). As a monogeneticist, Varnhagen believed that the *Tupi* were not only God's children, but also the product of immigration, therefore they must come from civilized races. It would even be possible to find the footprints of this civilized American race under Brazil's extensive tropical forests, covered by slime and patinas, as had happened in Mexico and Peru. It would not be necessary to waste money and time with archaeological expeditions to find them, the fragments of civilization would come out during the process of planting or while they built new roads. Civilization itself would find it is own traces.

Therefore the *Tupi* could be a part of the National Identity. For this to happen, however, their past, hidden in the forests of the Atlantic, in the myths whispered by their language, in the baroque notations of colonial chroniclers, and in scientific naturalism, would have to point to a historical civilized course. Varnhagen, as did other IHGB's intellectuals, saw Indians from another point of view. He sought their civilized side although today they may be degenerate, the "ruin of the people", in Martius' (1844) terms. So Lieutenant Varnhagen, following the example of the first Portuguese settlers, did not see another solution to civilize the Indians except through the use of "force" (1975[1854]: 212–222). It was because of a "misunderstood philanthropy" (1975[1854]: 220), first by the Jesuits and then by the King's pity, that the Indians had been brought to civilization through the slow process of catechism. After all, if the laws had allowed for the first settlers' greed, it would not have been necessary to gather and transport Africans to Brazil, who although the increased public wealth, also corrupted local customs because they were unbecoming, audacious and unashamed (Varnhagen, 1975[1854]: 225). With these degenerated races already populating the "blessed Brazilian soil" (Varnhagen, 1975[1854]: 30)—and Varnhagen's geographical descriptions are like a romantic version of Caminha's letter— one could not understand how there were poets who admired the

Genebra's philosopher, because it is known that with no laws and civilization, men are inclined to barbarity and anthropophagy (Varnhagen, 1975[1854]: 52).

Therefore, Varnhagen abandons Rousseau's argument of perfectibility, and with it, the I-*Juca Pirama and the Deprecação*, poems of Gonçalves Dias, allegories of indigenous suffering caused by the arrival of the Portuguese in Brazil. In a letter to the Emperor Pedro II, Varnhagen rejected Gonçalves Magalhães' poem financed by the State to be used as a national epic and called *A Canção dos Tamoios:*

> ... Unfortunately the poem is far from the honors of the National epic of Pedro II's century. Not even the subject of that bestial confederation is truly epical...
> (Letter to the Emperor Pedro II, September, 24, 1856, quoted in Lessa, 1961).

There is nothing better to the historian of ideas than a good polemic.

Allegro Spirituoso: D. J. Gonçalves de Magalhães, the Perfectibility, and the Non-Perfectibility

> ... Not even our historian alone will think in a different way; however, in his excessive love to civilization, he wants to attribute to it all goods deeds, he forgets for one moment that civilization is the result of the good human nature, that tends always to improve itself. (Magalhães 1860:17)
> ... Thus, the enquirer of truth, decide according to his particular opinion, and not according to the evidences of the documents... (Magalhães 1860:17)

In *Os indígenas do Brasil perante a História* (1860), Gonçalves de Magalhães criticizes the *História Geral do Brasil* (Varnhagen, 1975[1854]). His objective was the rehabilitation of indigenous people as part of the Brazil's population. As a philosophy professor at Pedro II School begins his reflections with methodological lessons. According to him, one cannot write the History of defeated and subjugated people who we see only through chronicles and documents of the conquerors, without another "indirect method" (Magalhães 1860: 4). One must be aware of contradictions within the documents and seek the truth through critics because the conquerors were always inclined to glorify their own acts as fair and to revile their victims with all kinds of imputations. Varnhagen, who did not use this indirect method, had gathered, joined together and forgiven all accusations against Brazilian savages. At the same time, according to most modern and best theories of History, Gonçalves de Magalhães considered the document an access point to the truth. To reach it, however, it was necessary to avoid the affirmations and insulting epithets about the defeated populations and accept only the good things that were spoken about them.

Nevertheless, Gonçalves de Magalhães did not restrain his criticism of Varnhagen's hermeneutic method. The author of *Canção dos Tamoios* also criticized Varnhagen's archaeological and Ethnographic interpretations and his philosophical erudition. Against Locke's opinion, whose innate ideas he wished to avoid, Gonçalves de Magalhães saw the Indians with the humanist's eyes of perfectibility. The professor thought Indians could resist the impositions of nature because the *bons sauvages*, as part of humanity, had an inborn inclination to development and civilization. Varnhagen's archaeological and ethnographic divagations thus appeared ridiculous. One could not say, based only in Ethnography and Archaeology, that our Indians were aliens who migrated from elsewhere. It was necessary to admit the geological fact that the human race had already inhabited all parts of the Earth before the universal flood or even before the last cataclysm. Therefore, in this dialogue with Cuvier, our professor said that while Ethnography and Archaeology could not determine the plurality of the human race, the most plausible way was to accept the biblical tradition of creation. One must recognize the unity of mankind, and this must be done without conceiving of the Indians as descendents of the Egyptians, Carthaginians or other known ancient civilizations.

Gonçalves de Magalhães thought that savagery was a kind of fiction or a temporary decadence of the normal condition of mankind which had escaped from its true nature. Anyway, between Lamarck's biological theories, false and degrading, and the studies of F. Schlegel, based on intellectual and moral nature of mankind, Gonçalves de Magalhães (1860: 37) preferred the latter. Thus was the basis of his criticism and, because of this, he stressed that Indians could be metaphysical. Indians lived in a regular social condition; they had arts, industries and scientific practices; they spoke differently because of sound, harmony and words that remind one of Homer's language; finally, they believed in a supreme God, which they called *Tupã*. This diversity of customs showed their metaphysical aspect: the religious respect for virginity until puberty; the protection of the family, including elders and orphans; the rules of matrimony; the stoicism in which they supported pain, work, and diseases; and as if all of this were not enough, anthropophagical rituals proved a "touch of virile dignity" (Magalhães 1860: 25), because the victim showed a sublime arrogance in their courage of facing death.

Therefore, Imperial counselor Gonçalves de Magalhães thought that the treatment given to the Indians in the *História Geral do Brasil* (1975[1854]) was partial. He also did not like the political and moral ideas of Varnhagen. After all, the historian, who promoted the idea of civilization, did not hesitate to encourage greed and use violence to subdue indigenous populations, because his method of civilization depended on the use of force (Magalhães 1860: 48). The Philosophy professor identified the influence of Thomas Hobbes on Varhagens' political schema. Gonçalves de Magalhães thought most important problem was imagining a civilization achieved through the power of guns. Instead, he argued) it was necessary to establish a social contract between the Imperial society and indigenous populations. In other words, population and territory, indigenous politics of integration and civilization of the country, provided the background for political debates within Gonçalves de Magalhães' work.

According to the Imperial counselor, Varnhagen followed Hobbes when he insisted that only war would bring the Indians to a social estate. Gonçalves de Magalhães, who was Secretary of the government, thought that conflict would not be necessary because Indians had already promoted economical prosperity and the union of the Nation in the past (1860: 49). The services rendered by the indigenous population to Brazil would be invaluable: they had helped in wars against the French and Dutch, they taught agricultural practices to the Portuguese and participated in the miscegenation process with the white settler, which contributed, and still contributes, to change Brazil into a 'white Nation'. Throughout all the Imperial provinces, one could see the Indians working for civilization in villages, towns, and farms as well as helping to tame the national territory through incursions to the interior of the country. Because of this, in the South provinces for instance, the *Guarani* differed very little or even did not differ from the Europeans, except in their athletic shapes. According to Magalhães, Mr. Varnhagen's geographical evaluations were also not correct, since Malthus' statistical axiom was not equivalent to a geometric proposition. If the development of population depends on sedentism and tilling the land, the same increased population would demands share of the land and, subsequently, intensification of agriculture. So, because of all this, the Empire reinforced the introduction of foreigner workers into the population, and should not wait for the population to multiply itself through the miracle of settlers.

A social contract with the Indians was therefore desirable and even possible because of the help they already rendered to civilization and of their inborn talent to develop intellectually. But one could not want the indigenous population increasingly abandoned to the villages' catechism without mixing them with foreigners. Black slaves were known to be able to absorb morality and civility as "spoiled meats helped to maintain health" (Magalhães, 1860: 56). The African slaves who were brought to Brazil by "sordid greed", were "stupid and submissive" (Magalhães, 1860: 57) and if they had been dismissed, perfectible Indian blood would not have been shed in such profusion. The tax payment of slavery contributed to Indian butchery. Gonçalves de Magalhães, commander of the Neapolitan Order of Francisco I, argued that if blacks had remained in Africa, more Indians would have been christianized and civilized and they would today represent a majority of Brazilian population—and above all would have stamped out the dark blend of the black race (Magalhães, 186: 61).

Allegro ma non Troppo: Gonçalves Dias, Civilization, and Decadence

...Oh! Who had, from the bowels of water,
The marine bones pulled up?
Our land demands, sniffs...
This monster
- what had he looked for here? (...)

It came to a bring heavy chains
which the *Tupi* tribe will moan
The elder will serve as slaves,
Even the *Piaga* shall be slave
(Gonçalves Dias, *O canto do Piaga*, in Ramos, 1997: 33–34)

. . . The Americans have an intellectual capacity inferior to that of the white race
(. . .) They have been converted to the faith like the Chinese and the Turkish,
people that we consider civilized . . . (Dias, 1867: 258)

Gonçalves Dias, well known as a poet, had been an active member of the IHGB since 1847 and where he had led for several years the
Archaeology and Ethnography section. He also engaged in numerous
political and strategic activities. In 1851, he was sent to study the public schools of the northern Provinces and collect historical and ethnographic documents from the archives of Bahia, Alagoas, Pernambuco,
Paraìba do Norte, Ceará, Maranhão and Pará. In 1856, he was nomi-
nated the Ethnography section's chief of the Brazilian Scientific Commission (1858–1861) which was organized by the Imperial government
and by the IHGB to study the resources of the northern Provinces. Another mission was reserved for him in 1858, once again in the north of
the country, where he was asked to study Brazilian Indians, obtain their
opinions about whites, and record any complaints they might have. He
should also study the archives, look for documents concerning Brazilian
History and Geography, and collect statistical information about trade
in the Provinces, especially concerning cultivated *versus* uncultivated
areas. Finally, in 1861, the poet was commissioned to supervise the
schools of the *Solimões* area. It was at that time that he went to Peru and
inspected the Management of Indian residing near the rivers *Madeira
and Negro*.

The poet published two ethnographic essays at the IHGB. In the
first, he responded to concern of Emperor Pedro II: were there or were
there not Amazons in Brazil?" (Dias, 1854: 599). Gonçalves Dias studied colonial documents and Indian's cosmologies to ascertain whether
Herodoto's warriors, the Amazons, had or had not been among the
Brazilian Indians (Cf. Dias, 1855: 5–66). In the second essay, *Brasil e
Oceania* (1867), Gonçalves Dias started an archaeological and Ethnographic discussion with clearly political goals. On the one hand, he
wanted to study the physical, moral and intellectual condition of the
Indians to ascertain how they had behaved during initial contact with
the Portuguese and to evaluate the facilities and difficulties that were
imposed on them by the policy of Indian integration. On the other hand,
he wanted to compare the Brazilian Indians with those of Oceania—a
region where, according to Gonçalves Dias, Malaio's people, Melane-
sians, Polynesians and New Zealanders, were gathered—to evaluate
which were more amenable to the teachings of civilization.

I will only touch on the first part of *Brasile Oceania* (1867), because
in this second essay, Gonçalves Dias recovers and extend the ideas
already stated in *Amazonas* (1855). I will only refer to the first issue
developed by the poet and choose not to discuss his ethnographic

comparisons because, although the author's thoughts are very clear, the first part of the essay is enough for us to understand the core of his political ideas.

Gonçalves Dias' formulations are characteristic of the discursive formation that guided the archaeological and ethnographic thought of IHGB. Like Varnhagen, one can notice that Gonçalves Dias' ethnography was also based on reading colonial chronicles and naturalists than on observations, *in situ*, of indigenous societies. By the same token, Philology, like Ethnography, continued to be considered important because it rallied the myths and Indian cosmology, and helped substantiate racial classifications. Archaeology at the time, however, did not seek to conduct excavations (this only occurred in Brazil after 1864); research on Indian origins and migratory routes were only deduced from myths and language studies. Thus, Archaeology, Ethnography and Philology, during the period focused on here, were epistemologically interchangeable. However, the concept of discursive formation distinguishes different events and above all, highlights how discursive groups articulate with others. We might even say that there are clear differences within the same formation (Foucault, 1986: 21–78). This explains Gonçalves De Magalhães' philosophical resistance to Ethnography and Archaeology, subjects with which he had to establish a dialogue (even if only to refute some of their points) in his moral and intellectual characterization of indigenous groups. It also explains how Varnhagen and Gonçalves de Magalhães established different criteria for validating the single origin point argument. It also explains the use Gonçalves Dias makes of craniometry in his attempt to describe the moral and physical condition of indigenous populations.

But let us see some of the poet's ethnographic and archaeological interpretations. According to both him and Varnhagen, the *Tupi* were a race of invaders from the North who came in successive migratory waves and occupied the entire Brazilian coast. Gonçalves Dias, however, differed from Varnhagen on two points. First, he felt the *Tupi* did not come from Caribbean populations, but had migrated from North America (thus the similarity between the *Tupi* and the *Iroquois*) and from the Andes. From these two centers, they traveled down the Amazon to finally occupy the Brazilian coast. This hypothesis can be observed in some verses of the poet, because according to him, Ethnography and Archaeology were useful, among other things, for a literary carpentry:

> my song of death,
> hearest thou, warriors:
> I am son of the jungles,
> In the forests I grew up;
> Warriors, *coming down*
> From the Tupi tribe.
>
> (...)I am brave, I am strong,
> *I am son of the North;*
> My song of death
> Hearest thou, warriors...
> (Gonçalves Dias. *I-Juca Pirama*, in Ramos, 1997: 124—emphasis mine)

Second, Gonçalves Dias, unlike Varnhagen, did not homogenize the whole Indian population of Brazil as *Tupi*. His racial analyses, in this point, were more sophisticated. According to the poet, when the first migrations happened, approximately during the XI century, the *Tupi* found primitive races in Brazilian forests. In order to occupy the best and more fertile land of the palm trees where the *sabiá* birds sang,[5] the *Tupi* were obliged to fight with these primitive races. The route from Andes to Brazil, moreover, was full of uninterrupted wars. The *Tupi* were thus a conquering and belligerent race. I call forth, once again, his verses:

The brave sons of yours, feared in war,
In the dawn of the morning, with strength have I seen them!
Death laid on the feather of the arrow,
On the sharp side of the club, on the Tupi's bow!
The brave sons of yours terrified,
Your sons fulfilled the edges of the sea,
The waves full of small boats,
Of arrows filling the spaces of the air.
(Gonçalves Dias, *Deprecação*, in Ramos, 1997: 35)

Two races therefore populated Brazil before the arrival of the Portuguese. By the color of the skin and by the physical characteristics the primitive races came from the Mongol race. The *Tupi*, however, had analogies with the lower, though noblest branches of the Caucasian race (Gonçalves Dias, 1867: 15). To Gonçalves Dias, some data confirmed the racial differences between the various Brazilian indigenous populations. In first place is philological evidence. While the *Tupi* used a language called by the first Jesuits and settlers as the General Language, the descendents of the Mongols spoke several dialects—constituting a kind of a tropical Babel. Ethnographic evidence proves that the *Tupi* populated the coast and the banks of the rivers, while the Mongols had already fought with them for part of this land. Their ornaments, the feathers on their arrows, their ceramics, their funeral rites, their different kinds of dwellings; in sum, both customs and artifacts were different between the two races. There was also another point of interest: while the *Tupi* sacrificed their prisoners and practiced anthropophagy because they loved revenge and glory, other populations have done it because they were barbarians and gluttonous.

The poet also examined moral and physical differences among the indigenous populations. His work was based not only on his personal observations, but also on craniometry literature and he concluded that there was a great mixing between the two races. Before the arrival of the Portuguese, miscegenation spread in the region 'where the birds sang like any place', resulting in the mixing of racial pedigree and the formation of the following groups: the *Mucuris*, the *Patachos*, the *Machados*, the *Coroados*, the *Botocudos*, the *Puris*, the *Aimores* and the *Tombiras*. These mixed groups were blamed for the degeneration of the *Tupi*, although they had remained unnoticed in the interior of Brazil and they defended themselves well and increased their population to fight against the *Tupi* for coastal sites—the most important part of the land

347
ARCHAEOLOGY,
ETHNOGRAPHY,
AND ROMANTISM

for all savages (Dias, 1860: 34). They became full of "old hates", with the instinct of "rapine birds", smelling the slaughter from many leagues away to feed their "starving appetite" (Dias, 1860: 53). So, before the Portuguese even established settlements, they encountered the entire coastal area populated by mixed communities and by decadent *Tupi*. As such, it was not Portuguese oppression that made *Tupi* civilization weak, but the mixed groups with whom they fought constantly for occupation of the coast. Before 1500, Brazil was already a territory filled with racial conflicts.

Actually, throughout his essay, Gonçalves Dias describes the qualities of the two races and the hybrid groups that resulted from their mixture. While the *Aimores* and the *Timbiras* were barbarians, revengeful and degenerated, the *Tupi* were almost stoic in their social institutions and in their morality. Gonçalves' *Tupi* were also close to Spartans, because of their concept of a warrior's honor in combats, and their virile strength and athletic constitution acquired years of conflict and hunting. The rhythms of this understanding of the contrasts between the mixed groups and the Tupi are also found in his verses:

> . . . Hast thou cried in the presence of death?
> In the presence of strangers hast thou not cried?
> Does not descend the coward from the strong;
> For thou hast cried, thou art not my son!
> Canst thou, damned descendant
> From a tribe of noble warriors,
> Begging to cruel foreigners,
> Be prey of vile *Aimores*
> (Dias, *I-Juca Pirama*, in Ramos, 1997: 133).

The poet thought the *Tupi*, in a distant past before the wars with others, had already built a civilization. Unlike Buffon and Von Martius, Gonçalves Dias did not feel the *Tupi* were already degenerate before the Portuguese arrived on Brazilian coasts. If they became decadent, it was because of unending wars with the mixed races that had inflicted the decrease and fragmentation of their populations. Second, least but not last, miscegenation with mixed and Mongol races perverted the fundamental physical, moral and intellectual purity of the *Tupi*. Finally, the *Tupi* decayed ultimately because of the erroneous policies practiced toward the Indians during the colonial period. The *Tupi*, because of their civilized past, should be allowed to associate freely, and be incorporated into a social contract that reshaped their customs and could give them a peaceful, farming and industrial life. In essence, less slavery and better civilization.

Gonçalves Dias' reflections about the past give us some lessons for the present. With a strategic imagination, the poet suggests that for the catechism and civilization of the indigenous people, one must specify whether the tribes surge towards a slow development or decadency. In the first case, it is necessary to oppose force with force and to have as a result from this the clash the annihilation of one or both forces. The clash of civilizations with slow development would be unavoidable. In the second case, a clash was unnecessary. It suffices to maximize and guide the decadency in the desired direction. In one word, less clash and better civilization.

Therefore, to the poet, the *Tupi* in a distant past were noble and brave. The *Tupi* of his present, however, were degenerated and mingled, amenable to a policy that guides them on an appropriated course toward the Empire's social schema. They could even be incorporated into the national identity, since they would thereby be reminded of their original condition. Actually, they could appear in the national identity, but only transformed into the rhythms and metaphors of romanticist poetry, only when rendered metrical, epic beings.

Conclusion

> ... This thought about the Guarani, from the musical critic of the Gazeta Musicale, is frustrating because the savage Brazilian maestro did not do a savage opera, he forgets the basic premise: from the moment that he writes an opera, a savage artist stops being a savage. Antithetically, Carlos Gomes wants to be recognized as a great musician, in his country and in the "civilized world"; *so becoming a European artist is the fastest and safest way of achieving what he wishes.* (Fonseca, 1994: 109)

The History of the Archaeology and Ethnography practiced in Imperial Brazil unveils a racist quality to the Brazilian romantic soul. The authors under consideration here, used a discursive formation which employed these disciplines, signified the Indian, and also took race as a fundamental category. In a moment when the unity of the nation was a priority, the racial issue introduces serious questions about a political scheme that intended to be, even if just a little, interested in integration: was it possible to civilize degenerated, belligerent, revengeful and savage populations? How could one civilize this "nomad and vagabond people"? These questions were the basis of reflection about a possible policy for the management of the Indian—a reflection in which the central point was supported by the binary opposition territory: population. It was necessary to civilize the Indians and at the same time, civilize the interior of the country. It was also necessary to assure the geopolitical unity of the territory and the development of its population. On the other hand, this reflection was also characterized by a biopower, power that controlled the life of indigenous populations; populations that were considered a problem in need of management in order to achieve the social goals of the State; that needed to be civilized, organized, multiplied, disciplined by work. Such populations were taken as a biological phenomenon, as a racial problem, degenerated and requiring Management to reconstitute them and, through this, regenerate the Brazilian population. Finally, populations over which one could use "power" and with whom one could not avoid a "clash"; populations that could be guided in their decadence, whose perfectible blood must be mixed with that of the foreigner and white settler. Thus, these authors declared the right to miscegenate, or the right to declare war.

The analysis of Archaeology and Ethnography as it was practiced in Imperial Brazil allows understanding of a fundamental period in our History. Precisely the moment in which we were constituted as a Nation, the period in which a kind of order was established, a kind of project, among many others that were left behind by through the various political conflicts, characterized, maybe still characterizes, our social identity in a deep way. In agreement with Benedict Anderson (1986), one could say that the XIXth century was characterized in general with a romantic soul for developing several techniques—among them Archaeology and Ethnography could be included—with the intention to building a Nation and a History of the Nations. Such construction demands not only a historical mistake, but also disappearance and occultation. In this way, the modern Brazilian identity, above all in the mass media, is still treated as a great melting pot, where civilization—now called "modernity"— is the main ingredient. The racist part of the Brazilian romanticism has vanished, as well as the civilization scheme that was developed for it.

Acknowledgements

I owe thanks to FAPESP for supporting my research and to the following colleagues who helped me in many different ways: Margarita Díaz-Andreu, Célia Marinho de Azevedo, Pedro Paulo Abreu Funari, Renata Garraffoni, Francisco Noelli, Ana Piñón, David Nogueira da Silva, José Alberione dos Reis. The ideas presented here are my own, for which I am therefore solely responsible. Translated by Renata Garrafoni and David Nogueira da Silva.

Notes

[1] For the relationship between Imperial Archaeology and Indian policy see Ferreira (1999; 2001) and Piñón (2000).

[2] For the relationship between Archaeology, race and identities see Jones (1997: 40–54); for the relationship between Racism and Archaeology see Trigger (1990: 110–147); for the relationships between Racism, Archaeology and Anthropology see Patterson (1997: 87–116); for the relationships between Race, Nation and State see Marx (1998); for relationships between Biology and Racism see Gould (1981).

[3] About the epistemological relationships between Archaeology and Philology see Funari (1999); about the relationships between History, Philology and Nation see Horsman (1981).

[4] See An Essay on the Principle of Population (1967).

[5] This passage refers to a well-known poem by Gonçalves Dias, Exile Song (Canção do Exílio), where he says "my land has palm trees, where the sabiá birds sings..." In Brazil, this poem is regarded as one of the best expressions of the missing one's homeland.

References

Anderson, B., 1986, *Imagined Communities: Reflections on the Origin and Spread of Nationalism*. Verso, London.

Barbosa, J. da C., 1839, Lembrança: sobre o que devem procurar nas províncias os sócios do Instituto Histórico e Geográfico Brasileiro, para remeterem à sociedade central do Rio de Janeiro. *RIHGB* 1: 141–143.

de Dias, G., 1855, Amazonas. *RIHGB* 18: 5–66.

1867, Brasil e Oceania. *RIHGB* 30: 5–271.

Ferreira, L. M., 1999, Vestígios de Civilização: O Instituto Histórico e Geográfico e a Construção da Arqueologia Imperial (1838–1870). *Revista de História Regional* 4(1): 9–36.

Ferreira, L. M., 2001, Arqueologia e Geoestratégia: As Fronteiras Imperiais e o Uso das Fontes Arqueológicas. *Vária História* 24: 149–171.

Fonseca, R., 1994, *O Selvagem da Ópera*. Companhia das Letras, São Paulo.

Foucault, M., 1986, *A Arqueologia do Saber*. Forense Universitária, Rio de Janeiro.

1988, *História da Sexualidade: A Vontade de Saber*. Graal, Rio de Janeiro.

1994a, Bio-Histoire et Bio-politique. *Dits et Écrits* 3: 95–97.

1994b, La Gouvernementalité. *Dits et Écrits* 3: 635–656.

1994c, Securité, Territoire et Population. *Dits et Écrits* 3: 719–723.

1994d, Naissance de la biopolitique. *Dits et Écrits* 3: 818–826.

1999, *Em Defesa da Sociedade*. Martins Fontes, São Paulo.

Funari, P. P. A., 1999, Lingüística e Arqueologia. *DELTA* 15(1): 161–176.

Gould, S. J., 1981, *The Mismeasure of Man*. W. W. Norton, New York.

Horsman, R., 1981, *Race and Manifest Destiny*. Harvard University Press, Cambridge.

Jones, S., 1997, *The Archaeology of Ethnicity: Constructing Identities in the Past and Present*. Routledge, London.

Lessa, C. R., editor, 1961, *Francisco Adolfo Varnhagen: Correspondência Ativa*. INL/MEC, Rio de Janeiro.

Magalhães, D. J. G. de., 1860, Os Indígenas do Brasil perante à História. *RIHGB* 23: 3–63.

Malthus, T. R., 1967, *An Essay on the Principles of Population*. Everyman's, London.

Martius, K. P. von., 1844, Como se Deve Escrever a História do Brasil. *RIHGB* 6: 389–411.

1907, O Estado do Direito entre os Autóctones do Brasil. *RIHGSP* 11: 20–82.

Marx, A. W., 1998, *Making Race and Nation: A Comparison of the United States, South Africa and Brazil*. Cambridge University Press, Cambridge.

Miles, R., 1989, *Racism*. Routledge, London.

Patterson, T. C., 1997, *Inventing Western Civilization*. Monthly Review Press, New York.

Piñón, A. S., 2000, La Arqueología y la Construcción de la Identidad en Brasil: el caso del los orígenes del hombre en Brasil. Master's Thesis, Universidad Complutense de Madrid.

Ramos, P. E. da Silva, editor, 1997, *Gonçalves Dias: Poemas*. Publifolha, São Paulo.

Trigger, B. G., 1990, *A History of Archaeological Thought*. Cambridge University Press, Cambridge.

Varnhagen. F. A., 1841, Memória: sobre a necessidade de Estudo e Ensino das Línguas Indígenas do Brasil. *RIHGB* 3: 53–63.

1849, Etnografia Indígena: Línguas, Emigrações, Arqueologia. Padrões de Mármore dos Primeiros Descobridores. *RIHGB* 11: 366–377.

1943 [1871], *História das Lutas contra os Holandeses do Brasil: desde 1624 a 1654*. Cultura, São Paulo.

1975 [1854], *História Geral do Brasil*. 9 edition. Melhoramentos, São Paulo.

20

Brazilian Archaeology

Indigenous Identity in the Early Decades of the Twentieth Century

Ana Cristina Piñón Sequeira

Introduction

Identity is a symbolic construction that defines inclusion, relative position or exclusion of an individual or group in a determined society. Since it is a construction, identity presents two dimensions: first, as a reflection of the interests of the subject that generates it; second, as a pattern in which relationships operate, that is, as parameters within which a "subject" and "identified object" are articulated. It is this public dimension of a relational pattern that confers relevance to discussions concerning the creation of identities, for these identities are the bases for defining tangible dimensions of societies such as legislation or institutions. In other words, an analysis of the creation of a determinate identity enables investigation into the both the interests of the subject that creates the identity and the relation between the "subject" and the "identified object." Note should be taken of the intentional use of the word "object," for the problematic of contact between identities is posed traditionally as a question of otherness (Todorov, 1999). The point of using these terms is to place the emphasis on the author of the discourse; that is, on the relationship with otherness, where "one" and the "other", are in a symmetrical relationship and where different groups alternate in occupying one or other category. Nevertheless, to pose the matter in terms of "subject" and "object" reveals quite clearly where the discourse originates, where the familiar articulation comes from, be it historic or archaeological.

The debates in archaeology concerning issues like multicultural-ism (Oyuela-Caycedo, 1994), ethnicity (Funari, 1994), and its own func-tionality (Gnecco, 1999) call for reflection on the role of our science in the construction of identities, especially indigenous and national identi-ties. In this framework, this paper will seek to analyze the role played by Archaeology as a political tool, with a focus on the relationship between hegemonic representations of the social and political envi-ronment and the image of the indigenous as constructed by archaeo-logical discourse. We will conclude that archaeology was used in the formation of multiple social formations of identity as a tool for self-identification and differentiation, of which ethnic and national identity are only two.

Preservation and Loss: The Republican Project for Nationhood

At the beginning of the twentieth century, Brazil was characterized by a recently established Republic (1889). Republican forms of government represented a reaction to the excessive centralization that had been car-ried out by the previous imperial government, and a political response to changes in the Brazilian economy, such as unequal regional devel-opment and the emergence of incipient capitalism in the southeast of the country, around São Paulo (Ferreira et al., 1999).

Fully engaged in the problem of creating an independent state[1] in a multi-ethnic reality, efforts were made to forge and extend the idea of na-tion in a unitary and centralizing manner throughout the imperial period following independence. In the republican period, these efforts were in no way mitigated. Consolidating national unity continued to be of cru-cial importance; national identity was to be forged through distinctive traits that comprised and defined both Brazil and "the Brazilian", both understood to be homogenous, uniform realities.

In fact, any national identity involves a projection of homogeneity on the imaginary social unity formed by its members. This perception of homogeneity, which, as Chaui (2000) pointed out recently, persists in Brazil today, laid its foundations in this period. Belief in homogeneity serves to resolve, on an imaginary level, the real tensions of a multi-ethnic society spread out over an immense territory that is home to rad-ically different modes of life. This instrument for diluting conflicts and contradictions can be called, in the anthropological sense, the creation of a myth (Chaui, 2000: 7–9). This is the myth of the single Brazilian, who is the product of the putatively harmonious coexistence of three races (Indians, blacks and whites) which however never came to pass. The so-cially shared images of the ethnic groups making up the country and the relationships between them (such as miscegenation) are a part of this myth, and remain the key point of departure for Brazilian national iden-tity construction to the present day. Far from being an exclusive feature of any Republican project of nationhood, this imagined homogeneity of "Brazil" and "Brazilians" was fully rooted in the nineteenth century, changing only slightly in later periods.

During the Empire period, integration of an indigenous ethnic element into Brazilian nationhood was subordinated into a broader context of defining the frontiers of the nation itself. In tangible aspects of the state, its assimilation involved a denial of its existence, which was revealed in meager and ambiguous legislation and in the leading role taken by the Church in the indigenous question at the expense of the state. This denial was partly explained by the widespread belief that the Amerindian was doomed to disappear, a belief that followed certain evolutionist principles such as the Haeckelian perspective. Haeckalian evolutionism held that according to the natural laws of evolution, weaker peoples must give way to stronger ones, suggesting that indigenous people, considered weak, would disappear in the foreseeable future.

In contrast, the Republican period seemed to suggest an open acknowledgement of Brazil's multi-ethnic reality. One example is the project for a constitution for the Republic implemented in 1889, which contains the following definition of Brazil: "The Republic of the United States of Brazil (. . .) is comprised of two classes of confederated states (. . .) which are as follows: the Brazilian states of the west that are systematically confederated and which originate in the fusion of the European element with the African and aboriginal elements; and the Brazilian American states (. . .) comprised of the fetishistic hordes scattered throughout the Republic." (in Gagliardi, 1989: 56). This text, even though it was not approved as it reads here, reveals the positivist inspiration of the political elite, while its ultimate rejection shows the division of opinion existing in society. In fact, such positivist premises in Brazil were even further consolidated at a later date.

Indeed, in the few years of the existence of the Republic, still in the first decade of the twentieth century, with positivism gaining more followers, a significant social debate began concerning the indigenous question. Broadly covered by the Brazilian press, the debate occurred between the then director of the *Museu Paulista*, Herman von Ihering, who upheld Haeckelian ideas, and several positivists, including several from the Congregation of the *Museu Nacional*, headed by Sergio de Carvalho, director of the Anthropology department (Gagliardi, 1989: 74).

The controversy started by von Ihering himself confronted, on the one hand, Haeckalian evolutionists, standard-bearers of nineteenth century evolutionary theories. Surveying Brazil's ethnic diversity in terms of a racial pyramid in which the indigenous people were at the bottom, they advocated extermination. On the other hand resided the positivists, who were grounded in the evolutionary humanism of August Comte. Although these individuals also placed the indigenous people on the lowest position in their ranking of social classification—where progress, especially technological, was a sign of human "growth"—they favored preservation of the indigenous people.

The final word in this debate came from von Ihering, who announced that his would be the last chapter to discuss the indigenous question. In it, von Ihering accused the State of neglecting indigenous affairs. In this regard, von Ihering was correct, for the Republic was characterized by a relative decentralization and the indigenous question was relegated to the regions and placed under the power of the governor of each state in the federation. This state of neglect was inherited from the imperial era, yet changed circa 1910, heralding what was to be a new era in indigenous policy, and most of all a new era in the construction of ideas of nationhood.

The concept of preservation, as shown by the debate on the indigenous question, was fundamental to positivist thought. However, the positivist current expressed an ambiguous relationship between the loss and preservation of Brazilian indigenous identity. This ambiguity existed in the three temporal dimensions of past, present and future, and encompassed not only the indigenous people as human beings but their material culture as well.

In other words, the extermination of indigenous people that had begun with colonization continued at the onset of the Republic, as armed conflicts and territorial disputes continued between the indigenous population and other Brazil social groups. In 1910, in an attempt to put a halt to this extermination and normalize relations with indigenous peoples, the State created a national institute for the protection of Indians, the *SPILT* (*Serviço de Proteção ao Indio e Localização de Trabalhadores*). As its very name indicates, however, the categories of indigenous and worker were linked, reflecting the underlying intent of transforming indigenous peoples into workers.

From a positivist perspective, the integration of indigenous people was part of an inevitable advancement towards civilization. Thus, the indigenous were seen as a future "non-Indian," i.e., a future Brazilian, a potential worker, a being meant to become a citizen sooner or later. This attitude is first revealed by a decree of 1911 stating: "(hereby enacted are) . . . respect of Indian tribes as peoples with the right to be themselves, to profess their own beliefs, to live in the only manner they know: that which they have inherited from their ancestors and which can be *changed* only slowly." (in Ribeiro, 1996: 158, emphasis mine), and subsequently, by the words of Cándido Mariano da Silva Rondon, the first director of the SPILT, who stated: ". . . we must redeem the indigenous people from their state of neglect and bring them into full possession of their rights, respecting their fetishist social organization, and await their evolution." (in Cunha, 1986: 161).

This preservationist attitude, which on the surface contrasts with nineteenth century premises by not calling for the extermination of indigenous peoples, nevertheless foresees a similar destiny, for they would ultimately be transformed and disappear as a consequence of their own evolution. Clearly, preservation in practice translated into a integrationist policy that did not involve passively waiting but actually envisaged subtle action for acculturation, slowly but surely, through education, which would enable Indians to achieve the same positive stage of civilization as whites: this constituted the so-called "pacification."

Pacification involved continuing to use, as in the previous century, educational policy as the key to changing indigenous people. However, whereas in the Imperial era education was a byword for evangelization, now, and even more so in the 1930s, civic education was charged with the task. In addition to Brazilian history (which would supposedly cultivate a feeling of belonging to the Brazilian nation among the indigenous), civic education included agriculture, in order to transform the indigenous ethnic element into productive workers for the nation and integrate it by means of the labor market.

Now, as already noted, the ambiguity implicit in the preservation of the contemporary Indian was also reflected in the treatment of their material culture. At first sight, conservation as a positivist ideal seems to predominate in social policy and ideology: within a short time of instituting protection of Indians (1910), bills of law are drafted for the conservation of their "archaeological heritage," such as the law presented in 1920 by Alberto Childe, curator of the Museu Nacional de Rio de Janeiro.

The idea of preservation and inclusion of the indigenous people in the present and future of the Brazilian nation necessarily encompassed the other temporal axis—the past—through their incorporation into the memory of the nation. Thus, the concept of heritage and the existence of legislation for the preservation of heritage exist as complementary aspects of a discursive modality engaged in a process of constructing a nation that is imagined and projected by Republican discourse.

So began an era of construction of the national memory that included the indigenous people of the past as inalienable parts of Brazil. In the words of Rodrigo Melo Franco de Andrade, the first director the Service of Historic and Artistic Heritage (SPHAN, founded in, 1937): "The heritage of products of the now long line of our predecessors will, by linking Brazilians of today to the peoples that preceded them whether they be native peoples or have come from other continents—authenticate and affirm the existence of Brazil."

It can be stated, as pointed out by Renato Ortiz (in O. Souza, 1994), that Brazilian identity was created through a search for an aspect of differentiation from the European element, as such differentiation was necessary for the formation of identity, and indigenous material culture distinguished Brazil from other nations.

By means of this distinctive trait, the Indian became a national symbol among diverse strata of the intellectuals. Such was the case in the arts, whereby indigenous people were assimilated as a theme into the Modernist Movement and upheld as a sign of "Brazilianness," thereby reducing them to a merely aesthetic or rhetorical dimension with little relation to reality. The image of the Indian, still partially anchored in nineteenth century romanticism, was thus instated as a national symbol, and, therefore, a source of pride.

It is no coincidence that years later, in approximately 1936, Mario de Andrade, one of the most prominent intellectuals of the Modernist Movement, was the author of a draft law on national heritage that named indigenous material culture as an archaeological and ethnological "good."

A certain ambiguity can be seen in the conservation of indigenous material culture and its inclusion in the patrimony of the nation: on the one hand, this culture is valorized in relation to its conservation and recovery; on the other, this same culture is subject to contempt and considered a symbol of savagery and primitive origins of civilization. At the same time, at a general theoretical level of heritage creation, this ambiguity lies in the very act of recovery because the reconstruction and exhibition of objects from a certain culture in another context—such as museums—implies a loss of meaning. Moreover, in terms of archaeological cultures, whenever materials are recovered, an attempt is being made to preserve and recapture something that is now irremediably lost in time.

It is this context of an ambiguous policy of preserving indigenous peoples, while also seeking to change them and their culture, which enables us to comprehend that the inclusion of 'the indigenous' as a part of the nation was not grounded in what indigenous peoples in fact were, but in what they could potentially become, or rather, what they could represent.

An example that illustrates this procedure well is the book *Noções de História do Brasil*, which was officially adopted as a textbook in 1920 in primary schools of the then Federal District, Rio de Janeiro. Written by Osorio Duque-Estrada, it devotes two chapters to the indigenous peoples of the pre-colonial era and describes their customs and cultural objects in considerable detail; it also makes a value judgment on them and their practices. At a time when learning history relied on memorization, the fact that the author provides long lists of material objects would suggest a genuine desire to disseminate such information, which, in the view of the school authorities, must be learned by the white student population. However, the evaluation that follows the list of material culture and its social reconstruction involves value judgments that place both the materials and indigenous people themselves at the lowest level of human development.

More concretely, the following is a quote from page 76 of the book: "Domestic objects: the *panicú* (straw basket), the *hamaca, the cuia,* the *igaçaba* (container for wine). Hunting instruments: arrows, bow, lassos, traps. For fishing: bait, nets, arrows (*setta*). Weapons of war: bow and arrow, *tacape* (club) and *murucú* (wooden lance). Instruments: maraca, *inubia* (horn), *uai* (drum), *memby* (pipes). They were vengeful and cruel." Throughout these two chapters the descriptive tone remains the same: a succession of materials followed by value judgments that are conveyed through adjectives applied to the indigenous peoples, such as: savage, fierce, rough, given to sweets, vengeful, cruel, idol-worshipping (Duque-Estrada, 1920: 74–76).

In like manner, the author devotes a chapter to contemporary indigenous peoples that reveals the scope of positivist thought in the era. Referring to the policies of the Republic on the indigenous question, Duque-Estrada (1920: 183) says: "... inspired by the most logical and rational principles, which counsel avoiding a sudden conversion of indigenous peoples to our customs, and our civilization, but allowing the operation to go forth gradually and over several generations, as they will for now maintain their own customs, family, ideas and habits of life and work, all in accordance with the theories of the great ethnologist Couto de Magalhães."

359
INDIGENOUS
IDENTITY IN THE
EARLY TWENTIETH
CENTURY

Race and Culture in Brazilian Archaeology

Heritage having been so constructed, both archaeology and ethnology mediated this relationship with the 'object' (the other), seeking the indispensable assimilation of the indigenous through generating distinctive traits of an imaginary community whose self-same tradition—i.e., heritage—was also being invented. As such, these sciences generated not only the elements of identification of the nation, but these same elements of the indigenous.

As a result of the intervention of these sciences in defining the elements that would serve as the basis of identity and the image that would be socially accepted of the indigenous, a close relationship developed between the theoretical principles guiding archaeology and other sciences involved and the values that thrived in Brazilian society at the time. This linkage means that we must speak of social or ideological values more than theoretical or scientific principles as the pillars of archaeology and, by extension, of indigenous identity.

In circulation since the nineteenth century, evolutionism sustained the concept of race in the Western world and its science as it sought to classify phenotypic differences in indigenous and white populations. The Indian became a well-defined scientific category. Thus Humboldt stressed at the beginning of the nineteenth century: "the nations of America, except those neighboring the polar circle, are of a single race, which is distinguished by the configuration of its cranium, its skin color and its flat, straight hair . . . a single organic type of the human race can be recognized, modified by circumstances that will forever be unknown to us" (in Souza, 1991: 55). This text reveals how indigenous racial uniformity, which does not exist in reality, was viewed as an unquestionable fact, not only from a strictly scientific, objective point of view, but also as a social reality. 'The Indian', therefore, was considered a subdivision of the human race, with singular, hereditary biological features.

The contribution of the twentieth century, and more specifically, of positivism, lies in a new conception of indigenous identity. This identity was no longer grounded in racial or phenotypic criteria, but rather in cultural ones. In other words, in the early decades of the last century there was a change in how the indigenous was conceptualized, distinct from that of the nineteenth century, when the categorization was essentially rooted in biology. Now, cultural criteria performed this task. As a result, to define an Indian involved the application of a cultural standard and not a racial one: that is, insofar as these individuals maintain a tribal form of organization, religions, languages, and, most of all, technologies and modes of subsistence that are different from those in Brazilian culture, they will be considered Indians; when these qualities change, they will be just like any other Brazilian. That is, an individual was considered Indian when they retained certain cultural elements that were foreign to white civilization, such that these cultural elements became, in a general way, the defining elements of "Indianness." Nevertheless, and despite this difference of criteria, the indigenous were still situated at the bottom of the prevalent social ranking as a result of a socially extended value system where progress, particularly technological progress, and "civilization" were considered key elements of human advancement.

In practice, this distancing from the racial premises of the nineteenth century meant that positivism partially recovered the romantic vision of the Indian, thus justifying his "cultural backwardness" not because of his incapacity as a race, but rather as a result of the social difficulties of integration. Consequently, policies of inter-ethnic contact sought to attain the assimilation of indigenous peoples into other segments of Brazilian society through governmental protection and aid, with the certainty that providing the material means necessary would suffice to move their "evolutionary stage" towards civilization.

According to positivist logic, evolution is not measured by racial or biological factors, but rather by a complex of cultural factors. Thus, while the leading scientific trends in Brazilian archaeology since the nineteenth century grounded themselves in studies of physical anthropology, positivism directed its attention to the definition of archaeological cultures and the setting up of relative chronologies, as in the case of the study of the "Culture of Marajó"[2] (Baldus, 1954).

Positivism thus brought about a thorough change in the study of "cultures." The concept of culture, having originated in Germany and spread among Anglo-American investigators since the end of the nineteenth century (e.g., Tylor and Morgan) underwent a change of meaning by moving away from the concept of race and becoming linked to a universalizing vision of "the human character."

However, while new studies were beginning, Brazilian archaeology in the early decades of the twentieth century showed a certain continuity with the previous century. This continuity in themes mean that the main objects of debate would still be: the origin of the Amerindian, the origin of the shell mounds and the "race" of Lagoa Santa.

This apparent thematic continuity has led some prestigious investigators of the history of the discipline such as Prous (1992) or Souza (1991) to characterize the early decades of the twentieth century as an essentially sterile period for archaeology. Nevertheless, this feeling of inertia hides a growing phenomenon within the archaeological community: a profound interest in the formation of the modern Brazilian people and its roots in time. Thus, the three central themes dealt with by archaeology inevitably ended up leading to a reflection on Brazil and "Brazilianness."

First, the theme of the "race of Lagoa Santa," supposedly inhabitants of the interior regions of prehistoric Brazil, in contrast to a coastal counterpart "the man of the sambaquis (shell mounds)," came to represent the model for the first settlement of Brazil. Here, indigenous roots were transported in time and connected to present national borders, such that indigenous people became the link between the Brazil of the past and the territory whose boundaries were being established in the twentieth century.

Moreover, going back even further in archaeological time, the subject of the origin of the Amerindian took root as a relevant question for the process of creating a common historic memory. By seeking alleged remains of lost civilizations and past colonization, above all Oriental ones like the Phoenician, Egyptian or even fantastic ones like Atlantis, Archaeology essentially sought to assign the nation a glorious past with origins in advanced civilizations-whether real or imaginary. In addition, the Twentieth Century began with the publication of the book by Cándido Costa entitled As duas Américas in 1900, which tried to prove settlement of Brazil by the Vikings, Greeks and Phoenicians prior to 1500 (Souza, 1991: 78). Since positivist principles assigned Indians an inferior position to that of white people, it became quite appealing in this perspective to search for the origins of a nation in settlement by more "noble" groups. This task of search had the special support of institutions such as the Instituto Histórico, Geográfico e Etnografico Brasileiro (Souza, 1991: 76).

Finally, regarding the third theme, the origin of shell mounds, a debate arose that lasted until practically the second half of the twentieth century; material was still being published on the subject in 1940.[3] This debate revolved around whether shell mounds were to be considered a natural or anthropological phenomenon. Both interpretations, which already existed in the nineteenth century, became more flexible in the twentieth century and gave rise to a third, so-called "mixed", trend that held that shell mounds originated in a combination of anthropological and natural events. An important representative of this alternative idea was Roqucte-Pinto, the director of the Museu Nacional (Gaspar, 2000: 13), while the director of the Museu Paulista, the above-cited Herman von Ihering, was an unconditional defender of naturalist theory.

As a result, an archaeology that was cloistered in activities of recovery and formation of the national heritage, when taking on an interpretative dimension, ended up echoing the negative social perceptions of the Amerindian. For instance, the stereotype of indigenous laziness served as the context for the debate on the origin of the shell mounds as an argument for an "artificialist current," which sustained that the formation of these piles of shells was due to the Indian's lazy disregard for clearing up leftover food that subsequently piled up (Gaspar, 2000: 12); but it also provided an argument to the "naturalist current," which believed that shelling and transporting food was not possible due to the indolent nature of indigenous people (Souza, 1991: 78).

In both cases, archaeologists assumed the role of the observer, distancing themselves from the "other"—which has thus become an object—because of their own prejudices, or in more generous language, scientific premises. They created a vision of "archaeological cultures," and even of "the culture of others," as outside history, isolated, homogeneous, free of conflicts and above all static, just like its members.

Ultimately, and speaking archaeologically, the term 'culture' referred both to the entire mode of life of a people and the people themselves.

Thus, in a certain manner, positivists also distanced themselves from the present state of indigenous people: there is hardly a mention of the question in the writing of these authors. In fact, during this period, the indigenous question was more a matter of military and national security, rather than of archaeology. As noted by Darcy Ribeiro (1996: 161–162), "indigenous social problems would not usually be dealt with by archaeology or ethnology, since they were both shut up in museums, confined within the role of theoretical disciplines, upholding an attitude of "academic pedantry," whose scientism, at most, would give rise to positions such as those of the director of the *Museu Paulista*, Herman von Ihering". Turning them into mere "objects of study" and taking a distance from the political responsibility to be assumed for their preservation.

Conclusion

A close relationship existed between the values that underpinned Brazilian society in the early decades of the twentieth century and the theoretical principles that guided archaeology: both were decisive in the construction of Brazilian indigenous identity.

The form of inclusion of the indigenous into the national community found a justification in the identity ascribed to them by scientific discourse. It was owing to the appropriation indigenous otherness and its conversion into an object of aesthetics and of study that the dominant ethic group, cut off from its European origins, was able to discover the self-defined trait that was needed for Brazilian national identity.

The elaboration of scientific discourse, in this case archaeological, distanced the indigenous from the present, while it attempted to assimilate them into the nation by means of the concept of heritage. The creation of national heritage involved a complex relationship of conservation and loss as regards the indigenous people and their material culture. This difficult relationship existed on two levels: first, to the extent that at effort was made to preserve that which was known to be disappearing or believed to be disappearing, that is, the indigenous people themselves, and second, to the extent that an effort was made to preserve and recover that which was already lost in time, and, by recovering it, integrate it into the present of the nation: the material culture of the indigenous peoples of the past.

In this context of the creation of a common memory for Brazil, archaeology as an activity with findings that would have political consequences, developed its classificatory dimension (until then it had been descriptive and accumulative), attaining the status of a science. In its work of classifying "objects," and ranking them according to their supposed complexity, archaeology placed indigenous culture, in its universalizing schema of human cultures, in an utterly inferior position. As a consequence, what had been the white's image of the Indian, became their own identity at broader levels—legally, socially, politically, and even scientifically. Identify created in this manner made fantasies—in the sense of mixing signifier, image and object—into a reality.

Notes

[1] As in other geographic contexts, such as Europe, the construction of the state was closely linked to concepts of nation and territory.

[2] The Culture of Marajó, discovered by Nimuendaju, became an important object of study at the time. In 1909 and 1913–14 excavations were made on the island and the results published in Ars Americana. In the following year, between 1914–16, the investigator Farabee from the Museum of Philadelphia also worked in the area.

[3] The debate on the shell mounds was extremely important for Brazilian archaeology, not only because it generated a bibliography of more than thousand titles, but also because legislation enacted in 1961 concerning archaeological patrimony, and which remains in force today, was drafted with this sort of excavation in mind (Carle, 1999: 255).

References

Baldus, H., 1954, *Bibliografía crítica da etnología brasileira*. Comissão do IV Centenario, São Paulo.

Chauí, M., 2000, *Brasil: mito fundador y sociedad autoritaria*. Editora Fundação Perseu Abramo, São Paulo.

Duque-Estrada, O., 1920, *Noções de Historia do Brasil*, 2nd edition. Livraria Francisco Alves, Rio de Janeiro.

Ferreira, A. et al., editors, 1999, *Encontros com a História*. UNESP, FAPESP, ANPUH/SP, São Paulo.

Funari, P. P. A., 1994, Rescuing Ordinary People's Culture: Museums, Material Culture and Education in Brazil. In *The Presented Past: Heritage, Museums and Education*, edited by P. Stone and B. Molyneaux, pp. 120–136. Routledge, London.

Gagliardi, J.M., 1989, *O indígena e a República*. HUCITEC, São Paulo.

Gaspar, M., 2000, *Sambaqui: arqueologia do litoral brasileiro*. Jorge Zahar, Rio de Janeiro.

Gnecco, C., 1999, Archaeology and Historical Multivocality: A Reflection from the Colombian Multicultural Context. In *Archaeology in Latin America*, edited by G. Politis and B. Alberti, pp. 258–270. Routledge, London.

Gonçalves, J. R. S., 1996, *A Retórica da Perda*. Editora UFRJ—IPHAN, Rio de Janeiro.

Oyuela-Caycedo, A., 1994, *History of Latin American Archaeology*. Worldwide Archaeology Series, vol. 15. Newcastle-upon-Tyne.

Prous, A., 1992, *Arqueologia Brasileira*. Editora Universidade de Brasilia, Brasilia.

Ribeiro, D., 1996, *Os índios e a civilização: a integração das populações indígenas no Brasil moderno*. Companhia das Letras, São Paulo.

Souza, A. M. De, 1991, *Historia da Arqueología Brasileira*. Pesquisas, n°46, Instituto Anchietano de Pesquisas, São Leopoldo.

Souza, O., 1994, *Fantasia de Brasil: as identificações na busca da identidade nacional*. Ed. Escuta, São Paulo.

Souza Filho, C. F. M., 1998, O direito envergonhado: O direito e os índios no Brasil. In *Índios no Brasil*, edited by L. Grupioni, pp. 153–178. Global Editora, São Paulo.

Todorov, T., 1999, *A conquista da América. A questão do outro*, 2nd edition. Martins Fontes, São Paulo.

21

Discussion

A Response from the 'Core'

Matthew H. Johnson

First let me thank the editors for the opportunity to comment on these papers. Frankly, I learned a lot from them, particularly about the theoretical basis of Latin American archaeology, about which I was only dimly aware. In some ways, any concluding comment, of whatever kind, is presumptuous. The majority of the contributors to this volume speak from the 'periphery'; and the editors are correct in stating in their Introduction that '(peripheral) conditions tend to produce critical thought'. This response is written very definitely from the core. I sit, writing these words, in a pleasant study in a comfortable middle-class home in England; a location far from peripheral, whatever definition one cares to choose. Such comfortable conditions, by implication, will tend to produce sloppy, uncritical thought.

Critical or uncritical, moreover, any concluding comments I might make implicitly serve to package these papers in a marginalizing and possibly trivializing way. 'These papers from the periphery are important', writes the discussant: 'they are important because I, a writer from the core, says so. I will tell you now what they really mean, I will summarize for you what the authors are really trying to say; I will explain to you why you should give them attention'.

The alternative to speaking of these papers, however, is silence, and silence of a most unsatisfactory nature. The most trivializing response of all would be to choose not to respond in the face of a group of papers that pose a series of challenges to the way we think about, and do, archaeology in the 21st century.

In any case, contributors to the volume take up a very definite, if implicit, position with regard to the issue of core versus periphery. They situate themselves rhetorically in the periphery, but go out of their way to state explicit alliances with 'core' thinking. In their Introduction, the editors isolate two horizons in the history of archaeological thought: the new archaeology, and what they call 'postprocessual, contextual or interpretive archaeology'. Both these horizons, of course, are primarily Anglo-American in nature. Indeed, they have a certain symmetry derived from this cross-Atlantic nature. Much, though not all, of the impetus behind New Archaeology came from North America; conversely, much, though not all, of the impetus behind postprocessualism came from Britain.

Writing from the periphery, these papers could choose to reject such a structure, perhaps claiming that it serves to marginalize non-Anglo contributions to the development of archaeological thought. Instead, and somewhat to my surprise, most authors appear to be not unhappy to orient and place their own work within it. Funari, Zarankin and Stovel state quite explicitly that this volume is part of this second horizon of postprocessual, critical or contextual archaeology. They cite the formation and subsequent history of the World Archaeological Congress (WAC) in this context.

Other contributors are more cautious in their affiliation to wider debates. Guarinello comes closest to outright rejection of interpretive models, even advocating a return to Hawkes' levels of inference. (The editors take care to assimilate Guarinello into the rest of the volume by stressing his insistence on the importance of context [Introduction], but on my reading of his paper, I am not so easily persuaded that Guarinello himself wishes to be brought back into the postprocessual fold in this way.)

Both New Archaeology and postprocessual archaeology came from the core. If one had to specify which was the more influential over the long term, I think one would have to say it was New Archaeology. New Archaeology opened up theoretical debate in the discipline; claims that wide-ranging theoretical debate existed before the New Archaeology have never been entirely convincing (Johnson, 1999; Trigger, 1989). This made it possible to debate the aims and methods of archaeology in an explicitly self-conscious and reflective way for the first time. It is of course true that theorizing was not absent from culture history, and that Renfrew's characterization of the period before 1960 as 'the long sleep of archaeological theory' was an oversimplification at best. (In this context, it is also worth noting that such a view was a distinctly Anglo one.) Nevertheless, the need to make one's theoretical basis clear, rigorous and explicit was notable by its general absence before 1960, particularly in the European world.

Once this need was established by New Archaeology, it had consequences that were entirely unintended. Explicit theory was accepted as necessary, but it was soon apparent that this did not have to be the specific form of positivist theory advocated by New Archaeology. The Pandora's Box of unrestrained theoretical reflection and debate had been opened. The early move away from logical-positivism was followed, in the next decade, by the postprocessual move away from the profession of any kind of professed positivism at all.

I am arguing here *contra* Shanks and Tilley (1987a, b), who claim that it was the 1980s rather than the 1960s that marked the true critical break with existing epistemological traditions in archaeology. They are of course correct to stress that in terms of *content*, postprocessualism was the more profound epistemological break, in terms of its rejection of positivism and objectivism, and also in terms of its affiliations in the wider world with an emergent postmodernist thought. However, in terms of its style, rhetoric and context within archaeological thought as a whole, postprocessualism was nevertheless first and foremost a reaction to New Archaeology. It is revealing that it is the writings of Binford and Renfrew, not primarily an earlier generation of culture historians, that are chosen for critical savaging in early postprocessual texts. And this deliberate choice of intellectual target unwittingly reveals just how dependent postprocessualism was on an intellectual and rhetorical horizon set by New Archaeology. Of course, it was also an intellectual context set by the course of core Anglo thought in its stress on Science and on a single way of knowing.

This does not mean that postprocessual ideas are lessened in their impact; they unquestionably do question existing, apparently mundane and accepted ideas and categories in a more radical way. This radical questioning is amply evidenced by a number of papers in this volume. Alberti's comments on the sex/gender split, derived in part from the thinking of Judith Butler, show just how far we have come in moving beyond accepted ideas and categories in thinking about the body, gender and sexuality. Again, Hakan Karlsson addresses 'the most fundamental question of all'—why there is material culture rather than nothing. It is impossible to conceive of either chapter being published, at least in the archaeological rather than philosophical world, thirty years ago. One of the defining features of recent thinking is the way it strikes at the heart of most core assumptions about the nature of archaeology and the nature of humanity.

Contributors to this volume writing from the 'core' maintain existing trends in postprocessual thinking, though in some respects they deepen the postprocessual critique, showing just how fundamental its implications are. Thomas and Karlsson discuss a range of theoretical issues around the theme of materiality, continuing the shift in recent thinking away from models based on the textual analogy for material culture towards a more embodied and phenomenological view of the archaeological record and of human action. Alberti discusses gender and the body, again moving towards more radical and de-centered ideas of sexuality and embodiment. Lazzari develops a social view of exchange relationships, moving beyond and de-centering the ecological models of Halstead and O'Shea. Orser discusses issues of scale and agency in his proposed network theory, relating very small scale interpersonal transactions outwards to state and world systems.

This group of papers, in many ways, does not develop new theory in a particularly radical or revolutionary way, but rather 'roll out' existing general propositions and current themes from broadly post-processual thinking. They take these established themes and apply them to specific themes of archaeological enquiry—space, trade and exchange, the relationship between agency and structure at a variety of scales, and so on. They show how a variety of new critical perspectives actually work out in terms of method—how they have implications for the way we think about specific issues in the archaeological record.

I have argued then that the critical difference between processual and postprocessual thought, particularly in the context of this volume led from the periphery, is not a strictly epistemological one but rather one of context. Postprocessualists at least paid, and continue to pay, lip-service to ideas of pluralism and multivocality. Postprocessualists were partly successful in their arguments that New Archaeology's stress on Science as a single way of knowing, and insistence on a certain model of 'testability' and 'objectivity' as a means of evaluating archaeological argument, did add up to an archaeology of NO: and that as such, it was open to a well-established postcolonial critique, namely that Science in this context was inevitably implicated in ethnocentric and colonialist practices. Now postprocessualists may have been hypocritical in this; their own work has been criticized as ignorant of non-Anglo intellectuals; my own work has been criticized in this regard. Nevertheless the claim was made, and was reinforced by historical circumstance. Pandora's Box was opened up for a second time, this time to let out the political possibility of a non-Anglo critique of and contribution to archaeological theory. The 1980s also saw the 'one world' aspirations of the World Archaeological Congress, and postprocessual ideas became coupled with this.

This volume shows Latin American archaeologists eager to take the rhetorical and practical opportunity afforded by such claims of plurality and to turn this opportunity to their advantage. The papers by Alberti and Politis are a good example of this. Drawing on recent thinking in feminist and gender theory, they move the debate forward: in Alberti's case, questioning the sex/gender split, for Politis, in addressing the question of a fully theorized archaeology of childhood. However, I want to focus on a particular area in which this challenge is opened up: the possibility of a postcolonial critique of historical archaeology.

Postcolonialism, Artifacts, and Texts

The debate within historical archaeology over the relative status of archaeological and documentary evidence is an old and in many respects a sterile one. It has recently been summarized, and indeed thrown into perspective, by John Moreland (2001). While I do not agree with much of Moreland's argument, particularly his dismissal of much of North American historical archaeology and the ritualistic denunciation of his caricature of an unrestrained postmodernism, his comments on the 'archaeology versus history' debate are acute ones that open up avenues for an historical archaeology informed by postcolonial theory.

Alberione dos Reis takes up the challenge of the 'tension' between historical documents and archaeological evidence. I agree with his assertion that 'through the game of opening words . . . we end up not coming to a conclusion'; much fruitless writing in historical archaeology has concerned itself with an attempt to settle once and for all what such a relationship should be. I read his essay as an attempt to open up a dynamic and shifting relationship between two 'classes of evidence' that are themselves dynamic and shifting in nature. In a phrase, they exist in a dialectical relationship to one another. Again, Felix Acuto's paper demonstrates indirectly how fruitless this opposition has become. By the time one has finished his paper, the opposition is meaningless.

Neither dos Reis nor Acuto, however, discuss at any length one of the major dimensions of the document/artifact debate: that the document is often taken as the voice of the colonizer, and the artifact is taken by some to offer a way into the world-view of the colonized, the 'people without history' (Wolf, 1982). Such a statement, taken without qualification, is of course simplistic: colonized need not equal illiterate, and as Wolf's and others' work shows, documentary evidence can be used to construct convincing accounts of the experience of the colonized. However, it remains a valid and useful opposition in broader terms, extending even to the use and appropriation of language itself. The numerous postcolonial readings of Shakespeare's The Tempest center on the image of the shackled 'native' monster Caliban screaming at his colonial master: You taught me language/And my profit on't is, I know how to curse' (Said, 1993: 256–257).

Funari and Orser come closest to discussing these themes, developing a comparative archaeology of Hispanic settlement on the one hand, and exploring the implications of Carrithers' network theory on the other (Carrithers, 1992). However, I remain surprised that few authors in this collection of papers take up the challenges of more radical and wide-ranging postcolonial critiques (see for example Bhabha, 1994; Said, 1978) pen up our readings of text and artifact, and the relationship between them.

Conclusion

Writing from the core, it is both easy and perhaps ironic for me to urge a bolder postcolonial reading from the periphery. I see in the relation between text and artifact one of several avenues for opening up a genuinely postcolonial archaeology. Many of the papers in this collection point the way forward; as dos Reis points out, these future paths are located in present tensions—between acceptance of an Anglo-American model of theory and rejection of it, between text and artifact, between the Latin American and 'core' contributors to this volume. These tensions are creative ones, ones to be embraced and to be the subject of critical focus. I look forward to seeing the future development of the themes opened up in this volume and their establishment as a diverse yet coherent platform.

Acknowledgements

I thank Pedro Paulo Funari for asking me to write this discussion, and Maria Senatore and Andrés Zarankin for discussions on these and related themes during their time at Durham.

References

Bhabha, H., 1994, *The Location of Culture*. Routledge, London.
Carrithers, M., 1992, *Why Humans Have Cultures: Explaining Anthropology and Social Diversity*. Oxford University Press, Oxford.
Johnson, M. H., 1999, *Archaeological Theory: An Introduction*. Blackwell, Oxford.
Moreland, J., 2001, *Archaeology and Text*. Duckworth, London.
Said, E., 1978, *Orientalism: Western Conceptions of the Orient*. Penguin, London.
Said, E., 1993, *Culture and Imperialism*. Chatto and Windus, London.
Shanks, M., and Tilley, C., 1987a, *Re-Constructing Archaeology: Theory and Practice*. Cambridge University Press, Cambridge.
Shanks, M., and Tilley, C., 1987b, *Social Theory and Archaeology*. Polity, Oxford.
Trigger, B. G., 1989, *A History of Archaeological Thought*. Cambridge University Press, Cambridge.
Wolf, E., 1982, *Europe and the People without History*. University of California Press, Berkeley.

Index

371